Innamincka Words
Yandruwandha dictionary and stories

Innamincka Words
Yandruwandha dictionary and stories

compiled by Gavan Breen

ANU

eView

ANU
eView

Published by ANU eView
The Australian National University
Canberra ACT 0200, Australia
Email: enquiries.eview@anu.edu.au
This title is also available online at http://eview.anu.edu.au

National Library of Australia Cataloguing-in-Publication entry

Title:	Innamincka words: Yandruwandha dictionary and stories / compiled by Gavan Breen.
ISBN:	9781921934216 (paperback) 9781921934223 (online)
Subjects:	Innamincka language--Dictionaries.
	Yandruwandha (Australian people)--Languages--Texts.
	Queensland--Languages.
	South Australia--Languages.

Other Creators/Contributors:
    Breen, Gavan, compiler.

Dewey Number: 499.15

Original cover concept by Ciril's Printers. Cover by Ivo Lovric and layout by ANU Press.

This book can be purchased from http://eview.anu.edu.au

Table of contents

Acknowledgments

Naturally, I owe most to Ben Kerwin for the many hours of his time that he gave me for little financial reward over the years. I am indebted also to my other teachers, Tim Guttie, Maudie Naylon and her husband Bob, Willy and Alfie Harris and Hector Harrison, for work that was congenial to some of them but not all.

I am grateful to those members of Ben Kerwin's family who helped me in one way or another, in particular to his daughter Barbara and her husband Kevin Allen, of Burra, South Australia (later Broken Hill, New South Wales), and his daughter Joan and her husband Ron Dennis, of Roma, Queensland, with whom he was living during the periods when the major part of the fieldwork was carried out. They were friendly, cooperative and interested at all times. Ben's great-grandson Aaron Paterson was interested in recent years and helped with some useful information.

I thank my wife Rosalie, who came with me (with small children after the first year) on some field trips and kept me fed and washed. Also the many linguists whose brains I have picked over the years (including Claire Bowern, who gave me a copy of her unpublished work on Nhirrpi) and the anonymous referee who read the manuscript for Pacific Linguistics.

I wish to thank also the Australian Institute of Aboriginal Studies (now Australian Institute of Aboriginal and Torres Strait Islander Studies) for financing all of the fieldwork and most of the analysis, and helping in other ways, and Monash University for equipment, typing and office accommodation during that time. The Burran and later Muda Aboriginal Corporations paid me for a little over a year, during which time the Institute for Aboriginal Development, Alice Springs, provided me with office accommodation and other services. The Queensland Herbarium, the Royal Botanic Gardens and National Herbarium, Sydney and the Royal Botanic Gardens and National Herbarium, Melbourne helped with information on plants. Thanks also to Helen Tolcher for some information, and to Brenda Thornley for the map.

Preface

Innamincka Words is one of a pair of companion volumes on Yandruwandha, a dialect of the language formerly spoken on the Cooper and Strzelecki Creeks and the country to the north of the Cooper, in the northeast corner of South Australia and a neighbouring strip of Queensland. The other volume is entitled *Innamincka Talk: a grammar of the Innamincka dialect of Yandruwandha with notes on other dialects.*

Innamincka Talk is a more technical work and is intended for specialists and for interested readers who are willing to put some time and effort into studying the language. *Innamincka Words* is for readers, especially descendants of the original people of the area, who are interested but not ready to undertake serious study of the language. It is also a necessary resource for users of *Innamincka Talk.*

These volumes document all that could be learnt from the last speakers of the language in the last years of their lives by a linguist who was involved with other languages at the same time. These were people who did not have a full knowledge of the culture of their forebears, but were highly competent, indeed brilliant, in the way they could teach what they knew to the linguist student. Although the volumes document only a small part of a rich culture, they are a tribute to the ability and diligence of the teachers.

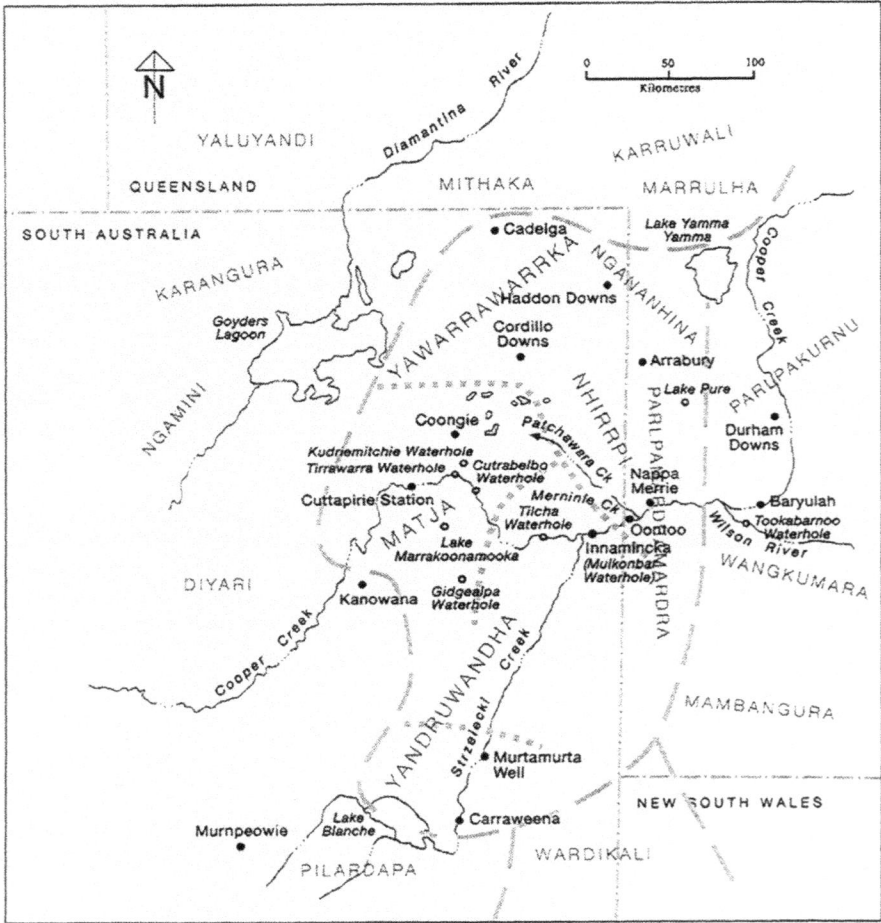

Map: Yandruwandha and neighbouring languages

Tim Guttie (Nelly Parker) with Fred McKellar at Windorah (1967)

Bob and Maudie Naylon with Gavan Breen and son Frank, Birdsville (1973)

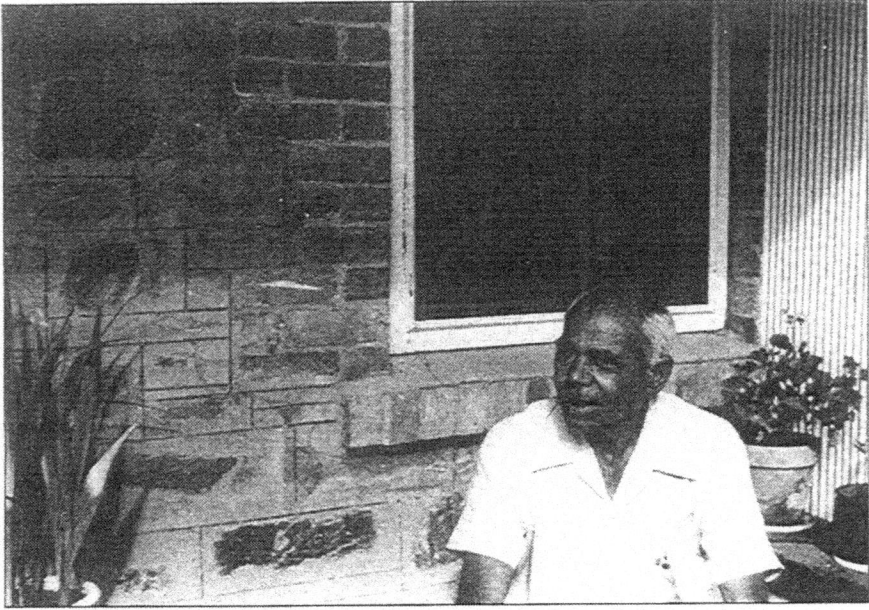

Benny Kerwin at Princess Royal Station, Burra (1972)

Benny Kerwin and Bill Gorringe in 1932

1 *Introduction*

The Yandruwandha were one of a group of tribes speaking dialects of the same language and living in the Lakes Country of northeastern South Australia. Other names referring to people speaking other dialects of this language are Yawarrawarrka, Nhirrpi, Matja, Parlpamardramardra, Ngananhina, Ngapardandhirri and Ngurawola. Very little is known about some of these groups, and what detail we have is given in the introductory chapter of the grammar, which also gives more information on the speakers who provided the words, sentences and stories that are the basis for these two volumes.

The bulk of this dictionary has been compiled from Yandruwandha language recorded from Tim Guttie in 1967–68 and from Bennie Kerwin from 1968 to 1976. It is primarily in the dialect spoken around Innamincka. However, words from the Strzelecki dialect and from Yawarrawarrka also have been added; these were obtained mainly from Maudie Naylon, from 1970 to 1976, but some Yawarrawarrka was recorded also from Willy and Alfie Harris and their brother Hector Harrison in 1967. The material from the two latter dialects is less reliable; Maudie Naylon tended to confuse the two to some extent — excusable for a person who was probably closer to ninety than to eighty at the time and who was trying to give information in what was probably her fifth or sixth language, while the other three were much younger and much less knowledgeable. There are also a few Nhirrpi words from Alice Miller (recorded by Stephen Wurm in 1957 and transcribed by Claire Bowern).

There are a number of words spelt in two different ways. In some of these cases one of these ways may not be correct, but I am not able to determine this from the recorded data. There may also be inconsistencies in the writing of some lexical items as one word or as two; for example, whether 'finger' is *marawitju* or *mara witju*. These words may be pronounced both ways, and the Yandruwandha people may decide on a rule for the way they are to be written. I have used hyphens to break up long words at the end of lines, but not much otherwise — only to break up reduplications of words of three syllables or longer (so *paladi-paladi*, but not *palapaladi*), to separate a couple of endings (*nyadi* 'like' and *ngada* 'while') and for a few special compounds like *ngarndri-ngapiri* 'parents'. Hyphens could be used more often if people prefer this.

All of the information on the words is given in the first part, Yandruwandha to English. The second part, English to Yandruwandha, is intended just for finding words. You should then go to the first part to get further information on the word, including example sentences (which are preceded by •) and additional notes (which are preceded by #). This is particularly important if an English entry has two or more Yandruwandha equivalents,

1

because these might be quite different. For example, two words are given for 'grandfather': *papa* and *tjindra*. But if you find these words in the first part you will see that *papa* is 'mother's father' and *tjindra* is 'father's father'. They both have other meanings too. Another example: two words are given for 'him', *yinha* and *nhunggani*. But *nhunggani* only means 'him' in expressions like 'to him', 'for him', 'with him' (in which it has an ending attached to it). In a sentence like 'I saw him' you couldn't use *nhunggani* for him, only *yinha*.

The form of an entry in the Yandruwandha-to-English section is: head word (the Yandruwandha word), its meaning or meanings in English, sometimes a note preceded by # giving further information, such as saying what dialect the word belongs to, often example sentences, each preceded by • and with the Yandruwandha sentence followed by an English translation and occasionally also by a more literal translation of all or part preceded by the abbreviation 'lit.'; after the example sentences comes often the symbol # followed by further information about the word, often referring the reader to other words with the same or similar meaning. If an example sentence is not in Innamincka Yandruwandha it is labelled, for example (SY) (see final paragraph below). In the English-to-Yandruwandha section the headword is in English and Yandruwandha equivalents follow.

When the meaning of a word is given as two or more words (or phrases) separated by commas, these are thought of as just different aspects of the meaning or different ways of saying the same thing, although between them they should give a better idea of the range of meaning of the Yandruwandha word than any one of them would give. Some examples are 'argue, have a row' and 'river, creek'. When the words are separated by semicolons they are thought of as different meanings, although closely related; for example 'yawn'; 'hiccough'; 'burp'. In these cases example sentences illustrating various meanings are not separated. Sometimes in such cases the different meanings are labelled with a letter, (a), (b) etc., and in these cases examples illustrating (a) are given before (b) is introduced, and so on. Letters are used also to separate off meanings that apply only to some dialect(s) other than Innamincka Yandruwandha. Numbers — (1), (2) etc. — are used instead of letters when the meanings are rather more divergent, as for example in the *kamiri* entry. When there are two words with the same form but meanings that seem to be completely unrelated they are given as quite separate entries; for example, *nhinda* 'shame', 'shyness' and *nhinda* 'size'; 'shape'; 'appearance'. Sometimes my judgment about these may be different from someone else's, and, more importantly, may be different from what the native speakers would have thought (especially for a case like that of *kamiri*).

Occasionally the head word in an entry is something that has never been heard except in compounds; in these cases it is given in brackets and no meaning may be given for it. An example is (*kaldri*). This is then followed by subentries for compounds that include it.

The example sentences contain large numbers of endings on words, and these are listed separately and very briefly explained in the dictionary. They are explained in detail in the grammar, and will be explained in a less technical way in the following section. Occasionally an example sentence contains a word or part of a word which I do not understand or could not hear properly. These are marked with question marks, in brackets which may also enclose the part of the word concerned or, if it is a whole word, just follow it.

Abbreviations used in the dictionary include:

Eng (English)
Nh (Nhirrpi)
Wngu (Wangkangurru)
Yn (= Yandruwandha)

AWH (material from A.W. Howitt's 'Native tribes of south-east Australia')
BK (= Benny Kerwin, used especially when he gave something in Yawarrawarrka)
H (= material from one or more of the younger Yawarrawarrka informants)
MN (used sometimes for material from Maudie Naylon)
RYn (= material in Yandruwandha from J.G. Reuther's massive late 19th-century
  work on the Diyari or Dieri[1] who lived to the west of the Yandruwandha)
SY (= material in Strzelecki Yandruwandha from Maudie Naylon)
TG (= Tim Guttie)
Yw (= material in Yawarrawarrka from Maudie Naylon)

When an abbreviation follows # it means that it applies to the preceding word; when it is in parentheses and following • it applies to the example sentence which follows; when it is in parentheses and preceding an alternative form of a word it applies to that alternative. So, for example, # SY, Yw • (SY) means 'this word occurs in Strzelecki Yandruwandha and Yawarrawarrka; the following example is from Strzelecki Yandruwandha'; *warrayi*, (Yw) *warranyi* means the Yawarrawarrka version is *warranyi*. The sign = in an entry means 'same as'. Yandruwandha information from Benny Kerwin (which forms the bulk of the dictionary) and Tim Guttie (whose dialect is the same as Benny's, apart from the odd word) is not identified. Strzelecki Yandruwandha and Yawarrawarrka words are identified only when they are different from Innamincka Yandruwandha or when there is no corresponding Innamincka dialect word known (in which case the odds are fairly high that the Innamincka dialect word is the same).

1.1 A short introduction to the Yandruwandha language

(a) The pronunciation of Yandruwandha words

The spelling system of Yandruwandha uses seventeen of the letters in the English alphabet, but a couple of these are used only as part of digraphs (pairs of letters that are used together to represent a single sound, like *sh* and *th* in English). The alphabet is, as one would expect, much less suitable for a language like Yandruwandha than it is for English (and it is far from ideal for English too). One result of this is that there are many more digraphs in Yandruwandha than in English, and there are two trigraphs — sounds written with three letters (**rdl, rdr** below). Yandruwandha has fewer vowel sounds than English, but more consonants.

The following are the consonants of Yandruwandha and their approximate pronunciations. They are not listed in alphabetical order, but are in groups of similar sounds. Some of them are not like any sounds in English and require some practice to learn.

---

[1]   See the References in *Innamincka Talk*.

p, like *p* in English but not pronounced as strongly, more like *p* in *spot* than *p* in *pot*.

b, like English *b*.

k, like *k* (or hard *c*) in English but not pronounced as strongly, more like *c* in *Scot* than *c* in *cot*.

g, like English *g*.

t, like *t* in English but not pronounced as strongly, more like *t* in *stop* than *t* in *top*.

d, like English *d* when it comes at the beginning of a word or after **n**, but pronounced with a quicker movement of the tongue when it comes between vowels, the way some people pronounce *r*.

th, not like English *th* but more like the combination of *t* and *th* in, for example, *got them* (pronounced quickly). The tongue touches the back of the front teeth.

dh, something like the combination of *d* and *th* in, for example, *had them* (pronounced quickly). The tongue touches the back of the front teeth.

tj, something like *ch* in English but cut short.

dj, something like *j* in English but cut short.

rt, like **t** except that the tongue tip touches the roof of the mouth not just behind and above the upper front teeth, as in **t**, but further back.

rd, like **d** except that the tongue tip is further back, as for **rt**.

m, as in English.

ng, as in English *hangar*, not like in *finger* (this combination of sounds is spelt **ngg** in Yandruwandha) or in *danger* (this combination of sounds is spelt **ndj** in Yandruwandha). Often comes at the beginning of a word, and this can be a problem for English speakers.

n, as in English.

nh, like **n** but pronounced with the tongue touching the back of the front teeth, not above them. Like *n* in *tenth*.

ny, like the *ny* in *canyon*.

rn, like **n** except that the tongue tip touches the roof of the mouth not just behind and above the upper front teeth, as in **n**, but further back.

l, as in English.

lh, like **l** but pronounced with the tongue touching the back of the front teeth, not above them. Like *l* in *filth*.

ly, like *lli* in million.

rl, like **l** except that the tongue tip touches the roof of the mouth not just behind and above the upper front teeth, as in **l**, but further back.

dl, as in English *fiddler*.

rdl, like **dl** except that the tongue tip touches the roof of the mouth not just behind and above the upper front teeth, as in **dl**, but further back.

rr, a rolled *r* sound, like what you might hear in Scottish English.

dr, starts as a **d** and ends up as a **rr** (rolled *r*).

rdr, starts as an **rd** and ends up as a **rr** (rolled *r*).

w, as in English.

y, as in English.

r, as in Australian English.

The vowels in Yandruwandha can be written with just three letters, **a**, **i** and **u**. Sometimes you hear sounds like *e* or *o*, but these are just variants of other vowels influenced by the consonants near them, just as, for example, the first vowel of English *wallaby* is written with *a* but pronounced like *o* because of the influence of the *w*.

a is generally pronounced like English *u* in *cut*, but can be more like *o* after **w** and more like *a* in *cat* after **y**.

i is normally like *i* in *hit*.

u is generally like *u* in *put*.

Some minor simplifications are made in the spelling of Yandruwandha words. Certain consonant clusters (pairs of consonants together) are simplified in the spelling in that a *h*, a *y* or an *r* are left out. Thus *nth* (a cluster of *nh + th*) is written instead of *nhth*, *ndh* instead of *nhdh*, *lth* instead of *lhth*. The others are *ntj* instead of *nytj*, *ndj* instead of *nydj*, *ltj* instead of *lytj*, *rnt* instead of *rnrt*, *rnd* instead of *rnrd*, *rndr* instead of *rnrdr*. Another simplification is the omission of the first *r* when the sounds *rd* and *rdr* occur at the beginning of a word. So, for example, *drama*, not *rdrama*, 'cut'. When there is a cluster of the sounds *n* and *g* a dot is written between them, to distinguish this combination from the single sound written *ng*. For example, *thawanga* means 'will go', *thawan.ga* 'went some time ago'.

The main stress (or accent) in Yandruwandha words is on the first syllable. So, for example, *kala* is more like *colour* in this respect than *galah* and *karta* is more like *cutter* than *catarrh*. It is in the three-syllable words that English speakers are most likely to get the stress wrong: *makita* has a tune like *marketer*, not like *mosquito*; *murali* like *morally* not *medallion*. It is very common in English for the first vowel to be weak and unclear: the first *o* in *tomato* is not at all like a clear strong *o* (as it is in *Thomas*), and hardly sounds different from the first *e* in *temerity*, the first *a* in *Tamara* or the first *i* in *timidity*. This never happens in Yandruwandha; the first vowel is always strong and clear.

(b) The grammar of Yandruwandha

A major difference in the way Yandruwandha works compared to English is that Yandruwandha makes far more use of suffixes (endings put on words, like *-ing* or *-ed* or *-ness* in English) to show the relationship between words in a sentence. For many of the functions that are performed by suffixes in Yandruwandha, English uses prepositions (words like 'in', 'by', 'from', 'through' that normally go before the word they refer to) or simply relies on the order of the words in a sentence.

For example, to show the location of something in English we use *in* or *at* or *on* or *between* or various other prepositions. Yandruwandha uses a suffix like *-yi*, which has the same function as some (not all) of those prepositions. In English we say 'He's hiding in the hole'; in Yandruwandha we might say '*Mingkayi nhutjadu purripandhirnanga*', literally 'hole-in he-there hide-down-is.doing'. To illustrate the function of word order in English we have the sentence: 'The dog killed a snake'. If we changed the order to 'A snake killed the dog' we would have a sentence with a quite different meaning, because the one that is mentioned first is the one that did the action. The only way we can change the order without changing the meaning is to make some other change at the same time, for example changing 'killed' to 'was killed by'. In Yandruwandha we can say '*Pandili kathikathi parndrina*', in which the word *pandi* 'dog' has an ending -*li* which specifies it as being the subject of the verb, the one that killed. If we say '*Kathikathi pandili parndrina*', putting the word for 'snake' first (which is less likely but quite possible), the meaning is still the same, because the word for 'dog' is still the one that has the suffix -*li*. (There are no words in the Yandruwandha sentence translated as 'the' or 'a'.)

If, say, the subject is a phrase with more than one word — say 'that dog' — we could say '*Pandi nhuludu kathikathi parndrina*' and this time we know that *nhuludu* goes with *pandi*, because it follows it, and that these two words express the subject of the sentence even though *pandi* doesn't have -*li* any more, because the word *nhuludu* has to be the subject or part of the subject of this type of sentence; if it was the object or part of the object it would be *yintjadu* instead. It is possible also for the words in the phrase to be separated, and then the *pandi* would need the ending to show that it belonged with *nhuludu*: '*Pandili kathikathi parndrina nhuludu*'. This is something like saying 'A dog killed a snake — that one did'.

The word *purripandhirnanga* in the first of the Yandruwandha sentences above illustrates another prominent feature of the language. It is made up of *purri* 'hide', *pandhi* 'down' and the suffix -*rnanga* 'is doing'. Because the hiding is being done in a hole it is likely that the person or thing is crouching, and so it is appropriate (but not obligatory) to augment the verb with *pandhi* to emphasise this aspect of it. This is very common, and a number of common words, such as the verbs *nhina* 'sit, stay', *thawa* 'go', *thika* 'return', *windri* 'go in', *thayi* 'eat' and the adverbs *thalka* 'up', *pada* 'in' and *yukarra* 'at night', are used in this way to add extra meaning to a verb.

The system of pronouns in Yandruwandha is more complex than that in English. Nominative personal pronouns (used as subject of a sentence) in English are *I*, *you*, *he*, *she*, *it*, *we*, *they*. Yandruwandha has *nganyi* 'I' (and *ngathu* when it is subject of a verb that has an object), *yini* 'you (one person)' (and *yundru* when it is subject of a verb that has an object), *yula* 'you (two)', *yuda* 'you (more than two)', *nhunu* 'he' or 'it', *nhani* 'she', *ngaldra* 'we (you and I)', *ngali* 'we (two, not including you)' (= 'he and I' or 'she and I'), *ngandra* 'we (more than two, including you)', *ngani* 'we (more than two, not including you)', *pula* 'they (two)', *thana* 'they (more than two)'. These pronouns are repeated in a slightly different order in the following table, which also has the object forms (corresponding to English 'me', 'you', 'him', 'her', 'it', 'us', 'them') and the genitive forms (corresponding to English 'my', 'your', 'his', 'her', 'its', 'our', 'their').

The genitives can combine with other endings that go on nouns. The third person pronouns, corresponding to English 'he', 'she', 'they' and so on, function also as demonstrative adjectives or demonstrative pronouns like 'this' and 'that' and take endings -*yi* meaning 'here' and -*du* (and some other variations) meaning 'there', so *nhunuyi* is 'this (male or thing)' and *nhunudu* (and the more common variant *nhutjadu*) means 'that (male or thing)'. Other roots that can combine with these endings -*yi* and -*du* (and others), but form only demonstrative adjectives and pronouns and not personal pronouns, are *nhinggi* and *nhuku*. For more detail see the dictionary entries or, better, the grammar volume, *Innamincka Talk*.

	Subject	Object	Genitive
first singular	*nganyi, ngathu*	*nganha*	*ngakani*
second singular	*yini, yundru*	*yina*	*yinggani*
third singular non-feminine	*nhunu*	*yinha*	*nhunggani*
third singular feminine	*nhani*	*nhanha*	*nhanggani*
first dual inclusive	*ngaldra*	*ngalunha*	*ngalungga*
first dual exclusive	*ngali*	*ngalinha*	*ngalingga*
second dual	*yula*	*yulhu*	*yulgani*
third dual	*pula*	*pulhu*	*pulgani*
first plural inclusive	*ngandra*	*nganunha*	*nganungga*
first plural exclusive	*ngani*	*nganinha*	*nganingga*
second plural	*yuda*	*yunhu*	*yunngani*
third plural	*thana*	*thanha*	*thanngani*

The following section is a list of all the suffixes that we know of in the language, with a short description of what the function of each is. A more detailed description of each, with examples, can be found in the grammar volume. The list is in alphabetical order, so I will list here the most common of the suffixes that are used on nouns and on verbs. On nouns, *-li, -ngadi, -yi, -nguda, -puru, -mindji, -pani, -ngurru*; on verbs *-na, -nhana, -lapurra, -rla, -nga, -malka, -yi, -ri, -rnanga, -rlayi, -ini, -ni, -padipadini, -yindri*. On all words the emphatic suffixes, especially *-la* and *-tji*, are very common. It is common for a word, especially a verb, to have two or three or more suffixes.

1.2 Alphabetical list of suffixes

Suffixes used only in Yawarrawarrka are usually cross-referred to the corresponding suffix in Yandruwandha. References such as 'See §11.14' are to relevant sections of the grammar volume, and are intended for readers who are sufficiently interested to study the particular point in more detail; others need not worry about them. The word or abbreviation, often in small capitals, given at the end of each description is the identification used for this suffix in interlinear translations in the grammar volume, *Innamincka Talk*, and in the stories.

-a- added to a verb stem preceding *-rla* to state that something which was not happening before is happening at the time of speaking. See §11.15. NOW

-ardi added to any word to add emphasis. See §18.4. EMPH

-ey distorts final vowel of a word, for emphasis. See §3.2.1 DISTORT

-du added to a third person or demonstrative pronoun or location word to show that the person(s) or thing(s) concerned is not close to the speaker. Can be translated 'there'. Same as *-tjadu*. THERE

-indri used in Yawarrawarrka with the same function as *-ri* in Yandruwandha. UNSP

-ini added to a verb stem ending in *a* to convert it into a form that can have noun endings added to it. See *-ni*. See §10.6. GER

-ipi added to a verb stem in Yawarrawarrka to warn that an undesirable event may occur. See *-yi*. POT

-irnanyi	used in Yawarrawarrka with the same function as *-rlayi* in Yandruwandha. Also *-rnanyi*. SIM
-itha	used in Yawarrawarrka with the same function as *-nhana* in Yandruwandha. NP
-iya	used in Yawarrawarrka with the same functions as *-nga* in Yandruwandha. FUT
-iyapurra	added to a verb stem in Yawarrawarrka to indicate that something used to happen. See §11.1. REMP
-ka	added to a noun stem or certain other words, to mean 'cause to be that thing'. See §13.7.4. CAUS
-ka	added to a verb to show that an action is being directed away from the speaker. See §11.14. AWAY
-kadi	a form of the ending *-ngadi* used on directional terms and *yila-* 'where'; see §9.7. DAT
-kala	added to a demonstrative pronoun or location word to show that the person(s) or thing(s) concerned is somewhere in the vicinity of some named or known place. Could be translated 'somewhere around'. May be added also to third person pronouns for emphasis. about
-kaldri	added to a verb stem and translated 'again'; it means that an action is repeated or that it restores the previous state of affairs. See §11.10. again
-ku	used in Yawarrawarrka with the same function as *-du* in Yandruwandha. THERE
-kurnu	used on nouns with the meaning 'other', 'another'. See §10.5.3. other
-la-	added to a verb stem preceding *-rla* to state that something which was not happening before is happening at the time of speaking. See §11.15. NOW
-la	added to any word to add emphasis. See §18.4. EMPH
-lapurra	added to a verb stem to indicate that something happened long ago. See §11.1. REMP
-ldra	added to a word to show that there is a contrast with something else; 'on the other hand', or 'contrary to expectation' or just 'but'. See §18.3.2. BUT
-ldrangu	added to any word and has the meaning 'again' or 'too'. Probably a compound of *-ldra* and *-ngu*. See §18.3.3. BUT-YET
-li-	added to a verb stem ending in *i* and preceding *-rla* to state that something which was not happening before is happening at the time of speaking. See §11.15. NOW
-li	added to a noun which is the subject of a transitive verb (and then it is not translated in English), and to a noun which denotes the instrument with which something is done (translated 'with'). See §9.1.3. ERG or INST
-li	added to a verb stem to show that two people are being told to do something. See §11.13. DUIMP

-lka   added to a few intransitive verb stems to form transitive verbs, meaning 'cause to do that action'. See §13.7.5. CAUS

-lu   added in Yawarrawarrka and Strzelecki Yandruwandha to a noun ending in *u* and has the same functions as the second *-li* above. ERG or INST

-ma   added to some intransitive verb stems to form transitive verbs, meaning 'cause to do that action'. See §13.7.4. CAUS

-ma   used in Yawarrawarrka with the same functions as *-ngadi* in Yandruwandha. DAT

-mada, -madani

            used on kinship terms with the meaning 'your', 'his', 'her'. Same as *-mala*. See §9.2, §10.5.8. 2KIN

-mala, -malani

            used on kinship terms with the meaning 'your', 'his', 'her'. May be followed by *-nyi*. See §9.2, §10.5.8. 2KIN

-malka   added to a verb stem to convey a weak command or permission to do the action. See §11.6. OPT

-mindji   used on nouns to mean 'having the thing or quality denoted by the noun'. See §10.5.4. PROP

-mini   used as part of a verb stem to denote that an action is performed in an interval between stages in a journey, or that the agent begins to go somewhere immediately after performing the action, or performs the action on completing his travelling, or performs an action, lasting a comparatively short time, while in motion. See §12.2. run

-na   added to a noun stem to mean 'become that thing' or 'come to have that quality', or to an intransitive verb stem to mean 'cause to do that action', or to a transitive verb to form a ditransitive verb (one that takes two separate objects), or to denote purposeful action. See §13.7.1. INCH or TVR or APP

-na   added to a verb stem to indicate that something has just happened in the very recent past. See §11.1. IP

-ndja   used on nouns to mean 'plural', i.e. 'more than two'. See §9.4, §10.5.2. PL

-ndji   added to a verb stem to mark an action that immediately follows another action. See §11.11. SEQ

-n.ga   added to a verb stem to indicate that something happened within the last few years. See §11.1. FARP

-nga   added to a verb stem, with a wide range of meanings, including future or intended action, action following on from another action, and also showing the purpose of another action. See §11.3. FUT

-ngadi   added to a noun or pronoun which denotes the purpose or aim or destination or beneficiary of an action, translated 'for' or 'to'. When used with a personal pronoun it is added to the genitive form. It is added to a noun also to mark the owner of something, and could then be translated or 'belonging to' or with apostrophe *s*. See §9.1.4. DAT

-*ngana*   added to a noun stem to mean 'become that thing' or 'come to have that quality'. Normally a separate word, not a suffix. See §13.7.2. do

-*ngari*   used as part of a verb stem to denote action directed downwards. See §12.13. down

-*ngi*   used on kinship terms with the meaning 'my'; also used on 'who' and on dual and plural words to mean 'belonging to'. See §9.2, §10.5.7. IKIN

-*ngu*   added to most types of words, and denotes that something is still the case ('still', or 'yet'), or that something else happened ('then', as in 'did this, then did that'). See §18.3.1. YET, THEN

-*nguda*   added to a noun or pronoun to show where something or someone is from, translated 'from'. When used with a personal pronoun it is added to the genitive form. See §9.1.6. ABL

-*ngurru*   used on kinship terms to refer to a group of people, one or more of whom is called by that term, and on other nouns to mean 'having with you'. See §10.5.6. COM

-*nhana*   added to a verb stem to indicate that something has happened within the last day or so. See §11.1. NP

-*nhina*   used as part of a verb stem to refer either to action continuing for some time or to something happening during the day. See §11.1, §12.8. sit

-*nhukada, -nhukadani*
        added to a verb stem to indicate that something happened within the last few days. See §11.1. RECP

-*ni*   added to a verb stem ending in *i* or *u* to convert it into a form that can have noun endings added to it. See -*ini*. See §10.6. GER

-*ni*   added to a verb stem in Yawarrawarrka to indicate that something has just happened in the very recent past. Same as -*na* in Yandruwandha. IP

-*ni*   added to a verb stem to show that more than two people are being told to do something. See §11.13. PLIMP

-*ni*   used in Yawarrawarrka with the same function as -*yi* (added to a noun) in Yandruwandha. LOC

-*nyadi*   can be added to almost any word, and shows that something resembles in some way or can be mistaken for the thing or action represented by that word. Translated 'like'. See §18.2. like

-*nyi*   used in Yawarrawarrka with the same function as -*yi* (added to a noun) in Yandruwandha. LOC

-*pada*   used as part of a verb stem with several functions, including to denote action carried out in or directed into a confined space, and action directed to the other side. See §12.12. in

-*padapada* used as part of a verb stem to denote habitual action, usually as a gerund -*padipadini*, which means 'used to'. See §12.9. HAB

-*pandhi*   used as part of a verb stem to denote action directed downwards. See §12.13. down

-pani	used on nouns to mean 'not having the thing or quality denoted by the noun'. See §10.5.5. It is also used on a verb stem to show that someone is being told not to do something. See §11.5.1. PRIV
-pika	added to a noun stem denoting some object, quality or state, to form a stem denoting someone who or something which is characterised by possessing or being affected by that object, quality or state. See §10.5.10. CHAR
-purra	added to a noun denoting a state or action, to denote 'one who is habitually in that state or performing that action'. See §10.5.9.
-puru	added to a noun or pronoun to show the cause of fear or of a precaution. There is no simple or regular translation in English. When used with a personal pronoun it is added to the genitive form. See §9.1.7. AVER
-rdaka	used as part of a verb stem and seems to denote motion in a different direction to the observer, but the meaning is not clear. See §12.16. (none)
-rduda	used as part of a verb stem to denote a continued or frequently repeated action carried out while the actor is travelling. See §12.1. along
-ri	added to a verb stem to indicate that the tense is not specified in the verb but is to be inferred from the context. See §11.8. UNSP
-rla	added to a verb stem to indicate that something is happening now or happens regularly. See §11.2 PRES
-rlayi	added to a verb stem in a subordinate clause to indicate that the action referred to is simultaneous with or the cause of (and continuing up to the time of) the action referred to in the main clause. See §11.12. SIM
-rnanga	added to a verb stem denotes a continuing action or state in the present, or if subordinate to a main clause it denotes action contemporaneous with, but extending over a longer time than, the action described by the main verb. In a story it denotes something happening at the period of the story. See §11.9. CONT
-rnanyi	used in Yawarrawarrka with the same function as *-rlayi* in Yandruwandha. Also *-irnanyi.* SIM
-thalka	used as part of a verb stem to refer to either action directed upwards or to something happening in the morning. See §11.4, §12.14. up
-tharra	used as part of a verb stem with a range of functions, including to refer to a person or thing moving away from the actor, and to denote completeness of an action. See §12.18. fly
-thawa	used as part of a verb stem to denote that an action is performed in an interval between stages in a journey, or that the agent begins to go somewhere immediately after performing the action, or performs the action on completing his travelling, or performs an action, lasting a comparatively short time, while in motion. See §12.2. go
-thayi	used as part of a verb stem to denote action performed for the actor's own benefit. See §12.17. eat

-thika   used as part of a verb stem to denote action directed back to or followed by a return to camp, or to some other point of recent origin of the actor, and in most cases also preceded by movement to the location of the action, or else it denotes action carried out on behalf of someone other than the actor. See §12.4. return

-thikathika used as part of a verb stem to denote action over a wide area or affecting many objects. See §12.6. everywhere

-thili   used on nouns to mean 'two'. See §9.4, §10.5.1. DU

-thudu   added to a noun or pronoun in Yawarrawarrka to show the cause of fear or of a precaution. There is no simple or regular translation in English. When used with a personal pronoun it is added to the genitive form. See §9.1.7. AVER

-tjadu   added to a third person pronoun to show that the person(s) or thing(s) concerned is not close to the speaker. Can be translated 'there'. Same as *-du*. THERE

-tji   added to any word to add emphasis. See §18.4. EMPH

-w   distorts final vowel of a word, for emphasis. See §3.2.1 DISTORT

-wa   added to a demonstrative pronoun or location word to show that the person(s) or thing(s) concerned is distant from the speaker. Can be translated 'over there'. THERE

-waga or *-wagawaga*
               used as part of a verb stem to denote motion located or directed around some object or place. See §12.7. around

-walpirri   used as part of a verb stem to denote action directed up and over some barrier. See 12.15. across

-warra   used as part of a verb stem to denote arrival. See §12.5. arrive

-windri   used as part of a verb stem to denote action (a) directed away from or (b) followed by movement away from the speaker or some other point of reference. See §12.3. enter

-y   distorts final vowel of a word, for emphasis. See §3.2.1 DISTORT

-ya-   added to a verb stem ending in *i* and preceding *-rla* to state that something which was not happening before is happening at the time of speaking. See §11.15. NOW

-yarndu   added to a verb stem, or more often following, to convey a weak command or permission to do the action. See §11.6. OPT

-yey   distorts final vowel of a word, for emphasis. See §3.2.1 DISTORT

-yi   added to a noun or pronoun to show where something or someone is at the time or is ending up as the result of an action, and translated 'at', 'in', 'on', 'into', 'onto'. When used with a personal pronoun it is added to the genitive form. See §9.1.5. LOC

-yi   added to a third person or demonstrative pronoun or location word to show that the person(s) or thing(s) concerned is close to the speaker. Can be translated 'here'. HERE

-yi   added to a verb stem to warn that an undesirable event may occur. See §11.6. POT

-yindri   used on verbs to mean 'doing to yourself', 'doing to one another', 'doing for your own benefit'. See §7.4, §14.1. RR

-yukala   meaning not known. See §18.5 (none)

-yukarra   used as part of a verb stem to refer to something happening during the night. See §11.4, §12.10. at night

2 *Yandruwandha-English dictionary*

D

daba hole, tear (for example, in a dress); torn # SY, Yw. See **purra**.

    dabaka open (door) # SY. See **pindri, pirika**.

    dabana get torn # SY

dadawa fan • *Maka nhandra yinhayi dadawarla.* 'She's fanning the fire.'

daka make # Yw. Heard only in speaking of making a boomerang. See **ngana, nhapi, wathi**.

dakamirri pelican • *... palha ngala thana dakamirri, marrumarruyitji.* '... they [catch] pelicans in the lake country.' # H *ngagangaga*

(daku)

    dakuka, dakurdakuka fix, repair, make good # Also **patjika**.

    dakuma do properly, make sure of • *Wawana ngathu yinha kanpa dakuma.* 'I saw it properly.' # This is the only example, and it is not clear what part of speech *dakuma* is.

    dakunpa catch (a ball); hit (for example, with bullet), do well or successfully • *Ay dakunpana nhuludu!* 'Oh, good catch!' (or good shot, or whatever). # RYn has it as meaning 'do carefully'.

Dalan.garanyi Dullingari Waterhole (?).

Dalindji Daringie Well (?).

dambu, kurni dambu testicles.

damburdambu(ra?) ball (of flour and water).

Dampunu Dampoona Waterhole # Yw (BK).

dandhirri turkey bush # Perhaps *Eremophila gilesii*. According to Reuther, this is saltbush. See **pundri**.

dan.ga (a) find • *Kali ngathu nhanha dan.gana.* 'I've found her.' • *Minhanganhana nhunu, dan.ganhanangu yuda?* 'What happened to him; did you find him?'; (b) have (a baby) • *Muduwa thidharri dan.ganhana.* '[That woman] had a baby yesterday.' # Yw *mankamanka*; See also **kurra, yadhi kurra, ngama mana, ngathanika**.

dangguda dream # SY. See **pukudu**.

    dangguda pardra dream about # SY Lit. 'dream hold'.

danthu, danthurdanthu soft, supple (as a tanned skin) # See **miltjamiltja, tjampa, paltja**.

dapa shut (mouth) • *Yandhinipurra nhutjadu karrukarru, walya marna dapini.* 'That old man's a good talker, he can't shut his mouth.' # See also **munma, ngapu**.

dapa sore # SY. See also **withi**.

dardirdardima tell someone not to do something, stop someone doing something (by telling) • *Nganha nhulu parndrinhana, ngarndra, minhangadi yundru walya dardirdardimanhana?*

'He hit me, mum, why didn't you stop him?'

darla skin, shell of egg • *Ngapala tjukurru darla karna parrkululi pula wathili pinyiyinkali walthangatji.* 'Two men carry the kangaroo skin [waterbag] on a stick resting on their shoulders.' • *Ngapala pakathikarnanga darla pirnngandji yinha, yilayarndutji kara.* 'Well, they carry them back to camp and skin them — I don't know how.' # See also the first **darlamurru** example. See also **nyindi**.

darlamurru bark • *Ngala pani-pani(kari?) muku palgupalgu dukininguda, ngapala dultharri darlamurru windrimari, paltjikini-ngaditji yina, pirtipirtikari darlatji yinha.* 'After they take out all the bone and muscle they put bloodwood bark in to make it supple and it makes the skin red.' • *Kathi thukali, walya kalpurru thalpali or walya darla-murruli, ngarru kathi thukali mandrirnanga.* 'We don't spoon it up with a coolibah leaf or with bark, only with a mussel shell.'

darnu weak (of person) # SY *wamiyami.*
darnurdarnu weak (of string)

darra cook, roast, burn # SY, Yw. See also **thangkana, mangga, ngarrtji, pidli, kudla, parndraka.**

darrka blow (wind) • *Wathara nhutjadu darrkarla.* 'The wind's blowing.' # See also **ngaka.**

darrpi stop (and turn around?)
darrpingari, darrpipandhi turn back (down) • *Thawapandhina kinipapa-ngadi, ngala nhunu darrpipandhiri thikathalkanga yadala.* 'He was going to the river, but he stopped and came back up.'
darrpithika turn back • *Yidlanggi kara nganyi darrpithikangatji.* 'I don't know where I'll turn back.'

dida the two front teeth # Compare *dida* 'mouth' in Mithaka. See also **marnardraku, waka.**
didamangga yawn # Also **kagayindri.**

didamarra new # SY • *nhipa didamarrayi* 'with a new husband' # See **kayidi.**

Didawalkali Derawalkillie Waterhole # Yw (BK)

Didawandrini Derawantana Waterhole.

didjipirri jump # TG only; See also **kulkupa.** Unlike *kulkupa, didjipirri* was not used for kangaroos hopping, so perhaps does not actually mean 'jump'.

digirdigilyarra dotterel # perhaps related to *dikilyarra* 'slipping', as it runs about in the mud. See also **thanpathanpa.**

dikarri black duck # See also **kunapika.**

dikilyarra slipping # SY • *Dikilyarra ngathu warrkani.* 'I slipped down.'
dikilyarra warra slip along # SY

(dinga)
dingayindri open (eyes) # SY. Compare *thinga* 'pull'. See also **pindri, pirika, tjalka, piltja.**

dinmi see **dirrmi.**

dintji shine # SY • *'Minha nhunurra dintjirla?' 'Oh, minha kara nhulurra warrkani.'* 'What's that shining over there?' 'Oh, something someone threw away.' # See also **para, tjarnma.**

diparri ribs, side # SY, Yw. See **pangki.**

Diradi Dieri, Diyari (language name) • *Ngarrungu nhunu Diradili nganha yakapadanga nga walypala yawarrili, 'Yilangginguda yiney?'* 'Then he just asked me in Dieri, and then in whitefellow language, "Where are you from?"'

(dirrka)
dirrkapandhi turn off (the way or track) • *Walya ngathu yinha*

wawiningadi yurarla. Dirrkapandhirla nganyi, paladila warrakurnula thawanga. 'I don't want to see him. I'll turn off and go on the other side.'

dirrmi   coot # BK; MN (SY) gave *dinmi*, which must be the same word, for a type of waterhen, perhaps purple swamphen. See **kilki, maltjimarrini**.

dirrpa   vulva # Also **ngunutjarrpa**.

ditji   sun # SY, Yw. See **dritji**, which was also used.   H *diyi*

ditjipa   put in the sun to dry • *Ngapala thikaringu ditjipawindriringu thana pirlitji thanha ngapa kadawayi.* 'Then they go back and spread the net out on the bank to dry in the sun.' • *Mulhakuna thayipadipadini ditjipininguda ngapala ngunkunhapiri.* 'They used to eat a brown-nosed one which they dried in the sun and rolled into a ball.' # See also **witjipa**.

ditjirdunka   sunrise # SY

ditjipurri   fall # See also **warlka**.

diyi   see **ditji**.

dragurdragu   (a) spotted # See also **malkamindji**; (b) coarse (not fine).

draka   stab, prick, poke; weave; write; cause pain; (SY) spear • *Kuluwali nganha drakana.* 'The needlewood pricked me.' • *Mitji ngathu drakana marawitju pulyali.* 'I poked my eye with my little finger.' • *Ngapala wirnitji yamatji thana drakaringu wathili kunyali.* 'They weave it into a cross net with a stick and a spindle.' • *Drakarnanga yarnduldrangu wirnikamuratji yiwangaditji pirnaldra, karriningadi panikaldra nhambalkayindrindji.* 'On the one hand they make a big one [hair-string apron] for women, to tie on to cover themselves completely.' • *Pipatji drakininguda nhandra, yilanggi kara nhunu.* 'I don't know where the letter is that she wrote.' • *Thundru drakarla nganha mulhudu pirna thayininguda.* 'I've got a bellyache from eating too

much.' # The subject of *drakarla* is omitted in the last example, but could be, say, *mulhuduli.* See **pipa, karrpa**.

drakardraka   (a) peck; (b) cause pain # SY • *Nganha thundru drakardrakarla mulhuduli.* 'The tucker is giving me a bellyache.'

dralyardralya   squashed

dralyama   squash something (as when you sit on an egg)

drama, dramardrama   cut, cut up • *Kathi yintjadu thatjili dramapandhi.* 'Cut the meat with a knife.' • *Ngapala thana kathi nayilbali-nyadi dramirdraminguda kilkari.* 'You would think it had been cut up with a steel knife.'

dranga   dance, sing, beat time • *Ngapala pula pakarila thanha, ngapirimaladitji mudalatji yina drangarnanga pantjinayindririlatji.* 'Well then they took all their fathers, and they had a corroboree and circumcised one another.' • *Minhangadi yintjadu wani kurnu yundru parndripadapadarla, walya wani kurnunguka drangini. Ngarru kurnungu yundru kilkarla.* 'Why do you always sing that same song, and never sing any other. Is that the only one you know?' • *Wani ngathu drangarla yadali.* 'I'm beating time with boomerangs.' # See **thambana, parndri**.

drangana   sing for someone • *Wani nganha drangana.* 'Sing me a song.'

drangayindri   sing to yourself • *Ngapala nhulu wani dranga-yindrirnanga ...* 'Well, he sang songs to himself ...'

drangka   sweep, wipe • *Nga ngarru makathurrpala thana dringarnanga drangkanga ngananga.* 'When there are only hot ashes left they scrape and sweep them away.' # See also **wipa, wikana, wirrk(a)**.

drantha   (a) crotch # See also **thitha** (b) limb of tree.

wathi drantha forked stick, fork of tree • *... ya nhunggani yabali ngapala wathi drantha kurrari, blanket-li yinha purrilkatharranga, nga wathi thanggunari pantja thangguni-nyadi nhunu karna.* '... and, in his fear, put a forked log on the other side, and covered it over with a blanket, and stood a stick up so that it would look like a man's knee sticking up.' • *Wathi dranthayi nhuniyi ngarnma-yindrirnanga.* 'It's jammed in the fork.'

dranyi hit (throwing), shoot • *Wathili ngathu dranyina.* 'I hit him with a stick (that I threw).' • *Ngapala palha pula dranyindji, nga yadatji nhunu thikawarranga ngapayi warlkapandhinga.* 'They hit a bird, and the boomerang came back down and fell into the water.' • *Walya nhulu kilkanhana minha nganarnanga kara nhunu; walya yina nganha nhulu dranyiningadi. Yarndu nganha nhulu dranyinhanatji.* 'He didn't know what he was doing. He didn't intend to hit me. That's how he came to hit me.' • *Ngarrungu thangguthalkawarrandji dranyingalatji yadali.* 'The man just stands up and kills [one] with a boomerang.' # See **tjutama**.

dratji break off # heard only once, seemed to refer to a stick that stuck into someone and broke off, but not clear. See **kudra**.

drika call (someone something), name • *Maya nganha drikana.* 'Tell me his name.' • *Minha thayipilthirri ngala yundru drikarla kudrikudriningudatji.* 'You call the ones that have been smashed up *thayipilthirri*.' • *Ngala yamali thana ngunipika kurraringu, kalkayi, marripathi minipandhi-ngayayi mandrithalkanga karlukarlu-latji, ngampurru kara, ya kathi nharramindji kara, ya palha kara, ya kathi thanayi — minhaya yina, kathi — mayatji nganyi kurritharrarlala, kathi*

thukathayini, thana drikalapurrayi thanha. 'Well, with the cross net, they put it down in the daytime, in the afternoon, and next morning they run down and pull up the fish — maybe yellowbelly, or maybe a turtle, or maybe a bird, or maybe one of those animals — what is it? — I forget the name — mussel eater they used to call them.' # See also **ngandja**.

dringa grind (seeds) • *Ngala pawa ngala kalildra dringarnanga, pawa kalpurru, pawa wadlangurru, pawa mitjiyimpa, pawa ngadli, pawa pidriyiltharri.* 'Then they used to grind seeds as well — coolibah seeds, wadlangurru seeds, puppa-grass seeds, pigweed seeds, frosty-arse seeds.' • *Wikawikarnanga, pinakanga, ya dringangalatjardi, nga thayiyindri-ngala yartunanga, ngapali ngunku-kininguda.* 'They clean it, rock it, and grind it and then, after mixing it with water and making it into a ball, they eat their fill.' # = *thunga, kururrupa.* **Dringa** 'scrape' may be the same word.

dringa scrape • *Nga ngarru maka-thurrpala thana dringarnanga drangkana ngananga.* 'When there are only hot ashes left they scrape and sweep them away.'

dringatharra, **dringawaga** scrape all over.

drintha spit, spit at • *Drintha mayi!* 'Spit it out!' # See also **ngaltja**.

dritji sun, star, day • *Dritji nhunu dunkarila ngandjarri nganyanguda.* 'The sun's coming out from behind the clouds.' • *Dritji kurnuyitji, karna malkirri thawa-warrandji, ngalyila.* 'One day another group of black-fellows arrived.' • *Dritji parrkulu nganyi nhinanhukada.* 'I stopped there two days ago.' # See also **ditji, kurli, nguni**.

dritji dandra star # SY

dritjirdunka east # Also **witjukura**.

dritjiwindrini west • *Ngalyi thana thawana karawarra, ya ngalyitji thana thawana dritjiwindrinindra.* 'Some of them went north and some of them went west.'

dritjiwindripandhi sunset.

druka splinter, shatter • *pilthipilthirri drukininguda* 'after [the stones] have been splintered into small pieces' # See also **kudra, pilthipilthirrika**.

drukampada bullfrog # big green frog in swamp. See also **durrkuwantha, kutjarrku, kuyarrku**.

drulkurdrulkuna grunt • *Minha yini drulkurdrulkunarla?* 'What are you grunting about?'

drupa rope # from Eng # See **wirni, wilpuru**.

drupayinka a length of rope.

duka pull, pull out, take out • *Kali thana dukaringu ngapangudatji ya pirditjirranga thanha.* 'Then they take it out of the water and strip it.' • *Ngala panipani(kari?) muku palgupalgu dukininguda, ngapala dultharri darlamurru windrimari, paltjikiningaditji yina, pirtipirtikari darlatji yinha.* 'After they take out all the bone and muscle they put bloodwood bark in to make it supple and it makes the skin red.' # See also **thinga, mandritharrapada**.

dukayindri take off (your clothes), untie yourself, get loose

dukapada pull out

dukatharra pull to pieces

dultharri bloodwood • *Ngala pani-pani(kari?) muku palgupalgu dukininguda, ngapala dultharri darlamurru windrimari, paltjikiningaditji yina, pirtipirtikari darlatji yinha.* 'After they take out all the bone and muscle they put bloodwood bark in to make it supple and it makes the skin red.' # *Corymbia* (formerly *Eucalyptus*) *opaca*. SY said blood-wood was not in Yandruwandha country.

dulyi twist (for example, ankle), sprain • *Martardaku nganyi dulyinhana, nganyi ngurrangu thawarla.* 'I twisted my ankle but I kept on going.' # See also **wapa**. It appears that *dulyi* can have only a reflexive meaning (like 'sprain' in English), so that if you speak of twisting someone else's ankle it could not be used, but *wapa* could. Reuther has it as *drulyi*.

dunka go out, come out • *Minha nganarla yini nhinggudu muduwa, walpakurnuyitji? Dunka yada mayi!* 'What are you doing there, kid, in someone else's house? Come on out!' • *Ngala nhulu walypalakurnutji ngarari ngapala nhunu dunkawindrirnangala yita.* 'Well he heard the other whitefellow and started to sneak out.' • *Ngarrungu nhunu kulkupathalkari purtu mandringa dunkawindringa nhunu windriwarrinitji yada warli.* 'So he just jumped up and grabbed his swag and went out the door he had come in by.' • *Nga yarnduldrangu ngathutji wawana yina dunkarlayitji nga yabalildrangu winkanga yadamaningadila thannganiyi thudayukarranga.* 'And I saw you going out and I was frightened too and I ducked off down to the horses and spent the night with them.'

dupurdupu round, curled up • *Dupurdupu yini thudarla, thutjutjunyadi.* 'You're lying curled up like a dog.'

dupurdupuka bend (arm?) # See **kundikundika**.

dupurdupuna fold (including legs).

durrkuwantha type of frog # little green frog, in swamp, half the size of *drukampada*, spends dry times in a clay ball # or *drukuwantha?* or *durrkuwarnta*, in sandhill (TG). See also **kutjarrku**, **kuyarrku**.

durru back • *kankuna durruyi* 'in the back of the windbreak' # See also **thuku, thumu**.

durrukadi from the back, from behind • *tjukurru durrukadi warrkananhana* 'speared the kangaroo from the back' # Lit. 'to the back'.

durruli backwards • *durruli thikathikanarla* 'walking backwards'

durrurdurruna, durruthanggu stoop, bend down • *yumbu durrurdurrunarlayi* 'with his head down'

durruyi behind • *Durruyi ngakani thawawarranhanatji nhunu.* 'He sneaked up behind me.' # See **ngalpirri, ngardra**.

K

ka # probably a short form of **kara**. See **kayidinguda**.

kabow see **kapow**.

kabuta hat • *Kabuta nhuludu ngakani nhangkana, madlamadlantjikarila yinha.* 'That fellow stood on my hat and ruined it.' # Also heard as *kabuda*.

kadawa edge, bank • *Ngapala thikaringu ditjipawindriringu thana pirlitji thanha ngapa kadawayi.* 'Then they go back and spread the net out on the bank to dry in the sun.' • *Palha purla pirnanarlayitji, ngapala yarru wathinaritji, marru kadawayi ...* 'When the young birds are getting big, they build a yard for them on the bank of the lake ...' # See also **ngudulu, wida, thadri**.

kadhi be proud, be happy • *Kadhirla nganyi muduwayitji.* 'I'm proud of that kid.' • *Muduwa thana kadhinhana ngapiritji thikawarrininguda.* 'The kids were happy when their father came home.'

kadi chase, drive • *kurrakurrari nhutjadu, muduwa kadikadini* 'that madman who's always chasing the kids' • *Kadipadanhana ngani, purrkapadanga, Kinipapayitji.* 'We drove the cattle across the river.' • *Pirritjampanarlayi nhunu karrtjipandhinga pulyatji nhunu nga thikanhinanga thundingadi, ngala thana kadirlayi palha ngalyitji, pirnapirnatji, ngapala thana windrimawarraringu wathininguda yarrutji thanngani.* 'If a little one gets tired it turns around and heads back to the island, while they hunt the rest of them, the biggest ones, on and put them in the yard that they have built for them.' # See also **thilpa**.

kadiyindri argue, have a row # contrast *thirri* 'have a fight' and see also **kaldriyindri**.

kadla, kadlaka see **kala, kalaka**

kadli wear # = *thulka, thurrka*.

kadlinayindri put on (clothes) • *Tjawurra nganyi kadlinayindrirla.* 'I'm putting my trousers on.'

kadli see **kali**.

kadra louse # SY says *kata*, which is the word in some neighbouring languages

kadrantji big brown snake

kadri river, creek # H. See **karirri, wipa, kinipapa**.

Kadrimitji Kudriemitchie Waterhole # where circumcision started

Kadripariwirlpa Cutrabelbo Waterhole # Lit. 'creek-sky'. According to AWH this is the name for the Milky Way.

Kadripayirri Cuttapirie Station # *Matja*; lit. 'long creek'.

kagarrali see **kakarrili**.

kagayindri yawn; hiccough; burp • *Marna kagayindrirla nganyi mukali.* 'I'm yawning, sleepy.' # See also **didamangga**.

kaka close, near • *Thibila ngala nhunu, maka kaka!* 'It's the devil, near the fire!' • *Nga yarnduldrangu nhinda,* *pirli ngunthuya mayi, minhangadildra, wathi nhutjadu kakaldra, ngala wathi pirna puladu kalpurru thanggurla, yarndu nhinda ngulutji.* 'They make the net of such a size that it stretches right across from a coolibah on this side to a big one standing [on the other side].'

kakana go close • *Kakana yadaw dranyingalatji yinha kantutji.* 'Get up closer so you can shoot the wallaby.'

kakanguda (SY) close • *Puladu yundra nhunuyi kakanguda.* 'Two a long way off and this one close.'

kakarrili, kagarrali, kagarrirli cockerina, Major Mitchell cockatoo

kakayalba split the end (of a stick, to make a handle)

kaku (a) elder sister • *Thawanhina-nhukadani walya nganyi, wawanga kakumalanitji.* 'If I'd come yesterday I would have seen your sister.'; (b) sister (when relative age is not known or irrelevant) • *Nguthupani nhunu ngarru kaku.* 'He's got no brothers, only sisters.'

Kakurrthunggayi Gidgealpa Oilfield # 'dead marpoo bush'

kala, kadla share, part; even; back; in turn • *Kalala yinha ngathu nganari* 'I told him back', (answered him). • *Parndripadanhana nhulu yina, yundru kadlala walya parndrithikari.* 'He hit you and you didn't hit him back.' • *Ngapiringi ngathu thayirla kathi nhunggani kadlatji.* 'I'm eating my father's share of the meat.' • *'Thawarla nganyi, kathi parndrithikanga.' 'Kawu, kala ngathu maka kinikarlayi.'* 'I'm going out hunting.' 'OK, for my part I'll get a pile of firewood ready.' • *Kadla ngaldra manu patjikayindrina.* 'We're even now [after hitting one another] and friends again.' • *Maka yundrutu wangathalkana, ngala maka kadlalatji ngathu wanganga.* 'You lit the fire this

morning; I'll light it [in my turn] now.' # The function of -*tu* on *yundrutu* is unknown. Reuther has *kadlala* 'reprisal (etc.)' and *kalapa* 'answer'. See **kidlali**.

kalaka, kadlaka get even • *Nganha yundru parndripadana, mirni wada, kalakiningadilatji ngathu.* 'You hit me, well just wait, I'll get even.'

kala there • *Nhunu kala yada, kanpana-larla!* 'There he is, he's showing up now!' # See also **nhinggiwa, nhinggudu, nhukuwa, yita**.

kala see **wathi kala**.

kalamurru black goanna # SY. Also given for carpet snake. See **makapari**.

kaldrapantji see **kaldripantji**.

kaldri sour, bitter • *'Yigatji wayi patji?' 'Ay kaldringu thana. Walpi kara pirtipirtinangatji.'* '"What are the wild oranges like?" "Oh, they're bitter yet. Don't know when they're going to get ripe."'

(kaldri)

kaldriyindri argue # Also **kadiyindri**.

kaldripantji call out, sing out • *Kaldripantjina nhunu ngakaniyi ngapalatji ngathu milkiningadi.* 'He sang out to me and made me spill the water.' # Yw *kaldrapantja*, H *karlupandja*. See also **karrka, kandri, mirrtjakurra, ngarndapandji**.

kaldrithayi swear at • *Nhipa nhandru yina kaldrithayila, thikawarrarlayi kurriringanarnanga.* 'She's swearing about her husband coming home drunk.'

kaldrukaldru growl, bark (of a dog); rough (voice) # See also **warlu, wawurrka, marrtji**.

kaldrukaldruna bark (verb)

kalga loose; dim; lightly (of eating)(?); relaxed; quietly (speaking) • *Kalgali nhutjadu tjarnmarla.* 'It's shining dimly.' • *Mulhudu kalgali nhulu thayirla ...* 'He doesn't eat much ...' (unfinished, and changed to *Pulya nhuludu thayirla ...*) • *Ay kalgali nganyi.* '[I've done the work and now] I've got it easy.'

kalgaka loosen • *Mardramitjili kara ngathu yinhadu parndripandringa yinha, kalgakarilatji.* 'I'll hit it with a rock; that'll loosen it.'

kalhidi husband's mother, woman's daughter-in-law # possibly *kalidi*. See also **patjiri**.

kali, kadli now, already, just (then) • *Kali ngathu yibana.* 'I just had a drink of water [so don't offer me any]' • *Kali thana dukaringu ngapangudatji ya pirditjirranga thanha.* 'Then they take it out of the water and strip it.' • *Kali ngathu panmapandhina.* 'I've already put it out.' (in reply to 'Put the fire out!') • *Thawarla nganyi ngala nhunu kuthiwarrarlayitji ngardrathikarla. Kadli nganyi thawari.* 'I'm going now, and he'll be getting here later. I'll be already gone.' # See also **kayidi, ngala**.

kali paningu not yet # Also **walyangu**.

kali walya, kadli walya nearly • *Kadli walya nganyi warlkanatji.* 'I nearly fell down.' • *Muduwa thidharri kadli walya nhunu yandhayandharlatji. Ngarnma-ngarnmayindrirlangu nhunu.* 'The baby can nearly talk, but he still gets stuck.' # Yw *ngampu*

kalipilhipilhi butterfly

kalka (a) afternoon • *Ngala yamali thana ngunipika kurraringu, kalkayi, marripathi minipandhingayayi mandrithalkanga karlukarlulatji ...* 'Well, with the cross net, they put it down in the daytime, in the afternoon, and next morning they run down and pull up the fish ...' • *Yakayindrini kalkayi, 'Mayi, karlukarlutji wayinila*

ngandra?'. 'In the afternoon they ask one another, "How many fish did we get?".'; (b) evening sky # SY • *Marrarla nhuniyi kalka.* 'The sky's getting red.' # Reuther 'evening'.

kalkanyi, kalkaalkanyi yesterday # Yw

kalkayi, kalkaalkayi yesterday # SY. See **ngananhinanhukada**.

kalkamarra get light, become daylight # SY, Yw. See **marra** and **padla marra**.

kalka, kalkayindri wait # SY, Yw. • *Watja kalkayindri nhunggananyi.* 'Don't wait for him.' • *Mirni nganha kalka.* 'Will you wait for me.' See **wada**; also **mirni, thakurru**

kalpurru coolibah # *Wathi kalpurru* would mean a coolibah tree, and *pawa kalpurru* coolibah seeds. • *Nga yarnduldrangu nhinda, pirli ngunthuya mayi, minhangadildra, wathi nhutjadu kakaldra, ngala wathi pirna puladu kalpurru thanggurla, yarndu nhinda ngulutji.* 'They make the net of such a size that it stretches right across from a coolibah on this side to a big one standing [on the other side].' • *Ngala pawa ngala kalildra dingarnanga, pawa kalpurru, pawa wadlangurru, pawa mitjiyimpa, pawa ngadli, pawa pidriyiltharri.* 'Then they used to grind seeds as well — coolibah seeds, wadlangurru seeds, puppa-grass seeds, pigweed seeds, frosty-arse seeds.'

kalta blue-tongue lizard # Doubtful; *kalta* is shingleback lizard in some other languages. Not found in Innamincka country, but to the south.

kaltja acacia bush # probably *Acacia victoriae*, but see also **wayaka**.

kaltjantada type of lizard, possibly barking gecko, *Underwoodisaurus milii* # SY. Yellow, spotted, stumpy tail, stand up and bark at you like a dog.

kalu liver # Also **ngarangara**.

Kalumurayi place name # 'quiet heart'

kalu bow vine # Yw, see **punggu**.

kalumarra be greedy # SY. Seems to be literally 'liver to get red'.

kaluwa dip up, scoop up (water) # SY. See **marndra**.

Kalyamarru Callamurra Waterhole # 'wide waterhole'

kalyu type of wattle

kamanti my, mine # Yw, H. See **ngakani**.

kamarra top # See also **kandra, kudu**.

kamba anthill

kambada or **kambadi** red ochre # SY. See **milthi**.

kambarri at the front; first • (SY) *Yini yita kambarri thawa*. 'You go first.' # See also **ngakamarra**.

kambu type of coolamon # Compare **nharrakambu**.

kamburru river wattle # like willow but red limbs

kami grandmother, father's mother, grandchild, woman's son's child, cousin, mother's brother's child, father's sister's child # H also 'sister-in-law'

kamiri (1) social division, totem ('meat') • *Minha kamiri yini?* 'What "meat" are you?' # People were divided, according to descent through the mother, into two groups (moieties), called something like *Thiniwa* and *Kulpurru* (but the exact pronunciations are not known). A person married someone from the other moiety. Each was further divided into a dozen or so totems, each given the name of some creature or thing, such as kangaroo, emu, eaglehawk, goanna, pitchery, red ochre, rain. See also **mardu**; (2a) smell (especially, perhaps, characteristic smell, as of a person) • *kamiri madlantji* 'unpleasant smell';

(2b) taste, flavour, sweetness • (SY) *Kamiri nhunuyi ngapa kuntha*. 'This tea's sweet.'

kananggu or **kanunggu** type of witchetty grub • *Ngarru kathi kananggu ngala dukarnanga kulanga makamuduyitji, mardra thakili parndrininguda*. 'And they pulled out witchetty grubs from trees, after chopping them out with a stone axe, and cooked them in hot ashes.'

kanbi take the part of someone (in a fight or argument) # Yw • *Nhuluku windrali drakitha, nguthu kanbiri*. 'He speared [the other man] on account of his brother.'

kanda shallow, light # See also **ngawada, ngalba, putha**.

kandama count # from Eng

kandatjiri kite hawk, black kite

Kandipantjini Pandie Pandie # Yw

kandjipulu policeman # SY, from Eng. See also **pilimpara, pilitjimani, thandjipulu, yulya**.

kandirrtha wasp, hornet or dragonfly # SY

kandra top, high • *walpa kandrayi* 'on top of the humpy' • (SY) *warliyi kandra* 'on top of the house' • *Kurrarnanga kandratji mirndithanminingaditji thana yamatji, karnan.gu yina*. 'They put reeds on top of the cross net so that it will float.' • *Wathi windra ngathu warrkanhana kandraldra, walya ngathu warrkapadipadini yarndu-kalatji*. 'I threw the spear very high; I never used to throw it like that.' • *Padlayi yina kurnutji kurrari ngala kandraldra nhambalkayindriri kurnulitji*. 'They put one on the ground and cover themselves over with another.' # See also **kamarra, kudu**.

kandrakandra (a) high • *kuka kandrakandra* 'head held high'; (b) upstream • *Kandrakandranguda,*

Ngapamiringuda kara nhunu thawawarrana. 'He came from upstream, maybe from Nappa Merrie.'

kandraka, kandrakandraka lift • *Mardra pudlupudlu kandrakarla ngathu.* 'I can't lift that rock.'

kandrana go up, ascend # Yw

kandratjanggu be glad

kandri call; send for • *Walya ngathu yinha kandrinhana, ngala nhunu thawawarranangu.* 'I didn't call him but he still came.' • *Nganyi thangguthikana nga walya thana nhinanhinarlayitji, kadlitji nganha kandrininguda.* 'I went to visit them but they weren't there, after sending for me.' # See also **mirrtjakurra, ngarndapandji.**

kandri palku beefwood gum # SY. See also **pirntathangka.**

kan.ga man! (as a term of address) # Possibly vocative form of *kan.gu,* but note that *kan.gu* was not heard in IY.

kangu warm • *Tjukurru parrkulu kara, parrkulu parrkulu kara karrpininguda nga kangu yukarrangatji.* 'It might be two skins, or maybe four and then they are warm at night.' • *Warrayi nhanudu nhinanhinapadaw kanguyi.* 'Let her stop inside in the warm.' # SY, Yw also 'sweat' which could be incorrect; See also **kanyi.**

kan.gu boy # SY. See also **walhini.**

kani, kathi kani carney, bearded dragon # See also **kurla.**

kankunu windbreak • *Nga kankunu pirna nhulu kurranga.* 'He put up a big wind-break.' • *Ngapala, kurrupu karrukarru pundrayi kara, makamakayi kara, ngapala ngarru kankunu kurraringa makawarrkanga kunawarrkutji thudayukarrangatji.* 'Well, the olden-days women and men, in winter or summer, only put up a windbreak, throw some firewood down and sleep all night crossways.'

kanpa present, in sight, plainly visible, in the open • *Kathi marngali ngathu wanthirla, walyawalyakanga yinha, kanthayi. Ay, nhutjadu kanpala.* 'I was after a goanna but I lost it in the grass. Hey, it's turned up!' • *Wawana ngathu yinha kanpa dakuma.* 'I saw it properly.' • *Thayinhana walya ngathu, kanpayi ngada.* 'I didn't eat it while it was there [and now it's gone].' • windratji *kanpa wirlpayi* 'a spear sticking out through a hole [in the wall]' • *Dan.gana ngathu walya yundra, kanpayi nhunu thudanhinarlayardi.* 'I found it nearby; it was lying in the open (easily seen).'

kanpaka be born • *yadhi thundriyi, muduwatji kanpakari* 'the afterbirth is in the stomach (= womb) when the baby is born'

kanpana show up, appear • *Nhunu kala yada, kanpanalarla!* 'There he is, he's showing up now!'

kanpanawarra appear

kanpa (1) very; (2) susceptible to • *kanpa kudrini* 'brittle, easily broken' # Reuther has *kanpa* 'real, really' (Yw)

kanpamuthu very • *Karna wirlpa kanpamuthu nhutjadu minirla yabayi.* 'That man ran off really fast in his fear.' # See also **muthu.**

kanpangu first time, straight away • *Ngapala nhunu thangguthalkawarrari nga dranyinga. Kanpangu, purnda yina dranyiri.* 'Then he would stand right up and kill one [emu]. He hits it right then, on the back of the neck.' • *Minithalkawarrarlayi ngala ngapayi mini warrkanapandhiri yita, kanpangu kara, nyalkari kara.* 'When they came up from the water they would spear them; they might get one straight off or they might miss.' • *Ngapala miniyukarrarlayi thana warrkanapadarlayildrangu, kanpangu.*

'They chase them at night too and
spear them then, straight off.'

kanpapardra first shot • *Muduwa
thanayi ngakanili kilkarla mardramitjili dranyiri kanpapardra.* 'My kids
think [I can] hit [a bird] with a stone
first shot.' * See also **kayidi pardra**.

kanta a word or ending that sometimes
follows a word that tells where or
which one; its meaning is not clear,
but it has been translated 'over there'.
See also **widi, walha, waka**.
• *yundra kanta* 'over there in the
distance, way over' • *nhinggiwa kanta*
'over there' • *Thawanhana nhunu
ngakaningadi yandhayandhanga-
nyadi nhinggiyi, walyangu nhunu
thawawarrana, nga yini thawa
mayi yandhayandhanga nhunggani
nhingguwa kantanga.* 'I thought he
was going to come here to talk to me.
He hasn't arrived yet, so you go and
talk to him over there.'

kantha grass; the bush • *Kantha mangga
mayi, pulkapada mayi.* 'Burn the
grass! Blow it (so it burns)!' • *Wilyaru
thana pardraringu pakangalatji
kanthayi warrkathikanga.* 'They
took him into the bush and left him.'
• *Ngapala thana kurrupulila
mandrithikathalkangardi kantha
pudlapudlarnanga thanha, ya wathi
karlitji.* 'Well, the women get grass
and separate the seeds, and limbs
of trees.' • *Kathi marngali ngathu
wanthirla, walyawalyakanga yinha,
kanthayi. Ay, nhutjadu kanparla.* 'I
was after a goanna but I lost it in the
grass. Hey, it's turned up!' # See also
kurrkari.

kanthakantha grassy country
• *Mirni, kirri yintjadu yaka, walpi
nhunu thawanga kanthakanthangadi.*
'Can you ask him when he's going to
the bush [lit. grassy place].'

kanthiri rubbish # SY. Used in the
context of talk about winnowing grain,

so may mean more specifically chaff
and/or husks and/or pods.

kantu, kathi kantu rock wallaby
• *Marripathi kara nganyi thawanga
parndrithikanga kathi kantu kurnula.*
'Tomorrow I might go out and get a
wallaby.'

kanyi sweat • *kanyi ngakarnanga*
'sweating (lit. sweat running)' # See
also **kangu**.

kanyini grandmother, mother's mother,
grandchild, woman's daughter's child

kapa lower part of body of kangaroo
Contrasts with *kuldru*; does not
seem to include hindquarters

kapada come on! • *Kapada thiliyi
ngakani nhinanga.* 'Come and sit
beside me.' • *Kapada ngaldra
thutjutjuli thawarla, tjukurru
parndringa.* 'Come on, we're going
with the dogs to kill a kangaroo.'

kaparri root of tree # See also
yunggudu.

**kapi, kapiyindri, kapikapi, kapikapi-
yindri** follow, track # The person
or thing being followed is marked
as locative if *-yindri* is used, and
as accusative if it is not.
• *Thawapadapadarla nganyi, pandili
nhulu kapiyindrirnanga ngurra.
Kapikapiyindrirnanga ngakaniyi
ngurra.* 'Wherever I go that dog
follows me. He's always following
me about.' • *Ngathu yinha kapirla,
yakayakanga yinha mardra ngakani
winkamanhana, ngunyithikanga kara
nganha nhulu, pani kara.* 'I'm going
to follow him and ask him whether
he took my money and whether he'll
give it back to me or not.' # May be
used with the word *thina* 'foot, track'.
• (Yw) *Ngathu yinhaku thina
kapikapirla.* 'I'm tracking him.'

kapitharra track # SY. See **palthu,
thina, wardayapa**.

kapitharrapada follow (someone)
inside

kapi, karlu kapi, karlukarlu kapi small catfish

kapitha bandicoot # SY

kapow look out! # Also **kabow**. 'Dog might be coming across to bite him, the other bloke sees him and he sings out, *Kapow!*'

kapukapu possibly gall on coolibah and the grub inside it # SY

kapurru, kapurrukutja armpit • *Mirra-mirrayindrirla nganyi, kuka kara, kapurru kara, pangkithirri kara.* 'I don't know whether I'm scratching my head, or under the arm, or my ribs.' # Recorded as *kapurra* from SY. Reuther has *kapurrukutja* as 'underarm hair'.

kara (also pronounced **kayi**) maybe, might, or, I don't know, how about? # Used often with a set of alternatives. • *Thawawarrarla kara nhunu, pani kara.* 'He might come, and he might not.' • *Man.garri kara, karruwali kara?* or *Man.garri kara karruwali?* 'Is it a boy or a girl?' • *'Yilangginguda nhutjadu?' 'Ngalaaku.' 'Yakapadala yinha mayi.' 'A'ey, nhindalitji nganyi yundru kayi.'* "Where's he from?" "I don't know." "Well, ask him." "Uh-uh, I'm shy, you do it."' • *Minhayangadilatji karlukarlu yukiningadi kara, ya kinipapayi kara kurriningadi, karlukarlu kara yamali.* 'That's what they're for, for catching fish while swimming in the water, and for putting across the river [to catch] fish in the cross net.' • *Punggu murrpiningudatji ngapala kurrari ngapayi, wiki parrkulu kara, thungganiningadi.* 'They cut the bow vine and put it in water for maybe two weeks, so that it will rot.' • *Miniwarrkanapandhiri yita, kanpangu kara, nyalkari kara.* 'They spear them on the run [too], and they might get one straight off or they

might miss.' # See also **mirni, kirri, ngalaaku**.

karadaka light (a fire) # SY. # See also **wanga, pulkapada, thalpapada**.

karawarra north • *Thawana thanawaka karawarrakadi.* 'They went north.' • *Ngalyi thana thawana karawarra, ya ngalyitji thana thawana dritji-windrinildra.* 'Some of them went north and some of them went west.'

karditjidi cheek # Also **ngulku, kidakida**.

kardra yam • *Kurrupu thana paku-padipadini kardra.* 'The [olden-days] women used to dig yams.'

kardri brother-in-law, wife's brother, husband's brother • *Puladu kardri-ngurru, wiriwinmanhana puladu ngathadi man.garri, nhipakiningadi.* 'Those two are brothers-in-law; they gave each other their young sisters to marry.' # See also **yimadi**.

kari, karithalka climb • *Muduwa wathiyi nhutjadu karirla.* 'The kid's climbing the tree.' • *Walya wathiyi karithalka.* 'Don't climb that tree.' # See also **walki, kathi**.

karingkarra sand goanna # Yw, H

karirri creek, river • *Karirri pandhiwaka karlukarlu mandriyindrirla.* 'He's down at the creek fishing.' # See also **karitjurru, kadri, kinipapa, wipa**.

karitjurru creek, river # Yw. • *Karitjurru nhunuyi pirnala.* 'The river is wide here.' # See also **karirri, kadri, kinipapa**.

Karitjurru Coongie Lake (doubtful)

karla empty # Yw. See also **marakarla**.

karlaka yower, mungeroo, wild onion (These are the nodules on the roots of the sedge *Cyperus bulbosus*.) • *Ya karlakala pakurnanga malkirri thana kulanga makakanyayildrangu.* 'They dig yowers and cook them in hot ashes too.'

karlantji bicycle lizard (type(s) of dragon lizard) # SY. See **yaliyali**.

karli (a) hair (of head), # SY, Yw *pada* (b) limb (of tree) # See **drantha**.

kuka karli hair (of head) • *Kuka karli payirri nhutjadutji yiwa-nyadi; nhindapani.* 'That fellow's got long hair like a woman. Got no shame.'

wathi karli limb of tree
• *Ngapala thana kurrupulila mandrithikathalkangardi kantha pudlapudlarnanga thanha, ya wathi karlitji.* 'Well, the women get grass and separate the seeds, and limbs of trees.'

karlku bulrushes • *Karlkuli ngala yamatji mikimana, nganalapurra thana yamali ngala karlkuli.* 'Well they made nets of bulrushes; they used to use nets made of bulrushes.'

karlukarlu fish • *Karlukarlungadi nganyi thawarla.* 'I'm going fishing.'
• *Ngapala pula karlukarlungadi yada thawari nga yandhanga nhinanga karlukarlu parndrirnanga pula thadri padawadaldra, ngala nganyitji thadri yitapandhiwarraldra nhinarlayi.* 'Two of them came down to do some fishing. They sat and talked and caught fish on the other bank, while I was camped on the bank that sloped down opposite them.'
• *... ngala ngarndri ngapirili thanha walthanarlayi karlukarlutji, ngunyinga nhinggikala yarruyi.* '... while their parents bring fish and give them to them in the yard.'
See also **kuya**.

karlu kapi, karlukarlu kapi small catfish

karlukarlu pardi type of fish # See under **kuya**.

karlupandja see **kaldripantji**.

karna (Aboriginal) person; man • *Ngala nhunu karnakurnutji thawawarrarlayi kilkarnanga yina karnatji yabapika.* 'Then this other man arrived and knew that this fellow was frightened.'
• *Ngala karna thana nhinarlayi, thundiyi.* 'Meanwhile there were some blackfellows camping on an island.'
• *Malkanpanguda nhutjadu karna.* 'That fellow's from Innamincka.'
• *Thayiyindringa palhatji yarndu thana parndripadipadini karnalitji, palhatji ngala drakininguda ngala paladi.* 'That's how the Aborigines used to catch birds to eat, with a special type [of net] they had woven.'

karnakurnu-karnakurnu everybody, anybody • *Karnakurnu-karnakurnu ngarru palthu kurnuyi thawarnanga ngapangadilatji pakuninguda thana matja.* 'Anyone using this road can get water from the well they dug long ago.'

karnapalha devil, (H) ghost
• *Ngapala nhunu nguthangutharnangala katjakatjarlayilatji parndriyindrininguda nganggali karnapalha-nyadi wawawawari.* 'Well, he stretched out his leg because of the pain, because he had hit himself, thinking it was a devil he had seen.'
• *... karnali thana nganha nganganga mardrangumuyi karnapalha nhinarlayi.* '... people told me there's a devil in the cave.' # See also **kurnki**, **yarrkamarta**.

karna parndrini murderer

karnan.gu reeds (on river bank)
• *Kurrarnanga kandratji mirndi-thanminingaditji thana yamatji, karnan.gu yina.* 'They put reeds on top of the cross net so that it will float.'

karndilkatha porcupine, echidna

karra tie, tie up • *Ngapala pirnta-thangkali nyanmari, marapardrini, wirnili ngukanguka pirntathangkali, karrangalatji yina.* 'I'll bind the handle on with string and seal it with beefwood gum (mixed with the string).' • *Ngala nhunu yadamani* *mapayindrirlayi milimanityéyi thikaringu yada, ya warlitji kuthiwarranga ya yadamani nhulu karrathikathikarnanga thanha windripadanga.* 'Meanwhile the mailman was rounding up his horses, and then he came back to the hut and tied up all the horses and went in.' • *Karraringu thanha mulpininguda warnta, payipayirru yina, mara witjunyadi.* 'They tie them on after cutting them into short lengths, about the size of a finger.'

karrakarra bandage (verb)

karrapandhi tie up

karrapada tie on, tie up

karramini tie here and there

karrawa eaglehawk

karriwara eaglehawk # SY, Yw, H

karrka call out, yell • *Minhangadi nhutjadu muduwa karrkarla?* 'Why is that kid yelling out?' • *Karrkapadanhana nhulu ngalinha padawadangudali.* 'He sang out to us from across the river.' • *Karrkarla ngathu nguthingi, ngali kandrakiningadi.* 'I'll call my brother and we'll lift it.' # See also **kaldripantji, kandri, mirrtjakurra, ngarndapandji.**

karrpa sew, weave • *Ngathu wawatharrana karlukarlungadi yukiningadi pirli yama yina karrparlayi.* 'I saw them make a bag net for catching fish while swimming in the water, and a cross net.' • *Ngapala thana karrparnanga thirrithirri-nyadi yina walypalali kurrarlatji thana, thirrila karrpiningadi mirrka.* 'Then they weave it just like the cotton white people use for making their clothes.' • *Ngapala windrimari karrpangalatji.* 'Then they put it [the kangaroo sinew] in and sew it.' # SY, Yw also 'tie'. See also **milpi, draka.**

karrpa, karrpakarrpa mend (for example, a torn dress) # SY

karrtji roll over

karrtjikarrtjima whirl (something) around, turn (something) over and over; tell (a story) • *Ngapala yina wathi thinbanari mandawarra, ya wirni thurrpanari yinha mulhudungadilatji nhunu thawathalkiningadi warrkanga wathilatji yina karrtjikarrtjimari.* 'Well, he would cut and shape a stick from a plum bush and tie a string to it and whirl it around, so that someone would come and leave some food for him.' • *Kurrapandhiri purtutji yinhanga makali yina karrtjikarrtjimawarranga wathi witjuli.* 'He put the swag down by the fire and started to turn [the ashes] over with a twig.' • *Karrtjikarrtjimanhana nhulu, patjikurnungu.* 'He told the story the right way.' # See also **wirni, purrilka.**

karrtjimawagawaga swing (something, such as a rope) around

karrtjingari, karrtjipandhi turn back, turn around • *Pirritjampanarlayi nhunu karrtjipandhinga pulyatji nhunu nga thikanhinanga thundingadi ...* 'If a little one gets tired it turns around and heads back to the island ...' • *... karrtjipandhinga parndringala yina.* '[They'll be good to you one minute and then] they'll turn around and kill you.'

karrtjiwaga turn around

karrtjiwagawaga go round and round • *Wathi nhuniyi karrtjiwagawagarla.* 'This machine (tape recorder) is going round and round.'

karru, karna karru (initiated, Aboriginal) man • *Ngala yiwalitji kardrarda pakurlayi, ngala ngarru karruli thana pawatji kudrarlayi.* 'Only the men crush the seeds, while the women dig yams.' • *Wanitji ngathu wawangala, karrula yina nganyi.* 'I can watch the corroboree now because I'm a man.'

karruka making a man of someone, initiating • *Mirni ngaldra ngapirila ngalungga karrukanga.* 'Come on, we'll go back and make a man out of our father.'

karrukarru (1) old man (often used as a term of address), olden-days men • *Karrukarruyi yintjadu ngathu mama-thikana wathi windra.* 'I took the spear off that old fellow over there.' • *Ngapala nhunu ngarru yankula mandriri, nga warrkapandhinga ngapala pulkanga ngala nhulu, marnali pulkarnanga nhulu ngala nhulu karrukarrukurnulitji ngararila.* 'So he just got some [dry] leaves and threw them down [on the hot coals] and started to blow them, and while he was blowing them the other old man heard him.' • *Yilayarndu kara thana pirnngipadipadinitji mara patjikurnuli yina karrukarrutji nhinapadipadini ngapangaditji.* 'I don't know how they did it, but the olden-days men used to be good hands at skinning [kangaroos] for water [bags].'; (2) male (animal) • *Pandi thanayi nhiwa karrukarru thawathawarla.* 'Dogs and bitches are wandering around.'

karrukarru, palha karrukarru diver (bird)

karrukarruna get old (of a male) • *Karrukarrunarla nhutjadu, madlantji ngananarla.* 'He [dog] is getting old and useless.'

karrupakarli flood bird

karruwali little boy • *Karruwali nhina-lapurratji pinthapurru.* 'They were still boys, with foreskins.' • *Man.garri kurnu ngala thana ngalyitji ngarru karruwalildra.* 'There's one girl and all the rest are boys.'

karta crack, cracking sound, bang, banging sound

kartaka make a cracking or banging noise • *Kartakarlayi ngathu ngarana.* 'I heard a bang.'

kartakanmana make something make a cracking or banging noise • *Wubu nhuludu kartakanmanarnanga.* 'He's cracking the whip.'

kartakarta saltbush species (probably bladder saltbush; they crack when you walk on them and the name means 'crack crack')

kartamatha belt, whack

kartiwirri dive, swoop • *Ngapala palhatji kartiwirriringu. Minhayapuru yina? Palha thirripuru.* 'Then the birds dive down. What for? Because [they think] it is a chicken hawk.' # See also **winkapandhi**.

kathi meat, animal • *Kathi ngathu pardranhana nhinggiyi.* 'I had some meat here.' • *Kathi thungga ngathu thayina.* 'I ate rotten meat.' • *Kathi tjukurrutji, ngarru wathi windralildra warrkanarnanga.* 'As for kangaroos, one way is to just kill them with a spear.' # See also **palgupalgu**. *Kathi* is often used with the name of an animal that is eaten, for example, *kathi tjukurru* 'kangaroo', *kathi warruwitji* 'emu', *kathi pundha* 'mouse', *kathi nharramindji* 'turtle', *kathi thuka* 'mussel' but not *kathi kananggu* 'witchetty grub'. It is also used with the name of an edible part of the animal, as in *kathi pangkithirri* 'rib-bone meat'.

kathi dramirdramini butcher

kathi parndrini butcher, hunter

kathi pirnngini butcher

kathikathi, pardi kathikathi snake • *Yabali yini kathikathipuru?* 'Are you frightened of snakes?' • *Pardi kathikathitji kali windrinhana pundrayi.* 'The snakes have gone in (to hibernate) because of the cold.' # It was said that you hear thunder when the winter is coming on, and when they hear this the snakes and goannas go into hibernation. Then about the end of August you hear thunder again, and that's when they come out. # *kathikathi* is probably used only for poisonous (and inedible) snakes.

kathi climb # Yw • *Kathi ngakaniyi thumuyi.* 'Get on my back [to a baby].' # See **walki, kari.**

Kathipidi Cuttaberrie Lake # Yw (BK)

katjakatja sting, pain, hurt # The person or thing feeling the pain is the subject. However, the person or thing appears as an object if the body part in which the pain is felt is specified (in which case the part appears as a subject, not an agent) or even if it is thought of. The cause of the pain is included only as a peripheral constituent or in a separate clause. • *Wayiludunguda nganyi katjakatjarla.* 'I'm stinging from a mosquito [bite].' • *Wayiluduli nganha mathana, katjakatjana nganyi.* 'A mosquito bit me; it [the place where I was bitten] stung.' • *Maltji nganha katjakatjarla.* 'My leg's stinging.' • *Ngurrangu nhunu yingkirla; katjakatjarlayi kara.* 'He's still crying. Must be still hurting him.' • *'Minhangadi nhutjadu muduwa maltji pardrayindrirla?'* *'Katjakatjarla yinha.'* 'What's that boy holding on to his leg for?' 'It's hurting him.' • *Ngapala nhunu ngutha-ngutharnangala katjakatjarlayilatji parndriyindrininguda nganggali karna palha-nyadi wawawawari.* 'Well, he stretched out his leg because of the pain, because he had hit himself, thinking it was a devil he had seen.' # See also **mundjaka, thalpa.**

kawalka crow # BK once gave the name of a totem as *wakiri* and translated it as 'crow', but it comes from one of the languages just to the north. Perhaps words from other languages were used to name the totems. See also under **pitjidi.**

kawu yes # Also heard as *ngawu;* also **ngaandi.**

kayakaya (woman's or sister's) daughter's daughter's child; perhaps also mother's mother's mother # SY, Yw (given also for mother's mother, woman's daughter's child, sister's child, daughter-in-law, mother-in-law). See also **ngarlu.**

kayarri tea tree # See also **thayarri.** One of these may be a mistake. SY *wawu.*

kayi = **kara**

kayidi now, directly, soon, new, lately • *Kayiditji walyala thana nhinarla.* 'They aren't living any more.' • *Kayidi nganyi papanangarirla.* 'I'll start directly.' • *Kayidila thanadu thawawarranhana, yilangginguda kara.* 'They [rabbits] have only come lately — I don't know where from.' • *Thidharri yini yingkilapurra; pirnapirnala ngala yini kayiditji.* 'You used to cry [a lot] when you were a baby, but you're big now.' • *Thawarla ngandra, kayidi, malthiyi ngada.* 'We'll go now, while it's still cool.' • (Yw) *Ngathu yinhayi puka nhapirla. Kayidi yinha ngathu makanga kurriya.* 'I'm making this damper. I'm just putting it into the fire now.' # See also **kali, ngala.**

kayidi-kayidi now and then • *Kundrukundrunhana nhutjadu kayidi-kayidi.* 'He was coughing now and then.' # See also **marndakurnu-marndakurnu.**

kayidinguda new • *Kayidingudali ka matjangudali?* '[Did you use] the new one or the old one?' # SY *didamarra*

kayidi pardra first time • *Kayidi pardra ngathu mandripadarla ngan.gutji.* 'I'm just now getting hold of the words [of Yandruwandha].' • *Kayidi pardra ngathu wantjana.* 'That's the first time I tried it.' # See also **kanpangu, kanpapardra.**

kayinta dry (something) # See also **muyaka, puruduka**.

kidakida cheek # SY. See **ngulku, karditjidi**.

kidla next; in return • *Ngapa yundru kidlala marndrathikanga.* 'You get the water next time [because I got it before].' • *Puka paka ngathu ngunyinhana, kathila nhulu nganha pakanathikandji kidlatji.* 'He brought me back some meat in return for the tobacco I gave him.'

kidlali in turn • *Kidlali waltha.* '[You] take a turn to carry [it].' • *Kidlalila ngathu waltharla.* 'I'll take a turn to carry [it].' # See also **kala, kadla**.

kidra see **kirdra**.

kilangkila galah # SY. See **nhadipintha**.

kilka, kilkalilka, kilkayilka know, recognise, think, suppose; think about • *Ngala nhunu karnakurnutji thawawarrarlayi kilkarnanga yina karnatji yabapika.* 'Then this other man arrived and knew that this fellow was frightened.' • *Kilkarla ngathu yintjadu, ngarndri-ngapiri ngala nguthu-ngama.* 'I know him, and his parents and relations.' • *Yundra ngathu yina wawana walya yina kilkanga.* 'I saw you a long way off and I didn't recognise you.' • *Walya nhulu kilkanhana minha nganarnanga kara nhunu; walya yina nganha nhulu dranyiningadi. Yarndu nganha nhulu dranyinhanatji.* 'He didn't know what he was doing. He didn't intend to hit me. That's how he came to hit me.' • *Kilkalikarla thawanga ngapangaditji, ngarru pulyala pakari tjukurru darla yibiningadi palthuyukala yitalayi thawarnanga.* 'They know it is there and they need carry only a small kangaroo skin [waterbag] for drinking from while they are going along.' • *Ngapala thana kathi nalybali-nyadi dramirdramininguda kilkari.* 'You would think it had been done with

a steel knife.' • *Ngala thanayi kilkarla, ngarru yarawarrangu thawathawapadipadini ...* 'People now think they used to walk about naked ...' • *Ngurra ngathu yinha kilkarla.* 'I'm always thinking of him.' • *Kilkana ngathu warlkiningadi-nyadi.* 'I thought I was going to fall.' # *kitka* in Yawarrawarrka, *kittja* in Matja. See also **kukathanggu**.

kilkakilka knowledgeable about something • *palthu kilkakilka* 'someone who knows the road' • *Pakanhana nganinha padla kilkakilkali.* 'He led us; he knows the country.'

kilkanhina think about • *Kilka-nhinarlala ngathu wanitji ngandra thambanininguda.* 'I'm thinking about that corroboree we danced.'

kilki waterhen # See also **dirrmi, maltjimarrini**.

kilkirri shoulder # Yw • *Nhandradu tjiwarali waltharla yinha purla kilkirrinyi.* 'The woman's carrying the baby on her shoulder.' # See also **pilpiri, pinyi, thapini, wiliwili**.

kilpa cold, winter # SY. May not be Yandruwandha. See **malthi, pundra**.

kilthi juice, juicy, soup, melted fat • (Yw) *Yundru yinhaku marni kurritha, makanyi, kalila nhunuyi kilthila.* 'You put the fat into the fire; now it's melted.' # See also **mitji kilthi**.

Kilyalpa Gidgealpa Waterhole

kilyikilyika (Yw), **kilyikilyipa** (SY) tickle # See **thithidika**.

kima lump, blister # Yw *malyu*

kimana swell • *Mulhudu ngathu pirna thayipandhina, thundrutji nganyi kimanarla.* 'I ate too much and my stomach is swollen.'

kima pour • (SY) *ngaltja kimari* 'dribbling' # See also **pirrpa, pudla**.

kimana, kimapandhi pour out
• *Ngapa ngathu kimapandhirla ngakani.* 'I'm going to pour out a drink of water for myself.'

kimba raw # Also **purda**.

kini group, cluster, heap, pile # See also **ngami, wadla**.

kinika heap up • *Kinikangatji ngala yiwalila yambarriyi kurranga.* 'The women heap them [seeds] up on the flat ground.' • *'Thawarla nganyi, kathi parndrithikanga.' 'Kawu, kala ngathu maka kinikarlayi.'* 'I'm going out hunting.' 'OK, for my part I'll get a pile of firewood ready.'

kinikinika stock up with, store up • *Mulhudu ngandra kinikinikanga ngapa yulpurrupuru.* 'We'd better get some extra tucker in in case the river floods.'

kinipapa river (in general) • *Minhaya-ngadilatji karlukarlu yukiningadi kara, ya kinipapayi kara kurriningadi, karlukarlu kara yamali.* 'That's what they're for, for catching fish while swimming in the water, and for putting across the river [to catch] fish in the cross net.' # See also **karirri, kadri, wipa**.

Kinipapa Cooper's Creek, Cooper Creek • *Yundra nhuniyi Kinipapangudatji.* 'This place is a long way from Cooper's Creek.'

kinirdaka scorpion # SY

kintha nose • *Man.gili nhunu mundja, patjarla, thawanhana nhunu, kirri-ngadi, kintha yunggudu ngakarnanga.* 'Benny's sick, his nose is bleeding and he's gone to the doctor.' • *kintha ngakarla* 'nose is running' • *Kintha pulkayindri!* 'Blow your nose!' # See also **mulha**.

kintha ngamburru snot, nasal mucus # SY said *kintha ngamurru* or *kintha ngamudu*.

kintha, kinthakintha shrimp

kinyi stealth; dishonesty

kinyili stealthily, dishonestly • *Kinyili nganha mirrka winkama-kanmananhana.* 'They stole my blankets.'

kinyikanpa, kinyipurra thief # SY gave it for 'liar'.

kinyi ngunyingunyi corrupt, make dishonest

kinyiwinka run away (stealthily) # Yw. See also **miniwindri, putharrkawindri, winka, winkapani**.

kirdra squeal, squeak, scream • *Pukurruli nhutjadu kirdrarla.* 'He screamed in his dream.' # Also heard as *kidra*. SY(?) *ngalamarra* **kirdrakirdrana** make squeal

kirrapara catfish # SY. See **wakuwaku**. May be Wngu.

kirrayindri be thin, get thin

kirri clever; doctor • *Man.gili nhunu mundja, patjarla, thawanhana nhunu, kirringadi, kintha yunggudu ngakarnanga.* 'Benny's sick, his nose is bleeding and he's gone to the doctor.' # Yw 'doctor' also *karna kirri*

kirrikirri (a) lively, active; (b) able, capable # SY • *Yini kirrikirri kathi parndrini.* 'You're a good butcher.'

kirri (1) can you?, will I?, how about? • *Mirni, kirri yintjadu yaka, walpi nhunu thawanga kanthakanthangadi.* 'Can you ask him when he's going to the bush [lit. grassy place].' • *Kirriya nganha dramana, wantjiningadi, parndrala kara.* 'Will you cut [the meat] for me so I can see if it's cooked.'; (2) if • *Kirri thawarlayi yuda ...* 'If you go ...' # See also **mirni, kara**.

kirriwali prentie, perentie # Not in Innamincka country; some at Arrabury.

kirrki type of hawk, probably kestrel # SY. See **pirrki**.

kitka know # H. See **kilka**.

kittja know # Matja. See **kilka**.

kiwada emu # Yw, H. See **warruwitji**, **maltharrimindji**.

kubala bottle • *Mirni kubala ngathu parrkulu mandrithikarla ngalungga.* 'I'll take home a couple of bottles [of beer] for us two [me and my wife].'

kudawarrala cloud # See also **nganya**, **ngandjarri**, **pariwirlpa**.

kudhi hide (yourself) # Also **purri**.

   kudhikudhi hidden, stealthy, sneaky • *Thikawarrarlatji nhaniyi kudhikudhi windriwarranga, walya ngathu nhanha wawarlayi. Purrtjinawarrari nganha nhandra.* 'She came back and sneaked inside and I didn't see her. She gave me a fright.'

   kudhikudhi, kudhikudhina hide (yourself), plant

   kudhikudhima hide (something) # Also **purrilka, wamba, winkama**.

   kudhithika go and hide

   kudhitharra get lost; hide behind someone who is going ahead # See **nyulkayindri**.

   kudhiwindri sneak off

kudi mussel # SY. May be Wngu. See **thuka**.

kuditharra forget • *Ngalyitji nganyi kuditharrarlala pawa thana dinga-padipadini.* 'I forget the other seeds they used to grind.' • *Ngala yamali thana ngunipika kurraringu, kalkayi, marripathi minipandhingayayi mandrithalkanga karlukarlulatji, ngampurru kara, ya kathi nharra-mindji kara, ya palha kara, ya kathi thanayi — minhaya yina, kathi — mayatji nganyi kuditharrarlala, kathi thukathayini, thana drikalapurrayi thanha.* 'Well, with the cross net, they put it down in the daytime, in the afternoon, and next morning they run down and pull up the fish — maybe yellowbelly, or maybe a turtle, or maybe a bird, or maybe one of those

animals — what is it? — I forget the name — mussel-eater they used to call them.'

kudla, kula burn (someone, something, not as being consumed by a fire but as being injured by a fire or heat), cook (something) • *Makamuduli kulari, mulhudu patjikurnutji.* 'They cook them in hot ashes, and they are good tucker.' • *Pirnapirna thanhayi, tharriningaditji nganarlayi, purndaparndringa kudlanga yina thayiyindrirnangatji.* 'The biggest ones, that are nearly ready to fly, they kill and cook and eat.' • *Kathi paladi parndriparndriyindrirnanga, ngala makatji wangininguda kathi yuka kara kuliningadi, ya karlukarlu kuliningadi.* 'They kill their own meat, and light a fire to cook their meat or maybe to cook fish.' • *Thiparili nganha thina kudlarla; makamakali nganha thina kudlarla.* 'The sand burns my feet; the hot [sand] burns my feet.' # See also **parndraka, darra**.

kudlapandhi cook (in a ground oven?)

kudlawagawaga, kudlathikathika cook for everybody

kudlayindri cook • *Kathi kudlayindrirla* 'The meat is cooking.'

kudlayukarra cook overnight • *Kathi ngali parndrinhana, nga kudlayukarranga yinha. Pandrala ngali walthathikana.* 'We killed [a kangaroo], and cooked him overnight, and then carried him home cooked.'

kudra, kudrakudra break something, break it off • *Pitji yina nhulu ngakani kudranhana.* 'He broke my coolamon.' • *Patjikurnutji makala ngala thana wangapandhirnanga ngapala ngapa kurrari mardrayi thana kudrakudrari makamakaniningudatji.* 'They light a good fire on the rock and after it has heated up they put water on it, to shatter the rock.' • *Ngala yiwalitji* *kardrarda pakurlayi, ngala ngarru karruli thana pawatji kudrarlayi.* 'Only the men crush the seeds, while the women dig yams.' # See also **dratji, druka, pilthipilthirrika.**

kudrayindri break, get broken • *Maltji nganyi kudrayindrina.* 'I broke my leg.' • *Minhangadi yundru wathi nhuludutji yada thinbarla; ngarru kudrayindrini yina nhutjadutji wathi.* 'What do you make a boomerang out of that wood for? It only breaks, that wood.'

kudrakudrayindri shatter, come apart • *Darnurdarnu nhuniyi wirni, kudrakudrayindrirla.* 'This string is weak, it's coming apart.'

kudrininguda broken • *Walya nganha ngunyi kudriningudatji.* 'Don't give me the broken one.'

kudra fall # Yw. See **warlka, ngurli.**

kudri swan

kudrikudrina (?) split, break # See **yalba.**

kudru hole ('straight down') • *Ngapala kudru pakuri ngari, nga yankula kurrawagandji nga windripandhinga palha mukuli.* 'They dig a hole and put boughs around it and [a man] goes down into the hole with a bird bone.' • *Kudru thana yarndu pakupurringarini.* 'That's how they make the wells deeper.' # Compare **mingka, thuka, wirlpa.**

kudrukudrunga see **kundrukundru.**

kudu top # Yw. See **kamarra, kandra** • *Kawalka nhunuyi nhinarla kudunyi.* 'There's a crow sitting on top [of the house].'

kudukudu unawares, without looking, without seeing # SY, Yw • *... nhuluku parndrinhana yinha kudukuduyi.* '... he hit him when he wasn't looking.' • *Walya ngandra wawanhana yinhayi thawarlayi, kudukudu nhunu thawanhana.* 'That fellow walked straight past us, without seeing us.'

Also heard as *kurrukurru.* Reuther has "*kurukuru*" 'hidden' (Yw).

kuka head • *Mirramirrayindrirla nganyi, kuka kara, kapurru kara, pangkithirri kara.* 'I don't know whether I'm scratching my head, or under the arm, or my ribs.' # SY also used **kungka.**

kukali thanggu be upside down, stand on head # See **purri.**

kukapidri crown of head, top (of hill)

kuka pipi grey hair # ? MN (for SY) gave *pipi* for 'brains'.

kukapira cushion for carrying coolamon on head # doughnut shaped, 8cm thick, made of hair-string

kukathanggu think # See **kilka.**

kuka thangka brains # See also **puwa, tjuru.**

kukawarnu knitted string cap

Kukatha name of a tribe and language • *karna Kukathangadi* '[going] to the [country of] the Kukatha people'

kukiyi cook # SY. From Eng. See **makawarlawagini.**

kuku deep • *Ngala ngapa kukuyitji ngari, wararriyitji, mardramitji karrininguda malkirri pardrangarini- ngadilatji thanha, paltjakiningadi.* 'They tie a lot of stones [to go] deep down in the water, on the bottom of the net, to weigh it down and keep it tight.' # SY 'hollow (in tree)'; See also **kukunu, mikiri.**

kukunka kite hawk, black kite (*Milvus migrans*)

kukunu hollow in tree • *Kukunu ngathu kupuli pardrapardranhana.* 'I felt in the hollow [for a possum].' • *wathi yinha parndriparndriri, kukunumindji- nyadi kara* 'banging a log to see if it's hollow'

Kukuyi Cooquie Waterhole

kula see **kudla.**

kulayada thigh # Yw. See **thadamuku, wandikila, ngalpa.**

kuldru brisket; upper part of body (for example, of kangaroo) • *Ngarru kuldru nganha yada ngunyi.* 'Just give me the brisket [of the kangaroo].'

kulikuliyada peewee, mudlark # SY. See also **martimarti, pathada-pathada**(?).

kulkupa, kulkuma jump # SY also 'boil' • *Ngapa nhunuyi kulkumarlala.* 'The water's boiling now.'

kulkupanhina hop (as a kangaroo) • *Tjukurru nhunudu kulkupanhinala.* 'The kangaroo's hopping along.'

kulkupathalka jump up • *Ngarrungu nhunu kulkupathalkari purtu mandringa dunkawindringa nhunu windriwarrinitji yada warli.* 'So he just jumped up and grabbed his swag and went out the door he had come in by.'

kulkupathalkawarra jump out (as from a hole)

kulkumathawa hop along (kangaroo) # SY

kulkumawalpirri jump across

kulkupawindri hop away (as a kangaroo) • *Tjukurru ngathu warrkananhana windrali, walya yinha nhadikangatji, kulkupawindringa nhunu wathi windra ngurru.* 'I speared a kangaroo, but I didn't kill it and it hopped away with the spear [still in it].'

kulpina round up, surround

kulpinayindri, kulpinawaga surround • *Wawarnanga ngapangadi ngari thawarlayi karna kulpinayindrirlayila ngapatji yibarlayi nga wathi windrali warrkananga.* 'Well, when they see them going to the water the men surround them, and then spear them while they're drinking.'

kuluwa needlewood # *Hakea ivoryi* • *Kuluwali nganha drakana.* 'The needlewood pricked me.'

kuma shaking legs, shaking knees (in corroboree, after a death) # See also **ngalpa**.

kumani pitchery bundle • *Wiriwinma-rnanga karna thana pitjidi kumaningurrutji.* 'The people with the bags of pitchery exchanged [them].' • *Pawathungini ngala pitjidi kumaningaditji ngunyiyindrirnanga yarndukalangu thana nhinapadipa-dinitji.* 'They traded grinding stones for bags of pitchery; that's how they used to live.'

kuna faeces; guts (probably a generic term)

kuna kadli small intestine

kuna ngarndri paunch, tripe # Compare *ngarndri* 'mother'.

kunathika defecate • *Kunathikanga nganyi thawarla.* 'I'm going to have a shit.'

kunakunana grumble • *Minha yini kunakunanarla?* 'What are you shitty about?'

kunapampu ball (of string) # probably *kuna + pampu* 'egg'

kunapampuka make into a ball

kunapampuna curl up • *Thudarla yini kunapampunarnanga, pandi-nyadi.* 'You're lying curled up like a dog.'

kunapantjiri green, blue # Yw. See also **kundakunda, pulayarra, kurrkari**.

kunapika wood duck # Also given for black duck but see **dikarri**.

Kunathi Coonatie Waterhole

kunawarrku crossways, across • *Ngapala, kurrupu karrukarru pundrayi kara, makamakayi kara, ngapala ngarru kankunu kurraringa makawarrkanga kunawarrkutji thudayukarrangatji.* 'Well, the olden-days women and men, in winter or summer, only put up a windbreak, throw some firewood down and sleep all night crossways [with heads towards the windbreak].' # *palthu kunawarrku thudanhan*a could mean 'lay across the path' or 'lay crossways to the path'.

kunawarrkuka cross • *maltji kunawarrkukari* 'crossing your legs'

kundakunda green # SY. See **pulayarra, kunapantjiri, kurrkari**.

kundangali wind • *Kundangali paltjapaltja pulkarla.* 'the wind's blowing hard.' • *Thawarla ngaldra kundangalipuru wardamayi nhinanga, yandhiyandhiningadilatji.* 'Let's go and sit in the car and talk out of the wind.' # See also **thayirri, wathara**.

kundi house, hut # Also **warli**.

kundi muda church

kundikili a ball • *Ngapala kundikilili thana thurrparitji.* 'Then they roll it [the string] into a ball.' # See also **ngambu, ngunku, damburdambu(ra?), kunapampu, kurndikurndi**.

kundrukundru cough, cold, flu • *Paldrinhana nhunu kundrukundruli.* 'He died of the flu.' # Yw *kurrungkurru*

kundrukundruna cough • *Kundrukundrunana nhutjadu kayidi-kayidi.* 'He was coughing now and then.' # SY *kudrukudrunga*

kun.ga gut, clean (the guts out of a carcase)

kungka hobble # SY • *Malantji nganani nganyi pantja. Nganyi kungkanga nganarla, pirtapirtali.* 'My knee's got sore, but I'll hobble along with a walking stick.'

kungka see **kuka**

kunirri plain # SY. See **yambarri**

kunparri lucky (for example, as a fisherman) • *kunparri pirna* or *kunparri patji* 'very lucky'

kuntha (1) pennyroyal (*Mentha australis*, a strong-smelling plant that grows on the edge of waterholes); (2)

tea • *Ngapa kuntha ngali wangarla.* 'We're making a drink of tea.'

kunthi mosquito # Also **wayiludu**.

kuntji hit with something flexible (as a whip or flexible stick) # = *warlpa*

kunuputha dust # See also **puthurru, thayirri**.

kunya spindle (a long stick with four short cross pieces near one end used for spinning fibre into string), walking stick • *Ngapala kururruparnanga nga nhurrpanga ngarrpayi kunya payirrili.* 'Then they rub it with stones and spin it on their thighs, using a long spindle.' • *Wirni payirrikari yinha nga kunyayi kurranga.* 'They make the string long and put it on the spindle.'

kunyama roll up • *Ngapala nhunu thangguthalkawarrananga patjipatjingu nga purtu nhulu kunyamanga, nga kupuyi yinha kurrapadaringu mungkayindriri yina purtutji.* 'Then he got up, very carefully, and rolled up his swag and put it under his arm.' # See also **nhapi, thurrpa, pampuka**.

kupitji wave # The person you wave to may be marked as dative or locative • *Warangi yini kupitjina?* 'Who did you wave to?' • *Nhipayi nganyi kupitjina.* or *Kupitjina nganyi nhipangadi ngakani.* 'I waved to my wife.' # = *kupu warrka*

kupu arm • *Kukunu ngathu kupuli pardrapardranhana.* 'I felt in the hollow [for a possum].' • *Ngapala nhunu thangguthalkawarrananga patjipatjingu nga purtu nhulu kunyamanga, nga kupuyi yinha kurrapadaringu mungkayindriri yina purtutji.* 'Then he got up, very carefully, and rolled up his swag and put it under his arm.' # See also **nguna**.

kupu warrka wave # = *kupitji*. Given once; not accepted on another occasion.

kupu warrkapada wave to someone going away

kura, ngandjarri kura storm

kurdikurdirri winding, crooked • *palthu kurdikurdirri* 'winding road' # Also heard as *kutikutirri*.

(kuri)

> **kurikapada, kuriyirrika, kuritharra** clean # Each heard once • *Purru ngathu yinha kuriyirrikana.* 'I cleaned it all over.'

kurla (1) burr, bindieye; (2) carney, bearded dragon # See **kani, manharri**.

> **kathi kurla** carney
>
> **kurla kilthi** roly poly, buckbush
>
> **kurla kurrumpa** burr on sandhills
>
> **kurla puntjiwarra** galvanised burr
>
> **kurla purralku** goathead burr

kurli day • *... ngapala thana, kurli parrku, mandrithayi pilthirri thana warrkathalkangatji.* '... after a couple of days, they pick up the broken pieces of rock and throw them out of the hole.' # Also used by SY and Yw as an alternative word for 'sun' • (SY) *Kandrala nhunuyi kurli.* 'The sun's high.' See **dritji, nguni**.

kurndikurndi crooked, bent # SY, Yw; see **kurdikurdirri, kundikili**.

> **kurndikurndika** bend # SY; see **dupurdupuka**.

kurni penis, tail, lightning • *Kathi marngali ngathu kurni pardranhana.* 'I caught a goanna by the tail.' # In a similar sentence SY used the suffix *-li* on the word for tail — *nhura* in that dialect. # See also **parrikara, nhura**.

> **kurni dambu** see **dambu**

kurnki devil • *Ngandra yaba ngunyinhana nganha yundru ngathutji purtupa walthawindrinhana winkarnanga yinggani kurnkipuru.* 'Oh! You frightened me and I took my swag away and ducked off for fear of you being a devil.' # SY also 'doctor'. See also **karnapalha, yarrkamarta**.

kurnu one; alone, on your own
• *Dritji kurnuyitji, karna malkirri thawawarrandji, ngalyila.* 'One day another group of blackfellows arrived.'
• *Nga yadala thana thinbari, yadatji thinbininguda nga wirlpa kurranga, mulha kurnuyi.* 'Then they make a boomerang and put a hole in one end of it.' • *Ngapala ngapatji walthayindringangu maltjitji kurnu karrininguda thiltjali.* 'They carry water in it, after tying up one leg with sinew.' • *Thawanhana, yini thangguthikanga thannganiyi, karna thulayitji. Parndriyukala yina walya kurnulitji thawarnanga. Parndriyila kara — parndriyila yina, kurnutji thawarlayi. Walya kurnutji thawala.* 'You went to visit those strangers. They might have killed you, going without someone else, on your own. ... Don't go on your own. • *Ngarndri-ngapiri nhunggani paldrin.ga, muduwa yina kurnula warrkawindriri.* 'His parents died and left the child on his own.'; another • *Mirniwa! Nhuniyi kurnula purtu.* 'Wait a minute! Here's another swag [to put on the truck].' # See also **paladi**.

> **kurnukurnu** alone, on your own
> • *Walya mabaabiyi thawa kurnukurnutji.* 'Don't go on your own in the dark.' • *Kurnukurnu nhutjadu yandhayandharla nganggali.* 'He's talking to himself.'
>
> **kurnu nguka** another, something
> • *Minhangadi yintjadu wani kurnu yundru parndripadapadarla, walya wani kurnu nguka drangini? Ngarru kurnungu yundru kilkarla?* 'Why do you always sing that same song, and never sing any other? Is that the only one you know?' # See also **minha kurnu nguka**.

kurra, kurrapandhi (a) put, put down, put up (in the sense of erect)
• *Kurrapandhiri purtutji yinhanga makali yina karrtjikarrtjimawarranga*

wathi witjuli. 'He put the swag down by the fire and started to turn [the ashes] over with a twig.' • *Punggu murrpiningudatji ngapala kurrari ngapayi, wiki parrkulu kara, thungganiningadi.* 'They cut the bow vine and put it in water for maybe two weeks, so that it will rot.' • *Nga kankunu pirna nhulu kurranga.* 'He put up a big windbreak.' • *Nga yadala thana thinbari, yadatji thinbininguda nga wirlpa kurranga, mulha kurnuyi.* 'Then they make a boomerang and put a hole in one end of it.' (b) give birth • *Mingkayitji nganha kurralapurra.* 'I was born at Minkie.' # See also **ngathanika, yadhi kurra, dan.ga, ngama mana.** (c) let, allow # Yw • *Minhama yundru yinhaku kurrani nganha parndrinima?* 'What did you let him hit me for?'

kurrakurra make camp • *Kurra-kurrawarranga warli matjayitji.* 'He made camp at an old hut.' • *Miringuda ngani ngatjada kurrakurranhana yundra.* 'We camped a long way from the sandhills.'

kurrapada put in, put under • *Ngapala nhunu thangguthalka-warrananga patjipatjingu nga purtu nhulu kunyamanga, nga kupuyi yinha kurrapadaringu mungkayindriri yina purtutji.* 'Then he got up, very carefully, and rolled up his swag and put it under his arm.' # Also **windrima, winma.**

kurrathalka put up • *Kathi tjukurru-purutji, ya mardra pirrapirra kurra-thalkaniya(?) kandratji.* 'They get a flat stone and put it over the top [of the well] to keep kangaroos out.'

kurrawaga put around • *Ngapala kudru pakuri ngari, nga yankula kurrawagandji nga windripandhinga palha mukuli.* 'They dig a hole and put boughs around it and [a man] goes down into the hole with a bird bone.'

kurrawindri leave behind • *Mardra ngathu kurrawindrinhana, walpayiyi, nguni parrkulu.* 'I left my money in the house for two days.' # Compare **ngardrawarrka, wawathawa.**

kurrayindri breed • *Ngurra yina kurrayindrirla mayi, purla, palhatji thana.* 'Those birds are breeding all the time.'

kurrakurra work out, make out, see properly • *Warnu kara thawa-warrarla; karru kara, nga yiwa kara. Walyangu ngathu kurrakurrarlatji.'* I don't know who they are coming; might be men or might be women. I can't figure them out yet.'

kurrakurrana teach • *Nguthingi ngamangi nganha nganalapurra, kurrakurranarnanga yina, ngan.gu yandhiningadi.* 'My brother and uncle told me what to say, and taught me.' # Also **ngana, warlparaka.**

kurrantjala whitewood (*Atalaya hemiglauca*) # SY. May be Wngu, see **ngurraputha.**

kurrari cranky, mad, drunk, (SY) stupid # Also heard as *kurrayi.*

kurrari ngana be cranky, be mad, be drunk • *Karrukarru, nhuniyi pada, ngapakaldringuda, yibanhana nhuluyi, thudarla nhunu, kurrari nganarnanga, kurrari nganarla.* 'This old fellow is inside, he's been drinking rum and now he's lying down, dead drunk.'

kurrakurrari madman • *Minithika-thikarla nhunu kurrakurrari-nyadi.* 'He's running round like a madman.' • *kurrakurrari nhutjadu, muduwa kadikadini* 'that madman who's always chasing the kids'

kurrikira rainbow # Also **mira.**

kurrkari grass; green # See **kantha.**

kurrpa trunk (of tree) • *kurrpali thangguri* '[tree is] upside down'

kurrthi thalpa fallen leaves around a tree

kurrtjarrku see **kutjarrku**.

kurrumpala spinifex

kurrungkurru a cough # Yw. See **kundrukundru**.

> **kurrungkurruka** cough # Yw
>
> **kurrungkurru ngunyi** make (someone) cough # Yw

kurrupakula flood bird, rain bird, channel-billed cuckoo # SY

kurrupu old woman, olden-days woman • *Ngapala, kurrupu karrukarru pundrayi kara, makamakayi kara, ngapala ngarru kankunu kurraringa makawarrkanga kunawarrkutji thudayukarrangatji.* 'Well, the olden-days women and men, in winter or summer, only put up a windbreak, throw some firewood down and sleep all night crossways.' • *Kurrupu thana pakupadipadini kardra.* 'The [olden-days] women used to dig yams.'

> **kurrupu ngana** get old (of a female) # Yw

kurtukurtu rough # See **thitathita**.

kururrupa grind; rub (hard) • *Ngapala kururruparnanga nga nhurrpanga ngarrpayi kunya payirrili.* 'Then they rub it [fibre] with stones and spin it on their thighs, using a long spindle.' # See **dringa**, **thunga**.

kuta coat # from Eng

kutawirri rotten • *Patjala nganyi kathi kutawirri thayininguda.* 'I'm sick because I ate rotten meat.' # Also **thungga**.

(kuthi)

> **kuthipada** (1) leave early in the morning; (2) join someone
>
> **kuthithika** have been before • *Kilkarla yundru kathi tjukurru ngaldra yinha parndringa, yini kuthithikanga?* 'Do you remember that kangaroo we killed when you were here last time?'
>
> **kuthiwarra** come, arrive • *Thawarla nganyi ngala nhunu kuthiwarrarlayitji ngardrathikarla. Kadli nganyi thawari.* 'I'm going now, and he'll be getting here later. I'll be already gone.' • *Ngapala nhunu purtu mandrimandrirnanga milyaruyi, nga thawawindringa ngatjada kurnungadila, withi ngabayi-ngada, ya kuthiwarrarila mayi.* 'Well, he packed his swag in the dark and walked on to the other camp, while the injury was still fresh, and he got there.' # Also **thawawarra**.

kuthikuthidi squeaky • *Ngan.gu kuthikuthidi nhinda ngunyingunyirnanga yinha. Yarndu nhunu walyatji yurarla yandhiningaditji.* 'His squeaky voice makes him shy. That's why he doesn't like talking.'

kutikutirri see **kurdikurdirri**.

kutja, palha kutja wing, wing feathers # See also **nguna**.

kutjarrku, kathi kutjarrku type of frog # little green frog, in water • *Ngathalki ngakani kathi kutjarrku yurarla pardriningadi.* 'My kids like catching frogs.' # Also heard as *kurrtjarrku*. Information about which frog is which is not consistent. See also **drukampada**, **durrkuwantha**, **kuyarrku**.

kuwukuku pigeon # perhaps a general term for pigeons and doves, or possibly the name of the diamond dove

kuya fish # See also **karlukarlu**.

> **kuya pardi** type of fish # red, poisonous — if it pricks your hand it will poison it; also called *karlukarlu pardi*.
>
> **Kuyapidri** place name, Queerbidie # 'fish's bum'; the place where a fish dreaming track starts

kuyarrku type of frog # green frog with stripe . See also **drukampada**, **durrkuwantha**, **kutjarrku**.

M

maadha see **mayatha**.

mabaabu = **mabumabu**

mabaabuna = **mabumabuna**

mabumabu night, dark • *Ngapala mabaabuli nhunu kuthiwarrarnanga nga kurrakurrawarranga purturduka-rdukarnanga yadamani papurlaka-tharrari yita.* 'Well it was dark when he arrived, and he unloaded his things and hobbled the horses.' # See also **milyaru**, **marri**, **waruwaru**.

mabumabuna get dark • *Pakali nganamalkardi, mabaabunala-rlayinardi.* 'Do it quickly, it's getting dark.' # Yw *marringana*

Madlali Mudlalee Waterhole

madlantji bad, no good, useless
• *Madlantji nhutjadu; karna nhuludu yuparla.* 'He's no good, he's cheeky.'
• *Pandi nhutjadu marna waka madlantji.* 'That dog's got bad teeth.'
• *Karrukarrunarla nhutjadu, madlantji nganananarla.* 'He [dog] is getting old and useless.' # See also **manha**.

madlantjika, **madlamadlantjika** spoil, ruin • *Kabuta nhuludu ngakani nhangkana, madlamadlantjikarila yinha, or madlantjikarila yinha.* 'That fellow stood on my hat and ruined it.' • *Puka nhulu kudlanhana, nga minheya ngarrkanga yinha, madlantjikarila yinha.* 'He cooked the damper and what did he do to it, he spoilt it.'

madru abdomen

maka fire, firewood • *Maka ngathu parndringa.* 'I'm going to chop some wood.' • *Ya maka nhulu thangkaka ya thudapandhiringu thapa thayininguda.* 'Then he made a fire and had his supper and went to bed.' • *Ngapala mardra thana warrkapandhiwarrka-pandhingala makayi.* 'Then they throw all the stones into the fire.'

maka kantha bushfire # Yw

maka kanya hot coal, hot ashes • *Ya karlakala pakurnanga malkirri thana kulanga maka kanyayildrangu.* 'They dig yowers and cook them in hot ashes too.'

makamaka hot, heat, summer
• *Pipinhinanga nganyi makamakayi yina.* 'I'll have a rest while it's hot.'
• *Ngapala, kurrupu karrukarru pundrayi kara, makamakayi kara, ngapala ngarru kankunu kurraringa makawarrkanga kunawarrkutji thudayukarrangatji.* 'Well, the olden-days women and men, in winter or summer, only put up a windbreak, throw some firewood down and sleep all night crossways.'

makamakali hot

makamakana get hot • *Patjikurnutji makala ngala thana wangapandhi-rnanga ngapala ngapa kurrari mardrayi thana kudrakudrari makamakaniningudatji.* 'They light a good fire on the rock and after it has heated up they put water on it, to shatter the rock.'

maka matji match

maka mudu hot ashes • *Maka muduli kulari, mulhudu patjikurnutji.* 'They cook them in hot ashes, and they are good tucker.'

maka mukuru hot coal • *Kathi thanayi pulkapulkaringu maka mukuruli-nyadi, ngala mardra mitjili ngala.* 'They grill their meat on the stones and you would think it had been grilled on the coals.'

maka paru firelight • *Walya karna wawini; ngarru ngathu maka paru wawanhana ngapa kurnayitji. Walya thawapandhini.* 'I didn't see anyone (while I was away). I only saw the light of a fire at a waterhole. I didn't go down.'

maka thirra firestick • *Winka-yukarranhana nhunu, makathirralila* *ngani wanthiyukarranhana.* 'He disappeared in the night and we were looking for him with a firestick.'

maka thupu smoke

maka thurrpa hot ashes • *Nga ngarru maka thurrpala thana dringarnanga drangkana ngananga.* 'When there are only hot ashes left they scrape and sweep them away.'

makawarlawagini a (good) cook

maka warnta log # SY, Yw? # See **thinka, wathi, muku.**

makawarrka, makawadhawarrka stack firewood • *Ngapala, kurrupu karrukarru pundrayi kara, maka-makayi kara, ngapala ngarru kankunu kurraringa makawarrkanga kuna-warrkutji thudayukarrangatji.* 'Well, the olden-days women and men, in winter or summer, only put up a windbreak, throw some firewood down and sleep all night crossways.' # Not clear what the function of the -*wadha* is.

makapari black goanna # See also **kalamurru.**

makita gun # SY makiti. From Eng 'musket'.

maku lower part of shin (?)

makudaka pigeon-toed

makumandri (1) trip someone • *Kadli walya nganyi warlkana, mardrali nganha makumandrirlayi.* 'I nearly fell when the stone tripped me.'; (2) lift # Yw, = *kandraka* • *Ngathu yinhaku pulu makumandrirla. Pirna nhunuku.* 'I can't lift it, it's too heavy.'

Makulpi Marqualpie Waterhole

makumarda whirlwind # *makukarda* (?) in Yw; also **thurrpu.**

malantji see **madlantji.**

malka mark, picture; stripe • (SY) *mara malka kurrari* 'putting a mark on [your] hand'

malkamalka piebald

malkamindji spotted, striped # See **dragurdragu.**

malka well! # Also **mayi, ngandra.**

Malkanpa Innamincka, Mulkonbar Waterhole

malkirri many, a lot • *Dritji kurnuyitji, karna malkirri thawawarrandji, ngalyila.* 'One day another group of blackfellows arrived.' • *Ngapala yamalitji mandriri malkirri.* 'They got a lot [of fish] in the cross net.' • *Mulha malka, yundru wawanga malkirri thanayi ngakani, mulha malka mandrininguda yina, walypalali.* 'I've got a lot of photos here that have been taken by a white man, if you'd like to look at them.' # See also **ngami, wamba.**

malparu flock pigeon # SY. AWH gives this name for "a crane [= heron?], black with white on wings".

maltharri emu feathers

maltharrimindji emu # lit. the one with emu feathers. See **warruwitji, kiwada.**

malthi cold, winter; year • *ngapa malthi* 'cold water' • *Mara malthi yini.* 'Your hands are cold.' • *Malthi parrkulu nganyi nhinan.ga Mardrapirnangi.* 'I stayed at Planet Downs for two years.' • *Ngala malthilitji nganari, kali windripadamalka walpayi.* 'If you're cold go and sit inside.' # SY also 'wind', perhaps only 'cold wind'. See **kilpa.**

malthika cool (someone, something) down # SY, Yw

maltji leg • *Maltji withi.* '(My) leg is sore.' • *Maltji nganyi kudrayindrina.* 'I broke my leg.' • *Ngapala ngapatji walthayindringangu maltjitji kurnu karrininguda thiltjali.* 'They carry water in it, after tying up one leg with sinew.' # *Maltji* is used for both thigh and lower leg, although there are separate words for thigh (*wandikila*) and lap (*ngalpa*). RYn gave *maltji*

for 'shinbone' and SY (for Yw) said
it was 'shin'. See also **maku**.

maltjimarrini waterhen, black-tailed
native hen # SY; 'red legs'; See also
kilki.

maltjimuku lower leg # SY

maluda shag, cormorant (*malurra* black
shag, cormorant # SY) Also
ngukumindji.

malyu lump # Yw. See **kima**.

mama, mamathika steal; take by force
• *Kathi ngathu mamana pandipuru.*
'I took the meat from the dog.'
Perhaps taking the meat was a
precaution against the dog's eating it.
• *Karrukarruyi yintjadu ngathu
mamathikana wathi windra.* 'I took
the spear off that old fellow over
there.' • *Nguthingi nganha mamana.*
'My brother took (it) from me.' # See
also **winkama**.

mambu humpy # SY. See also **walpa**,
walparda, **punga**.

mampa front # See also **marna**.

mampali hard, vigorously, animatedly
• *wakanarla mampali* 'working hard'
• *thirrirla mampali* 'fighting hard'
• *yandhayandharla mampali* 'talking
like anything' # Difference from
pidipidi not clear. *Mampali* is much
preferred in some cases, such as the
second example.

mana give # SY, see **ngunyi**.

mandawarra plum bush • *Ngapala
yina wathi thinbanari mandawarra,
ya wirni thurrpanari yinha mulhudungadilatji nhunu thawathalkiningadi
warrkanga wathilatji yina karrtjikarrtjimari.* 'Well, he would cut and
shape a stick from a plum bush and tie
a string to it and whirl it around, so
that someone would come and leave
some food for him.' # See **patjiwara**.

mandhirra marpoo bush # probably
Acacia ligulata

mandri pick up, get, take • *Ngapala
nhunu ngarru yankula mandriri, nga
warrkapandhinga ngapala pulkanga
ngala nhulu ...* 'So he just got some
[dry] leaves and threw them down
[on the hot coals] and started to blow
them ...' • *Ngapala yamalitji mandriri
malkirri.* 'They got a lot [of fish] in the
cross net.' # See **pardraka, mapa**.

mandrika, mandrina, mandriyindri
get

mandripandhi muster, get together
Also **mapa, marnduna**.

mandripada, mandriyindripada
marry # See also **nhipaka**, and note
mandripada also in • *Mandripadaka
yita!* 'Get that over there!'

mandrithalka pick up, pull up

mandritharrapada take out • *Kathi
yintjadu mandritharrapada mirrkayi
nhunggatjaduyi.* 'Take the meat out of
the bag.' # Also **duka**.

mandrithawa, mandrimini pick up
on the way • *Wilpadali nganyi thawa-
lapurra, mandrithawari nganha
walypalali.* 'Once I was travelling in
a wagon — some white men picked
me up.'

mandrithawa mandrithawa pick up
here and there

mandrithayi get for yourself, win
• *Mardrangadi, mandrithayinga pirna.*
'They're going to win a lot of money.'

mandrithika go and get

manga woma, sandhill snake, carpet
snake # Also **wama**; see also
mulhana.

man.garri little girl • *Man.garri kurnu
ngala thana ngalyitji ngarru karruwalildra.* 'There's one girl and all the
rest are boys.' # possibly also 'female',
see **kardri** # SY and H sometimes
man.garra

mangawarru widow

mangga burn • *Kantha mangga mayi,
pulkapada mayi.* 'Burn the grass!

Blow it [so it burns]!' # See also **thangkana, darra, ngarrtji, pidli.**

manggarduda burn along (as a bushfire)

manggana get burnt • *Ngapiringi walpa mangganana.* 'My father's house got burnt.'

mangga scatter • *Walthayindrithikangala kathi thana manggarlayila yabalilatji.* 'They carry the meat back to camp while the rest of the emus go for their lives.'

manggamanggakurra share out • *Ya manggamanggakurraringu.* 'They share them [the birds they have caught] out.' # See also **wandukudra, yalba.**

mangkiri happy # SY

manha bad, no good; dirty # Yw, H; SY(?). May not be correct Yandruwandha. See **madlantji.**

manhamanha wrongly, the wrong way # Yw • *Manhamanhala nganyi thawanhana.* 'I went the wrong way.' # See also **yikayika.**

manhawakura get old and feeble • *Parndripadipadini ngani, ngurra thawarnanga; manhawakurarla ngani.* 'We used to go hunting all the time, but we're getting too old now.'

manhawakuru old and feeble

manharri bindieye, Bogan flea (*Calotis hispidula*) # See also **kurla.**

mankamanka find # Yw • *... karnali ngandranha mankimankiya.* '[We'll wait here and] someone will find us.' # See also **dan.ga.**

manma, manmana tell (a lie), pretend • *Manmarla nhutjadu ngakaniyi, minhangadi kara.* 'I don't know why he's telling me lies.' # perhaps also 'steal'. See also **munga.**

manmini kanpa liar # SY # See **mungini.**

manpakurra squat, sit on heels (with knees on the ground), sit (as emu)

manthi bed • *manthi yawapandhi* 'spread bedding out'

manu heart (perhaps only in the figurative sense) • *Walya nhutjadu yurayindrirla. Manu madlantji nganarnanga.* (Only example; given as translation of 'He's sad.' Second part translated as: 'His heart's not too good — about it'.)

manu patjika reconcile • *Kadla ngaldra manu patjikayindrina.* 'We're even now [after hitting one another] and friends again.'

manyanguda long ago # SY, Yw. See **matja, pandja.**

manyu, manyumanyu good, well • *Manyuldra nganha yundru nganana.* 'It's a good job you told me.' # See **patji, ngumu.**

manyu kurnu a good thing, a good job • *Manyu kurnu nhulu thayina kathitji ngakani.* 'It's a good job he ate my meat [because he's my dog].' • *Manyu kurnu yundru nganha nganana pandipurutji nhunggani, wathila ngathu mandrina, yaba ngunyingalatji yinha.* 'It's a good job you warned me about that dog; I got a stick and frightened it.'

manyuna get better • *Kadli nhunu manyunalarla; kadli walya nhunu paldrinhana.* 'He's getting better now; he nearly died.'

mapa, mapamapa, mapaapa, mapathika, mapathikathika gather, pick up, muster • *Ngala ngarru pawala thana mapaapanga pinakaringu pitjiyilayi.* 'They just gather up the seeds and rock them in the coolamon.' • *Yadatji ngathu mapanhana ngala nhunu winkarlayila.* 'I picked up the boomerang and he ran away.' • *Ngala thana ngarndri-ngapirilitji mulhudu mapaapininguda yinba-tharrapandhingalatji nhunggani.* 'His parents sent down food that they had collected for him.' • *Ngala nhunu* *yadamani mapayindrirlayi milima-nityéyi thikaringu yada, ya warlitji kuthiwarranga ya yadamani nhulu karrathikathikarnanga thanha windripadanga.* 'Meanwhile the mailman was rounding up his horses, and then he came back to the hut and tied up all the horses and went in.' • *Palha purla pirnanarlayitji, ngapala yarru wathinaritji, marru kadawayi, ngapala thawarnanga puka windritharranga ngapa marruyitji palha purla thanhayi mapathikanga.* 'When the young birds are getting big, they build a yard for them on the bank of the lake and then go down into the water and herd the baby birds back [into the yard].' # See also **mandri.**

mara hand; five • *Mara malthi yini.* 'Your hands are cold.' • *Mara ngathu pardrarla padlangurru.* 'I've got a handful of sand.' • *mara parrkulu* 'ten'

marakarla empty-handed # SY, Yw. See **karla.**

maramitji finger # See also **witju.**

maramuku fist

mara ngunpurru fingernail, claw # Also **marapirri, marapuku.**

mara pabu clapping of hands • *mara pabu parndriyindrirla* 'clapping hands'

mara pani empty handed • *Thika-warrana nganyi, kathi mara pani.* 'I came home empty-handed.'

marapardrini handle • *Ngapala pirntathangkali nyanmari, mara-pardrini, wirnili ngukanguka pirnta-thangkali, karrangalatji yinha.* 'I'll bind the handle on with string and seal it with beefwood gum (mixed with the string).'

mara patji, mara patjikurnu expert ('good hand at') • *Yilayarndu kara thana pirnngipadipadinitji mara patjikurnuli yina karrukarrutji nhinapadipadini ngapangaditji.* 'I don't know how they did it, but the

olden-days men used to be good hands at skinning [kangaroos] for water [bags].'

mara payirri, marawutju payirri second finger

marapirri fingernail

marapuku fingernail • *Mirra-yindrina nganyi marapukuli.* 'I cut myself with my fingernail.'

marapundji let go (of something held) # SY

marathangka palm of hand

marawitju, marawutju fingers • *Mitji ngathu drakana marawitju pulyali.* 'I poked my eye with my little finger.' • *Karraringu thanha mulpininguda warnta, payipayirru yina, mara witju-nyadi.* 'They tie them on after cutting them into short lengths, about the size of a finger.' • *marawutju payirri* or *mara payirri* 'second finger' • *marawutju milarri* 'third finger' • *marawutju pulya* 'little finger' • *marawutju pirna* 'thumb'

marayilka miscarry, lose (unborn) baby # Also **thundruyilka.**

Maramilya Merrimelia Waterhole

marangkarra spider

mararrala crab # Also **mundrupa.**

Mardamarda Murtamurta Well

mardanpa type of lizard (on stones, 15cm, red head)

mardipirri type of tree # possibly 'mulga' in Yawarrawarrka. See **marlka.**

mardra stone, rock, money, (SY) bullet • *Mardrangadi, mandrithayinga pirna.* 'They're going to win a lot of money.' • *Ngapala, pakuthawakaldriri mardra minhaya.* 'While they're going along, they dig out [the holes in] the rocks again.' • *Ngapala mardra thana warrkapandhi-warrkapandhingala makayi.* 'Then they throw all the stones into the fire.'

mardrakipani rockhole

mardrakupu grinding stone # the small one, held in the hand • *ngardu parndriparndrirnanga mardrakupuli* 'crushing nardoo with a grinding stone'

mardra mani money • *Mardra mani nhanggatjadu nhuniyi.* 'This money belongs to her.'

mardramitji stone, gibber, bullet # = *mardrathandra* • *Mardramitjili nganha dranyina.* 'He hit me with a stone.' • *Ngala ngapa kukuyitji ngari, wararriyitji, mardramitji karrininguda malkirri pardrangarini-ngadilatji thanha, paltjakiningadi.* 'They tie a lot of stones [to go] deep down in the water, on the bottom of the net, to weigh it down and keep it tight.' • *Kathi thanayi pulkapulkaringu makamukuruli-nyadi, ngala mardra-mitjili ngala.* 'They grill their meat on the stones and you would think it had been grilled on the coals.'

mardrangumu cave in hill • *... karnali thana nganha ngananga mardrangumuyi karnapalha nhina-rlayi.* '... people told me there's a devil in the cave.'

mardra nhiwa grinding stone # the big one, that seeds are ground on

mardra pawa thungini grinding stone

Mardrapirna Planet Downs or Tibbooburra

mardra puru hailstone

mardra thaki tomahawk • *Ngarru kathi kananggu ngala dukarnanga kulanga makamuduyitji, mardra thakili parndrininguda.* 'And they pulled out witchetty grubs from trees, after chopping them out with a stone axe, and cooked them in hot ashes.'

mardrathandra stone, bullet # = *mardramitji*

mardra thayi grinding stone

mardra thayithayi axe; grinding stone # SY. The use for 'axe' was possibly a mistake, but it was heard several times.

mardra wita hill, mountain

mardrawuldru narrow gap between rocks, the gateway a spirit goes through after a person dies

Mardrandji Mudrangie Waterhole

mardri heavy, dense • *Puka ngathu nhapipandhina mardri.* 'I mixed a thick damper.' • *Mardri kara nhunu ngakanipuru.* 'Maybe it's too heavy for me [to move].' • *Walya kandraka — mardri nhutjadu yiwangaditji.* 'Don't lift it, it's too heavy for a woman.'

mardringari weigh down

mardu social division, totem ('meat') • *Minha mardu yini?* 'What "meat" are you?' # This is the Dieri word; see **kamiri**.

mardumanha gidgea # SY; may be Wngu. See **mawurra**.

marla more • *Maka ngakani nhulu mulpamulpana, ngala nhulu parndrirla marla nganggalila.* 'He cut wood for me, and now he's cutting more, for himself.' # See also **nguka**.

marlka red mulga # *Acacia cyperophylla* • *Marlkali ngathu thinbanhana.* 'I made it [a boomerang] out of mulga.'

marna mouth; front, door • *Ngapala nhunu ngarru yankula mandriri, nga warrkapandhinga ngapala pulkanga ngala nhulu, marnali pulkarnanga nhulu ngala nhulu karrukarrukurnulitji ngararila.* 'So he just got some [dry] leaves and threw them down [on the hot coals] and started to blow them, and while he was blowing them the other old man heard him.' • *Ngapala marnatji nhinari mayi pulapulayarra thayini-ngudatji padri mulhakunatji.* 'Their mouths were green after eating the brown-nosed grub.' • *walpamarnayi* 'at the front of the humpy' # See **mampa**.

marna yiba kiss # *marna thapa* in Yw; See also **ngandja**.

marnamimi lip

marnamirri, marnamidi full # See also **yartu**, **pirna**.

marnaminina become full
• *Ngandjarri warlkarnanga ngapala nhunu ngapa marnamininari.* 'When it rains the water fills it to the brim.'

marnangadika put into the mouth
• *Kathi thukali ngala thayirnangatji marnangadikinitji mandrirnanga.* 'We eat it by spooning it into our mouths with a mussel [shell].'

marnardraku tooth # See also **dida**, **waka**.

marnayi in front

Marnanhi Merninie Creek

marnathunga tomorrow # Yw, = *marripathi, ngaranhina nhukadani*

marnda halfway • *Thawalapurra milimani nhunu Tibuparanguda, nga thudathawanga marndayitji Thanangarrpira.* 'A long time ago, a mailman was travelling from Tibooburra, and he spent the night halfway, at Tenappera.' # See also **thanu**.

marndakurnu halfway
• *Marndakurnu nhunu nhinanhina-rlatji, minhayi kara.* 'I don't know why he's sitting down halfway.'

marndakurnu-marndakurnu here and there, now and then • *Nhinggiyi ngathukurapandhirla, marndakurnu-marndakurnu.* 'I'm putting them down here and there.' # See also **kayidi-kayidi**.

marndakurra stop halfway
• *Thawanhana nhunu, marnda-kurranga thanu.* '[He] was coming, but he stopped halfway.' • *Ngala pulyatji marndakurrapandhirlayi, nga walya yinha wawatharranga,*

karrtjipandhiyila thana paninarla. 'When the little ones stop halfway they don't take any notice of them, for fear the whole lot will turn back.' # Yw 'turn back from halfway'

Marnda a waterhole near Innamincka

marndikila ripples, waves # Also **ngamanyalpi**.

marndra body # See also **parlaka**, **yiwari**.

marndra, marndraka get, dip up, scoop up (water); carry (water)
• *Nhipali ngakani ngapa marndrarla.* 'My wife will get us water.' • *Ngapa ngathu marndranga maka yinhayi panmapandhiningadi.* 'I'm going to get water to put out the fire.' # SY *kaluwa*.

marndrathika bring back (water), go and get (water) • *Karna kurnu nhulu ngapa marndrathika.* 'One of you blokes better go and get some water.'

marndra, marndrapandhi paint • *Wani thambaniningadi marndrapandhirla nganyi.* 'I've got to paint myself for a corroboree.' # *Marndra* seems to be intransitive here, but it is also used in a reflexive or reciprocal form, *marndra-yindri* 'paint yourself' or 'paint one another'. # See also **windri**.

marndu together (for example, feet); alike, close (in appearance) • *Walpa puladu nguya marndu.* 'Those two houses look exactly the same.' # See also **yala**.

marnduka, marndumarnduka join together, put together • *Mirrkatji milpirnanga, marndumarndukana pulhu tjukurru thiltjali.* 'They sew two [skins] together with kangaroo sinew [to make] the blanket.'

marnduna, marndumarnduna get together, join up • *Kuka mandunarla pulayi.* 'They've got their heads together.' # See also **mandripandhi**.

marndunangu alike, in a similar way • *Thawananga pula marndunangu.* 'They both walk the same way.'

marngali, kathi marngali yellow goanna • *Kathi marngali ngathu wanthirla, walyawalyakanga yinha, kanthayi. Ay, nhutjadu kanpala.* 'I was after a goanna but I lost it in the grass. Hey, it's turned up!'

marni fat (the substance) • *Kudlini ngathu yurarla, minhangarrkana yundru marnitji?* 'I want it cooked; what did you do with the fat?' • (Yw) *Marnili nganha windrima, thumu.* 'Rub my back with some fat.'

marnimarni fatty • *kathi marnimarni* 'fatty meat'

marnipirna, marnipika fat (person or animal) • *... tjukurru ngathu warrkananhana windrali, kathi marnipirna ...* '... I speared a kangaroo, a fat one ...'

marnipikana, marnipirnana fatten up, get fat • *Marnipirnanarlayi thana parndriyindrindji, pirnapirnatji.* 'When they have got fat they kill them, the biggest ones.'

marnipirnaka fatten • *Marnipirna-kiningaditji, ngapala thana parndriri thayingalatji.* 'After they fatten them they kill them and eat them.'

marnka cracked (for example, cracked mud) # Also **thaltha**.

marnkana crack, become cracked

marnka, marnkamarnka slow, slowly • *Marnka yandhow!* 'Say it slowly!' # See also **thakurru**.

marnkaka slow (someone or something) down, make slow

marnkamarnkali (SY) slowly

marnkunu meat ant # Also **pardi mirrka**.

marnngani crayfish, yabby

marra get red

marri (a) next day; (b) dark, in the night # Yw • *Marri nhunu thawitha.*

'He went away in the night.' # See **milyaru, mabumabu, waruwaru**.

marrikudhi do early, get up early in the morning • *Minha yini marrikudhi-warrarlayey?* 'What are you coming in here so early for?' • *Marrikudinhanala yini yilanguda?* 'Where did you come from to get here so early?' • *Yakayakarlayitji nhulu nganandji yinha, 'Ay marrikudhinhana nhunu'.* 'If he asks you tell him, "Oh, he went early".'

marrikudukudu early, early morning • *Ngapala kurrarla, marripathi thana marrikudukudutji minipandhiringu mandrithalkangalatji karlukarlu, pitjanka yina.* 'Then they put it in [at night] and next morning, very early, they run down and pull up the fish — bony bream.' # Also heard as *marrikurukuru*.

marringana get dark # Yw • *Marri-nganarnanyi, nganyi yabali nganari.* 'When it got dark I got frightened.' # See **mabumabuna**.

marriparrkulu two days later • *Ya thudathawa-thudathawanga marriparrkulu kara marriparrkulu kara thudathawari kakupani, ngarru tjukurru darlali walthininguda.* 'They might have only two or three nights on the road with no water, apart from what they carry in the waterbag.'

marripathi tomorrow, next day • *Kathi marripathingadi nhutjadu.* 'That meat's for tomorrow.' • *Ngala yamali thana ngunipika kurraringu, kalkayi, marripathi minipandhingayayi mandrithalkanga karlukarlulatji ...* 'Well, with the cross net, they put it down in the daytime, in the afternoon, and next morning they run down and pull up the fish ...' • *Marripathi kara nganyi thawanga parndrithikanga kathi kantu kurnula.* 'Tomorrow I might go out and get a wallaby.' # Yw also 'this morning'. See also

ngaranhina nhukadani,
marnathunga.

marriyungka(?) early in the morning

marrka, marrkali camping out
• *Marrkali ngani thudathikanhana.*
'We went out camping.'

marrka, marrkamarrka crawl • *Ay,
minha kara nhuniyi marrkathalkarla
maltji ngakani.* 'Hey, something's
crawling on my leg.' • *Nhunu
thangguthangguningadi yurarla,
ngarnmangarnmayindrinanga ngala.
Ngarru marrkamarrkarlangu nhunu.*
'He wants to stand up but he can't.
He's only crawling yet.'

Marrkulpi Markulpi Waterhole

Marrpu Marpoo Waterhole

marrpu, marrpuwithi long # See
payirri.

marrtji bark; call out (as a galah)
• *Pandi nhuniyi ngurra marrtjirla,
karna ngalyi ngala nhulu walya
matharla.* 'This dog's always barking,
but he never bites anybody.' # Some
creatures *yandhari* or *ngampari*; for
example brolga, magpie, willy wagtail;
some, including ducks, *marrtjiri*; some
mirrtjari or *mirrtjakurrari*, including
cattle, emus, crows and hawks. A
horse *yingkiri*. There are several
words for sounds made by dogs
(including *mirrtjari*). nOther words
for 'bark' are *warlu, kaldrukaldru,
wawurrka.*

marru lake • *Palha purla pirnanarlayitji, ngapala yarru wathinaritji,
marru kadawayi, ngapala thawarnanga puka windritharranga ngapa
marruyitji palha purla thanhayi
mapathikanga.* 'When the young birds
are getting big, they build a yard for
them on the bank of the lake and then
go down into the water and herd the
baby birds back [into the yard].' # Yw
mitka.

marrumarru lake country, area with
a lot of lakes • *... palha ngala thana*

dakamirri, marrumarruyitji. '... they
[catch] pelicans in the lake country.'

Marrukatjani Lake Maroocutchanie

Marrukuthani place name

Marrulha name of a people and
language, northeast of Yandruwandha

martardaku ankle • *Martardaku
nganyi dulyinhana, nganyi ngurrangu
thawarla.* 'I twisted my ankle but I
kept on going.' # See also
mukunkirri.

martimarti (1) peewee, mudlark # See
also **kulikuliyada, pathada-pathada**
(2) quarrion, cockatiel

matha bite • *Pandi nhuniyi ngurra
marrtjirla, karna ngalyi ngala nhulu
walya matharla.* 'This dog's always
barking, but he never bites anybody.'
• *Muduwa thika yada ay, pandilila
yina mathayi.* 'Come back here, or the
dog will bite you.'

matja long ago, not for a long time;
old; before, on a previous occasion
• *Kurrakurrawarranga warli
matjayitji.* 'He made camp at an old
hut.' • *Karnakurnu-karnakurnu
ngarru palthu kurnuyi thawarnanga
ngapangadilatji pakuninguda thana
matja.* 'Anyone using this road can
get water from the well they dug
long ago.' • *Rabitipani yina thana
nhinapadipadini matjardi.* 'They
didn't have any rabbits in the old
days.' • *Matja nhinggiwa ngaldra
nhinanhukada.* 'We were there
before.' • (H) *padla matja* 'a long time
ago' # See **manyanguda, pandja.**

matjanguda old; in the past
• *Windra matjanguda.* 'It's an old
spear.' • *Matjanguda nganyi nhinggiyi
thangguthikan.ga.* 'I've been here
before.'

matjurra greenhead ant

mawa hunger; empty (belly) • *thuru
mawa* 'empty belly'

mawakanpa hungry person

mawali hungry • *Ngurrangu nganyi mawali nganarla.* 'I'm still hungry.'

mawamawa fasting(?) # Yw

mawa ngunyi, mawa ngunyingunyi make you hungry # SY *mawa manamana*

mawapika person with a big appetite • *Mawapika nhatjadu, mulhudu pirna thayini — patjangarirla nhani mulhudungudа.* 'She's got a big appetite; she ate too much and now she's sick from it.'

mawurra, mawuda gidgea # *Acacia cambagei* # Also **mardumanha**

maya name • *Minha maya nhutjadu?* 'What's the name of that thing?' • *Thudathawari padla maya Thanangarrpira.* 'He camped at this place called Tenappera.' • *Maya ngathu yinha yakana.* 'I asked him his name.' # Yw also **tharla**.

mayatha boss # from Eng 'master'; also heard as *maadha* • *Mayathali nhulu parrkulu pulhu mandrithikanhana, kathi puluka mapiningadi.* 'The boss went and got two blokes to go and muster cattle.'

mayi (often spelt **may**) emphatic particle, not always translated, used often with commands and with questions; eh!, eh?, what!, what?, what now?, well • *Kantha mangga mayi, pulkapada mayi.* 'Burn the grass! Blow it (so it burns)!' • *Mayi minha ngala yini yurarla yakanga nganha.* 'What do you want to ask me now?' • *'Yilangginguda nhutjadu?' 'Ngalaaku.' 'Yakapadala yinha may.' 'A'ey, nhindalitji nganyi yundru kay.'* '"Where's he from?" "I don't know." "Well, ask him." "Uh-uh, I'm shy, you do it."' • *Mayi, wawathikana yundru pani? Yidlayi nhunukukalangu thana?* 'Well, did you see anybody? Whereabouts are they?' • *Yakayindrini kalkayi, 'Mayi, karlukarlutji wayinila ngandra?'.* 'In the afternoon they ask

one another, "How many fish did we get?".' # See also **malka, ngandra**.

mayikurru rat

mayiputha fog

mikiri deep # SY, Yw. May be Wngu. See **kuku**.

mila, milarri hook • *Padritji dukari thana milali.* 'They pull the grubs out with a hook.' # See also **nguku**.

   milarrika hook, make a mesh (net), knit

milimani mailman

milimiliwaduka float off into the air # used in a description of what happens to souls after death. Also **thinawaduka**. Given by BK in response to a question about a word (probably the same, but not recorded on tape) given by TG as 'angel'. Given by AWH as *mili waruka*. See also **Palkarrakarani**.

milka, milkapada pinch • *Warlu nganha milkapadana?* 'Who pinched me?'

milkiwaru or **milkiwari** type of hawk, probably whistling kite # SY

milparri company • *Thawanga nganyi ngambuyi, milparri.* 'I'll go along with my mate, keep him company.' [example suggested and accepted]

milpi sew • *Mirrkatji milpirnanga, marndumarndukana pulhu tjukurru thiltjali.* 'They sew two [skins] together with kangaroo sinew [to make] the blanket.' # Also **karrpa**.

milthi red ochre; paint • *Parrkulu wathi yundru wawarlatji; milthipani nhunu kurnutji, ngala milthimindjildra nhunu kurnutji. Ngala milthimindjitji nhunu, nganyi yurarlatji.* 'You see two things, one with paint and one without paint. I want the painted one.' # SY *kambada*.

miltjamiltja soft # Yw See **danthu, tjampa**.

milyaru night, dark • *Ngapala nhunu purtu mandrimandrirnanga milyaruyi,* *nga thawawindringa ngatjada kurnungadila,* ... 'Well, he packed his swag in the dark and walked on to the other camp, ...' • (Yw) *Watja nhina milyarunyi, thawa yada ngathu yina wawinima.* 'Don't sit in the dark, come this way so I can see you.' # See also **mabumabu, waruwaru, marri**.

mimi lip; point • *mimi tjalpatjalparri windra* 'sharp point on the spear' # See **mudra**.

marnamimi lip

mindimulpa cut in halves

mindithanma float • *Kurrarnanga kandratji mindithanminingaditji thana yamatji, karnan.gu yina.* 'They put reeds on top of the cross net so that it will float.'# See **ngupa, tharraka**.

mindra navel # SY also *pidra*, Yw *pirda*

mingka cave, hole # 'like a burrow' in contrast to *kudru* 'straight down' • *Karrukarru nhutjadu mingkayi nhinarla.* 'That old man lives in a cave.' • *Thawawarranga thanggu-wagawaganga, ngala karna nhunu purrinhinarlayi ngari mingkayi.* 'They go and stand around the hole, while the man hides in it.' # See also **wirlpa, thuka**.

mingkanguda, palha mingkanguda mountain duck # Also **ngapami-ngkanguda**.

Mingkayi Minkie Waterhole # 'in the hole'

minha, minhaya what, which, something • *Minha maya nhutjadu?* 'What's the name of that thing?' • *Minhaya ngala?* 'What next?' • *Walya nhulu kilkanhana minha nganarnanga kara nhunu; walya yina nganha nhulu dranyiningadi. Yarndu nganha nhulu dranyinhanatji.* 'He didn't know what he was doing. He didn't intend to hit me. That's how he came to hit me.' • *Kuditharrala nhukada ngathu, minhala ngathu yina nganangatji.* 'I forgot it before, what I

told you.' • *Minha karna yini?* 'Who are you?' [Lit. 'What person you?'] • *Minha windrali nhulu warrkanana?* 'Which spear did he spear [it] with?' • *Minhali yundru parndrinhana?* 'What did you hit it with?'

minha kara, minhaya kara something, I don't know what • *Minha kathi kara nhutjaduwaka.* 'There's some sort of animal over there.' • *Ay, minha kara nhuniyi marrkathalkarla maltji ngakani.* 'Hey, something's crawling on my leg.'

minha kurnu nguka something else, another one; (with negative) anything • *Walya ngathu ngananhinanhana, minha kurnu ngukatji.* 'I didn't make [that], that's another one.' • *Walya ngathu ngananhinanhana minha kurnu ngukatji.* 'I never did anything at all.'

minhama why, what for # Yw **minhamindji** strange # See **thula**.

minhangadi, minhayangadi why, what for # the *-ngadi* is sometimes dropped • *Minhangadi nhutjadu muduwa karrkarla?* 'Why is that kid yelling out?' • *Minha yini marrikudhiwarrarlayey?* 'What are you coming in here so early for?' • *Ngandjarri thana nganya thawa-thalkarlala, nga walya ngandjarritji warlkanga, minhaya kara.* 'Those clouds come up, but it won't rain. I don't know why.'

minhangana do what; what happen to • *Walya nhulu kilkanhana minhanganarnanga kara nhunu.* 'He didn't know what he was doing.' • *Minhangananhana nhunu, dan.ganhanangu yuda?* 'What happened to him; did you find him?'

minha ngarrka, minhaya ngarrka do what (to someone or something) • *Puka nhulu kudlanhana, nga minhaya ngarrkanga yinha, madla-ntjikarila yinha.* 'He cooked the damper and what did he do to it, he spoilt it.' • *Minhangarrkanhana ngala nhuludu yina?* 'What effect did it [a food he had tried for the first time] have on you?' • *Minha ngarrkanga kara ngandra? Yilakadi ngandra pakanga?* 'What are we going to do with her? Where will we take her?'

minhayarndu what is it? # Yw. Used when trying to remember a name.

mini run • *Ngapala ngathu wawana thirrirlayi thanha; ngapala nganyi miniri pirnpinga thanha.* 'Then I saw them [kids] fighting, and I ran down and scattered them.' • *Ngapala kurrarla, marripathi thana marri-kurukurutji minipandhiringu mandri-thalkangalatji karlukarlu, pitjanka yina.* 'Then they put it in [at night] and next morning, very early, they run down and pull up the fish — bony bream.'

minilka run away with # SY. See **winkama**.

minimandrithika go and get

miniminithika run around

mininhina drive along (in a car)

minithika run back, go back • *Muduwa, ngarndringadi minithika may!* 'Kid, go back to your mother!' # See also under **thika**.

miniwarra come (of a car)

miniwindri run away • *Thinaputa-panindra nhunu miniwindriri yabali, ...* 'He ran away without his boots, frightened, ...' # See also **putharrkawindri, winka, kinyiwinka**.

miniwarrkana run and spear • *Miniwarrkanapandhiri yita, kanpangu kara, nyalkari kara.* 'They spear them on the run [too], and they might get one straight off or they might miss.'

mira, ngandjarri mira rainbow • *Ngandjarri mira yita wawaka!* 'Oh.

look over there, there's a rainbow!' # Also **kurrikira**.

mirdiwiri maggot # SY. See **parndilka**.

miri sandhill • *Miringuda ngani ngatjada kurrakurranhana yundra.* 'We camped a long way from the sandhills.' • *Kathi puluka walpirri miriyi thanggukarlatji.* 'Tailing cattle over the sandhill.'

miriwita sandhill • *miriwita wartakanga* 'to go over the sandhill'

mirni in a while, by and by, wait on!; take it easy; before, a while ago; how about # often not translated; perhaps often like English 'excuse me' to introduce a question or request • *Muduwa ngathu yingkiyingkinana, mirni yada mandrithikangay.* 'I made the baby cry, will you come and get it.' • *Mirni nganha wadangay thawarlayi nganyi.* 'Will you wait while I go?' • *... mirni ngathu yina ngananga, pirnayila.* '... I'll tell you later, when you're grown up.' • *Mirni, kirri yintjadu yaka, walpi nhunu thawanga kanthakanthangadi.* 'Can you ask him when he's going to the bush [lit. grassy place].' • *Mirni thawa-malkangatji.* 'Wait a while and go later.' • *Thudanhana mirni nhunu, yingkilarla nhutjadu.* 'He was asleep before but now he's crying.' • *Tjukurru mirni ngani thayipadi-padini.* (repeated without *mirni*) 'We used to eat kangaroo.' • (SY) *Mirni ngakaniyi yandha mayi.* 'Say it slowly.' # See also **kirri, kara**.

mirni kara by and by, don't know when

mirnimirningu (a) in time, with time to spare • *Thawawarranhanatji ngani, waningaditji, mirnimirningu yina.* 'We got there, plenty of time, for the corroboree.'; (b) later on

mirniwa wait! • *Mirniwa! Nhuniyi kurnula purtu.* 'Wait a minute! Here's another swag [to put on the truck].'

• *Mirniwa ngapunarlayi!* 'Wait till they stop talking!' [Lit. 'Wait till (they're) quiet!']

mirra, mirramirra scratch • *Mirramirrayindrirla nganyi, kuka kara, kapurru kara, pangkithirri kara.* 'I don't know whether I'm scratching my head, or under the arm, or my ribs.'

mirrka bag, blanket, clothes • *Kathi yintjadu mandritharrapada mirrkayi nhunggatjaduyi.* 'Take the meat out of the bag.' • *Ngapala thana karrparnanga thirrithirri-nyadi yina walypalali kurrarlatji thana, thirrila karrpiningadi mirrka.* 'Then they weave it just like the cotton white people use for making their clothes.' • *Ngarru mirrka ngala thana kathi tjukurru darlali.* 'They have only a kangaroo skin for a blanket.' • *Mirrkatji milpirnanga, marndumarndukana pulhu tjukurru thiltjali.* 'They sew two [skins] together with kangaroo sinew [to make] the blanket.' • *Ngala thanayi kilkarla, ngarru yarawarrangu thawathawapadipadini, mirrka thana* (word not clear) *karrpapadipadini paladi.* 'People now think they used to walk about naked, but they used to sew their own clothes.' # See also **pirli**, **paltja**, **thandji**, **yakutha**.

mirrkapiki rag • *Mirrkapiki thatamindji yinhadu yada ngunyi.* 'Hand me that greasy rag.'

mirrtja noise, noisy; make a noise • *Pandi nhuliyi parndrina yinha, ngurra mirrtjarlayi.* 'He hit the dog because it's always making a noise.' # See **yindri**.

mirrtjakurra make a noise, call • *Warruwitji ngathu ngarana mirrtjakurrarlayi.* 'I heard an emu calling.' • *Mirrtjakurra thanha muduwa!* 'Call those kids!' # See also **marrtji**, **ngampa**, **yandha**, **kandri**, **ngarndapandji**.

mirrtja ngana be noisy, make a noise • *Muduwali thanayi mirrtjanganarla.* 'The kids are making a noise.' # SY

mirrtjapika, mirrtjapurra, (SY) **mirrtjapirna** noisy

mithinti type of carpet snake, possibly the Children's python # SY. AWH gave it for 'slow-worm' (= blind snake)'. See **nyungumarlinya**.

mithipudanda smallest type of black ant

mitji eye, seed • *Mitji ngathu drakana marawitju pulyali.* 'I poked my eye with my little finger.' • *Warlu yina mitji yimpakanhana?* 'Who gave you a black eye?' • *Yambarriyi kurranga, padla paltjapaltja yina wipinginingudatji yinha, patjikaringu padla, padla thaka mitji ngukangukayindriyi.* 'They put them on the hard flat ground, after sweeping it to make it clean so that the seeds don't get mixed with clay.' # Also appears as the second part of compounds, possibly with a reference to smallness and roundness; see **mardramitji**, **maramitji**, **thinamitji**, **purndamitji**.

mitji kilthi tears # SY. See **mitjiyindri**.

mitjiyimpa puppa-grass, or seeds of type of bush # Lit. 'black seed' • *Ngala pawa ngala kalildra dingarnanga, pawa kalpurru, pawa wadlangurru, pawa mitjiyimpa, pawa ngadli, pawa pidriyiltharri.* 'Then they used to grind seeds as well — coolibah seeds, *wadlangurru* seeds, puppa-grass seeds, pigweed seeds, frosty-arse seeds.'

mitjiyindri tears # SY *mitji kilthi*

mitji padna button # from Eng

mitjiparlu white-eyed duck

mitjipilpa eyebrow, eyelash

mitjithulkini glasses

mitka lake # Yw (BK); see **marru**.

Mitkakaldrithili Mitkacaldratillie # Yw (BK), 'two bitter lakes'

Mitkapatjithili place name # Yw (BK), 'two good lakes'

muda corroboree; corroboree ground, church; initiation ceremonies • *Ngapala pula pakarila thanha, ngapirimaladitji mudalatji yina drangarnanga pantjinayindririlatji.* 'Well then they took all their fathers, and they had a corroboree and circumcised one another.' # See **wani**.

mudamuda story

muda yalkura God # see **yalkura**.

muda bad cold # Yw • *Mudamindji nhunuyi kurrunggurru.* 'He's got a bad cold.'

mudlu bean tree • *Thudathawanhana nganyi padla mudlu malkirriyi.* 'I camped last night in a place with a lot of bean trees.'

mudra point, end # Also **ngulu, mulha, mimi.**

ngan.ga mudra point of beard, chin

mudra yamstick

mudranganku butt of a yamstick

Mudrangankuthili place near Scrubby Camp Waterhole

mudu ashes # Also **thurrpa.**

muduna burn away to ashes • *Makatji nhunu mudunamalkaya.* 'Let the fire burn away to ashes.'

muduwa child, baby • *Muduwa nhutjadu yingkirla.* 'The baby's crying.' • *Minhangadi nhutjadu muduwa karrkarla?* 'Why is that kid yelling out?' • *Muduwa pulyali ngathu wawatharrana kurrupu karrukarrutji nhinarlayi ya thayiyindrirlayi padri yuka thanha.* 'When I was a little boy I saw how the old people lived and how they ate those grubs.' # See also **thidharri.**

muka asleep, sleep, sleepiness • *Walya nganyi yinha yurarla wawiningadi nganha. Nganyi yukarrapandhirla, muka-nyadi nganha nhulu kilkiningadi.* 'I don't want him to see me.

I'll lie down and make him think I'm asleep.'

mukaka put to sleep # Yw • *Nhunuwa purla yingkirla, ngathu ngandjarla yinha mukakiya. Yingkirlanyi.* 'The baby's crying; I want to put him to sleep. Because he's crying.'

mukali sleepy • *Marna kagayindrirla nganyi mukali.* 'I'm yawning, sleepy.'

mukapurra sleepyhead • *Mukapurra nhatjadu.* 'She's always asleep.'

muka ngunyingunyi make (someone) sleepy # possibly also **muka ngunyi.**

muka thuda sleep, camp • *Karna nhunu thawalapurra muka thuda-thawanga.* 'This man, a long time ago, was travelling, and camped along the way.' • *Walya yinha yirrtjinatjay, muka yina nhutjadu thudarla.* 'Don't wake him up, let him sleep.'

muki or **muku** smoke # from Eng. See **thupu.**

muku bone, log • *mukuli drakari* 'pointing the bone' • *Mukupika yina thana pitjankatji.* 'Those bony bream are the very bony ones.' • *Ngapala kudru pakuri ngari, nga yankala kurrawagandji nga windripandhinga palha mukuli.* 'They dig a hole and put boughs around it and [a man] goes down into the hole with a bird bone.' # See **thinka, wathi, maka warnta.**

mukurduka pull bones out • *Thana mukurdukalapurra thanha, ngarru ngaga yina nhunu pirnatji wirlpa.* 'They took the bones out through a hole only as big as the throat.'

mukukarta thin # 'rattly bones'. See also **ngawada.**

mukunkirri ankle # SY. See **martardaku.**

mukuru charcoal • *maka mukuru* 'hot coals'

mulapada crested pigeon

mulha face, nose, end (of something) • *Nga yadala thana thinbari, yadatji thinbininguda nga wirlpa kurranga, mulha kurnuyi.* 'Then they make a boomerang and put a hole in one end of it.' • *Kinipapa nhulu mulhatji wawangarirla.* 'He's facing towards the river.' • *Mulha wawayindrini, nhunu wawayindrinhana, nga yaba ngunyiyindringa.* 'He saw his face [as a reflection], he saw himself and got frightened.' • *palthu mulha* 'end of a road' # See also **mudra, ngulu, kintha.**

mulhakuna an edible green grub with a brown nose and a sharp tail • *Mulhakuna thayipadipadini ditjipininguda ngapala ngunkunhapiri.* 'They used to eat a brown nosed one which they dried in the sun and rolled into a ball.' • *Ngapala marnatji nhinari mayi pulapulayarra thayiningudatji padri mulhakunatji.* 'Their mouths were green after eating the brown nosed grub.'

mulhakurnu-mulhakurnu all sorts

mulha malka photo (of a person) • *Mulha malka, yundru wawanga malkirri thanayi ngakani, mulha malka mandrininguda yina, walypalali.* 'I've got a lot of photos here that have been taken by a white man, if you'd like to look at them.'

mulhapundra south • *Thawarla nganyi mulhapundra.* 'I'm going south.' • *Thawawarranhana nhuniyi mulhapundranguda.* 'This fellow comes from the south.' # SY and Yw *wakarramuku*

mulhayimpa (1) black-headed python; (2) saltbush

mulhana carpet snake # in hill country. SY. See also **manga, wama.**

mulhudu food, tucker • *Makamuduli kulari, mulhudu patjikurnutji.* 'They cook them in hot ashes, and they are good tucker.' • *Mulhudu ngathu pirna*

thayipandhina, thundrutji nganyi kimanarla. 'I ate too much and my stomach is swollen.' # See also **puka.**

mulpa egret

mulpa cut off, cut through, sever; shear • *Mara nhunu mulpayindrina.* 'He cut off his own finger.' • *Punggu mulpiningudatji ngapala kurrari ngapayi, wiki parrkulu kara, thungganiningadi.* 'They cut the bow vine and put it in water for maybe two weeks, so that it will rot.' • *Karraringu thanha mulpininguda warnta, payipayirru yina, mara witjunyadi.* 'They tie them on after cutting them into short lengths, about the size of a finger.' • *Kathi thambaka ngathu kilkarla; ngathu wakanarla thannganitjadu kathi tjipiyitji, minhayangadi yina, yamunu thana mulpiningadi, tjidali.* 'I know all about sheep; I work with those sheep, for whatsaname, for them to cut their wool, the shearers.'

mulpamulpa cut up

multhipa wash # Yw. See **yika, yirra.**

munba lichen (?)

Munba Lake Moonba

mundha, mundhapani greedy

mundja sick • *Man.gili nhunu mundja, patjarla, thawanhana nhunu, kirringadi, kintha yunggudu ngakarnanga.* 'Benny's sick, his nose is bleeding and he's gone to the doctor.' # *Mundja* and *patja* are often used together. See, for example, **warnta** entry. See also **wariwari.**

mundjana become sick • *Ngarru ngala thana ngapali nhinapadipadinitji. Ngawu, karna paltjapaltja nhinanga, walya mundjanini, ngarru nhinanga thipingu.* 'They only used to live on water [they didn't have tea]. Yes, they were strong people, never got sick; they were really alive.'

mundjaka, mundjamundjaka hurt, injure; make sick • *Walya yinha*

*ngurratji pardrapardraw,
mundjakayila yundru yintjadu.*
'Don't keep on handling it, you'll
hurt it.' # See **katjakatja**.

mundja ngunyingunyi make sick

mundju fly

mundjungunku a cake or ball of flies
(which is what people get to eat when
they go to Hell)

mundjurrunga blowfly

mundrupa crab # Also **mararrala**.

munga tell a lie # Also **manma**.

mungini liar # See also **manmini
kanpa**.

mungini orphan # ? Contradictory
information

mungka hug; carry under arm

mungkayindri hug one another, hug
(something) to yourself • *Ngapala
nhunu thangguthalkawarrananga
patjipatjingu nga purtu nhulu
kunyamanga, nga kupuyi yinha
kurrapadaringu mungkayindriri
yina purtutji.* 'Then he got up, very
carefully, and rolled up his swag and
put it under his arm.'

munma shut (mouth) # SY. See also
dapa, ngapu.

munthu bottom or back of net (**pirli**)

muntji smother • *Thupulu nganinha
muntjirla.* '[The fire]'s smothering us
with smoke.'

munumunu curly (or **munhumunhu**)

karli munumunu, kuka munumunu
curly hair

mura drink; thirst # Often used with
ngapa 'water': *ngapa mura*.

murakanpa thirsty person

murali thirsty • *Yibathawanga yita
ngapa muralitji nganari.* 'They drink
it when they get thirsty.' • *Karnatji
ngathinha dan.ganhana paldringala
nganarlayi ngapa murali.* 'When I
found that man he was nearly dying
of thirst.'

mura ngunyingunyi make thirsty
• *Ngapa kaldri nhanha(?) ngathu
yibanhana, ngapa mura ngunyi-
ngunyinga nganha.* 'I drank salty
water and it made me thirsty.'
SY *mura manamana*.

murda finish, stop • *Kali thanadu
murdana.* 'They've stopped [playing].'
• *ngandjarri murdininguda* 'after it
had stopped raining' • *Kali ngaldra
murdana, kurrathikapadaringu
purtutji thanhadu. Yingganiyi
walthayindrithikangaldra yini.*
'We've finished now, I'll put those
things away. You take yours home.'
See also **parndriyindri** and under
pani.

murla quiet, tame, inoffensive • (Yw)
Murla kamanti. 'My (horse) is quiet
(and wouldn't throw its rider).'

murlathi type of lizard, possibly military
dragon, *Ctenophorus isolepis* • *Walya
murlathi yintjadu parndrini!* 'Don't
kill that lizard!'

murna, murnathitha chest
• *murnathithangadi ngapa* 'chest-deep
water' • At initiations the boys had to
sit up all night without sleeping. To
keep them awake they would hit
them on the chest and say: *Kapow!
Yurlawarrali yina murna parndrina.*
'Bang! The night owl hit you in the
chest.'

murnakaldra chest # Yw

murnamandriyindri meet (one
another)

murnampirri chest # SY

murnapaka lie on front

murnurru gentle slope # SY gave
munarra 'high bank'. See also
ngarnarri.

murrupurlu poor hunter # TG only

murrumpadi black cockatoo

muthu very, well; real, true, proper;
really; (with negative) not at all
• *tjarnmarla muthu* 'shining brightly'

• *madlantji muthu* 'very bad'
• *Purrtjinana muthu.* '[He] really frightened [me].' • *Yabapani muthu nhutjadutji.* 'He's not a bit frightened.'
• (Yw) *Karrukarru muthu ...* 'He's very old ...' • *Windripada muthu may!* 'Go right in!' • *karna muthu* 'a real person' (See Text 8 Sentence 10 in §5.2, 'Yandruwandha stories') # See also **yurlu**, **kanpa**.

muthuka (1) get (spear, shoot etc)
• *Kadli walya ngathu muthukana.* 'I nearly got it.' # opposite of *pudlupudluka*; (2) prove, show to be true

mutuka, **wathi mutuka** motorcar

mutuka pakini driver

muya dry # SY, Yw, H. See **purudu**, **kayinta**.

muyaka dry (something) # SY

N

nalyba, **nayiba** knife # from Eng
• *Ngapala thana kathi nalybali-nyadi dramirdramininguda kilkari.* 'You would think it had been cut up with a steel knife.' SY and Yw *nayipa*. See also **thurla**, **thatji**.

nga and, then; but • *Ngapala kururruparnanga nga nhurrpanga ngarrpayi kunya payirrili.* 'Then they rub it with stones and spin it on their thighs, using a long spindle.'
• *Wirni payirrikari yinha nga kunyayi kurranga.* 'They make the string long and put it on the spindle.'
• *Pirritjampanarlayi nhunu karrtji-pandhinga pulyatji nhunu nga thikanhinanga thundingadi ...* 'If a little one gets tired it turns around and heads back to the island ...'
• *... thudiningarilatji ngani, nga pukapani ngala ngani thawanhana.* '... we wanted to camp, but we had come without food.' # See also **ya**.

ngaandi, **ngaani** yes • *A 'ay yundra-nguda nganyi, ngaandi, mayi yundra-ngudanga.* 'Oh, I'm from a long way away, yes, a long way.' # Also **kawu**.

ngaba, **ngabangaba** wet, fresh
• *Ngabakana nganha, ngabangabala thikawarrana nganyi.* '[The rain] wet me and I came home wet.' • *Ngapala nhunu purtu mandrimandrirnanga milyaruyi, nga thawawindringa ngatjada kurnungadila, withi ngabayi-ngada, ya kuthiwarrarila mayi.* 'Well, he packed his swag in the dark and walked on to the other camp, while the injury was still fresh, and he got there.'

ngabaka, **ngabangabaka** wet something • *... ngandjarritji warlkaringu ngabangabakaringu pulhu.* '... the rain came down and wet them both.'

ngabana, **ngabangabana** get wet
• *Walya ngabangabananitji!* 'Don't get wet!' (to kids)

ngada still # May be a clitic. See **ngaba** entry, second example. See also **ngurrangu**.

ngadlari see **ngalari**.

ngadli pigweed • *Ngala pawa ngala kalildra dingarnanga, pawa kalpurru, pawa wadlangurru, pawa mitjiyimpa, pawa ngadli, pawa pidriyiltharri.* 'Then they used to grind seeds as well — coolibah seeds, wadlangurru seeds, puppa-grass seeds, pigweed seeds, frosty-arse seeds.'

ngadra mother's father # Yw. See **papa**.

ngaga throat, neck • *Thana mukurduka-lapurra thanha, ngarru ngaga yina nhunu pirnatji wirlpa.* 'They took the bones out through a hole only as big as the throat.' # See also **ngayimala**, **yutju**.

ngagangaga pelican # H. See **dakamirri**.

ngagapardra choke (someone or something) # Also **puma**.

'for us' etc.) • *ngalingga nhunggani.*
'It belongs to me and him.' • *Muduwa
yini wanthiyindrirla; nhuniyi nhinarla
ngalinggayi.* 'You're looking for the
boy; he's sitting down here with me
and him.' # Yw also **ngalini**.

ngalinha us (two, not including
person spoken to) • *Karrkapadanhana
nhulu ngalinha padawarrangudali.*
'He sang out to us from across the
river.'

ngalini our, ours, belonging to us
(two, not including person spoken to);
us (as in 'with us', 'for us' etc.) # SY
and Yw = *ngalingga(ni).*

ngalpa (a) the lap, the two thighs
• *Kapada nhinanga ngalpayi.* 'Come
and sit on [my] lap.' • *Ngapala
kururruparnanga nga nhurrpanga
ngalpayi kunya payirrili.* 'Then they
rub it with stones and spin it on their
thighs, using a long spindle.'; (b) type
of dance movement, dance 'shake-a-
leg' • *ngalpa thambanana* 'danced
shake-a-leg' # See also **kuma**.

ngalpirri behind, on the other side
(not visible) # or *walpirri*, which see
• *Ngalpirriwaka miri; miriyi ngalpirri.*
'[They are] on the other side of the
sandhill.' # See **durruyi, ngardra**.

ngaltja spit, saliva • *Ngaltja drinthana
nganhala muduwali.* 'The kid spat at
me.'

ngalungga, ngalunggani our, ours,
belonging to us (two, including person
spoken to); us (as in 'to us', 'for us'
etc.) • *Waranu kara nhuniyi thawarla
ngatjada ngalungganingadi.*
'Someone's coming to our camp.'
• *Thawawindrirla nhunu ngalungga-
puru.* 'He's walking away from us.'

ngalunha us (two, including person
spoken to) • *Mirni ngaldra yandhayandharla, walya ngariningadi
ngalunha ngalyilitji.* 'Let's have a
talk [here], [where] the others won't
hear us.'

ngalyi some, a few, a little, any, others
• *Karna ngalyi nhulu walya matharla.*
'He (dog) never bites anybody.'
• *Thudayukarranga warrarnanga
thakumani ngalyila.* 'He camped
overnight while he waited for some
stockmen.' • *Dritji kurnuyitji, karna
malkirri thawawarrandji, ngalyila.*
'One day another group of blackfellows arrived.' • *Thanayildra
pakangala ngalyitji, thanayildra
(word not clear), thanayildra yarndu.*
'Each group takes a few.' • *Ngalyi
thana yadali dranyirnanga.* 'Some
people kill them with boomerangs.'
• *Pirritjampanarlayi nhunu karrtjipandhinga pulyatji nhunu nga thikanhinanga thundingadi, ngala thana
kadirlayi palha ngalyitji, pirnapirnatji,
ngapala thana windrimawarraringu
wathininguda yarrutji thanngani.* 'If a
little one gets tired it turns around and
heads back to the island, while they
hunt the rest of them, the biggest ones,
on and put them in the yard that they
have built for them.' • *Man.garri
kurnu ngala thana ngalyitji ngarru
karruwalildra.* 'There's one girl and
all the rest are boys.' # See **nganya,
pulya, ngariyuka**.

ngama breast, milk, teat (for example,
of kangaroo) • (SY) *Ngama nhuluyi
thaparla muduwali.* 'The baby's
sucking the breast.'

ngama mana # SY give birth, have
(a baby) # ? Lit. 'give breast' or 'give
milk'; see **yadhi kurra, ngathanika,
dan.ga**.

ngama mother's brother, uncle; father-
in-law • *Ngama ngakani paldrilapurra
matja.* 'My uncle died a long time
ago.' # See also **tharu**.

ngamanyalpi ripple, wave # Also
marndikila.

ngambu mate • *Ngaranhana ngathu
ngambunginguda.* 'I heard about it
from my mate.' # a kinship term.

ngambu, ngambungambu ball (for
example, of clay)

ngamburru see **kintha ngamburru**.

ngamburu see under **pitji**.

ngami group, mob, flock • *Kathi purlatji
thanadu ngamiyi.* 'The young ones
are [together] in a group.' • *Ngami
thanadu tharrarla.* 'They're flying in
a flock [for example, ducks, pelicans].'
See also **kini, malkirri**.

ngamikularri dogwood # SY. See
thayamarni.

ngampa pus, matter (in boils and sores)

ngampa talk, speak; make its natural
sound (for example, a bird to call)
Also **yandha**.

ngampu nearly # Yw. See **kali walya**.

ngampurru yellowbelly, golden perch
• *Ngala pirlili ngampurrungaditji
paladildrangu thana drakininguda,
kurrarla yarnduldrangu kinipapayi
kurrapadari yita.* 'They use a net that
they have woven with a different
mesh, and that they put into the water
in the same way, for yellowbelly.'

ngamudu see **kintha ngamudu**.

ngamurru orphan • *Ngarndri-ngapiri
nhunggani paldrin.ga, muduwa yina
kurnula warrkawindriri. Ngamurru.*
'His parents died and left him on his
own. An orphan.'

ngana tell, say, be, do, cause, teach,
explain, become, make, use, ask, get
ready, be about to, intend to • *Ngathu
yinha nganana nhinapandhiningadi.*
'I told him to sit down.' • *Minha
yundru nganarlay?* 'What did you
say?' • *Ngurrangu nganyi mawali
nganarla.* 'I'm still hungry.'
• *Ngapala pula nganayindrirnanga
'Yilanggniguda nhutjadu?'* 'Well
they asked one another "Where's he
from?"' • *Ngararnanga pulhu walya
ngathu pulhu nganandji.* 'I understood
them but I didn't tell them.'
• *Nhindalila pula nganalapurratji.*

'They had been very shy.' • *Kalkuli
ngala yamatji mikimana, nganalapurra thana yamali ngala kalkuli.*
'Well they made nets of bulrushes;
they used to use nets made of
bulrushes.' • *Pirnapirna thanhayi,
tharriningaditji nganarlayi, purndaparndringa kudlanga yina thayiyindrirnangatji.* 'The biggest ones,
that are nearly ready to fly, they kill
and cook and eat.' • *... nganyitji
thangguwindringala nganarla
thawiningadi.* '... I was just going to
go.' • *Thawiningadi-nyadi nganyi
ngananhana, ngala ...* 'I was going
to go but ...' • *Karnatji ngathinha
dan.ganhana paldringala nganarlayi
ngapa murali.* 'When I found that
man he was nearly dying of thirst.'
• *Nganayindringa nganyi, walya
yabalitji ngana may.* 'I told myself not
to be frightened.' • *Pakali nganamalkardi, mabaabunarlarlayinardi.* 'Do it
quickly, it's getting dark.' # In SY and
Yw this word in its present tense or
simultaneous action form is often used
in the formation of future tense, and
often seems to mean 'want, intend'.
• (Yw) *Nganyi yulganiyi thawanga
nganarla.* 'I'm going [to go] with you
two.' # It clearly means 'want' in:
• (Yw) *Nganyi nganarla muka parriya.*
'I want to sleep.' # It can only denote
future tense in • (Yw) *Ngandjarra
warlgiya nganarla kayidi.* 'It'll rain
soon.' # See *yabaka* for an example
of *ngana* apparently meaning 'want'.
Many other verbs share one or more
of the meanings of *ngana*.

ngananhinanhukada yesterday, day
before yesterday • *Thirrinhana pula
nganahinanhukada.* 'They had a fight
yesterday.' • *Ngananhinanhukada
nhani thawanhanatji.* 'She went the
day before yesterday.' # May refer
only to daytime. See also **kalkayi**.

nganathalkana this morning

nganathika tell someone back

nganathikathika tell everyone

nganayukarranhukada last night

nganamayindri clench (fist) • *mara nganamayindri* 'clench the fist' # Also **ngarndamayindri**.

Ngananhina language name (Arrabury area)

ngandala handle (as of axe) # from Eng

ngandithirri waddy, two-handed fighting stick

ngandja name, call (someone something) • *Kanyini nhandradu ngandjarla.* 'She calls [me] granny.' # Also **drika**.

ngandja like; kiss # SY, Yw. *Yura* was not accepted for 'like', but used (optionally) with the negative *walya* to say 'don't like'. • (SY) *Ngathu yinhaku ngandjarla.* 'I like him.' • (SY) *Walya nganyi nhungganiyi karnayi yurarla.* 'I don't like that man.' • (Yw) *Watja ngathu ngandjarla kulanga.* 'I don't like cooking.' # See **marna thapa, marna yiba**.

ngandjarri rain, clouds • *Ay ngandjarri kara warlkanga nganyi thawarla warli matjayi thudanga.* 'Oh, it looks like rain, I'll go and sleep in the old hut.' • *Ngandjarri warlkarnanga ngapala nhunu ngapa marnamininari.* 'When it rains the water fills it to the brim.' • *Muduwa yada winkapadani ngandjarripuru.* 'Kids, come inside out of the rain.' # MN (SY and Yw) and H more often said *ngandjarra*. See also **nganya, pariwirlpa, kudawarrala**.

ngandjangandjarri cloudy

ngandjarri kura storm

ngandjarri mira rainbow

ngandjarri mitji thunder cloud # (H) hailstorm

ngandjarri nganya cloud • *Dritji nhunu dunkarila ngandjarri nganyanguda.* 'The sun's coming out from behind the clouds.'

ngandra oh!, well! • *Ngandra maka ngala nhunuyardi thangkanarla ngurrangu.* 'Oh! Well this fire's still alive!' # See also **mayi, malka**.

ngandra we (more than two, including person spoken to) • *Minha ngarrkanga kara ngandra? Yilakadi ngandra pakanga?* 'What are we going to do with her? Where will we take her?' • *Yakayindrini kalkayi, 'Mayi, karlukarlutji wayinila ngandra?'.* 'In the afternoon they ask one another, "How many fish did we get?"'

ngandrarni our, ours, belonging to us (more than two, including person spoken to); us (as in 'to us', 'with us' etc.) # SY, = *nganungga(ni)*

ngandrangandra hunt, search # Yw

ngandrawandra death adder # SY

ngan.ga beard • *Ay ngan.gamindji ngathu wawanhana.* 'I saw [a man] with a beard.'

ngan.ga mudra chin, point of beard # See also **nganka, tjindra**.

nganggali or **nganggalhi** by oneself; own, owner; having rights over; for oneself • *Ngapala nhunu nguthangutharnangala katjakatjarlayilatji parndriyindrininguda nganggali karna palha-nyadi wawawawari.* 'Well, he stretched out his leg because of the pain, because he had hit himself, thinking it was a devil he had seen.' • *Yarndukala ngali yinha thulathulakanhana ay karna nganggalitji nhutjadu.* 'How could we reckon he was a stranger, when he's one of our own people.' • *Walpanganggalili wawayila yina winkamarlayi kara yundru.* 'The owner of the house might see you and think you are stealing something.' • *Nganggalhildra thana wani thambanapadipadini, walya yiwali wawiningadi, yirrbantji yina.* 'They [the men] dance their own corroboree and the women don't watch, it's forbidden.' • *Minhangadila yundru parndrinhana yintjadu, nganggali-nyadi.* 'Why did you hit him, you had no right to.' • *Kurnukurnu nhutjadu yandhayandharla nganggali.* 'He's talking to himself.' • *Maka ngakani nhulu mulpamulpana, ngala nhulu parndrirla marla nganggalila.* 'He cut wood for me, and now he's cutting more, for himself.' # SY and Yw *nganggili.* See also **thula**.

nganggalika own (something) • *Minhangadi pandi nhuliyi nganggalikarla parndriningaditji?* 'Why does he own a dog if he's just going to belt it?'

ngan.gu word, speech; voice • *Nganyi yandharla ngan.gu yina, karna yawarri Yandruwandha.* 'Well I'm talking the language, Aboriginal language, Yandruwandha.' • *Kali nhutjadu ngan.gu yinggani patjikurnu.* 'That's right [what you say].' • *Nguthingi ngamangi nganha nganalapurra, kurrakurranarnanga yina, ngan.gu yandhiningadi.* 'My brother and uncle told me what to say, and taught me.' • *Ngan.gu kuthikuthidi nhinda ngunyingunyirnanga yinha. Yarndu nhunu walyatji yurarla yandhiningaditji.* 'His squeaky voice makes him shy. That's why he doesn't like talking.' # *ngan.gu* is not 'language', like *yawarri*, but 'what you say'. See also **parlpa, yindri, yawarri, ngaru**.

nganha me • *Pandi malkirrili nganha kadina.* 'A mob of dogs chased me.' • *Ngandra yaba ngunyinhana nganha yundru ngathutji purtupa walthawindrinhana winkarnanga yinggani kurnkipuru.* 'Oh! You frightened me and I took my swag away and ducked off for fear of you being a devil.' • *Wilpadali nganyi thawalapurra, mandrithawari nganha walypalali.* 'Once I was travelling in a wagon — some white men picked

me up.' • *Nga Kinipapayi nganha warrkawindringa ngapa yulpurru yina ngakarlayi.* 'They left me at Cooper's Creek because the river was in flood.'

ngani we (more than two, not including person spoken to) • *Marrkali ngani thudathikanhana.* 'We went out camping.' • *Walyala ngani purrka-padayi wilpadalitji, ngarrungu pula thawandji, thantjiyipa-ngadi, nganyi nhinapadapadarlayi nhinggikala Kinipapayi.* 'We mightn't have got across with the wagon so they went on without me, to the town, and I stayed there at the river.'

nganingga, nganinggani our, ours, belonging to us (more than two, not including person spoken to); us (as in 'to us', 'with us' etc.) • *Yandhayandharla nhutjadu nganinggani.* 'He's talking to us.' • *Muduwa nhutjadu winkawindrina nganinggayi.* 'That kid's running away from us.'

nganinha us (more than two, not including person spoken to) • *Thupulu nganinha muntjirla.* '[The fire]'s smothering us with smoke.'

nganini our, ours, belonging to us (more than two, not including person spoken to); us (as in 'to us', 'with us' etc.) # SY

nganka chin # SY. See **ngan.ga mudra, tjindra**.

nganku butt # See **mudra, warta**.

nganungga, nganunggani our, ours, belonging to us (more than two, including person spoken to); us (as in 'to us', 'with us' etc.) • *Walypalangadi mulhudu madlantji nganunggangaditji.* 'Whitefellows' tucker is no good for us.'

nganunha us (more than two, including person spoken to) • *Ngarndapandjina ngaldra yinha, ngala nhulu walya ngararlayi ngalunha.* 'We called out to him, but he didn't hear us.'

nganya cloud • *Ngandjarri thana
nganya thawathalkarlala, nga walya
ngandjarritji warlkanga, minhaya
kara.* 'Those clouds come up, but it
won't rain. I don't know why.'
• *Nganya thanadu yimpanapadalarla.*
'The clouds are getting black.' # See
also under **ngandjarri, pariwirlpa,
kudawarrala**.

nganya little bit # See also **pulya,
ngalyi**.

nganyi I (subject of intransitive verb
or in a sentence without a verb)
• *Pundrali nganyi yirrikarla.*
'I'm shivering with the cold.'
• *Pipinhinanga nganyi makamakayi
yina.* 'I'll have a rest while it's hot.'
• *Karlukarlungadi nganyi thawarla.*
'I'm going fishing.' • *Kali thana
wirninarnanga warnu nganyi.* 'They
told them who I was.' # See **ngathu**.

nganyipuntha mouse # SY. = *pundha,
puntha*

ngapa water, source of water • *Nhipali
ngakani ngapa marndrarla.* 'My wife
will get us water.' • *Walarri nganyi
wawayindrirla ngapayi.* 'I can see
myself in the water.' • *Ngapa yundra
nhunu ngatjadayi.* 'The water's a
long way from the camp.' • *Punggu
murrpiningudatji ngapala kurrari
ngapayi, wiki parrkulu kara,
thungganiningadi.* 'They cut the
bow vine and put it in water for
maybe two weeks, so that it will rot.'

ngapa kaldri rum, whisky, anything
bitter • *Karrukarru, nhuniyi pada,
ngapa kaldringuda, yibanhana
nhuluyi, thudarla nhunu, kurrayi
nganarnanga, kurrayi nganarla.*
'This old fellow is inside, he's been
drinking rum and now he's lying
down, dead drunk.'

ngapakuku bottom of the water

ngapakurna deep water, waterhole
• *Ngapakurnangadi nganyi thawarla,
makita ngala ngathu pakarla,*
palhanguka ngathu wawayi. 'I'm
going to the waterhole; I'll take my
gun just in case I see any birds
(meaning ducks).' • *ngapakurna
muthu* 'very deep (water)'

ngapa mandrini waterbag • *Ngapala
ngapa marndrinilatji thanngani yulpu
thawiningadi, padla yundrawaka
ngapapaniyi.* '[They use] their waterbags when they go on a journey in
remote waterless country.'

ngapa mingkanguda mountain duck
Also **mingkanguda**.

Ngapamiri Nappa Merrie # 'water-
sandhill'

ngapangarrka (river) crossing

ngapa palyakini sugar # SY and Yw
thipi

ngapa yulpurru flood

ngapatjili soak

Ngapatjiri Lake Apachurie

Ngapawirni Nappaoonie # 'water-
string'

ngapala then, and then, connective
(often not translated) • *Ngananga
kurranga kinipapayitji, ngapala thana
mirndithanmari.* 'Then they put them
in the river and they float.' • *Palha
purla pirnanarlayitji, ngapala yarru
wathinaritji, marru kadawayi, ngapala
thawarnanga puka windritharranga
ngapa marruyitji palha purla thanhayi
mapathikanga.* 'When the young birds
are getting big, they build a yard for
them on the bank of the lake and then
go down into the water and herd the
baby birds back [into the yard].'
• *Mulhakuna thayipadipadini
ditjipininguda ngapala ngunkunhapiri.*
'They used to eat a brown-nosed one
which they dried in the sun and rolled
into a ball.' # See **ngala**.

ngapardalku wood adder (type of
gecko)

ngapardi see **ngapiri**.

ngapiri father, father's brother, (cross-) cousin's son • *Yada nhutjadu ngapiringi.* 'That boomerang is my father's.' # Yw and H *ngapardi.*

ngapiri pirna father's elder brother

ngapiri pulya father's younger brother

ngapitja spirit of a person, soul • *Paldriri, ngapala nhunu ngapitja thawari Kuntjidingaditji.* 'When [someone] dies, the spirit goes to Kuntjidi (a place in Pilardapa country).'

ngapu, ngapungapu quiet # See also **pilpangurru.**

ngapuka shut (mouth) # Yw • *Marna yinhaku ngapuka!* 'Shut your mouth!' # *Ngapuka* would presumably also mean 'quieten, make quiet'. See also **dapa, munma.**

ngapuna be quiet, become quiet; be shut (mouth) • *Mirniwa, ngapunarlayi.* 'Wait till [they] shut up [before you try to tell me].' • (Yw) *Marna nhunuyi ngapunarla.* 'His mouth's shut.'

ngara hear, understand • *Minhala yini yurarla ngariningadi nganyi yandharlayi?* 'What do you want to hear me say?' • *Ngaranhana ngathu ngambunginguda.* 'I heard about it from my mate.' • *Ngapala nhunu ngarru yankula mandriri, nga warrkapandhinga ngapala pulkanga ngala nhulu, marnali pulkarnanga nhulu ngala nhulu karrukarru-kurnulitji ngararila.* 'So he just got some [dry] leaves and threw them down [on the hot coals] and started to blow them, and while he was blowing them the other old man heard him.' • *Ngapala Diradili pula yandha-rnangatji ngala ngathutji ngararlayi pulhu.* 'Well they were talking in Dieri, and I understood them.' # SY and Yw *panga.*

(ngara)

ngaranhina nhukadani tomorrow # Also **marripathi, marnathunga.**

ngarathalkana this morning

(ngara)

ngarangara (a) liver; (b) heart; (c) breathing # SY (but this was corrected to *pulhanga* on one occasion). See **thupurru, kalu.**

ngarawantina breathe hard, be out of breath # Yw

ngardra behind, at the back; before; later • (SY) *Ngardrayi thawa.* '[I'll go first], you come behind.' • *Thawanhana ngani waningadi, ngala thana kadli thambanari, ngardratjila ngani thawawarranhana.* 'We went for the corroboree, but they had already danced; we arrived later.' # Its meaning in • *Ngarru nhutjadu Yandru-wandha ngardra yandhayandharla.* 'Only half talk; he can half talk Yandruwandha.' is not clear. # See **durruyi, ngalpirri.**

ngardratjika, ngardratjikala behind • *Thawarla nganyi ngala nhunu kuthiwarrarlayitji ngardratjikala. Kadli nganyi thawari.* 'I'm going now, and he'll be getting here later. I'll be already gone.' # *-la* may be the emphatic ending.

ngardrawarrka leave behind, pass • *Pirnalatji nhunu payirrila. Ngardra-warrkangala kara yina.* 'He's big and tall now. He might pass you (in height).' # Compare **kurrawindri, wawathawa, wanthathawa.**

ngardrawarrkathawa leave behind, pass

ngardu nardoo # the plant *Marsilea drummondii*, a small plant growing on low-lying areas after rain, and also the flour prepared from the spore cases of this plant • *Ngardu ngala, parndringa ngandra nga pinakanga nhulu pitjili.* 'Then there is nardoo; we crush it and then rock it in the coolamon.' # SY *ngardru*

**ngarduparndrini, mardra ngardu-
parndrini** stone for grinding nardoo
• *Pawangadi, pawa thungini
ngunyirnanga ya ngarduparndrini
ngunyirnanga.* 'They gave grinding
stones, for seeds, and nardoo
pounders.'

ıngari down, the bottom; inside
• *Ngapala kudru pakuri ngari, nga
yankula kurrawagandji nga windripandhinga palha mukuli.* 'They dig
a hole and put boughs around it and
[a man] goes down into the hole with
a bird bone.' • *Ngala ngapa kukuyitji
ngari, wararriyitji, mardramitji
karrininguda malkirri pardrangariningadilatji thanha, paltjakiningadi.* 'They tie a lot of stones
[to go] deep down in the water, on
the bottom of the net, to weigh it
down and keep it tight.' # Also
pandhi, pada.

ngari widi, ngaritji widi down there

ıngariyuka the rest, others # See also
ngalyi.

ıngarlakurra, ngarlangarlakurra the
sound of the bullroarer

ngarlakurraka make the sound of
the bullroarer (transitive)

ngarlangarlakurrana make the
sound of the bullroarer (intransitive)

ıngarli gully, small watercourse # SY,
Yw. See **thurrka.**

ıngarlu great grandmother, mother's
mother's mother, mother's mother's
mother's brother, great grandchild,
woman's daughter's daughter's child
SY and Yw *kayakaya.*

ıngarnarri steep slope # See also
murnurru.

ıngarnda forehead # See also **ngurlu.**

Ngarndaparlu placename, Arrabury
Means 'white forehead', name of a
large sacred rock there.

ıngarndama, ngarndangarndama block
• *... wathi malkirrili nganha ngarnda-*
ngarndamaritji. '... the trees blocked
me [from getting through].' # SY and
Yw also 'shut, be shut (door, eyes,
etc.)'. See also **nyandama.**

ngarndamayindri shut (eyes), clench
(fist) • *Mara ngarndamayindri* 'Clench
your fist.' # Also **nganamayindri,
ngupina(?).**

ngarndapandji call, sing out to
• *Ngarndapandjina ngaldra yinha,
ngala nhulu walya ngararlayi
ngalunha.* 'We called out to him, but
he didn't hear us.' # See also **kandri,
mirrtjakurra, kaldripantji.**

ngarndri mother • *Ngarndri nganyi
wanthiyindrirla.* 'I'm looking for my
mother.' *Nganyi thawarla muduwa
ngarndringa.* 'I'm going to have a
baby.'

ngarndri yipi, yipi mother's sister

ngarndri-kaku relations # Probably
only female relatives in a person's own
moiety; see **nguthu-ngama, kamiri.**

ngarndri-ngapiri parents
• *Ngala thana ngarndri-ngapirilitji
mulhudu mapaapininguda yinba-
tharrapandhingalatji nhunggani.*
'His parents sent down food that they
had collected for him.' • *Kilkarla
ngathu yintjadu, ngarndri-ngapiri
ngala nguthu-ngama.* 'I know him,
and his parents and relations.'
• *... ngala ngarndri-ngapirili thanha
walthanarlayi karlukarlutji, ngunyinga
nhinggikala yarruyi.* '... while their
parents bring fish and give them to
them in the yard.'

ngarnma grip, hold tight # See also
pangkithirri, thundru.

ngarnmayindri be stuck together,
be jammed, be stiff (for example, leg),
be cramped • *Thiltja ngarnmayindrirla
nganyi ngurra nhinininguda.* 'I've
got a cramp from sitting a long time.'
• *Wathi dranthayi nhuniyi ngarnma-
yindrirlanga.* 'It's jammed in the fork.'

ngarnmangarnmayindri hang on to one another; jib; be stuck for words, be hard to follow (of someone's speech); be unable to walk freely or stand (because of stiff or paralysed leg or because of age) • *Muduwa thidharri kadli walya nhunu yandhayandharlatji. Ngarnmangarnmayindrirlangu nhunu.* 'The baby can nearly talk, but he still gets stuck.' • *Yadamana nhuniyi ngarnmangarnmayindrirla, walya thawini.* 'The horse is jibbing; he won't go.' • *Nhunu thangguthangguningadi yurarla, ngarnmangarnmayindrinangu ngala. Ngarru marrkamarrkarlangu nhunu.* 'He wants to stand up but he can't. He's only crawling yet.'

ngarra shiver, shake # Yw. See **yandjiyandji, yirrika.**

ngarrka do • *Minha ngarrkanga kara ngandra? Yilakadi ngandra pakanga?* 'What are we going to do with her? Where will we take her?' • *Puka nhulu kudlanhana, nga minhaya ngarrkanga yinha, madlantjikarila yinha.* 'He cooked the damper and what did he do to it, he spoilt it.' # See also **ngana.**

ngarrtji burn • *Maka nhutjadu ngarrtjirla.* 'the fire's burning.' # Also *thangkana.* SY also 'cook' . See also **darra, mangga, pidli.** • *Ngathu parnimarla, minha kara, ngarrtjirlayi, kathi kara.* 'I can smell something cooking; must be meat.'

ngarrtjirduda burn along (as a bushfire) # = *manggarduda*

ngarru only, just; for nothing, for no reason • *Ngapala nhulu drangayindrirnanga yirrtjinakaldri yina karnakurnutji, pani ngala nhunu karnatji ngarru wathildra thudarlayi.* 'Well he was singing to himself, to keep the other man awake, but there was no other man, only the log lying there.' • *Ngapala nhunu ngarru yankula* mandriri, nga warrkapandhinga ngapala pulkanga ngala nhulu ... 'So he just got some [dry] leaves and threw them down [on the hot coals] and started to blow them ....' • *Yawarri pulganili walya yawarri ngakanili, ngarru walypalayingu yawarri yandhayandharitji nganyi nganarnangatji pulhu.* 'I hadn't spoken to them in their language or in mine, only in the whitefellows'.' • *Ngarrungu thangguthalkawarrandji dranyingalatji yadali.* 'The man just stands up and kills [one] with a boomerang.' • *Thana mukurdukalapurra thanha, ngarru ngaga yina nhunu pirnatji wirlpa.* 'They took the bones out through a hole only as big as the throat.' • (Yw) *'Minhanganarla yini?' 'Ngarru nganyi thawathawanhinarla.'* 'What are you doing?' 'Just walking about (for no reason).'

ngaru voice • *ngaru kuthikuthidi* 'squeaky voice' • *ngaru pirna* 'deep voice' • *Ngaru ngakani ngaranga thanayi muduwalitji.* 'These kids will hear my voice [on tape] 'when I'm dead and gone'. # Also **ngan.gu.**

(ngatha)

ngathadi younger brother, younger sister • *ngathadi man.garri* 'younger sister' • *Ngapala pardra-pardrarnanga-thili, nganandji nhulu ngathadimaladinyi, 'Thangguthalka wawayindringalatji.'* 'Well, the two of them were feeling about (for the boomerang) and he told his brother, "Stand up and look at yourself."' # See **kardri.**

ngathalki child (of a man), brother's child • *Ngathalki ngakani kathi kutjarrku yurarla pardriningadi.* 'My kids like catching frogs.' • *Ngathalki ngakani thawawindrina nhani, nhipangurru.* 'My daughter went away with her husband.'

ngathani child (of a woman), niece, nephew, sister's child • *Yiwa nhatjadu yingkirla ngathaningadi.* 'That woman's crying for her baby.'

ngathanika give birth to • *Ngarndrili nganha ngathanikalapurra Malkanpatji.* 'I was born at Innamincka. (Lit. My mother made me a child at Innamincka)' • *Malkanpa ngala nhunu, ngathanikalapurratji yintjadu.* 'He was born at Innamincka.' # See also **kurra**, **yadhi kurra**, **ngama mana**, **dan.ga**.

ngathinha I (subject) him (object), I (subject) that (object) (compound of *ngathu* and *yinha*) • *Karnatji ngathinha dan.ganhana paldringala nganarlayi ngapa murali.* 'When I found that man he was nearly dying of thirst.'

ngathinhayi I (subject) him here (object), I (subject) this (object) • *Pudlupudlu ngathinhayi thilpathilparla.* 'I can't get this horse going.'

ngathu I (subject of transitive verb) • *Tjukurru ngathu windrali warrkanana.* 'I speared a kangaroo with a spear.' • *Kilkarla ngathu yintjadu, ngarndri-ngapiri ngala nguthu-ngama.* 'I know him, and his parents and relations.' # See **nganyi**.

ngathuna I (subject) you (object) (compound of *ngathu* and *yina*) • *Ngathuna nganarla.* 'I'm telling you.' • *Kapada thumbalkarla ngathuna kardratji pakuningadi, padla yundru kilkiningadilatji.* 'Come on, I'll show you where to dig the yams, so you'll know the place.'

ngatjada camp • *Ngapa yundra nhunu ngatjadayi.* 'The water's a long way from the camp.' • *Ngapala nhunu purtu mandrimandrirnanga milyaruyi, nga thawawindringa ngatjada kurnungadila, ...* 'Well, he packed his

swag in the dark and walked on to the other camp, ...' # Also **nguda**.

ngawada thin, light # See also **kanda**, **ngalba**, **mukukarta**.

ngawu see **kawu**.

ngayana iron # from Eng
  wathi ngayana something made of iron

ngayimala throat # Yw also *ngayimala yutju*; see **yutju**, **ngaga**.

ngidla sorrow
  ngidlali sorry (for someone) • *Ngidlali nganyi, nhunggatjadu karrukarrungadi.* 'I'm sorry for that old fellow.' # you could say *karrukarruyi* instead of *karrukarrungadi*.
  ngidlali ngana be sorry • (SY) *Nganyi ngidlali nganarnanga ngakani muduwayi.* 'I'm sorry for my boy.'
  ngidla ngunyingunyi make (someone) sorry
  ngidlayi poor fellow # SY. See also **ngurrani**.

ngindra breathe • *ngindrangindrarla pirnala* 'breathing hard' • *Marnali nhutjadu ngindrarla.* 'He's breathing through his mouth.' # See **pulhanga**.

nginyaru gruie apple, moalie apple, emu apple (*Owenia acidula*) (has red cherries)

nguda camp # Also **ngatjada**.

ngudani see **ngurrani**.

ngudhangudha see **nguthangutha**.

ngudulu edge # Also **kadawa**.

nguduthalpa stare

nguka, ngukanguka (1) too; other, more • *Yinhayi nguka.* '[Put] this one [on] too.' • (Yw) *Ngali parrkulu thawanga. Yini nguka?* 'Us two are going. How about you?' • *Kurnungukala yada ngunyi.* 'Give me another one [of the same].' • *Ngapala pirntathangkali nyanmari, marapardrini, wirnili ngukanguka pirntathangkali,* *karrangalatji yinha.* 'I'll bind the handle on with string and seal it with beefwood gum (mixed with the string).' # See also **marla**; (2) in case • *Wathi nganha yada ngunyi kathikathi nguka ngathu parndriningadi.* 'Give me a stick in case I have to kill a snake.' # See also **kurnu nguka**, **minha kurnu nguka**, and **yuka**.

nguka, ngukanguka mix • *... mitji thaka ngukangukayindriri ...* '... the seeds mix with the clay ...' # May be related to *nguka* 'too'. See also **nhapi**, **warlawaka**.

nguku hook # possibly from Eng 'hook'; see **mila**.

ngukumindji black shag, cormorant # 'because he's got a hooky mouth'. See also **maluda**.

ngukuwarra, ngukuwada vomit • *Kathi thungga ngathu thayina, ngukuwarrana nganyi.* 'I ate stinking meat, and I heaved it all out.'

ngulku cheek # Also **karditjidi**, **kidakida**.

ngulu end • *Nga yarnduldrangu nhinda, pirli ngunthuya mayi, minhangadildra, wathi nhutjadu kakaldra, ngala wathi pirna puladu kalpurru thanggurla, yarndu nhinda ngulutji.* 'They make the net of such a size that it stretches right across from a coolibah on this side to a big one standing [on the other side].' # Also **mudra**, **mulha**.

nguluka peep out # Perhaps derived from *ngulu* 'end'

ngulukayindriwaga peep around • *Purrirla nhunu; ngulukayindriwaganga, ya winkathikapadakaldri.* 'He's hiding; he peeped out and then ducked back in again.'

nguluwarnda kangaroo rat

ngulyi gum (from tree) # SY. See **tjirarri**.

ngumu good # SY. See **patji**, **manyu**.

nguna arm, wing, branch # See **kupu**.

palha nguna wing # SY also **nguna kutja**. '*Nguna* is the wing itself and *kutja* is the feathers'

ngunamarnda elbow # Also **thintipidi**.

Ngunapirnta Oonabrinta Creek # 'wing-fighting stick'

nguna warrku left hand # Also **wannganyi**.

nguna wathi branch of tree

nguni day, daytime, light, daylight • *Walya yilyirri nganatji mayi, nguni pirnangu ngaldra.* 'Don't hurry, we've got all day yet.' • *Ay thawarla ngali kathi parndriparndriyindringa, nguni walya pipini* 'We go hunting; we don't miss a day.' # See also **dritji**, **kurli**, **padlakanpa**.

ngunikurnu-ngunikurnu every day

ngunipika middle of the day, not late • *Kuthiwarranga ngaldra ngunipikangu yina.* 'We'll get there in plenty of time.' • *Ngala yamali thana ngunipika kurraringu, kalkayi, marripathi minipandhingayayi mandrithalkanga karlukarlulatji ...* 'Well, with the cross net, they put it down in the daytime, in the afternoon, and next morning they run down and pull up the fish ...'

nguni pirna middle of the day, not late • *Nguni pirnanguwardi.* 'There's plenty of time yet.'

ngunku ball (for example, of tobacco or pitchery mixed with ash, or dough) • *Makamuduyi ngalyitji kudlari, ngunku pirnatji, ngala ngarru ngunku pulya thanha thayirnanga kartitji.* 'They bake some of them in hot ashes, the big balls, only the little ones are eaten raw.' # See also **mundjungunku**.

ngunkuka make into a ball • *Wikawikarnanga, pinakanga, ya dringangalatjardi, or thungangalatji, nga thayiyindringala yartunanga, ngapali ngunkukininguda.* 'They clean it, rock it, and grind it and then, after mixing it with water and making it into a ball, they eat their fill.'

ngunkunhapi make into a ball • *Mulhakuna thayipadipadini ditji-pininguda ngapala ngunkunhapiri.* 'They used to eat a brown-nosed one which they dried in the sun and rolled into a ball.'

ngunpurru nails, claws # See also **mara ngunpurru, thina ngunpurru.**

ngunu women's genitals

ngunutjarrpa vulva # Also **dirrpa.**

ngunuwirlpa vagina

ngunyi, ngunyika, ngunyingunyi give • *Pandi yintjadu kathi ngunyi.* 'Give the dog some meat.' • *Pawangadi, pawa thungini ngunyirnanga ya ngarduparndrini ngunyirnanga.* 'They gave grinding stones, for seeds, and nardoo pounders.' • *Ngapala wiki parrkulu wiki parrkukurnu kara nhinapadapadarnanga thayirnanga palhatji thanha, ngala ngarndri-ngapirili thanha walthanarlayi karlukarlutji, ngunyinga nhinggikala yarruyi.* 'Then for two or maybe three weeks they camp there, living on birds, while the birds feed on fish that their parents bring them and give them in the yard.'

ngunyiyindri exchange, swap • *Pin.gi pin.gi thana ngunyiyindripadipadini yarndu.* 'That's how they used to trade things.' # See also **wiriwinma.**

ngunyiwindri give to someone who is going away

ngunyithika give back • *Ngathu yinha kapirla, yakayakanga yinha mardra ngakani winkamanhana, ngunyithikanga kara nganha nhulu, pani kara.* 'I'm going to follow him and ask him whether he took my money and whether he'll give it back to me or not.'

ngunyithikathika give around, distribute

ngupa, ngupangupa swim, float • *Walya ngupa nhunggudutji.* 'Don't swim there.' # See **thanma, mindithanma, tharraka.**

ngupina shut (eyes) (?) # SY. See **ngarndamayindri.**

ngurli fall # Yw. See **warlka, ditjipurri, kudra, pundji.**

ngurlu forehead or upper part of head (perhaps not including the crown) # See also **ngarnda.** The difference between the two is not clear.

ngurluyapidi headband # made from dingo tail

ngurlu short • *Ngurlu nhutjadu, ngala payirrika yintjadu, thadri-palapalangatji karriningadi.* 'It's [too] short, make it longer so you can tie it [to trees] on both banks [of the river].' # See **warnta.**

ngurluka cut short, shorten

ngurlupulya little pieces

ngurlupulya mulpamulpa cut into little pieces

ngurra often, a lot, for a long time, all the time; always, before • *Thiltja ngarnmayindrirla nganyi ngurra nhinininguda.* 'I've got a cramp from sitting a long time.' • *Pandi nhuluyi ngurra parndrirla.* 'He's always hitting his dog.' • *Ngurra yina kurrayindrirla mayi, purla, palhatji thana.* 'Those birds are breeding all the time.' • *Ngala ngapatji pararlayi ngurra.* 'Then the water stays there for a long time.' # See also **purra.**

ngurrangu still • *Ngandra maka ngala nhunuyardi thangkanarla ngurrangu.* 'Oh! Well this fire's still alive!' # See also **ngada.**

ngurrangurra for good, altogether • (SY) *Mama yinhaku ngurrangurra.* 'Take it away altogether.'

ngurrani kangaroo rat # SY, Yw?. Small, on claypan, bushy tail, in burrows, fast

ngurrani poor thing, poor fellow # Yw, also heard as *ngudani*. See also **ngidlayi**.

ngurraputha whitewood (tree, *Atalaya hemiglauca*) # SY(?) *kurrantjala*

ngurraru straight # See also **yurlu**.

ngurru, ngurrungurru hard, strong # SY = *paltja, paltjapaltja*

ngurru ngana get hard # SY

ngurrungurruna get strong, be strong; be strong enough (to cope with a situation) # Yw • *Watjala nganyi warlgaritji, ngurrungurrunarila nganyi.* 'I didn't fall; I saved myself.'

ngurrukutha sit with legs straight out

nguthangutha stretch (arm, leg) out • *Ngapala nhunu nguthangutharnangala katjakatjarlayilatji parndriyindrininguda nganggali karna palha-nyadi wawawawari.* 'Well, he stretched out his leg because of the pain, because he had hit himself, thinking it was a devil he had seen.' # Also heard *ngudhangudha*

nguthu (a) elder brother • *Nguthu ngakani yidlanggiyi?* 'Where's my brother?' • *Thawarla nganyi nguthingiyi.* 'I'm going with my brother.'; (b) brother (when relative age is not known or irrelevant) • *Nguthupani nhunu ngarru kaku.* 'He's got no brothers, only sisters.'

nguthu-ngama male relatives in a person's own moiety # See **kamiri** • *... mulhudutji yina thana nguthu-ngamalitji pakanapandhimalka.* '... his relations would carry food down for him.' • *Kilkarla ngathu yintjadu, ngarndri-ngapiri ngala nguthu-ngama.* 'I know him, and his parents and relations.' # Translated 'relations' by BK; see also **ngarndri-kaku**.

nguya sort, size, appearance; reflection • *Walpa puladu nguya marndu.* 'Those two houses look exactly the same.' # See also **nhinda, walarri**.

nguyamindji well built

nguya yala the same • *Pandi puladu nguya yala.* 'The two dogs look the same.' # *nguya marndu may be the same as nguya yala.* See also **yala, yarnduldrangu**.

nhadi dead # Also **thinka**.

nhadika, nhadinhadika kill • *Tjukurru ngathu warrkananhana windrali, walya yinha nhadikangatji, kulkupawindringa nhunu wathi windra ngurru.* 'I speared a kangaroo, but I didn't kill it and it hopped away with the spear [still in it].' # See also **parndri, thinkaka**.

nhadina die • *Nhadinanhana, ya nhambana yinha kadli.* 'He died and they buried him.' # Also **paldri**.

nhadipintha galah • *Yiwa thanadu yandhayandharla nhadipintha-nyadi.* 'Those women are chattering like a mob of galahs.' # SY *kilangkila*

nhama (a) touch; (b) taste # SY; See **wantja**.

nhamba cover, bury • *Nhadinanhana, ya nhambana yinha kadli.* 'He died and they buried him.' # See also **thudri, purrilka, wamba**.

nhambalka cover # = *nhamba*

nhambalkayindri, nhambalkanayindri cover yourself • *Padlayi yina kurnutji kurrari ngala kandraldra nhambalkayindriri kurnulitji.* 'They put one on the ground and cover themselves over with another.' • *Drakarnanga yarnduldrangu wirnikamuratji yiwangaditji pirnaldra, karriningadi panikaldra nhambalkayindrindji.* 'On the one hand they make a big one [hair-string apron] for women to tie on, to cover themselves completely.'

nhambapandhi bury • *Pandili nhuludu nhambapandhina kathi.* 'The dog buried the meat.'

nhandra she, the (feminine) (subject of transitive verb) • *Nhandu nhandra wawarla wadlumpadali.* 'The white woman is looking at the horses.'

nhandradu she (there), that (female) (subject of transitive verb) • *Kanyini nhandradu ngandjarla.* 'She (there) calls [me] granny.'

nhandrayi she (here), this (female) (subject of transitive verb) • *Mirni ngaldra wawarla man.garri nhani thikawarriningadi, yakarlalatji ngathu, nhandrayi pardrarla nhinggiyi.* 'Wait on, we'll watch for that girl and I'll ask her; she's got it here.'

nhandu horse • *Nhandu nhandra wawarla wadlumpadali.* 'The white woman is looking at the horses.' # SY and Yw sometimes *nhantu*; see also **pirndiwalku, yadamani**.

nhanggani her, hers, belonging to her; her (as in 'to her', with her' etc.)

nhangganiyi her, hers, belonging to her (here); with her • *Thawarla nganyi yandhayandhathikanga nhangganiyi.* 'I'm going over to have a talk with her.'

nhanggatjadu her, hers, belonging to her (there); her (as in 'to her', with her' etc.) • *Mardra mani nhanggatjadu nhuniyi.* 'This money belongs to her.'

nhanggatjaduyi with her (there)

nhangka step on • *Thinamitji nganha nhuludu nhangkana.* 'He stepped on my toe.' • *Kabuta nhuludu ngakani nhangkana, madlamadlantjikarila yinha.* 'That fellow stood on my hat and ruined it.'

nhangkapandhi put on top of • *... nhangkapandhinhana kara yundru ...* '... you might have put [it] on top [of the coolamon].'

nhanha her, the (feminine) (object of verb) • *Thikawarrarlatji nhaniyi kuthikuthi windriwarranga, walya ngathu nhanha wawarlayi. Purrtjina-warrari nganha nhandra.* 'She came back and sneaked inside and I didn't see her. She gave me a fright.'

nhanhadu her (there), that (female) (object of verb) • *Wawalapurra ngathu nhanhadu, muduwa pulyayi.* 'I saw her a long time ago, when she was a little girl.' • *Walya ngathu nhipakari nhanhadutji, pirni nguru yina ngakani nhatjadu.* 'I couldn't marry that woman, she's the wrong relation to me.'

nhanhayi her (here), this (female) (object of verb)

nhani she, the (feminine) (subject of intransitive verb or in a sentence without a verb) • *Yiwa nhaniyi yilangginguda?* 'Where does this woman come from?' • *Nhipamindjila nhutjadu, nhinggiwangadi nhani nhinarla, Malkanpayi.* 'He's got a wife; she lives at Innamincka.'

nhanidu, nhanudu she (there), that (female) (subject of intransitive verb or in a sentence without a verb) (= *nhatjadu*) • *Warrayi nhanudu nhinanhinapadaw kanguyi.* 'Let her stop inside in the warm.'

nhaniwa she (in the distance) # SY

nhaniyi she (here), this (female) (subject of intransitive verb or in a sentence without a verb) • *Thikawarrarlatji nhaniyi kuthikuthi windriwarranga, walya ngathu nhanha wawarlayi. Purrtjinawarrari nganha nhandra.* 'She came back and sneaked inside and I didn't see her. She gave me a fright.'

Nhanthanini Yantandana Waterhole

nhantjadu her (there), that (female) (object of verb)

nhantu see **nhandu**.

nhanudu see **nhani**.

nhapi roll something up; mix; make (something that is made by mixing things) • *Ngapali wirdiwirdikari pukatji nhapinga.* '[They] stir the flour with water and roll it up.' • *Puka patji ngathunha nhapinhana, patjikurnu muthu.* 'I made a cake, a good one.' # See also **ngana, nguka, warlawaka, thurrpa, pampuka**.

nhapingari, nhapipandhi mix • *Puka ngathu nhapipandhina mardri.* 'I mixed a thick damper.'

nhardithi (possibly) stick insect # SY

nharra (1) coolamon, shovel • *Walthanhana ngathu nharra nhipangi.* 'I'm carrying the coolamon for my wife.' # See also **pitji** (2) turtle, tortoise (*kathi nharra*) # SY

nharrakambu coolamon (for carrying a baby, or water) • *Yiwali nhandradu walthayindrirla nharrakambuli.* 'That woman was carrying [the baby] in the coolamon.' (lit. 'with the coolamon')

nharramindji turtle • *Ngala yamali thana ngunipika kurraringu, kalkayi, marripathi minipandhingayayi mandrithalkanga karlukarlulatji, ngampurru kara, ya kathi nharra-mindji kara, ya palha kara, ya kathi thanayi — minhaya yina, kathi — mayatji nganyi kuditharrarlala, kathi thukathayini, thana drikalapurrayi thanha.* 'Well, with the cross net, they put it down in the daytime, in the afternoon, and next morning they run down and pull up the fish — maybe yellowbelly, or maybe a turtle, or maybe a bird, or maybe one of those animals — what is it? — I forget the name — mussel eater they used to call them.'

nharramuku (1) big coolamon; (2) turtle. # SY. AWH gives this name for 'rabbit bandicoot (= bilby)'. This seems unlikely.

nharrathitha shield

nharra hunt away

nharrpa (steel) knife # H

nharrtha (? *narrtha*) type of fruit, 'wild peaches' (in hills) # SY

nhatjadu she (there), that (female) (subject of intransitive verb or in a sentence without a verb) (= *nhanidu, nhanudu*) • *Yiwa nhatjadu mundja.* 'That woman's sick.'

nhilanhila mirage

nhina sit, stay, live; be • *Thiltja ngarnmayindrirla nganyi ngurra nhinininguda.* 'I've got a cramp from sitting a long time.' • *Walyala ngani purrkapadayi wilpadalitji, ngarrungu pula thawandji, thantjiyipa-ngadi, nganyi nhinapadapadarlayi nhinggi-kala Kinipapayi.* 'We mightn't have got across with the wagon so they went on without me, to the town, and I stayed there at the river.' • *Ngala karna thana nhinarlayi, thundiyi.* 'Meanwhile there were some black-fellows camping on an island.' • *Kayiditji walyala thana nhinarla.* 'They aren't living any more.' • *Karruwali nhinalapurratji pintha-purru.* 'They were still boys, with foreskins.' • *Pawathungini ngala pitjidi kumaningaditji ngunyiyindri-rnanga yarndukalangu thana nhina-padipadinitji.* 'They traded grinding stones for bags of pitchery; that's how they used to live.'

nhinalka have # SY • *Ngathu mulhudu yulgani nhinalkarla.* 'I've got some meat for you two.' • *Ngarru puka ngathu nhinalkarla thayingatji, kathipani.* 'I've only got bread to eat, no meat.' • *Ngarru man.garri ngathu nhinalkarla.* 'I've only got daughters.' # See **pardra**.

nhinana sit on something

nhinanhina stay a while • *Warrayi nhanudu nhinanhinapadaw kanguyi.* 'Let her stop inside in the warm.'

nhinapandhi sit down

nhinanhinathawa come and sit down for a while

nhinatharrathika go and visit • *Karrulatji thana nhinatharrathikarla.*

'They went and visited the men [in all the other places].'

nhinathika return

nhinathanggu do every day or do for some time # See §12.19 of *Innamincka Talk*.

nhinawagawaga sit around • *makayila ngaldra nhinawagiwagini-ngadi* 'and we'll sit around the fire'

ınhinda shame, shyness • *Kuka karli payirri nhutjadutji yiwa-nyadi; nhindapani.* 'That fellow's got long hair like a woman. Got no shame.'

nhindali ashamed, shy • *'Yilanggi-nguda nhutjadu?' 'Ngalaaku.' 'Yakapadala yinha mayi.' 'A 'ey, nhindalitji nganyi yundru kayi.'* 'Where's he from?' 'I don't know.' 'Well, ask him.' 'Uh-uh, I'm shy, you do it.'

nhinda ngunyingunyi shame, make ashamed, make shy • *Ngan.gu kuthikuthidi nhinda ngunyingunyi-rnanga yinha. Yarndu nhunu walyatji yurarla yandhiningaditji.* 'His squeaky voice makes him shy. That's why he doesn't like talking.' (Perhaps the second word should have the ergative suffix -*li*)

ınhinda size, shape, appearance • *nhindapani* "got no shape" • *Nga yarnduldrangu nhinda, pirli ngunthuya mayi, minhangadildra, wathi nhutjadu kakaldra, ngala wathi pirna puladu kalpurru thanggurla, yarndu nhinda ngulutji.* 'They make the net of such a size that it stretches right across from a coolibah on this side to a big one standing [on the other side].' # See also **nguya**.

ınhinggi location # See also **nhuku**.

nhinggikala over there, in the vicinity of a place that has been named or is known • *Ngarndaparlungi nganyi wakananhukada, nhinggikala.* 'I worked on Arrabury before.' • *Walyala ngani purrkapadayi wilpadalitji, ngarrungu pula thawandji, thantjiyipangadi, nganyi nhinapadapadarlayi nhinggikala Kinipapayi.* 'We mightn't have got across with the wagon so they went on without me, to the town, and I stayed there at the river.' • *Ngapala wiki parrkulu wiki parrkukurnu kara nhinapadapadarnanga thayirnanga palhatji thanha, ngala ngarndri ngapirili thanha walthanarlayi karlu-karlutji, ngunyinga nhinggikala yarruyi.* 'Then for two or maybe three weeks they camp there, living on birds, while the birds feed on fish that their parents bring them and give them in the yard.'

nhinggingu the same place • *'Karlu-karlu ngathu parndrinhana malkirri.' 'Yidlanggiyi?' 'Nhinggiyingutji, nhinggingutji, ngaldra parndrithika-nhukada.'* 'I caught a lot of fish.' 'Where?' 'In the same place where we caught them before.'

nhinggiwa there • *Yiwa thanadu thirrirla nhinggiwa ngari.* 'Those women are fighting down there.' • *Thawanhana nhunu ngakaningadi yandhayandhanga-nyadi nhinggiyi, walyangu nhunu thawawarrana, nga yini thawa mayi yandhayandhanga nhunggani nhingguwa kantanga.* 'I thought he was going to come here to talk to me. He hasn't arrived yet, so you go and talk to him over there.' # Also heard as *nhingguwa*. See also **kala, nhinggudu, nhukuwa, yita**.

nhinggiwangadi to there • *Nhinggiwangadi pitjidi kumani mandrithikanga.* 'They used to go over there to get bundles of prepared pitchery.'

nhinggiwanguda from there

nhinggiyi here • *Kathi ngathu pardranhana nhinggiyi.* 'I had some meat here.' • *Ngala yamunumindjildra nhinggiyitji nyinyimulpiningudatji.*

'But [our people] here [tan the hide] with the fur on, after turning the skin inside out.' • *Mirni ngaldra wawarla man.garri nhani thikawarriningadi, yakarlalatji ngathu, nhandrayi pardrarla nhinggiyi.* 'Wait on, we'll watch for that girl and I'll ask her; she's got it here.'

nhinggiyingadi to here • *Kathi tjukurru ngathu wawana thawarnanga nhinggiyingadi, parrkulu pulayi thika* 'I saw some kangaroos when I was coming here; two back here.'

nhinggiyinguda from here, local • *Kinipapa nhinggiyingudaldrangu.* 'He's from this river, Cooper's Creek.'

nhinggiyipada on this side # SY

nhinggudu there • *Kurrapandhi nhinggudu thanuthanu.* 'Put it down there, in the middle.' • *Minha nganarla yini nhinggudu muduwa, walpakurnuyitji? Dunka yada mayi!* 'What are you doing there, kid, in someone else's house? Come on out!' # See also **kala, yita, nhinggiwa, nhukuwa**.

nhinggudungadi to there

nhinggudunguda from there

nhingka, nhingkayindri look for # Yw. See **wanthi**.

nhipa wife, husband; father's sister's daughter • *Nhipali ngakani ngapa marndrarla.* 'My wife will get us water.' # Perhaps only a man calls father's sister's daughter *nhipa*, and a woman would use the term for mother's brother's son.

nhipaka marry • *Walya ngathu nhipakari nhanhadutji, pirni nguru yina ngakani nhatjadu.* 'I couldn't marry that woman, she's the wrong relation to me.' # See also **mandripada**.

nhipamindji married • *Pangga nhutjadu nhipamindji.* 'That young man is married.'

nhipa mulha unrelated, eligible to marry # Complement of *pirni nguru*

nhipangurru married couple

Nhirrpi language name # Heard as *Nyirrpi* from SY.

nhiwa female animal • *kathi nhiwa* 'female game animal, for example kangaroo' • *pandi nhiwa* 'bitch' • *kathi puluka nhiwa* 'cow' • *tjipi nhiwa* 'ewe' • *Pandi thanayi nhiwa karrukarru thawathawarla.* 'Dogs and bitches are wandering around.' # See also **yiwa**.

nhuku location # See also **nhinggi**.

nhukudu over there • *A karna wayini nhukudu waka?* 'How many men are over there?'

nhukuyi, nhukiyi here • *Wadana ngathu thawawarriningadi kara nhukuyi thana, ay paningu.* 'I waited for them to come here, but nobody yet.' • *Pulyala kara nhukuyi nhunu wathitji, yandhayandharlayitji nganyi nganarnangatji yunhu.* 'There must be only a little bit of tape left now, for me to talk to you fellows.' • *Thawarla nganyi nhukuwa, Ngarndaparlu kaka, thangguthikanga.* 'I'm going visiting, somewhere near Arrabury.' # Said on one occasion to mean 'here somewhere' (with *-yi*, or, 'there somewhere' with *-wa*) as opposed to *nhinggiyi* 'here' (and *nhingguwa* 'there').

nhukurra there in the distance ? # SY

nhukuwa there • *Pulganiyi nhunu nhinanhinarla nhukuwa, nhinggiwa nhunu.* 'He's with them two, over there.' • *Walya thana thirripadi-padinitji, pani, ngarru pinyayi, karna thula nhukuwanguda yada thawarnanga parndrithikangatji, minhayatji pinyalitji.* 'They never used to fight, except in a war. Strangers would come from over there [in their country] to kill and then go back. That's what they used to call war.' • *Thawarla nganyi nhukuwa,*

Ngarndaparlu kaka, thangguthikanga.
'I'm going over there, near Arrabury,
visiting.' # See also **kala, nhinggiwa,
nhinggudu, yita**.

nhukukala about there, around there
• *Ngala nhukukalangu, nhunu
thawathawarla kara.* 'He must be
walking around somewhere.' # Also
nhunukukala.

ɪ**nhulu** he, it, the (subject of transitive
verb) • *Karrkapadanhana nhulu
ngalinha padawadangudali.* 'He sang
out to us from across the river.'

nhuludu he (there), it (there), that
(subject of transitive verb) • *Parndrina
nganha nhuludu.* 'He hit me.' • *Pandili
nhuludu nhambapandhina kathi.*
'The dog buried the meat.' • *Purtutji
yinggani wawawawanaw, winkamayila
nhuludu.* 'Watch your things, or he'll
take them.'

nhuluyi, nhuliyi he (here), it (here),
this (subject of transitive verb)
• *Wirlpangudali nhuliyi nganha
wawarla.* 'He's peeping at me through
a hole.' • *Walarriyi ngali nhuliyi
pirripirrili nhinarla.* 'Me and this
white fellow sitting in the shade here.'

ɪ**nhunggani** his, its; him, it (as in
'to him', 'with him', 'for it' etc.)
• *Muduwa nhuniyi yabali nhungganiyi
walypalayi.* 'The boy's frightened of
this white bloke.' • *Yabali nganyi
nhungganipuru.* 'I'm frightened of
him.'

nhungganiyi his (here), its (here);
with him, with it

ɪ**nhunggatjadu** his (there), its (there);
him, it (as in 'to him', 'with him',
'for it' etc.) • *Ngidlali nganyi,
nhunggatjadu karrukarrungadi.*
'I'm sorry for that old fellow.'

nhunggatjaduyi with him (there)

nhunggu or **nhungku** location
• *Nhungkukalangu kara nhunu.* 'It's
somewhere over there, round about
there.'

nhuniyi he (here), it (here), this (subject
of intransitive verb or in a sentence
without a verb) • *Windra warangi
nhuniyi?* 'Whose spear is this?'
• *Thawawarranhana nhuniyi mulhapundranguda.* 'This fellow comes
from the south.' • *Muduwa yini
wanthiyindrirla; nhuniyi nhinarla
ngalinggayi.* 'You're looking for the
boy; he's sitting down here with me
and him.' • *Ngandjarri purra nhuniyi
padla.* 'This is a rainy place.'
• *Pudlupudlu ngathu nhandu yinhayi
thilpathilparla, pirritjampanarla
nhuniyi.* 'I can't get this horse going
because he's tired.'

nhunu he, it (subject of intransitive verb
or in a sentence without a verb), the
• *Makatji nhunu mudunamalkaya.* 'The
fire is allowed to burn away to ashes.'
Possibly used also to refer to a group
as a single entity; see line 46 of the
ethnographic text in §5.1.

nhunudu he (there), it (there) (subject
of intransitive verb or in a sentence
without a verb) (= *nhutjadu*)
• *Matjanguda nhutjadu, ay thipingu
nhunudu.* 'He's very old, but he's still
alive.'

nhunuwa he (in the distance), that
(distant) # SY

nhunuyi he (here), it (here), this
(subject of intransitive verb or in a
sentence without a verb) # SY, Yw.
See **nhuniyi**.

nhunukukala about there • *Mayi,
wawathikana yundru pani? Yidlayi
nhunukukalangu thana?* 'Well, did
you see anybody? Whereabouts are
they?' # Also **nhukukala**.

nhura tail (for example, of dog,
kangaroo, goanna) # SY, Yw. See
kurni.

nhurrpa spin (something) • *Ngapala
kururruparnanga nga nhurrpanga
ngarrpayi kunya payirrili.* 'Then they
rub it with stones and spin it on their

thighs, using a long spindle.' # May be the same as *thurrpa*.

nhurrpa, nhurrpanhurrpa quickly • *Nhurrpanhurrpala nhutjadu yandharla.* 'He's talking fast.' # See also **pakali, pawada**.

nhutjadu he (there), it (there), that (subject of intransitive verb or in a sentence without a verb) (= *nhunudu*) • *Ngapala pula nganayindrirnanga 'Yilangginguda nhutjadu?'* 'Well they asked one another "Where's he from?"'

nindri bag, net # See also **pirli, mirrka, paltja, thandji, yakutha**.

nyadi like # not normally pronounced as a separate word. See §18.2. *-yadi* in Yw.

nyalka, nyalkanyalka miss; make a mistake • *Miniwarrkanapandhiri yita, kanpangu kara, nyalkari kara.* 'They spear them on the run [too], and they might get one straight off or they might miss.' • *Dranyinhana nganha nhulu, nyalkari karnakurnu kilkarnanga.* 'He hit me by mistake; he thought I was someone else.'

nyandama block, block up • *Wirlpa-mindji nhunuyi, nyandamanhana ngathu yinha.* 'This had a hole so I blocked it.' # See also **ngarndama**.

nyangi moon, moonlight, month • *Nyangi kurnu ngaranhukadatji.* '[I] heard it a month ago.' • *Nyangiyi nganyi thawanga; nyangi pararlayi.* 'I'll go by moonlight, while the moon's shining.' # SY, Yw, Nh all *pira*

nyanma seal, plug • *Ngapala pirnta-thangkali nyanmari, marapardrini, wirnili ngukanguka pirntathangkali, karrangalatji yinha.* 'I'll bind the handle on with string and seal it with beefwood gum (mixed with the string).'

nyarna blunt, square-ended # Also **parntu**.

nyindi skin • *Thiltja thana tjukurru pardrarla, ngapala thanadu pirditjirraritji nga palha mukuli tjalparrikininguda wirlpakanga nyinditji.* 'They hold the kangaroo sinew and strip it and poke the holes in the skin with a bird bone that has been sharpened.' # Also **darla**.

nyinyimilpa, nyinimilpa skin (something), turn inside out • *Yilayarndu kara nyinimilpanga.* 'I don't know how they turn [the skins] inside out.' • *Ngala yamunumindjildra nhinggiyitji nyinyimulpiningudatji.* 'But our people [tan the hide] with the fur on, after turning the skin inside out.' # See **pirnnga**.

Nyirrpi see **Nhirrpi**.

nyulka squeeze # SY *yiga*

nyulka lose # SY. See **walyawalyaka, yikaka**.

nyulkana get lost # SY

nyulkayindri get lost, be lost # Yw

nyungumarlinya blind snake # See also **mithinti**.

nyunma drown someone/something • *Tjukurruli yinha nyunmanhana.* 'The kangaroo drowned [the dog].'

nyunmayindri drown • *Ngapali yulpurruli nhunu nyunmayindrinhana.* 'He got drowned in the floodwaters.'

nyununyunu wrinkly # the swallow is called *pulyurru nyununyunu* 'wrinkly mud' because its nest is like that

nyurdu body hair # Yw. See **yamunu**.

P

pabu clapping # See **mara pabu**.

pada, kuka pada hair of head # SY, Yw. See **karli**.

pada inside, under, underneath • *Karrukarru, nhunuyi pada, ngapa-kaldringuda, yibanhana nhuluyi, thudarla nhunu, kurrayi nganarnanga, kurrayi nganarla.* 'This old fellow is inside, he's been drinking rum and now he's lying down, dead drunk.' • *Thilthirri nhutjadu pada darlamurruyi.* 'There's a centipede under the bark.' # Also **ngari**.

pada, padangari, padawarra other side • *Thawapadarla ngaldra padawarrangadi.* 'We're going across the river.' • *Ya palhatji thana yurari parndringa, pirli thana paladildrangu drakininguda, nga wathiyi pada karranga warrakurnutji, thadripalapala yina.* 'If they want to catch birds they make a net of a different mesh and tie it on to a tree on each bank of the river.' • *Karrkapadanhana nhulu ngalinha padawadangudali.* 'He sang out to us from across the river.' • *Ngapala pula karlukarlungadi yada thawari nga yandhanga nhinanga karlukarlu parndrirnanga pula thadri padawarraldra, ngala nganyitji thadri yitapandhiwarraldra nhinarlayi.* 'Two of them came down to do some fishing. They sat and talked and caught fish on the other bank, while I was camped on the bank that sloped down opposite them.' # Also **warrkupada**. *Pada* seems to mean 'side' rather than 'other side' in *nhinggiyipada* 'this side'.

padhaka disbelieve, not believe someone

padla ground, country, place, dirt, sand • *Mara ngathu pardrarla padlangurru.* 'I've got a handful of sand.' • *Padlayi yina kurnutji kurrari ngala kandraldra nhambalkayindriri kurnulitji.* 'They put one on the ground and cover themselves over with another.' • *Thudathawari padla maya Thanangarrpira.* 'He camped at this place called Tenappera.' • *Kapada thumbalkarla ngathuna kardratji pakuningadi, padla yundru kilkiningadilatji.* 'Come on, I'll show you where to dig the yams, so you'll know the place.' • *Thawawarranhana nhunu,*

padla nganggali-nyadi kilkarnanga. 'He came in here just like he owned the place.' • (H) *padla matja* 'a long time ago' # See also **thipari**.

padlakanpa daylight • *Padlakanpayi nhunu thawawarrana.* 'He came in the morning just after sunrise.' • *Padlakanpayinyadi yini thawawarriningadi wadanhana ngathu yina.* 'I was expecting you to come early.' # See also **nguni**.

padlakurnu-padlakurnu everywhere • *Ngapala thawawagawagarnangardi karrukathikathikana padlakurnupadlakurnu.* 'They went everywhere and circumcised all the men in every place.' # Also **purru**.

padla marra dawn, become daylight # Also **kalkamarra**.

padla muthu sand # *muthu* 'true'; 'sand' as opposed to other meanings of *padla*

padlangarika throw (in wrestling)

padlapadla dirty • *Thayiyindrirnanga yartunarnangalatjini, walya padlapadla walya thurrpathurrpa, mardramitjingudatji.* 'They eat until they are full, [meat] from the stones, not dirty or ashy.' # Yw *palapala*

padla thaka clay • *Yambarriyi kurranga, padla paltjapaltja yina wipinginingudatji yinha, patjikaringu padla, padla thaka mitji ngukangukayindriyi.* 'They put them on the hard flat ground, after sweeping it to make it clean so that the seeds don't get mixed with clay.'

padla yundra another country, somewhere far away • *Thaltuwatanguda ngala nhunudu padla yundrangudatji.* 'He's from the sea then, from another country.' • *Ngapala ngapa marndrinilatji thanngani yulpu thawiningadi, padla yundrawaka ngapapaniyi.* '[They use] their waterbags when they go on a journey in remote waterless country.'

padlawarna heap of dirt(?)
• *Ngapala thudrirnanga yinhaya,
padlawarnaya(?) pirnakaringu …*
(probable translation) 'Well they bury
him [dead person] and then make a big
heap of dirt …'

padna, mitji padna button # from Eng

padupadu yellow # Yw. See also
parruparru.

pagi buggy # from Eng

paka quick • *Parndriri kathitji ngapala
kayidi pakanga nhulu dramardrama-
ritji.* 'When he kills the meat he cuts
it up quickly.'
pakali quickly, in a hurry,
immediately • *Pakali yada thawa!*
'Come here right now!' # Also
yilyirri, nhurrpa, pawada.
pakalika, pakapakalika hurry
someone up # Also **yilyirrika.**

paka take; lead, guide • *Ngapala pula
pakarila thanha, ngapirimaladitji
mudalatji yina drangarnanga
pantjinayindririlatji.* 'Well then they
took all their fathers, and they had a
corroboree and circumcised one
another.' • *Wilyaru thana pardraringu
pakangalatji kanthayi warrkathikanga.*
'They took him into the bush and
left him.' • *… mulhudutji yina
thana nguthu-ngamalitji pakanapandhimalka.* '… his relations would
carry food down for him.' • *Thanayildra pakangala ngalyitji, thanayildra
(word not clear), thanayildra yarndu.*
'Each group takes a few [of the ducks
that they caught].' • *Pakanhana
nganinha padla kilkakilkali.* 'He led
us; he knows the country.'
pakathika, pakanathika carry home,
bring back • *Puka paka ngathu
ngunyinhana, kathila nhulu nganha
pakanathikandji kidlatji.* 'He brought
me back some meat in return for the
tobacco I gave him.'

pakawarra bring • *Pula yadamani
pakawarranhana.* 'The two brought
some horses.' # Also **waltha.**

pakawindri carry away • *Nhunu
thawawindrina, mardratji paka-
windriri.* 'He ran away with the
money.'

paka, puka paka tobacco # from Eng

paka (meaning not clear, perhaps 'just,
exactly') # Yw • *karna-yadi* 'like a
blackfellow', *karna-yadi paka* 'just
like a blackfellow'

pakitjampa buckjumper # from Eng

paku dig • *Ngapala kudru pakuri ngari,
nga yankula kurrawagandji nga
windripandhinga palha mukuli.*
'They dig a hole and put boughs
around it and [a man] goes down into
the hole with a bird bone.' • *Ngapala,
pakuthawakaldriri mardra minhaya.*
'While they're going along, they dig
out [the holes in] the rocks again.'
• *Kurrupu thana pakupadipadini
kardra.* 'The [olden-days] women
used to dig yams.' • *Yiwa thawanhana
thana pakuthikanga kardra.* 'The
women went to dig yams.'
pakungari, pakupandhi dig down
pakutharra dig all around

paladi one, a certain one, particular, your
own • *Thayiyindringa palhatji yarndu
thana parndripadipadini karnalitji,
palhatji ngala drakininguda ngala
paladi.* 'That's how the Aborigines
used to catch birds to eat, with a
special type [of net] they had woven.'
• *Kathi paladi parndriparndriyindrirnanga, ngala makatji wangininguda
kathi yuka kara kuliningadi, ya
karlukarlu kuliningadi.* 'They kill their
own meat, and light a fire to cook their
meat or maybe to cook fish.' • *Ngala
thanayi kilkarla, ngarru yarawarrangu
thawathawapadipadini, mirrka thana
(word not clear) karrpapadipadini
paladi.* 'People now think they used to

walk about naked, but they used to sew their own clothes.' # See **kurnu**.

paladildrangu different, a different one • *Ngala pirlili ngampurrungaditji paladildrangu thana drakininguda, kurrarla yarnduldrangu kinipapayi kurrapadari yita.* 'They use a net that they have woven with a different mesh, and that they put into the water in the same way, for yellowbelly.'

paladi-paladi different, separate • *nguya paladi-paladi* 'different (in appearance)' • *Yandruwandha Yawarrawarrka ngan.gu paladi-paladingu, ngala ngarayindrirnanga ngala thana.* 'Yandruwandha and Yawarrawarrka are two different languages, and yet they can understand one another.' # *palapaladi* also accepted. Yw *punthipunthipa*.

palapala on both sides • *palthupalapala* 'both sides of the road' # Perhaps does not exist as a separate word. See also **thadripalapala**.

palapala see **padlapadla**.

palbarri flat, smooth; level, not sloping much • *Ngapa mandrithikapandhi palbarri nhutjadu.* 'Go and get water, [the bank] is not steep.' # See also **pali, pirrapirra, palurru**.

paldri die • *Pandi ngakani paldrinhana.* 'My dog died last night.' • *Walya ngandra yurarla paldriningadi nhinggiyi.* 'We don't want (him) to die here.' # Also **nhadina**.

paldritharra die out, all die • *Paldritharranhana yina thana panina karnatji.* 'They've all died out, the Aborigines [who lived in the old ways].'

palgupalgu meat, muscle; lean (meat) • *Ngala panipani(kari?) muku palgupalgu dukininguda, ngapala dultharri darlamurru windrimari, paltjikiningaditji yina, pirtipirtikari darlatji yinha.* 'After they take out all the bone and muscle they put blood-wood bark in to make it supple and it makes the skin red.' # See **kathi**.

palha bird • *Ya palhatji thana yurari parndringa, pirli thana paladildrangu drakininguda, nga wathiyi pada karranga warrakurnutji, thadripala-pala yina.* 'If they want to catch birds they make a net of a different mesh and tie it on to a tree on each bank of the river.' • *Ngapala palhatji kartiwirriringu. Minhayapuru yina? Palha thirripuru.* 'Then the birds dive down. What for? Because [they think] it is a chicken hawk.' • *Palha purla pirnanarlayitji, ngapala yarru wathinaritji, marru kadawayi, ngapala thawarnanga puka windritharranga ngapa marruyitji palha purla thanhayi mapathikanga.* 'When the young birds are getting big, they build a yard for them on the bank of the lake and then go down into the water and herd the baby birds back [into the yard].' • *Ngapala nhinari yartunarnanga palhangudatji, ya palha paninarlayitji.* 'They eat their fill of them until the birds are all gone.' • *Ngapala kudru pakuri ngari, nga yankula kurra-wagandji nga windripandhinga palha mukuli.* 'They dig a hole and put boughs around it and [a man] goes down into the hole with a bird bone.' # *palha* often precedes the specific name of a bird, thus *palha kawalka* 'crow', or *palha thirri* 'chicken hawk' in the example sentence above. Traditionally it may have included only flying birds and perhaps also bats, and excluded emus, as in many other Australian languages. BK said once that *warruwitji* 'emu' was *kathi*, and not *palha*, but also once described it as *palha*, perhaps influenced by English.

palha parlu corella # SY, H. Lit. 'white bird'

pali flat # SY # See also **palbarri, pirrapirra, yambayambarri**.

palika flatten # Yw

Palirdidakira or **Palitharrkara** Cordillo # Yw. The two names were given by the same person at different times.

Palkarrakarani the name of the sandhill from which the spirits of the dead float off into the air # BK's explanation. According to AWH it is a spring where the spirit has its last drink on its way to the home of the dead. Both may be correct. Originally given by TG as 'Heaven'. See also **thinawaduka, milimiliwaduka** and compare the word given by AWH as *"barku-balkala"* and translated 'peacefully'.

palki chip (a stone, to make a tool) • *Minhayali ngala thana, pirna palparrilitji mardra pilthirrili palkininguda.* 'Now what do they [skin animals] with: with a stone chip that has been broken off a big boulder.'

palku flesh # Yw

palparri boulder, bedded rock, big flat rock • *Minhayali ngala thana, pirna palparrinitji mardra pilthirrili palkininguda.* 'Now what do they [skin animals] with; with a stone chip that has been broken off a big boulder.'

palthu track, road • *palthupalapala* 'both sides of the road' • *Ngathu wawathawana yinha, palthuyi.* 'I passed him on the road.' • *Karnakurnu-karnakurnu ngarru palthu kurnuyi thawarnanga ngapangadilatji pakuninguda thana matja.* 'Anyone using this road can get water from the well they dug long ago.' # See also **wardayapa, kapitharra, thina.**

paltja (palyka?) bag • *Windrimapaday yintjadu paltjayi.* 'Put it in the bag.' # may be from Eng. See **pirli, mirrka, thandji, yakutha.**

paltja, paltjapaltja hard, strong, supple, tight, stiff • *Paltjapaltjali warrka mayi!* or *Paltjali warrka mayi!* or *Pidipidili warrka mayi!* 'Throw it hard!' • *Walya yina nganyi paltjapaltja.* 'I'm not strong enough.' • *Yambarriyi kurranga, padla paltjapaltja yina wipinginingudatji yinha, patjikaringu padla, padla thaka mitji ngukangukayindriyi.* 'They put them on the hard flat ground, after sweeping it to make it clean so that the seeds don't get mixed with clay.' • *Kundangali paltjapaltja pulkarla.* 'the wind's blowing hard.' # See also **pidipidi, ngurru, danthu.**

paltjaka, paltjapaltjaka strengthen, harden, tighten, make supple • *Paltjapaltjakari thana karlukarlungadi kurranga kinipapayitji.* 'They make it strong and put it across the river to catch fish.' • *Ngala panipani(kari?) muku palgupalgu dukininguda, ngapala dultharri darlamurru windrimari, paltjikiningaditji yina, pirtipirtikari darlatji yinha.* 'After they take out all the bone and muscle they put bloodwood bark in to make it supple and it makes the skin red.' • *Ngala ngapa kukuyitji ngari, wararriyitji, mardramitji karrininguda malkirri pardrangariningadilatji thanha, paltjakiningadi.* 'They tie a lot of stones [to go] deep down in the water, on the bottom of the net, to weigh it down and keep it tight.'

palurru, palupalurru smooth # See also **palbarri.**

palurruka smoothe • *Thilpithilpi palurruka!* 'Knock the spikes off!'

palya boggy, spongy (also 'sticky'?)

palyakini fruit on mistletoe

palyakini thapithapini honeyeater (or mistletoe bird?)

palyada type of animal # digs holes and makes little humpies. May be stick-nest rat. TG' s *kamiri* or totem (and note that the stick-nest rat is a totem in Dieri).

pampu egg • *Karruwalili thanayi pampu pardrakarla ...* 'These boys are getting eggs ...' • *Pampu nhutjadu purlamindji.* 'There's a chicken inside the egg.'

pampaampu (or **pampuwampu**, from **pampupampu**) rounded • *wathi kuka pampaampu* 'stick with a rounded end'

pampuka roll up into a ball (for example, string) # See **kunyama, nhapi, thurrpa.**

pandhi down, bottom • *Ngapala pandhi wirlpinhinarnanga, ngala kathi thana ngarangaraminirlayila warruwitjilitji.* 'Then he whistles down there, and the emus hear him.' # Also **ngari.**

pandhitji widi down there # probably *pandhi widi* with emphatic *-tji.*

pandi dog • *Pandili nhuludu nhamba-pandhina kathi.* 'The dog buried the meat.' • *Muduwa thika yada ay, pandilila yina mathayi.* 'Come back here, or the dog will bite you.' # See also **thirrtha, thutjutju.**

pandiwilka wild dog

pandiyapa wild dog

pandja a long time ago # = *matja, manyanguda*

pandjanguda old • '... *kayidi-ngudali?* ' *'Ahey! Pandjangudali.'* '... with the new one?' 'Uhuh! With the old one.'

panga caterpillar

panga hear # SY, Yw. Also heard as *pangga.* See **ngara.**

pangga, panggapangga young man • *Pangga nhutjadu nhipamindji.* 'That young man is married.' • *Kathi tjukurru ngathu parndrilapurra panggalitji.* ' I used to kill kangaroos when I was a young fellow.'

pangki side, ribs # SY and Yw *diparri*

pangkiparndri (make) gallop • *Maadhali nhulu yadamani pangkiparndrithalkana mardra*

withangadi. 'The boss galloped his horse up the hill.'

pangkithirri rib, side • *Pangkithirri nhulu yinha warrkananhana.* 'He speared it in the ribs.' • *Mirramirrayindrirla nganyi, kuka kara, kapurrukara, pangkithirri kara.* 'I don't know whether I'm scratching my head, or under the arm, or my ribs.' • *walpa pangkithirriyi* 'at the side of the humpy' • *Kathi pangkithirri nganha yada ngunyi.* 'Give me the rib-bones [of the kangaroo].' • *pangkithirrili thudarnanga* 'lying on your side' • *pangkithirri ngarnma* (also *thundru ngarnma*) 'to have a stitch'

pani (1) no, not, nothing, none, absence • *kathi pani* 'no meat' • *Kurnki ngala pani.* 'There was no devil at all.' • *Ngapatji panila.* 'There's no water (here).' • *Wadana ngathu thawa-warriningadi kara nhukuyi thanha; ay paningu.* 'I waited for them to come here, but nothing yet.' • *Thawaka, nga purnunukini pani.* 'Go away, don't tease me.' • *Matjanguda ngathu thayirla, paniyila yina.* 'I'm eating stale [food] because there's nothing [good].' [lit. 'in the absence of [anything good]'] # See also **walya**; (2) all # only in derived words. See **purduku, pulpa.**

pani kara or not • *Thawawarrarla kara nhunu, pani kara.* 'He might come, and he might not.' • *Yilayarndu kara nhulu parndrinhana kara pani kara.* 'I wonder how he went, whether he killed something or not.'

panika finish, do completely • *Panikakaldri thawakaldringa mapathika puthakurnula.* 'When they finish them off they go down again and muster some more.' • *Drakarnanga yarnduldrangu wirnikamuratji yiwangaditji pirnaldra, karriningadi panikaldra nhambalka-*

yindrindji. 'On the one hand they make a big one [hair-string apron] for women to tie on, to cover themselves completely.'

panina, panipanina all, everybody • *Ngandra thawarla panina.* 'We're all going.' • *Karna thana panipanina thawanhana, ngala yinitji minhayildra walya thawanhana?* 'Everybody went, so why didn't you go?' # See also **karnakurnu-karnakurnu.**

panina, paninatharra finish, end, die down; complete, do completely • *Kadli nhunu paninarlala.* '[The wind] is easing up.' • *Ngala pulyatji marndakurrapandhirlayi, nga walya yinha wawatharranga, karrtjipandhiyila thana paninarla.* 'When the little ones stop halfway they don't take any notice of them, for fear the whole lot will turn back.' • *Ngapala nhinari yartunarnanga palhangudatji, ya palha panina-rlayitji.* 'They eat their fill of them until the birds are all gone.' # See **murda.**

panipanika complete, completely • *Mapari panipanika thanha purlatji.* 'They muster all the young ones.' • *Panmana ngani, walya panipanika manggininguda.* 'We put (the fire) out before it burnt everything.'

panma wash (hands)

panma, panmapandhi put out (fire) • *Maka yintjadu panma!* 'Put that fire out!' • *Kali ngathu panmapandhina.* 'I've already put it out.'

panmayindri go out (fire) • *panma-panmayindrirnanga ngurra* 'going out all the time'

panthama smell (something) • *Minha kara panthamarla.* 'I can smell something.' • *Mirni kathi yintjadu panthama, walya thayini.* 'Smell that meat, it's no good to eat.' # SY and Yw *parnima*

pantja knee • *... ya nhunggani yabali ngapala wathi drantha kurrari, blanket-li yinha purrilkatharranga, nga wathi thanggunari pantja thangguni-nyadi nhunu karna.* '... and, in his fear, put a forked log on the other side, and covered it over with a blanket, and stood a stick up so that it would look like a man's knee sticking up.'

pantjakurra kneel

pantji circumcised

pantjika, pantjina circumcise • *Ngapala pula pakarila thanha, ngapirimaladitji mudalatji yina drangarnanga pantjinayindririlatji.* 'Well then they took all their fathers, and they had a corroboree and circumcised one another.'

papa grandfather, mother's father, grandchild, man's daughter's child, brother's daughter's child • *Muduwa pulya nhunuyi karruwali papa ngakani.* 'This little boy is my daughter's son.' • *Ngali pirnana-lapurra yulkuparluyi, papangi nganha pirnakalapurra.* 'We grew up on the Cooper's Creek. My granddad reared me.' # Yw *ngadra*

papana start • *Kayidi nganyi papana-ngarirla.* 'I'll start directly.'

papurla hobble (on a horse) # from Eng
papurlaka hobble (a horse) • *Ngapala mabaabili nhunu kuthiwarrarnanga nga kurrakurra-warranga purturdukardukarnanga yadamani papurlakatharrari yita.* 'Well it was dark when he arrived, and he unloaded his things and hobbled the horses.'

para (1) lie (of water) • *Ngala ngapatji pararlayi ngurra.* 'Then the water stays there for a long time.' • *Ngapa nhuniyi tjiri pararla.* 'There's a spring here.'; (2) shine • *Nyangiyi nganyi thawanga; nyangi pararlayi.* 'I'll go by moonlight, while the moon's

shining.' # See also **tjarnma, dintji.**
Note also Yw *parinyi* given for 'in the
creek', suggesting a noun *pari*. These
two meanings are found in one word
also in Warluwarra, far to the north.

para sneak up • *Paranhana nganyi,
nhinarlayi yinha warrkananga.*
'I sneaked up to spear it while it's
sitting.'

pararrka dead finish (tree, *Acacia
tetragonophylla*)

paratharra claypan, flat place # SY and
Yw *paritharra*. See also **wani.**

pardaparda suck # See **thapa,
yibayiba.**

  pardapardayindri suck • *Marawitju
nhani pardapardayindrirla.* 'She's
sucking her [cut] finger.'

pardi poisonous creature, snake
• *Thawarlayi yini wawarduda
pardipuru.* 'Watch out for snakes as
you go along.' # SY also 'white man'

  kuya pardi type of fish # See under
kuya.

  pardi kathikathi snake • *Pardi
kathikathitji kali windrinhana
pundrayi.* 'The snakes have gone in
(to hibernate) because of the cold.'

  pardi mirrka meat ant # Also
marnkunu.

  pardimardri bulldog ant

  pardingunthu water snake

Pardlaparli Burlieburlie Waterhole

pardra hold, catch; have • *Kathi ngathu
pardranhana nhinggiyi.* 'I had some
meat here.' • *Ngarru mulha malka
ngathu thanhayi pardrarla nhanggani.*
'I've only got these photos of hers.'
• *Pukurru ngathu yina pardranhana.*
'I had a dream about you last night.'
• *Ngarru pitjanka pardrarlatji.* 'They
only catch bony bream [in cross-nets].'
See also **nhinalka.**

  pardraka get • *Karruwalili thanayi
pampu pardrakarla ...* 'These boys
are getting eggs ...' # See **mandri.**

pardrapada hold, grab

pardrapardra feel (with the hand);
hold • *... minipandhiri pardra-
pardranga thanha.* '... ran down
and stopped them [fighting].'
• *Ngapala pardrapardrarnanga-thili,
nganandji nhulu ngathadimaladinyi,
'Thangguthalka wawayindringalatji.'*
'Well, the two of them were feeling
about (for the boomerang) and he told
his brother, "Stand up and look at
yourself".'

  pardrathalka hold up, hold high
• *Kupu nhulu pardrathalkarla.* 'He's
holding his hand up' [*kupu* 'arm'; you
could also use *mara* 'hand']

pardri edible grub, moth • *Muduwa
pulyali ngathu wawatharrana
kurrupu karrukarrutji nhinarlayi ya
thayiyindrirlayi pardri yuka thanha.*
'When I was a little boy I saw how the
old people lived and how they ate
those grubs.' # Also heard *padri*.

  pardri ngurraputhanguda grub in
butts of trees, especially whitewood

  pardri panga caterpillar

pari see **para.**

paritharra see **paratharra.**

pariwirlpa sky, cloud # See also
nganya, ngandjarri, kudawarrala.

parlaka, karna parlaka body • *Parlaka
madlantji nganyi.* 'I don't feel well.'
• *Marripathi kara, walpi kara. Mirni
nganyi karna parlaka patjinarlayi.*
'Maybe tomorrow, or some time.
As soon as I feel better. [Lit. when
my body gets good]' # Also **yiwari,
marndra;** See also **palku.**

  parlaka pirtipirti half-caste # Lit.
'red body'

parlayila willow # perhaps *Acacia
salicina*. See also **tjirri.**

parli father's sister, (cross-)cousin's
daughter; mother-in-law # See **patjiri.**

parlpa tongue; blade (of spear);
language • *parlpa pirrapirra* 'flat

blade' # See also **thanhani, tharli, yawarri, ngan.gu, yindri.**

Parlpakurnu language name, Durham Downs and other areas east of Yandruwandha (lit. 'other language')

Parlpamardramardra language or tribal name # Their area probably included Nappa Merrie and Lake Pure. Lit. 'stony language'.

parlu (a) white • *Warangi kara nhutjadu pandi parlutji.* 'I don't know whose that white dog is.'; (b) naked, bare # Yw • *Thanaku mirrkapani, parlu.* 'They've got no clothes on; they're naked.' • *kungka parlu pantjira* 'bald head' # Not clear what the *pantjira* means. See also **yarawarra.**

parndilka maggot # SY mirdiwiri

parndra cooked, ripe • *Kirriya nganha dramana, wantjiningadi, parndrala kara.* 'Will you cut [the meat] for me so I can see if it's cooked.' • *Kathi ngali parndrinhana, nga kudlayukarranga yinha. Parndrala ngali walthathikana.* 'We killed [a kangaroo], and cooked him overnight, and then carried him home cooked.' # See also **parrkini, pirtipirti.**

parndraka cook (something) # See also **kudla, darra.**

parndri hit, kick, kill; catch (animals, birds or fish); chop (wood); pound, crush; drive (a vehicle) • *Maka ngathu parndringa.* 'I'm going to chop some wood.' • *Ngapala pula karlukarlungadi yada thawari nga yandhanga nhinanga karlukarlu parndrirnanga pula thadri pada-wadaldra,* ... 'Two of them came down to do some fishing. They sat and talked and caught fish on the other bank, ...' • *Wirnikamalka puru-purriningudalatji thana parndringa* (word not clear) *wirningadi nga thurrpanga* ... 'They tease it up and make it into string by pounding it and then spinning it ...' • *Ya palhatji thana*

yurari parndringa, pirli thana paladi-ldrangu drakininguda, nga wathiyi pada karranga warrakurnutji, thadripalapala yina. 'If they want to catch birds they make a net of a different mesh and tie it on to a tree on each bank of the river.' • *Ngapala parndringa palhatji, walthayindrithikangalatji.* 'Well, they kill the birds and carry them back home.' • *Ngardu ngala, parndringa ngandra nga pinakanga nhulu pitjili.* 'Then there is nardoo; we crush it and then rock it in the coolamon.' • *Ngandjarrili nganha parndrina.* 'The rain fell on me.'

parndrinipurra bully

parndripada hit

parndripandhi kill

parndriparndri (1) crush • *Yarndu thana pawala dinganga, ya pawa parndriparndringa.* 'They grind the seeds, or crush them.'; (2) bang • *wathi yinha parndriparndriri, kukunumindji-nyadi kara* 'banging a log to see if it's hollow'

parndrithika hit back; go and kill and come back; go and catch (fish) and come back

parndriyindri (a) stop # See **murda;** (b) catch (fish); (c) chop; (d) hit yourself • *Ngapala nhunu nguthangutharnangala katjakatja-rlayilatji parndriyindrininguda nganggali karna palha-nyadi wawawawari.* 'Well, he stretched out his leg because of the pain, because he had hit himself, thinking it was a devil he had seen.'

parndri sing • *Minhangadi yintjadu wani kurnu yundru parndripada-padarla, walya wani kurnunguka drangini. Ngarru kurnungu yundru kilkarla.* 'Why do you always sing that same song, and never sing any other. Is that the only one you know?' # May

be the same word as *parndri* 'hit'. See
also **dranga**.

parni smell, have a smell, stink # SY
• *Minha kara thungga parnirla.*
'Something stinks.'

parnima smell (something) # SY, Yw
• (SY) *Ngathu parnimarla, minha
kara, ngarrtjirlayi, kathi kara.* 'I can
smell something cooking, must be
meat.' # See **panthama**.

parntu blunt • *Kadli walya nhunuyi
parntu.* 'It's nearly blunt' # Also
nyana.

parntuna become blunt

parra lie (down) # Yw, H

parrari underneath • *Wawa parrariyi.*
'Look underneath.' • *nhunutji
parrarildrala nganyitji kandraldra*
'him underneath and me on top'

parrikara lightning # Also **kurni**.

parrkini ripe # SY. Perhaps from a verb
parrka or *parrki* 'ripen'. See also
parndra, pirtipirti.

parrku, parrkulu two • *Nguthu
parrkulumindji nganyi.* 'I've got two
(elder) brothers.' • *Dritji parrkulu
nganyi nhinanhukada.* 'I stopped there
two days ago.' • *Pulya, ngapala, karna
parrkulu pula thanmaritji yukangatji.*
'It [the bag net] is a small one and two
men swim with it to catch [the fish].'
• *... ngapala thana, kurli parrku,
mandrithayi pilthirri thana warrkathalkangatji.* '... after a couple of
days, they pick up the broken pieces
of rock and throw them out of the
hole.' # *parrku* is rare but has been
heard alone and with the dual suffix,
thus *parrkuthili*; the usual word is
parrkulu. See also **pulpa, thili**.

parrkulu kurnu three • *Ngapala
wiki parrkulu wiki parrkukurnu kara
nhinapadapadarnanga thayirnanga
palhatji thanha ...* 'Then for two or
maybe three weeks they camp there,
living on birds ...' • *Ngarru dritji
parrkulu kurnu nhunu thawa-*

windrinhanatji. 'He went away only
three days ago.'

parrkulu-parrkulu four • *Tjukurru
parrkulu kara, parrkulu-parrkulu
kara karrpininguda nga kangu
yukarrangatji.* 'It might be two skins,
or maybe four and then they are warm
at night.' # Also accepted
parrkuparrkulu.

parrkuka tip up, spill • *Yundru nganha
nganana parrkukiningaditji ngapatji
ngakani.* 'You made me spill my
water.' # See also **pudla, yikaka,
yikayika**.

parrtjini (water) boil # Yw • *Kali
nhunuyi parrtjinirla. Ngapa kuntha
warrka!* 'The water's boiling. Throw
the tea in!'

parru yellow ochre, yellow

parruparru yellow # See also
padupadu.

parru bony bream # SY. See **pitjanka**.
May be Wngu

paru light • *nyangi paru* 'moonlight'
maka paru firelight, torch
mitji parumandri dazzle • *Dritjili
nganha mitji parumandrirla.* 'The
sun's dazzling me.'

pathada coolibah # Yw. See also
kalpurru.

pathada-pathada peewee, mudlark
(?) # SY. See **kulikuliyada,
martimarti**.

patja be sick, get sick • *Man.gili nhunu
mundja, patjarla, thawanhana
nhunu, kirringadi, kintha yunggudu
ngakarnanga.* 'Benny's sick, his
nose is bleeding and he's gone to
the doctor.' • *Patjala nganyi kathi
kutawirri thayininguda.* 'I'm sick
because I ate rotten meat.' • *Thawana
nganyi, thangguthikanga ngatjadayi,
muka ngala nhunu karrukarru
thudarla. Walya ngathu yinha
yirrtjinandji, patjala kara nhunu.*
'I went over to the old man's camp,

but he was asleep. He might be
sick, that's why I didn't wake him.'
Mundja and *patja* are often used
together. See, for example, the
warnta entry. See also **wariwari**.

patji good, well, properly • *Muduwa
thanayi patjingu nhinarla wawawawanarlayitji thanha.* 'The kids are
good while you're watching them.'
• *Walya nhandradu muduwa wawa-
wawanarla patji.* 'The mother's not
looking after the baby properly.'
• *'Yigatji wayi patji?' 'Ay kaldringu
thana. Walpi kara pirtipirtinangatji.'*
'"What are the wild oranges like?"
"Oh, they're bitter yet. Don't know
when they're going to get ripe."'
See also **manyu, ngumu**.

patjika, patjipatjika make good;
mend, fix, cure • *Yambarriyi
kurranga, padla paltjapaltja
yina wipinginingudatji yinha,
patjikaringu padla, padla thaka
mitji ngukangukayindriyi.* 'They put
them on the hard flat ground, after
sweeping it to make it clean so that
the seeds don't get mixed with clay.'
Also **dakuka**.

patjikurnu good, right; satisfied
• *Pandi patjikurnu ngurru nganyi.*
'I've got a good dog.' • *Patjikurnutji
makala ngala thana wangapandhi-
rnanga ngapala ngapa kurrari
mardrayi thana kudrakudrari
makamakaniningudatji.* 'They light
a good fire on the rock and after it
has heated up they put water on it, to
shatter the rock.' • *Makamuduli kulari,
mulhudu patjikurnutji.* 'They cook
them in hot ashes, and they are good
tucker.' • *Thayiyindrinhana mulhudu
nganyi, yartula nganyi nhinarla, patji-
kurnula.* 'I had a feed and I'm full
now, satisfied.'

patjikurnuka make good; mend, fix
patjili (do something) well # SY

patjina get better • *Marripathi kara,
walpi kara. Mirni nganyi karna
parlaka patjinarlayi.* 'Maybe
tomorrow, or some time. As soon as
I feel better. [Lit. when my body gets
good]'

patjipatji carefully • *Ngapala
nhunu thangguthalkawarrananga
patjipatjingu nga purtu nhulu
kunyamanga, nga kupuyi yinha
kurrapadaringu mungkayindriri yina
purtutji.* 'Then he got up, very
carefully, and rolled up his swag
and put it under his arm.'

patjiri son-in-law, woman's daughter's
husband, mother-in-law, husband's
mother (or wife's mother?) # Given
in Yw for 'father-in-law'. See also
kalhidi, parli.

patjiwarra tree with little black plums
tree is 'very snappy'. This may be
the Yawarrawarrka name of the
mandawarra.

Patjiwarra Patchawara Creek

pawa seeds (probably only edible seeds);
ground seeds, flour # The word *pawa*
is often used in combination with the
name of a particular plant to mean the
seeds of that plant, as in the following
example • *Ngala pawa ngala kalildra
dingarnanga, pawa kalpurru, pawa
wadlangurru, pawa mitjiyimpa, pawa
ngadli, pawa pidriyiltharri.* 'Then they
used to grind seeds as well — coolibah
seeds, wadlangurru seeds, puppa-grass
seeds, pigweed seeds, frosty-arse
seeds.' • *Pawangadi, pawa thungini
ngunyirnanga ya ngarduparndrini
ngunyirnanga.* 'They gave grinding
stones, for seeds, and nardoo
pounders.'

pawathungini grinding stone
• *Pawathungini ngala pitjidi
kumaningaditji ngunyiyindrirnanga
yarndukalangu thana nhinapadipadinitji.* 'They traded grinding stones

for bags of pitchery; that's how they used to live.'

pawada, pawada-pawada quickly # SY • *Pawada-pawada yinhaku walpa wathi, ngandjarri thawarla.* 'Build a humpy quickly, the rain's coming.' # See also **nhurrpa, pakali, pawada, yilyirri**.

pawayi, palha pawayi hawk (?)

payama buy # from Eng

payipaka whistle # See **wirlpi**.

payirri long, tall • *Ngapala kururrupa-rnanga nga nhurrpanga ngarrpayi kunya payirrili.* 'Then they rub it with stones and spin it on their thighs, using a long spindle.' • *Kuka karli payirri nhutjadutji yiwa-nyadi; nhindapani.* 'That fellow's got long hair like a woman. Got no shame.' • *Wathi payirriyi nganyi walkinhana kathi pildrangadi.* 'I climbed a big tree for a possum.' • *Pirnalatji nhunu payirrila. Ngardrawarrkangala kara yina.* 'He's big and tall now. He might pass you (in height).' # See also **marrpu**.

payirrika lengthen, make long • *Wirni payirrikari yinha nga kunyayi kurranga.* 'They make the string long and put it on the spindle.'

payipayirri shortish, not very long; a bit longer • *Payipayirrila mulpay! Payipayirrimalka!* 'Cut [them into] longer [pieces]! Make [them] longer!' • *Karraringu thanha mulpininguda warnta, payipayirru yina, mara witju-nyadi.* 'They tie them on after cutting them into short lengths, about the size of a finger.' (Note, the word was pronounced *payipayirru* on this occasion. The reason is not known.)

paynputu pannikin, pintpot # from Eng. See **tjampitji**.

paypa pipe # from Eng

pidipidi hard, vigorously; loudly • *minirla pidipidi* 'running hard' • *kukathanggurla pidipidi* 'thinking hard' • *ngindrarnanga pidipidili* 'breathing hard' • *pidipidili darrkarla* '(wind's) blowing hard' • *Pidipidili nhunu yandharla.* 'He's talking loudly.' • *Ngandjarri pidipidili warlkarla.* 'It's raining hard.' # Difference from *mampali* not clear; it is not acceptable in some cases, especially the third example. See also **paltja**.

pidli, pili burn # Yw • *Makathuru yada kapada, yini pidlipi.* 'Come away from the fire, you might get burnt.' # See **thangkana, darra, mangga, ngarrtji**.

pidri anus, backside, bottom • *Ngapa nhutjadu purudu ngananhana pidringadi.* 'The water dried up to the bottom.'

pidriyiltharri 'frosty-arse' (plant like pigweed, big yellow flower, on sides of sandhills, perhaps a type of pigface) • *Ngala pawa ngala kalildra dingarnanga, pawa kalpurru, pawa wadlangurru, pawa mitjiyimpa, pawa ngadli, pawa pidriyiltharri.* 'Then they used to grind seeds as well — coolibah seeds, wadlangurru seeds, puppa-grass seeds, pigweed seeds, frosty-arse seeds.'

pidriputha sandfly

pidrithitha crotch

pika spoil (?) # SY • *Nganha mukatji pikarla, nhuluyi thirrthali. Walya nganyi thudanhana.* 'He won't let me sleep, that dog. I didn't sleep.'

Pilardapa name of a people and language, south of Yandruwandha

pildra, kathi pildra possum • *Wathi payirriyi nganyi walkinhana kathi pildrangadi.* 'I climbed a big tree for a possum.' • *Ngala ngarru kathi tjukurruli thana nhinapadipadini, ya thalkaparlu, ya kathi pildra.* 'They only had kangaroo then, and kangaroo rat, and possum [to get fur from].'

pildripildri thunder # 'real rough one, severe one, after he's struck anything'. See also **yindri**.

pili see **pidli**.

pilimpara policeman # SY, Yw. See also **kandjipulu, pilitjimani, thandjipulu, yulya**.

pilitjimani policeman • *Matja nhina-padipadini pilitjimani*. '[He] used to be a policeman.' # from Eng. Heard as *pulitjimani* from H. See also **kandjipulu, pilimpara, thandjipulu, yulya**.

pirrpa pour # SY

pilpangurru quiet # Yw. See **ngapu**.

pilpangurrulu quietly # Yw

pilpiri shoulder # SY. See also **kilkirri, pinyi, thapini, wiliwili**

pilta belt # from Eng

pilthirri, pilthipilthirri broken piece(s) of stone • *... ngapala thana, kurli parrku, mandrithayi pilthirri thana warrkathalkangatji*. '... after a couple of days, they pick up the broken pieces of rock and throw them out of the hole.' • *Minhayali ngala thana, pirna palparrilitji mardra pilthirrili palkininguda*. 'Now what do they [skin animals] with: with a stone chip that has been broken off a big boulder.' # Compare **thayipilthirri**.

pilthipilthirrika shatter, split something into splinters # See also **druka, kudra**.

piltja, piltjapiltja open (your eyes, mouth) # SY, Yw. See also **pindri, pirika, dingayindri, tjalka, thangu**.

pinaka rock (as in a coolamon) • *Ngala ngarru pawala thana mapaapanga pinakaringu pitjiyilayi*. 'They just gather up the seeds and rock them in the coolamon.'

pindjipindjinhada bat # SY; same as Wngu

pindri open • *marna pindrininguda* 'open door' (lit. 'door that has been opened') # See also **pirika, dabaka, dingayindri, tjalka, thangu, piltja**.

pindri grasshopper # SY. See also **wamalurru**.

pin.gi possessions • *Pin.gi pin.gi thana ngunyiyindripadipadini yarndu*. 'That's how they used to trade things.'

pinhaniwa (or **pinhani**) on the right
pinhanikadi to the right

pinngapinnga sticky

pintaka tell # SY, heard only in *kinyili pintaka* 'tell a lie', but Reuther gave *pintaki* as the Yn and Yw equivalent of a Diyari word translated as 'to tell, relate; state, mention'. See **ngana, wirina**.

pintha foreskin; 'string' under penis
pinthapurru uncircumcised • *Karruwali nhinalapurratji pinthapurru*. 'They were still boys, with foreskins.'

pinthika, also heard as *pinthikani* shield shrimp

pintjidi tick or louse # SY

pinya war; soldiers, warriors • *Walya thana thirripadipadinitji, pani, ngarru pinyayi, karna thula nhukuwanguda yada thawarnanga parndrithikangatji, minhayatji pinyalitji*. 'They never used to fight, except in a war. Strangers would come from over there [in their country] to kill and then go back. That's what they used to call war.' # Soldiers might also be referred to as *karna pinya*. AWH translates pinya as 'blood-revenge party'

pinyanku budgerigar # SY See also **thilbirrutja, thilinkurru**.

pinyi, pinyimara shoulder # Yw. *Pinyimara* was once said to be 'my grandfather', perhaps referring to the use of body parts in sign language terminology for kin

pinyipinyi collarbone # SY

pinyiyinka shoulder • *Ngapala tjukurru darla karna parrkululi pula wathili pinyiyinkali walthangatji*. 'Two men carry the kangaroo skin [waterbag] on a stick resting on their shoulders.' # See also **thapini, wiliwili, kilkirri, pilpiri.**

pipa paper, letter # from Eng

pipa poke # SY gave it for 'point'. See also **draka.**

pipa draka write

pipi miss, have a spell • *Pipinhinanga nganyi makamakayi yina.* 'I'll have a rest while it's hot.' • *Ay thawarla ngali kathi parndriparndriyindringa, nguni walya pipini* 'We go hunting; we don't miss a day.'

pipina have a spell

pipi See **kuka.**

pira moon, month # SY, Yw, Nh. See **nyangi.**

pirapardri grub in roots of trees # Perhaps the Christmas beetle larva, which is named from its resemblance to the moon in some languages. (The order of the parts of this word is unexpected.)

pirda navel # SY, Yw. See **mindra.**

pirditjirra, pirditjinga strip • *Kali thana thukaringu ngapangudatji ya pirditjirranga thanha.* 'Then they take it [the plant used for making string for nets] out of the water and strip it.' • *Minhaya warrkarnanga pirditjirranga thanha, kathi thukali.* 'They cut them [bulrushes] down and strip them with a mussel [shell].' • *Thiltja thana tjukurru pardrarla, ngapala thanadu pirditjirraritji nga palha mukuli tjalparrikininguda wirlpakanga nyinditji.* 'They hold the kangaroo sinew and strip it and poke the holes in the skin with a bird bone that has been sharpened.' # Also **tjirra.**

pirdrithiwirdi hornet

piri between the legs • *Nhinapandhi kuka piriyi kurrapandhinga.* 'Sit down and put your head between your knees [when you feel sick].'

pirika open; be open # Yw • *Marna pirika!* 'Open the door!' • *Kali pirikarla nhunuyi walparda.* 'The door's open.' (lit. 'The house is open.') # See also **pindri, dabaka, dingayindri, tjalka, thangu, piltja.**

pirimayindri open your legs

pirithanuthanu in the space between the legs

piriyarra apart (of feet)

pirli net (in general), bag (in general), bag net • *Ngathu wawatharrana karlukarlungadi yukiningadi pirli yama yina karrparlayi.* 'I saw them make a bag net for catching fish while swimming in the water, and a cross net.' • *Ngala pirlili ngampurrungaditji paladildrangu thana drakininguda, kurrarla yarnduldrangu kinipapayi kurrapadari yita.* 'They use a net that they have woven with a different mesh, and that they put into the water in the same way, for yellowbelly.' • *Ngarru ngathu pirli tjapura yina wawalapurratji, thana drakininguda.* 'I only saw the pitchery bags they wove, a long time ago.' # *Pirli* can be used in combination with another word that refers to a particular type of net or bag, as in *pirli yama* in the first example and *pirli tjapura* in the last.

pirli mitji net, gill net

pirli nindri bag net

pirli tjapura pitchery bag

pirli yama bag net

pirli yurrkuyurrku dillybag # SY

pirli smoky cloud

pirna big, grown up; elder; full (of stomach); a lot; deep (voice); thick, wide • *Nga kankunu pirna nhulu kurranga.* 'He put up a big windbreak.' • *Mardrangadi, mandrithayinga pirna.* 'They're going to win a lot of money.' • *Thana mukurdukalapurra thanha, ngarru ngaga yina nhunu pirnatji wirlpa.* 'They took the bones out through a hole only as big as the throat.' • *Mulhudu ngathu pirna thayipandhina, thundrutji nganyi kimanarla.* 'I ate too much and my stomach is swollen.' • *... mirni ngathu yina ngananga, pirnayila.* '... I'll tell you later, when you're grown up.' • *ngindrangindrarla pirnala* 'breathing hard' • *Mulhudu ngathu wawanhana, wayi pirna kara.* 'I looked at the tucker, wondering how much there was.' • *ngama pirna* 'mother's elder brother' # Also appears as the second part of compounds, with a meaning like 'much' or 'very (well)'; see **marnipirna, mirrtjapirna, puthapirna, thirripirna, yuthapirna.**

pirnaka bring up, raise; initiate • *Ngali pirnanalapurra yulkuparluyi, papangi nganha pirnakalapurra.* 'We grew up on the Cooper's Creek. My granddad reared me.'

pirnana become big, grow # = *punka* • *Palha purla pirnanarlayitji, ngapala yarru wathinaritji, marru kadawayi ...* 'When the young birds are getting big, they build a yard for them on the bank of the lake ...'

pirnapirna biggish, not very big, comparatively big, bigger, biggest • *Thidharri yini yingkilapurra; pirnapirnala ngala yini kayiditji.* 'You used to cry [a lot] when you were a baby, but you're big now.' • *Pirritjampanarlayi nhunu karrtjipandhinga pulyatji nhunu nga thikanhinanga thundingadi, ngala thana kadirlayi palha ngalyitji, pirnapirnatji, ngapala thana windrimawarraringu wathininguda yarrutji thanngani.* 'If a little one gets tired it turns around and heads back to the island, while they hunt the rest of them, the biggest [of the young] ones, on and put them in the yard that they have built for them.'

pirnapirnana make big

pirndiwalku horse # SY, Yw. Apparently primarily a Mithaka word. See **nhandu, yadamani.**

pirni nguru related to one another in such a way that you can't marry one another • *Walya ngathu nhipakari nhanhadutji, pirni nguru yina ngakani nhatjadu.* 'I couldn't marry that woman, she's the wrong relation to me.' # complement of *nhipa mulha*

pirnnga skin, peel • *Ngapala pakathikarnanga darla pirnngandji yinha, yilayarndutji kara.* 'Well, they carry them back to camp and skin them — I don't know how.' • *... thana pirnngipadipadinitji mara patjikurnuli yina karrukarrutji nhinapadipadini ngapangaditji.* '... the olden-days men used to be good hands at skinning [kangaroos] for water [bags].' # Also **nyinyimilpa.**

kathi pirnngini butcher • *Kathi pirnngini nhutjadu patjikurnu, ngapala kathitji nhulu dramardramari.* 'He's a good butcher, he cuts up the meat.'

pirnpi scatter (them, for example, people) • *Ngapala ngathu wawana thirrirlayi thanha; ngapala nganyi miniri pirnpinga thanha.* 'Then I saw them [kids] fighting, and I ran down and scattered them.'

pirnta beefwood (*Grevillea striata*) # Also **tjin.gini.**

pirntathangka beefwood gum • *Ngapala pirntathangkali nyanmari, marapardrini, wirnili ngukanguka pirntathangkali, karrangalatji yinha.* 'I'll bind the handle on with string and seal it with beefwood gum (mixed with the string).' # Also **kandri palku.**

pirnta stick with a big knob on # used to stop a boomerang

pirrapirra flat • *Kathi tjukurrupurutji, ya mardra pirrapirra kurrathalka-(niya?) kandratji.* 'They get a flat stone and put it over the top [of the well] to keep kangaroos out.' # See also **palbarri, pali, yambayambarri**.

pirripirri (1) spirit # in Reuther's Diari Dictionary. (2) white man • *Walarriyi ngali nhuliyi pirripirrili nhinarla.* 'Me and this white fellow sitting in the shade here.' # See **walypala**.

pirritjampana get tired • *Pirritjampana-rlayi nhunu karrtjipandhinga pulyatji nhunu nga thikanhinanga thundingadi* … 'If a little one gets tired it turns around and heads back to the island …' • *Yandhayandharla yini ngurra, pirritjampanarla nganyi.* 'You're talking a lot, I'm getting tired.'

pirrki type of hawk # possibly a mistake; see **kirrki**.

pirrpa pour (something) # SY. See also **kima, pudla**.

pirta post, support (as for a humpy) # Yw. Also **wathi muku**.

pirtapirta walking stick # SY • *Malantji nganani nganyi pantja. Nganyi kungkanga nganarla, pirtapirtali.* 'My knee's got sore, but I'll hobble along with a walking stick.' # See **kunya, wathi witju, windawinda**.

pirtipirti red, ripe • *Windringa ngathu yinhayi pirtipirti.* 'I'm going to paint it red.' # See **parndra, parrkini**.

pirtipirtika make red • *Ngala pani-pani(kari?) muku palgupalgu dukininguda, ngapala dultharri darlamurru windrimari, paltjikini-ngaditji yina, pirtipirtikari darlatji yinha.* 'After they take out all the bone and muscle they put bloodwood bark in to make it supple and it makes the skin red.'

pirtipirtina ripen, get ripe • *'Yigatji wayi patji?' 'Ay kaldringu thana. Walpi kara pirtipirtinangatji.'* '"What are the wild oranges like?" "Oh, they're bitter yet. Don't know when they're going to get ripe."'

pithiri fart # possibly a verb

pitjanka bony bream • *Ngapala kurrarla, marripathi thana marrikurukurutji minipandhiringu mandrithalkangalatji karlukarlu, pitjanka yina.* 'Then they put it in [at night] and next morning, very early, they run down and pull up the fish — bony bream.' • *Mukupika yina thana pitjankatji.* 'Those bony bream are the very bony ones.' # See also **parru**.

pitji coolamon • *Ngala ngarru pawala thana mapaapanga pinakaringu pitjiyilayi.* 'They just gather up the seeds and rock them in the coolamon.' # SY also 'bark (of tree)'. See also **nharra**.

pitjimudalhi smallest coolamon

pitjingamburu middle-sized coolamon

pitjiwiritji coolamon # 'the one they rock with'

pitjidi pitchery • *Wiriwinmarnanga karna thana pitjidi kumaningurrutji.* 'The people with the bags of pitchery exchanged [them].' • *Yilanggitji kara thana pitjidi mandripadipadini, ngarlaku.* 'I don't know where they used to get the pitchery.' # SY *pitjirri*. BK's *kamiri* (and he pronounced it *pitjirri* when he named it as his *kamiri*. See also the note to the **kawalka** entry).

pitjipampu sugarbag, honey # SY. BK said there was none in his country

piyaka parli mother-in-law # SY, Yw. See **parli**.

puba smoke (tobacco) • *ngurra pubini* 'someone who's always smoking'

puda urine; urinate

pudathika urinate • *Thawarla nganyi thudathikanga.* 'I'm going to have a piss.' # See also **pudu**.

pudhukani melon, wild cucumber

pudla, pula spill, pour out, empty out # See also **kima, pirrpa, parrkuka, yikaka**.

pudlapudla knock or shake seeds off (a tree branch or a clump of grass) • *Ngapala thana kurrupulila mandrithikathalkangardi kantha pudlapudlarnanga thanha, ya wathi karlitji.* 'Well, the women get grass and separate the seeds, and limbs of trees.'

pulayindri spill; leak (as flour from a bag, not water) • *wirlpayi pulayindriri* 'leaking out through a hole'

pudlu, pudlupudlu can't • *Pudlu ngathu kandrakarla.* 'I can't lift it.' • *Pudlupudlu ngathu nhandu yinhayi thilpathilparla, pirritjampanarla nhuniyi.* 'I can't get this horse going because he's tired.' • *Mundja nhutjadu, pulu nhunu thawarlatji.* 'He's too sick to walk.'

pudlupudluka be unable • *Pudlupudlukana ngathu, nguthingi mandrithikarla ngathu warliminingadi nganha.* 'I can't do it; I'll get my brother to help me.'

pudu dew, frost # 'the Seven Sisters' piddle, see also **yiltharri**.

puduma urinate on • *Purtu yada windrimapada pandili pudumayi.* 'Bring the swag inside so the dog won't piddle on it.' # See also **puda**.

puka food, tucker, damper, dough • *puka thayiri* 'having a feed' • *Puka ngathu nhapipandhina mardri.* 'I mixed a thick damper.' # Also **mulhudu**.

puka kiki cake # SY. From Eng.

puka paka tobacco

puka patji good food (specifically used for cake by BK)

pukapuka, wathi pukapuka scrub; useless (small?) growth • *Thawanhana nhunu wathi pukapuka, walya ngala kilkarnanga yidlakadi kara nhunu thawarnangatji.* 'He wandered through the scrub without knowing where he was going.'

puka purda unripe fruit

Pukapurdayi Bookabourdie

pukudu dream • *Pukuduli nhutjadu yandharla.* 'He's talking in his sleep.' • *Pukudu ngathu yina pardranhana.* 'I had a dream about you last night.' • *Karna palha-nyadi wawarnanga nhinawarrarlayi ngakaniyi, pukuduli …* 'I thought I saw a devil sitting with me, in my dream, …' # See also **dangguda**.

pula they (two), two of them, the (two) • *Thirrinhana pula ngananhinanhukada.* 'They had a fight yesterday.' • *Ngapala pula karlukarlungadi yada thawari …* 'Two of them came down to do some fishing.'

puladu they (two, there), those two • *Ay yuriyi puladu yandhayandharla.* 'Those two are talking for a long time.'

pulayi they (two, here), these two • *Kathi tjukurru ngathu wawana thawarnanga nhinggiyingadi, parrkulu pulayi thika* 'I saw some kangaroos when I was coming here; two back here.'

pula see **pudla**.

pulayarra, pulapulayarra green • *Ngapala marnatji nhinari mayi pulapulayarra thayiningudatji padri mulhakunatji.* 'Their mouths were green after eating the brown-nosed grub.'

pulgani their, theirs, belonging to them (two); them (two) (as in 'for them', 'with them' etc.) • *Pulganiyi nhunu nhinanhinarla nhukuwa, nhinggiwa nhunu.* 'He's with them two, over there.' • *Yawarri pulganili walya yawarri ngakanili, ngarru walypalayingu yawarri yandhayandharitji nganyi nganarnangatji pulhu.* 'I hadn't spoken to them in their language or in mine, only in the whitefellows.'

pulganiyi their, theirs, belonging to them (two, here); with them (two); them (two, here) (as in 'for them', 'with them' etc.) • (SY) *Pulganiyi nhaniyi yabali.* 'She's frightened of those two.'

pulgatjadu their, theirs, belonging to them (two, there); them (two, there) (as in 'for them', 'to them' etc.)

pulgatjaduyi with them (two, there)

pulhanga breathe # SY, Yw • *marnali pulhangarla* 'breathing through the mouth' # See **ngindra**.

pulhiyi them (two, here), these two (object of verb) • *Ngarlaku, kilkarla yundru pulhiyi?* 'I don't know; do you know these two?'

pulhu them (two), the (two, object of verb) • *... ngandjarritji warlkaringu ngabangabakaringu pulhu.* '... the rain came down and wet them both.' • *Mirrkatji milpirnanga, marndu-marndukana pulhu tjukurru thiltjali.* 'They sew two [skins] together with kangaroo sinew [to make] the blanket.'

pulhudu them (two, there), those two (object of verb) • *Muduwa ngathu pulhudu wanthiyindrinhana.* 'I was looking for those two kids.'

pulitjimani see **pilitjimani**.

pulka blow (wind, or with mouth) • *Kantha mangga mayi, pulkapada mayi.* 'Burn the grass! Blow it (so it burns)!' • *Ngapala nhunu ngarru yankula mandriri, nga warrkapandhinga ngapala pulkanga ngala nhulu ...* 'So he just got some [dry] leaves and threw them down [on the hot coals] and started to blow them ...' • *Kundangali paltjapaltja pulkarla.* 'The wind's blowing hard.'

pulkayindri blow (nose) • *Kintha pulkayindri!* 'Blow your nose!'

pulka, pulkapulka grill • *Kathi thanayi pulkapulkaringu makamukuruli-nyadi, ngala mardramitjili ngala.* 'They grill their meat on the stones and you would think it had been grilled on the coals.'

pulkapada light (fire) # See also **wanga, thalpapada, karadaka**.

pulpa (1) all, the lot # IY See *purduku, pani* • *pulpa thanadutji* 'they all'; (2) two # SY. Also used in Yw. See **parrku**.

pulpapulpa four # SY

puluka, kathi puluka bullock • *Kathi puluka walpirri miriyi thanggukarlatji.* 'Tailing cattle over the sandhill.' # from Eng. Also **yuritjamindji**.

pulumuku hips # Also **wartamuku**.

Pulupulu Booloo Booloo Waterhole # *pulupulu* said to mean 'leg' in Parlpamardramardra.

pulya small, narrow; little bit; younger • *Mitji ngathu drakana marawitju pulyali.* 'I poked my eye with my little finger.' • *Pulyala kara nhukuyi nhunu wathitji, yandhayandharlayitji nganyi nganarnangatji yunhu.* 'There must be only a little bit of tape left now, for me to talk to you fellows.' • *Pulya, ngapala, karna parrkulu pula thanmaritji yukangatji.* 'It [the bag net] is a small one and two men swim with it to catch [the fish].' • *Pirri-tjampanarlayi nhunu karrtjipandhinga pulyatji nhunu nga thikanhinanga thundingadi ...* 'If a little one gets tired it turns around and heads back to the island ...' • *Muduwa pulya nhunuyi karruwali papa ngakani.* 'This little boy is my daughter's son.' • *ngama pulya* 'mother's younger brother' # See also **nganya, purla**.

pulyurru mud • *Mardramitji warrka-pandhina ngathu ngapayi, ngapala nhunu thawari pulyurrungadi.* 'I chucked a stone into the water and it went down into the mud.' # Also heard *pulyudu*.

pulyurru nyununyunu swallow (bird) # Perhaps fairy martin. See also **tjumpunya**.

puma choke • *Thirrinhana ngali,
ngapala ngali parrkulu ngunu(?)
warlkari, nhunutji parrarildrala
nganyitji kandraldra. Ngapala ngathu
yinha pumari.* 'We fought, then we
fell down, with him on the bottom and
me on top. I choked him then.' # Also
ngagapardra.

pumayindri wrestle

pundha, kathi pundha mouse # See
also **puntha, nganyipuntha**.

pundji fall (leaf or fruit from a tree)
• *thalpa pundjina* 'a leaf fell' # See
also **marapundji, warlka**.

pundra cold, winter • *Pundrali nganyi
yirrikarla.* 'I'm shivering with the
cold.' • *Ngapala, kurrupu karrukarru
pundrayi kara, makamakayi kara,
ngapala ngarru kankunu kurraringa
makawarrkanga kunawarrkutji
thudayukarrangatji.* 'Well, the olden-
days women and men, in winter or
summer, only put up a windbreak,
throw some firewood down and sleep
all night crossways.' # See **malthi**.

pundra ngunyingunyi make you cold

pundrapundra kidney # SY also
pundra.

pundri turkey bush # perhaps
Eremophila gilesii. See **dandhirri**.

pundrinya lignum # SY *wayirri*

punga humpy # Yw? May be Wngu.
See also **walpa, walparda, mambu**.

punggu bow vine # for fibres for net.
Not really a vine at all but a tall herb
growing in swamps, one or more
species of *Cullen*, formerly *Psoralea*.
See also **kalu** • *Punggu murrpiningudatji ngapala kurrari ngapayi,
wiki parrkulu kara, thungganiningadi.*
'They cut the bow vine and put it in
water for maybe two weeks, so that it
will rot.'

punka grow; grow up # = *pirnana*
• *thadripalapala punkarla* 'growing
on both sides (of the river)' • *Nganyitji*

*punkanga, karrutji, ngapala ngathu
kathi parndriri.* 'I'm going to be a
butcher when I grow up.'

punnga lungs # SY, RYn

puntha, punthapuntha mouse, possibly
the *kultarr, Antechinomys laniger*
SY. See **pundha, nganyipuntha**.

punthipunthipa separate # Yw
• *... nganyi puthanhana punthi-
punthipanga.* '[The dogs were fighting
so] I ran and separated them.' # See
paladipaladi.

puntjiwarra see **kurla**.

pupara fine, finely ground

puradlu bridle # from Eng

purda green, unripe; raw # Also **kimba**.

purdathayini plain turkey, bustard
• *Palha pirnaldra nhutjadutji
warruwitjitji, nga purdathayinitji
pulyaldra.* 'Emus are bigger than
turkeys.' # The name is said to refer to
a little bush with berries, growing on
sandhills; the turkeys eat the berries
before they are ripe.

purdru fruit tree # little bush, with lots
of little yellow fruit, in flooded
country

purduku all • *karna purduku*
'everybody' • *purduku thana* 'they all'
See **pani, pulpa**.

purdupa woman! (as a term of address)
• *Purdupa, minha yundru nganha
nganangaka?* 'Woman, what are you
going to tell me?'

purla small, young • *Palha purla pirnanarlayitji, ngapala yarru wathinaritji,
marru kadawayi, ngapala thawarnanga puka windritharranga ngapa
marruyitji palha purla thanhayi
mapathikanga.* 'When the young birds
are getting big, they build a yard for
them on the bank of the lake and then
go down into the water and herd the
baby birds back [into the yard].' # Yw
and H 'baby, child'; see **muduwa,
pulya**.

(purlka)

purlkali worrying; sorry # Yw. See **ngidla**.

purnda back of neck, nape • *Kanpangu, purnda yina dranyiri.* 'He hits it right then, on the back of the neck.' # SY wakarri

purndamitji back of neck

purndaparndri hit on the back of the head or neck; kill in this way • *Pirnapirna thanhayi, tharriningaditji nganarlayi, purndaparndringa kudlanga yina thayiyindrirnangatji.* 'The biggest ones, that are nearly ready to fly, they kill and cook and eat.'

purndapurnda girl

purndawalkini pillow

purnunu itchy, tickly feeling • *Purnunu maltjiyi ngakaniyi* 'I can feel something on my leg.'

purnunuka (1) be itchy # a transitive verb with the one who is itchy, or the part which is itchy, as the object, and no agent needing to be specified; (2) tease (someone) • *Karna ngalyitji nhulu purnunukari.* 'He teases the others.' • *Thawaka, nga purnunukini pani.* 'Go away, don't tease me.'

purra always; before # Perhaps not a separate word • *Ngandjarri purra nhunuyi padla.* 'This is a rainy place.' • *Mukapurra nhatjadu.* 'She's always asleep.' # Note also *-purra* as part of the remote past tense suffix, *-lapurra* (*-iyapurra*, which also functions as past habitual, in Yw). See **ngurra**, also **kinyipurra**, **mirrtjapurra**, **parndripurra**, **thirripurra**, **yuthapurra**.

purra tear # See **daba**.

purrapurrana, purrapurraka tear up • *Kaburda ngakani — pandili thambathambakanana — purrapurrananga.* 'My hat — the dog's playing with it — tearing it up.'

purrayindri be torn # SY • *Ngakani nhunuyi mirrka purrayindrirla.* 'My dress is torn.'

purralku brolga # See also **kurla**.

purrga cramp

purri, purrilayindri turn over, be upside down # See also **kukali thanggu**.

purrilka turn (something) over # See also **karrtjikarrtjima**.

purri, purrinhina, purripandhi crouch, get down on hands and knees; hide (yourself) • *Thawawarranga thangguwagawaganga, ngala karna nhunu purrinhinarlayi ngari mingkayi.* 'They go and stand around the hole, while the man hides in it.' • *Purrirla nhunu; ngulukayindri-waganga, ya winkathikapadakaldri.* 'He's hiding; he peeped out and then ducked back in again.' • *... mingkayi nhunu purrirla ...* '[The snake] hides in the hole [in winter].' # See also **kudhi**.

purrilka hide something, cover something • *... ya nhunggani yabali ngapala wathi drantha kurrari, blanket-li yinha purrilkatharranga, nga wathi thanggunari pantja thangguni-nyadi nhunu karna.* '... and, in his fear, put a forked log on the other side, and covered it over with a blanket, and stood a stick up so that it would look like a man's knee sticking up.' # See **nhamba, wamba, kudhikudhima, winkama**.

purrina drop # Yw

purringari stoop # SY

purrka leave (someone or something) # Yw

purrkapada cross, go across • *Walyala ngani purrkapadayi wilpadalitji, ngarrungu pula thawandji, thantjiyipangadi, nganyi nhinapadapadarlayi nhinggikala Kinipapayi.* 'We mightn't have got across with the wagon so they went on without me, to the town, and I stayed there at the river.'

purrtji frightened; to get a fright • *Purrtjina nhunu ngakani; thukayindrirlayi ngathu.* 'I was riding my [horse] and he shied.' # See also **yabali**.

purrtjina, purrtjinawarra frighten, give a fright • *Ngarru nhunu kulkupathalkawarrandji purrtjinanga nganha.* 'He jumped up and frightened me.' • *Thikawarrarlatji nhaniyi kuthikuthi windriwarranga, walya ngathu nhanha wawarlayi. Purrtjinawarrari nganha nhandra.* 'She came back and sneaked inside and I didn't see her. She gave me a fright.'

purrtjipurrtji, purrtjipurrtjini touchy (of horse) • *Warrkapandhiyila yini yina, purrtjipurrtjini yina nhutjadu.* 'You might fall off; he's very touchy.'

purru all over, everywhere, anywhere • *Purru ngathu yinha kuriyirrikana.* 'I cleaned it all over.' • *Purru thana thawawarrarla yilangginguda kara.* 'They've come from all over the place, I don't know where.' # Also **padlakurnu-padlakurnu**.

purtu belongings, swag, bundle, things, gear • *Ngapala nhunu purtu mandri-mandrirnanga milyaruyi, nga thawawindringa ngatjada kurnungadila, ...* 'Well, he packed his swag in the dark and walked on to the other camp, ...' • *Ngapala nhunu windripadari purtungurru.* 'Then he went inside with his swag.' • *Purtutji yinggani wawawawanaw, winkamayila nhuludu.* 'Watch your things, or he'll take them.'

purtupakini, purtuwalthini swagman, bagman • *Yadamani thannganiyi thudayukarraringula ngala nhunu walypala kurnutji purtu walthinitji, minhaya?* 'He spent the night with the horses, while the other white man, the swagman — what about him?'

purturdukarduka unroll swag • *Ngapala mabaabili nhunu kuthiwarrarnanga nga kurrakurra-warranga purturdukardukarnanga yadamani papurlakatharrari yita.* 'Well it was dark when he arrived, and he unloaded his things and hobbled the horses.'

puru end of a burrow or cave # but not the end or bottom of a vertical hole

purudu dry # See also **muya, kayinta**.

puruduka dry (something)

purudukayindri dry yourself • *Purudukayindrina nganyi.* 'I dried myself.'

purudungana dry, get dry • *Ngapa nhutjadu purudu ngananhana pidringadi.* 'The water dried up to the bottom.'

puruka dress # from Eng 'frock'

puruka pay # verb

purupurra tease (fibre) • *Wirnikamalka purupurriningudalatji thana parndringa (*unclear word*) wirningadi nga thurrpanga ...* 'They tease it up and make it into string by pounding it and then spinning it ...' # could also be used of a dog teasing the hair out of the tail on a bullock hide

putha race; gallop, move fast # this is the normal word for 'run' in Yawarrawarrka (Yw, H); see **mini**.

putharrkawindri run away, flee # Yw • *Ngathu kandrakarnanyi yinhayi windra, tjukurru putharrka-windriri.* 'When I raised the spear the kangaroo hopped away.' # See **miniwindri, winka, winkapani, kinyiwinka**.

puthapika fast • *Putha thana minithalkarla, marripathi, dritji parrkulu nhandu thanayi puthapika.* 'There's races on tomorrow, for two

days, these racehorses.' # See also
wirlpa.

puthapirna fast # faster than
puthapika • *Muduwa nhunggani
puthapika ngala muduwa ngakani
puthapirnaldra.* 'His kids can run
but mine can run faster.'

putha time, occasion

putha kurnu once

puthakurnu next, again • *Walyala
wawanga puthakurnu ngarru walypawalypala yina thana nhinarla kayiditji,
...* 'We won't see [that] again. They
just live like white people now, ...'
• *Panikakaldri thawakaldringa
mapathika puthakurnula.* 'When they
finish them off they go down again
and muster some more.' • *Walyala
ngathu puthakurnu thayinga kathi
thunggatji.* 'I'm not going to eat
stinking meat again.'

putha white (only in compounds, such
as *mayiputha* 'fog', *pidriputha*
'sandfly', *thundruputha* 'shag')

putha shallow # SY, Yw. See **kanda**.

puthurru dust, duststorm # See
kunuputha, thayirri.

puthurru, puthuputhurru dusty,
hazy

putiyita potato • *Putiyita-nyadi thayingatji.* 'They eat them [yams] like
potatoes.' # from Eng

putjaputja type of bird # MN thought
the name belonged to the pied butcher-
bird; if so it is probably from Eng

putju, mitji putju blind • *mitji kurnu
putju* 'blind in one eye'

putjuna be shut (eyes), be blind, go
blind # Yw • *Putjunarla nhunuyi.*
'His eyes are shut.'

puwa brains # SY. See **tjuru, kuka
thangka**.

R

rabiti rabbit • *Walya ngathu wawa-
lapurra rabiti-nyadi yina thana
walypalali nyinimilparla, darla
pirnngarnanga.* 'I never saw it, but
they might have done it like white men
turn rabbit skins inside out.' • *Rabiti-
pani yina thana nhinapadipadini
matjardi.* 'They didn't have any
rabbits in the old days.' # from Eng

T

thadamuku thigh # SY. See **wandikila,
kulayada, ngalpa**.

Thadani place name

thadjingumini mountain devil, thorny
devil (lizard)

thadra push

thadrarduda push along

thadri bank of river • *Ngapala pula
karlukarlungadi yada thawari nga
yandhanga nhinanga karlukarlu
parndrirnanga pula thadri
padawadaldra, ngala nganyitji thadri
yitapandhiwarraldra nhinarlayi.*
'Two of them came down to do some
fishing. They sat and talked and
caught fish on the other bank, while I
was camped on the bank that sloped
down opposite them.' # See also
kadawa, wida.

thadripalapala on both sides of
the river • *Ya palhatji thana yurari
parndringa, pirli thana paladildrangu
drakininguda, nga wathiyi pada
karranga warrakurnutji, thadripalapala yina.* 'If they want to catch
birds they make a net of a different
mesh and tie it on to a tree
on each bank of the river.' • *Ngapala
thana tharrapandhiri yada, ngala
karna nhunu(?) wadayindrirla
thadripalapala yadatji warrkanga.*
'Well, when they fly down towards

the net, the men waiting there on both sides of the river throw their boomerangs.' # 'on one side' would be *thadri kurnuyi*

thaka see **padla**; also given by SY for 'bank (of creek)'

thakumani stockman # from Eng

thakurru wait; slowly • *Tjukurru nhutjadu thakurru thayithayiyindrirla.* 'The kangaroo's feeding along slowly.' # See also **marnka**.

    thakuthakurru slowly • *Thaku-thakurru yandha.* 'Speak slowly.'

Thala Della Waterhole

thalka up; outside • *Minha nganalapurra yini nhinggiwa thalka.* 'What were you doing up there?' • *Walpayi nhutjadu thudarla, ngala thinatji nhunu yambarriyildra thalka.* 'He's lying asleep in the humpy with his feet sticking out.' # See also **wirdi**, **yambarri**.

    thalkatji walha, thalkatji widi up there • *Nhinarla thalkatji widi Yinimingka.* '[He] lives up there at Innamincka.'

thalkaparlu kangaroo rat (or perhaps bilby) • *Ngala ngarru kathi tjukurruli thana nhinapadipadini, ya thalka-parlu, ya kathi pildra.* 'They only had kangaroo then, and kangaroo rat, and possum.'

thalpa ear, leaf • *Wathi nhutjadu thalpa payirri.* 'That tree's got long leaves.' • *Kathi thukali, walya kalpurru thalpali or walya darlamurruli, ngarru kathi thukali mandrirnanga.* 'We don't spoon it up with a coolibah leaf or with bark, only with a mussel shell.'

    thalpapuru deaf # Yw *thalpakurru*

    thalpapuruka deafen • *Mirrtjali nganha thalpapurukarla.* 'That noise is deafening me.'

thalpa (a) strike (a match); (b) sting # See **katjakatja**.

thalpapada light (fire) • *Maka yundru thalpapadayi!* 'You light the fire!' # See also **wanga**, **pulkapada**, **karadaka**.

thaltha cracked (of ground) # Also **marnka**.

thaltu salt # from Eng

    thaltuwata sea • *Thaltuwatanguda ngala nhunudu padla yundrangudatji.* 'He's from the sea then, from a far country.' # from Eng 'saltwater'

thamba play (Yw) • *Purla, thambathika-yada! Thanaku watja wawinima, walpa thulanyi.* 'Little one, play back this way! So they won't see you at the stranger's humpy.'

    thambaka, thambathambaka play with • *Ngakani ngathu kaburdatji dan.ganhana, pandili nganha nhulu pakininguda. Thambathambakanga.* 'I found my hat that the dog had taken. He was playing with it.'

    thambana dance, play • *Thambana-thikawarrkana nganyi yita ngaka-marra.* 'I was dancing a while ago.' • *Wani thambanini nhutjadu.* 'He's a good dancer.' [or 'He can dance.'] # See also **dranga**.

    thambanawaga, thambanawaga-waga play around

    thambanayukarra dance at night • *Wani ngandra thambanayukarra-nhana.* 'We danced a corroboree last night.'

    thambathambana play • *Muduwa thanadu thambathambanarla.* 'The kids are playing.' • *Walya makayitji nhinawagawaga, kudlayindriyila yini. Makapani thambathambanakani mayi yambarriyi.* 'Don't stay near the fire, you might get burnt. Play away from the fire, out on the flat.'

thambaka see **tjambaka**.

thana they (more than two), the (more than two) • *Paltjapaltjakari thana karlukarlungadi kurranga* *kinipapayitji.* 'They make it strong and put it across the river to catch fish.' • *Mukupika yina thana pitjankatji.* 'Those bony bream are the very bony ones.' • *Man.garri kurnu ngala thana ngalyitji ngarru karruwalildra.* 'There's one girl and all the rest are boys.' • *Karna nhinggikala padlangudatji thana paldritharranhana panina.* 'The people from that country have all died out.'

thanadu they (more than two, there), those (more than two) • *Yiwa thanadu thirrirla nhinggiwangari.* 'Those women are fighting down there.'

thanayi they (more than two, here), these (more than two) • *Thanayildra pakangala ngalyitji, thanayildra (unclear word), thanayildra yarndu.* 'These take a few, and these, and these the same.' • *Ngala thanayi kilkarla, ngarru yarawarrangu thawathawapadipadini ...* 'People now think they used to walk about naked ...'

thandakalini type of lizard # perhaps *Diporiphora winneckei*

thandji bag; pouch # See also **pirli, mirrka, paltja, yakutha.**

thandjipulu policeman # Yw. See also **kandjipulu, pilimpara, pilitjimani, yulya.**

thandra nut in bloodwood tree # possibly the 'bush coconut', an insect gall on the tree, with edible flesh and an edible grub inside; however, the fact that *mardra thandra* (see under **mardra**) means 'bullet' and 'small stone' suggests that *thandra* means the fruit of the bloodwood (which is much smaller than the coconut)

thanggu stand, sit (in tree, of a bird); be (of something that typically stands, such as a tree) • *Nga yarnduldrangu nhinda, pirli ngunthuya mayi,*

minhangadildra, wathi nhutjadu kakaldra, ngala wathi pirna puladu kalpurru thanggurla, yarndu nhinda ngulutji. 'They make the net of such a size that it stretches right across from a coolibah on this side to a big one standing [on the other side].'

thangguka stand (someone, something) up; tail (stock) • *Kathi puluka walpirri miriyi thanggukarlatji.* 'Tailing cattle over the sandhill.'

thanggumini, thangguthawa stop for a minute on the way past (for example, to talk to somebody)

thangguminiwindri stand up and walk away • *Yunka nhunu thangguminiwindrina.* 'He stood up and walked away disgusted.'

thangguna lean (something on something), stand (something) up • *... ya nhunggani yabali ngapala wathi drantha kurrari, blanket-li yinha purrilkatharranga, nga wathi thanggunari pantja thangguni-nyadi nhunu karna.* '... and, in his fear, put a forked log on the other side, and covered it over with a blanket, and stood a stick up so that it would look like a man's knee sticking up.' # See also **wathi thirri.**

thangguthalka stand up • *Thangguthalkana nganyi palthu wawanga. Paningu nhunu.* 'I stood up and looked up the road. He's not coming yet.'

thangguthalkawarra stand right up • *Ngapala pula yadatji yina wanthirnangala nga kurnutji nhunu thangguthalkawarranga wawayindripandhiringu.* 'They were looking for the boomerang. Then one of them stood up and looked down at himself.' • *Ngarrungu thanggu-thalkawarrandji dranyingalatji yadali.* 'The man just stands up and kills [one] with a boomerang.'

thangguthanggu stand; walk about • *Malthi yini mirrkapani thanggu-*

thangguyukarrarla; walya yini pundrali? 'You walk around in the cold with nothing on; aren't you cold?'

thangguthika go to visit • *Nganyi thangguthikana nga walya thana nhinanhinarlayitji, kadlitji nganha kandrininguda.* 'I went to visit them but they weren't there, after sending for me.' • *Thawanhana, yini thanggu-thikanga thannganiyi, karna thulayitji. Parndriyila yina, kurnutji thawarlayi.* 'You went to visit those strangers. They might have killed you, going on your own …'

thangguthikathika be somewhere for a while

thangguwagawaga stand around • *Thawawarranga thangguwaga-waganga, ngala karna nhunu purrinhinarlayi ngari mingkayi.* 'They [emus] go and stand around the hole, while the man hides in it.'

thangguwindri get up to go • *… nganyitji thangguwindringala nganarla thawiningadi.* '… I was just going to go.'

thangka burn up, (start to) burn

thangkaka make (a fire), build up (a fire) • *Ya maka nhulu thangkaka ya thudapandhiringu thapa thayi-ninguda.* 'Then he made a fire and had his supper and went to bed.' • *'Thawarla nganyi, kathi parndri-thikanga.' 'Kawu, kala ngathu maka thangkakarlayi.'* 'I'm going out hunting.' 'OK, for my part I'll get a fire going.'

thangkakathalka light up (fire) • *Ngapala purtuwalthini nhulu purtu kunya-manga thikaminiwarranga warliyitji makala yina thangkaka-thalkanga.* 'Well, [next morning] the swagman rolled up his swag and went back up to the hut, and lit up the fire.'

thangkana burn # Also **ngarrtji**; See also **darra, mangga, pidli** • *Maka nhutjadu thangkanarla.* 'The fire's

burning.' • *Ngandra maka ngala nhunuyardi thangkanarla ngurrangu.* 'Oh! Well this fire's still alive!'

thangu open (mouth); be open (mouth) # SY, Yw • *Marna thangu!* 'Open your mouth!' • *marna thanguri* 'mouth [is] open' # See also **pindri, pirika, piltja**. Note also that MN sometimes pronounced the verb 'to stand' as *thangu* instead of *thanggu*, and it may be that this is that.

thanha them (more than two), the (more than two, object of verb) • *Ngapala palhatji thana thilparingu, karna malkirri thawininguda nga thilpanga thanha palhatji.* 'Then a lot of men go and chase the birds down.' • *Muduwa ngathu thanha wawarla nhinanhinarnanga wathi wartayi.* 'I'm sitting under the tree watching the kids.'

thanhadu them (more than two, there), those (more than two, object of verb)

thanhayi them (more than two, here), these (more than two, object of verb) • *Palha purla pirnanarlayitji, ngapala yarru wathinaritji, marru kadawayi, ngapala thawarnanga puka windri-tharranga ngapa marruyitji palha purla thanhayi mapathikanga.* 'When the young birds are getting big, they build a yard for them on the bank of the lake and then go down into the water and herd the baby birds back [into the yard].'

thanhani tongue • *Thanhani thaparla nhutjadu ngakaniyi.* 'He's poking his tongue out at me.' # See also **tharli, parlpa**.

thani copulate

thanma, thanmathanma swim • *Karirriyi nhutjadu thanmathanmarla.* 'He's swimming in the creek.' • *Pulya, ngapala, karna parrkulu pula thanmaritji yukangatji.* 'It [the bag net] is a small one and two men swim with it to catch [the fish].' # SY *thanma* also 'float'. See also **ngupa**.

thanmapada swim across

thanngani their, theirs, belonging to them (more than two); them (more than two) (as in 'for them', 'with them' etc.) • *Ngapala ngapa marndrinilatji thanngani yulpu thawiningadi, padla yundrawaka ngapapaniyi.* '[They use] their waterbags when they go on a journey in remote waterless country.'

thannganiyi their, theirs, belonging to them (more than two, here); with them (more than two, here) • *Nga yarnduldrangu ngathutji wawana yina dunkarlayitji nga yabalildrangu winkanga yadamaningadila thannganiyi thudayukarranga.* 'And I saw you going out and I was frightened too and I ducked off down to the horses and spent the night with them.'

thannganitjadu their, theirs, belonging to them (more than two, there); them (more than two, there) (as in 'for them', 'with them' etc.) • *Kathi thambaka ngathu kilkarla; ngathu wakanarla thannganitjadu kathi tjipiyitji, minhayangadi yina, yamunu thana mulpiningadi, tjidali.* 'I know all about sheep; I work with those sheep, for whatsaname, for them to cut their wool, the shearers.' • *Kalala yita yandhaka thannganitjaduyi* or *Kalala yini yandha thanngatjaduyi.* 'You take a turn at talking to them.'

thanpathanpa dotterel # Also **digirdigilyarra**.

thantjiyipa town • *Walyala ngani purrkapadayi wilpadalitji, ngarrungu pula thawandji, thantjiyipangadi, nganyi nhinapadapadarlayi nhinggikala Kinipapayi.* 'We mightn't have got across with the wagon so they went on without me, to the town, and I stayed there at the river.'

thanu, thanuthanu in the middle, halfway; between • *Thawanhana nhunu, mandakurranga thanu.* '[He] was coming, but he stopped halfway.' • *Kurrapandhi nhinggudu thanuthanu.* 'Put it down there, in the middle.' • *Nhutjadu nhinanhinarla yiwa thanuthanu.* 'He's sitting between the two women.' • *Pandi thanuthanu nhunu nhinarla.* 'He's sitting in the middle of a mob of dogs.' # See also **marnda**.

thapa (a) poke out tongue • *Thanhani thaparla nhutjadu ngakaniyi.* 'He's poking his tongue out at me.' (b) drink, suck, lick # SY, Yw, H, Nh • (SY) *Ngama nhuluyi thaparla muduwali.* 'The baby's sucking the breast.' # See **yiba**, **pardaparda**.

thapathapa lick

marna thapa kiss # SY

thapa supper • *Ya maka nhulu thangkaka ya thudapandhiringu thapa thayininguda.* 'Then he made a fire and had his supper and went to bed.' # from Eng

thapini shoulder # See also **kilkirri**, **pilpiri**, **pinyi**, **wiliwili**.

tharla name # SY, Yw, Nh. See **maya**.

tharli tongue # SY, Yw (but not H). See **thanhani**.

tharra fly • *Pirnapirna thanhayi, tharriningaditji nganarlayi, purndaparndringa kudlanga yina thayiyindrirnangatji.* 'The biggest ones, that are nearly ready to fly, they kill and cook and eat.'

tharraka float # Yw. See also **mindithanma**, **ngupa**.

tharrapada fly across

tharrapandhi fly down • *Ngapala thana tharrapandhiri yada, ngala karna nhunu(?) wadayindrirla thadripalapala yadatji warrkanga.* 'Well, when they fly down towards the net, the men waiting there on both sides of the river throw their boomerangs.'

tharrathalka fly up

tharratharra hurry

tharratharrawindri hurry away

tharrawagawaga fly in circles • *Palha pawayi tharrawagawagarla.* 'The hawks are circling.'

tharrawindri, tharrawinditharra fly away

tharralku duck (probably teal duck)

tharu father-in-law, husband's father, wife's father # A type of uncle. '*Tharu*, your uncle, the oldest fellow too, way back. They can't go into their camp. You keep away because he's your *tharu*.' See also **ngama**.

thata grease

thatathata, thatamindji greasy • *Mirrkapiki thatamindji yinhadu yada ngunyi.* 'Hand me that greasy rag.'

thathi step cut in tree trunk

thatji (a) clitoris; (b) stone knife • *Kathi yintjadu thatjili dramapandhi.* 'Cut the meat with a knife.' # See **thurla**.

thatjithatji tool for making (or grooving?) boomerang # SY

thawa go, walk, travel • *Yilakadi yini thawarla?* 'Where are you going?' • *Karlukarlungadi nganyi thawarla.* 'I'm going fishing.' • *Karna nhunu thawalapurra mukathudathawanga.* 'This man, a long time ago, was travelling, and camped along the way.' • *Wilpadali nganyi thawalapurra, mandrithawari nganha walypalali.* 'Once I was travelling in a wagon — some white men picked me up.' • *Ngapala thana kathi warruwitji-ngaditji thawari, kathi warruwitji yukatji parndringa.* 'They also go out for emus, to kill emus.' • *Ngandjarri thana nganya thawathalkarlala, nga walya ngandjarritji warlkanga, minhaya kara.* 'Those clouds come up, but it won't rain. I don't know why.'

thawaka, thawawindri go away • *Thawaka, nga purnunukini pani.* 'Go away, don't tease me.' • *Ngapala nhunu purtu mandrimandrirnanga milyaruyi, nga thawawindringa ngatjada kurnungadila, ...* 'Well, he packed his swag in the dark and walked on to the other camp, ...' # See also **yundrana**.

thawakaldri go again

thawaminiwarra come for a while

thawapada go across (to the other side) • *Nga thawapadanga thundiyi thannganiya thudaringu.* 'They went across to the island and camped with them.'

thawardakapada go across, go at an angle • *Palthuyi ngathu thina wawana, thawardakapadininguda nhunu.* 'I saw the tracks on the road, where he'd gone across.'

thawathawa walk around • *Ngala thanayi kilkarla, ngarru yarawarrangu thawathawapadipadini ...* 'People now think they used to walk about naked ...'

thawawarra come, arrive • *Ey walpi yini thawawarranhaneyey?* 'Hey, when did you get here?' # Also **kuthiwarra**.

thawirritji, thawurritji black bream

thawulu type of duck, possibly spoonbill duck (= blue-winged shoveller) # SY

thayamarni dogwood # perhaps *Alectryon oleifolius*. SY *ngamikularri*

thayarri tea tree # See also **kayarri**. One of these may be a mistake. SY *wawu*

thayi eat; chew (tobacco) • *Kathi thungga ngathu thayina.* 'I ate rotten meat.'

thayithayi chew • *Ngunku thayi-thayini nhutjadu.* 'He's always chewing pitchery.'

thayiyindri, thayithayiyindri feed (yourself), have a feed • *Pirnapirna* thanhayi, tharriningaditji nganarlayi, purndaparndringa kudlanga yina thayiyindrirnangatji. 'The biggest ones, that are nearly ready to fly, they kill and cook and eat.'

thayi, mardrathayi grinding stone

thayipilthirri chips from making of grinding stone • *Minha thayi-pilthirri ngala yundru drikarla kudrikudriningudatji.* 'You call the ones that have been smashed up *thayipilthirri.*'

Thayipilthirringuda Yandruwandha (or one group of them, the Innamincka people. So named because they come from the country where the quarries where the large grinding stones were made are located, and so from the country where all the chips left from shaping the stones are lying.)

Thayipin.gini Typingine Waterhole # Yw

Thayipingginyi waterhole on Patchawara Creek (?)

thayirri wind, dust # SY, Nh • (SY) *Thayirri nhunuyi ngakarla.* 'Wind's coming up now.' # See **kunuputha, puthurru, kundangali, wathara.**

thidharri baby • *Muduwa thidharri dan.ganhana.* '[That woman] had a baby yesterday.' • *Thidharri yini yingkilapurra; pirnapirnala ngala yini kayiditji.* 'You used to cry [a lot] when you were a baby, but you're big now.' # See also **muduwa.**

thidi see **thirri.**

thidri jealous; jealousy

thidrili jealous # SY

thidri ngunyingunyi make someone jealous

thidripika jealous

thika back; go back, come back • *Kathi tjukurru ngathu wawana thawarnanga nhinggiyingadi, parrkulu pulayi thika* 'I saw some kangaroos when I was coming here; two back here' • *Ngala*

nhunu yadamani mapayindrirlayi milimanityéyi thikaringu yada, ya warlitji kuthiwarranga ya yadamani nhulu karrathikathikarnanga thanha windripadanga.* 'Meanwhile the mailman was rounding up his horses, and then he came back to the hut and tied up all the horses and went in.' • *Pirritjampanarlayi nhunu karrtjipandhinga pulyatji nhunu nga thikanhinanga thundingadi ...* 'If a little one gets tired it turns around and heads back to the island ...'

thikathika, thikawarra go back, come back • *Mirni ngaldra wawarla man.garri nhani thikawarriningadi.* 'We'll watch for her to come home.' • *Ngapala palha pula dranyindji, nga yadatji nhunu thikawarranga ngapayi warlkapandhinga.* 'They hit a bird, and the boomerang came back down and fell into the water.'

thilbirrutja budgerigar # See also **thilinkurru, pinyanku.**

thili side # See also **thinka, warra.**

thiliyi at the side • *Kapada thiliyi ngakani nhinanga.* 'Come and sit beside me.'

thili two • *Ngapala yingkarnangala thili yabangunyiyindrininguda ngala pula walypalathili.* 'Well, they both laughed then, the two white men, at the way they had frightened one another.' # Usually used as a suffix. See **parrku, pulpa.**

thilinkurru budgerigar # See also **thilbirrutja, pinyanku.**

Thilka Tilcha Waterhole

thilpa chase, frighten • *Ngapala palhatji thana thilparingu, karna malkirri thawininguda nga thilpanga thanha palhatji.* 'Then a lot of men go and chase the birds down.' # See also **kadi.**

thilpathilpa make go • *Pudlupudlu ngathu nhandu yinhayi thilpathilparla, pirritjampanarla nhuniyi.* 'I can't get this horse going because he's tired.'

thilpawarra notify

thilpi, thilpithilpi spike, thorn

    wathi thilpi spiky stick

    wathi thilpithilpi spiky stick (as with a lot of twigs broken off, leaving spiky ends)

thilthirri centipede • *Thilthirri nhutjadu pada darlamurruyi.* 'There's a centipede under the bark.'

thiltja sinew • *Thiltja ngarnmayindrirla nganyi ngurra nhininguda.* 'I've got a cramp from sitting a long time.' • *Ngapala ngapatji walthayindringangu maltjitji kurnu karrininguda thiltjali.* 'They carry water in it, after tying up one leg with sinew.' • *Mirrkatji milpirnanga, marndumarndukana pulhu tjukurru thiltjali.* 'They sew two [skins] together with kangaroo sinew [to make] the blanket.'

thimbiltji type of yam # It is described as two or three inches long, like a sweet potato but white, dug up on claypans. • *Thimbiltji pakurnanga kulanga yarnduldrangu makamuduli.* 'They dig *thimbiltjis* and cook them the same way, in hot ashes.'

thina foot; track of foot • *Mardrali nganyi parndriyindrina thina.* 'I hit my foot on a rock.' • *Mayi ngapala nhunu thikangaldranguya ngala nhunu walypalatji thawarlayi yita thinalildra.* 'Well he went back while this white man was going that way, on foot.' • *Palthuyi ngathu thina wawana, thawardakapadininguda nhunu.* 'I saw the tracks on the road, where he'd gone across.'

    thinamitji toes • *Thinamitji nganha nhuludu nhangkana.* 'He stepped on my toe.'

    thina ngunpurru toenail, claw

thinapara spur # *para* from Eng 'spur'

thinapirri toenails

thinaputa boots • *Thinaputapanindra nhunu miniwindriri yabali, ...* 'He ran away without his boots, frightened, …' # *puta* from Eng

thinathundru sole

thinawaduka float off into the air #Lit. 'foot-hang'. Used in a description of what happens to souls after death. Also **milimiliwaduka**. See also **Palkarrakarani**.

thinawarta heel

thinathina type of frog, in sandhills # = *durrkuwarnta* (TG)

thinba chisel, cut and shape (wood), make (boomerang), 'clean' (or finish) (a spear) • *Marlkali ngathu thinbanhana.* 'I made it [a boomerang] out of mulga.' • *Ngapala pula yada thinbari nga palhangadi thawanga.* 'Well, they made a boomerang and went out hunting birds.' • *Ngapala yina wathi thinbanari mandawarra, ya wirni thurrpanari yina mulhudungadilatji nhunu thawa-thalkiningadi warrkanga wathilatji yina karrtjikarrtjimari.* 'Well, he would cut and shape a stick from a plum bush and tie a string to it and whirl it around, so that someone would come and leave some food for him.' • *Parndrithikana nhulu windra, thinbarla nhulu.* 'He cut the spear and he's cleaning it now.'

    thinbithinbini chisel, adze

thindrithindri willy wagtail

thinga pull; lead (a horse) # Also **duka**

    thingarduda drag

    thingapada pull in • *Ngapala pula thingapadanga yada.* 'They pull it [the net] in.'

thinka log # See also **wathi, maka warnta, muku**.

thinka side # See **diparri, pangki, thili, warra**.

    thinkali sideways • *Thinkali nganyi thudanhinarla.* 'I'm lying on my side.'

thinka dead # Also **nhadi**.

thinkaka kill • *Wawawawana
yintjadu, thinkakayila yina nhuludu.*
'Watch him, or he'll kill you.' # See
also **nhadika, parndri**.

thintipidi elbow # SY, Yw. See
ngunamarnda.

thipari sand • *Thiparili nganha thina
kudlarla; makamakali nganha thina
kudlarla.* 'The sand burns my feet; the
hot [sand] burns my feet.' # See also
padla.

thipi alive • *Matjanguda nhutjadu, ay
thipingu nhunudu.* 'He's very old, but
he's still alive.' • *Ngarru ngala thana
ngapali nhinapadipadinitji. Ngawu,
karna paltjapaltja nhinanga, walya
mundjanini, ngarru nhinanga thipingu.*
'They only used to live on water [they
didn't have tea]. Yes, they were
strong people, never got sick; they
were really alive.'

thipinhina live

thipi or **thipiwa** sugar # SY, Yw. See
ngapa palyakini.

thirri hit, fight; aggression • *Thirri kara
nhunu thawanhana.* 'He must have
come for a fight.' • *Yiwa thanadu
thirrirla nhinggiwangari.* 'Those
women are fighting down there.'
• *Walya thana thirripadipadinitji,
pani, ngarru pinyayi, karna thula
nhukuwanguda yada thawarnanga
parndrithikangatji, minhayatji
pinyalitji.* 'They never used to fight,
except in a war. Strangers would
come from over there [in their country]
to kill and then go back. That's
what they used to call war.'
• *Nharrathithangurru, thirri kara
nhunu thawanhana.* 'He went with a
shield [and other weapons], must have
been looking for a fight.' # Functions
both as a noun and as a verb. However,
in sentences like the last it has never
been heard with any inflectional suffix.
Heard as *thidi* in Yw.

thirripirna, thirripurra cheeky

thirrithirrina be wild, be sulky, be
savage • *Nhuludu windrali warrkananhana. Nguthuyi nhunu thirrithirrina-
nhana.* 'He speared him while he
was wild over his brother.' • *Pandi
karranhana yintjadu kathipani,
yarndungudala thuru mawa thirrithirrinarlatji.* 'The dog was tied up
without any meat, that's how he got
starved, and that's what made him
savage.' # SY *yunkana*

thirri, palha thirri chicken hawk
• *Ngapala palhatji kartiwirriringu.
Minhayapuru yina? Palha thirripuru.*
'Then the birds dive down. What for?
Because [they think] it is a chicken
hawk.'

thirri, thirritha, thirrithirri cotton #
from Eng 'thread'? • *Ngapala thana
karrparnanga thirrithirri-nyadi yina
walypalali kurrarlatji thana, thirrila
karrpiningadi mirrka.* 'Then they
weave it just like the cotton white
people use for making their clothes.'

thirripurdu feather, down

Thirriwarra Tirrawarra Waterhole # in
Matja country

thirrtha dog # SY, AWH. See **pandi,
thutjutju**.

thita knot (on tree), bump, knob

thitathita rough, knobby, knotty
• *mardra thitathita* 'rough stone or
rock' • *thilpi thitathita* 'a knotty stick'
See also **kurtukurtu**.

thitha, pidrithitha crotch, fork of legs
thitha also used in the formation of
other words denoting something flat
and hard: *murnathitha* 'chest',
nharrathitha 'shield'. See **drantha**.

**thithidika, thithithithidika, thithi-
yithidika** tickle • *Mirni ngathu
yinhayi muduwa thithithirrikarla
yingkaningadi.* 'I'm tickling this boy
to make him laugh.' See also
kilyikilyika.

thiwi blossoms # SY

thiwildraka magpie

thuburu bullroarer

thuda sleep, camp • *Nga thawapadanga thundiyi thannganiya thudaringu.* 'They went across to the island and camped with them.' # See also **muka**.

thudanhina be lying

thudapada lie inside

thudapandhi lie down • *Ngala nhunu thudapandhinga nhinggiyi maka warrakurnula.* 'Then he lay down on his side of the fire.' • *Ya maka nhulu thangkaka ya thudapandhiringu thapa thayininguda.* 'Then he made a fire and had his supper and went to bed.' # Also **yukarrapandhi**.

thudathawa, thudathawa-thuda-thawa, thudathawayukarra spend nights on the road while travelling • *Thawalapurra milimani nhunu Tibuparanguda, nga thudathawanga marndayitji Thanangarrpira.* 'A long time ago, a mailman was travelling from Tibooburra, and he spent the night halfway, at Tenappera.' • *Ya thudathawa-thudathawanga marri-parrkulu kara marriparrkulu kara thudathawari ngapapani, ngarru tjukurru darlali walthininguda.* 'They might have only two or three nights on the road with no water, apart from what they carry in the waterbag.'

thudathudanhina lie awake ? # SY

thudayukarra lie at night, camp the night • *Thudayukarranga wadarnanga thakumani ngalyila.* 'He camped overnight while he waited for some stockmen.' • *Nga yarnduldrangu ngathutji wawana yina dunkarlayitji nga yabalildrangu winkanga yadamaningadila thannganiyi thudayukarranga.* 'And I saw you going out and I was frightened too and I ducked off down to the horses and spent the night with them.'

thudri bury • *Kuldru pakuri, thudringatji nhaditji ...* '[They] dig a hole, and bury the dead person ...' # See **nhamba**.

thudu, kathi thudu euro, wallaroo # SY. Also **yuru**. TG said there were none in their country.

thuka hole, well # See also **mingka, thuka, wirlpa, kudru**.

thuka mussel • *Minhaya warrkarnanga pirditjirranga thanha, kathi thukali.* 'They cut them [bulrushes] down and strip them with a mussel [shell].' • *Kathi thukali ngala thayirnangatji marnangadikinitji mandrirnanga.* 'We eat it by spooning it into our mouths with a mussel [shell].' # See also **kudi**.

thukathayini, thukali thayini water rat • *Ngala yamali thana ngunipika kurraringu, kalkayi, marripathi mini-pandhingayayi mandrithalkanga karlukarlulatji, ngampurru kara, ya kathi nharramindji kara, ya palha kara, ya kathi thanayi — minhaya yina, kathi — mayatji nganyi kurri-tharrarlala, kathi thukathayini, thana drikalapurrayi thanha.* 'Well, with the cross net, they put it down in the daytime, in the afternoon, and next morning they run down and pull up the fish — maybe yellowbelly, or maybe a turtle, or maybe a bird, or maybe one of those animals — what is it? — I forget the name — mussel eater they used to call them.'

thuka carry • *Walya ngandra yurarla paldriningadi nhinggiyi, thuka-thikanga ngala ngandra.* 'We don't want him to die here, we'll have to carry him home.' # Also **waltha**.

thukayindri ride (a horse) • *Thawarla nganyi Malkanpangadi, nhandulu, thukayindrirnanga.* 'I'm going to Innamincka on horseback.' • *Yadamani ngathu yintjadu thuka-yindringatji. Pakitjampa yina* *nhutjadu, walya nganyi yabali nhunggatjaduyi.* 'I'm going to ride that horse. He's a buckjumper but I'm not frightened of him.' # The word for horse most commonly takes the instrumental suffix, *-li* or *-lu*, but has been heard with locative *-yi* and with no suffix. The word for the rider can be nominative or ergative.

thukayindrini good rider

thuku back • *Yadamani thukuli nganyi thawanga.* 'I'm going to go on horseback.' • (SY) *walpa thukuyi* 'at the back of the house' # See also **thumu, durru**.

thula stranger; strange, not belonging • *Thaltawatanguda nhutjadu karna thula.* 'He's a stranger, from the sea.' • *Yarndukala ngali yinha thula-thulakanhana ay karna nganggalitji nhutjadu.* 'How could we reckon he was a stranger, when he's one of our own people.' • (SY) *Kathi thula warrka, karru kurnungadi.* 'Leave that other fellow's meat alone.' # *Thula* here is the opposite of *nganggali*.

padla thula strange country # SY

thulka wear • *Ay kabuta ngapirimalangi yini thulkarla!* 'Hey, you're wearing your father's hat!' # = *kadli, thurrka*

thumba point, show • *Ngapakurna yundru wawari yintjadu, thumbarla ngathuna, mathanhukada nganha nhinggiwa ngapakurnayi.* 'That waterhole that you see, that I'm showing you; that's the waterhole where I got bitten [by a snake].' # MN (SY, Yw) did not accept this meaning, and said it means 'to call'. • *Windra thana thumbarla Yandruwandhali.* 'The Yandruwandha call a spear "windra".' See also **pipa**.

thumbalka, thumbatharra, thumbalkatharra show (by pointing) • *Kapada thumbalkarla ngathuna kardratji pakuningadi, padla yundru kilkiningadilatji.* 'Come on, I'll show

you where to dig the yams, so you'll know the place.' # Also heard as **thumbakatharra**.

thumbalkathikathika, thumbalkawagawaga show around

thumu back • *walpa thumuyi* 'at the back of the humpy' # See also **thuku, durru**.

thundi island • *Ngala karna thana nhinarlayi, thundiyi.* 'Meanwhile there were some blackfellows camping on an island.' • *Pirritjampanarlayi nhunu karrtjipandhinga pulyatji nhunu nga thikanhinanga thundingadi ...* 'If a little one gets tired it turns around and heads back to the island ...'

Thundilawarani Lake Toontoonawaranie

thundru stomach • *Mulhudu ngathu pirna thayipandhina, thundrutji nganyi kimanarla.* 'I ate too much and my stomach is swollen.' • *thundru ngarnma* or *thundru ngarnma thiltjali* (also *pangkithirri ngarnma*) 'to have a stitch' # Also **thuru**.

thundruka, thundruthuka lie on back

thundrumindji pregnant • *Thawanhana nhani, karnayi nhungganiyi, ngapala nhani thikawarralarla thundrumindjila.* 'She went off with that bloke, and now she's pregnant.'

thundruputha diver, pied shag

thundruyilka miscarry, lose (unborn) baby # Also **marayilka**.

thunga grind • *Pawangadi, pawa thungini ngunyirnanga ya ngarduparndrini ngunyirnanga.* 'They gave grinding stones, for seeds, and nardoo pounders.' • *Wikawikarnanga, pinakanga, ya thungangalatji, nga thayiyindringala yartunanga, ngapali ngunkukininguda.* 'They clean it, rock it, and grind it and then, after mixing it with water and making it into a ball, they eat their fill.' # = *dringa, kururrupa*

thungga, thunggathungga rotten, stinking • *Kathi thungga ngathu thayina.* 'I ate rotten meat.' # Also **kutawirri.**

thunggana rot, go bad, get mouldy • *Punggu murrpiningudatji ngapala kurrari ngapayi̠, wiki parrkulu kara, thungganiningadi.* 'They cut the bow-vine and put it in water for maybe two weeks, so that it will rot.'

Thuntjimintji placename, on the Cooper just downstream from Innamincka. # 'There's an island there.'

thuntjirri sneeze # SY, Yw

thupa soap # from Eng

thupari milk bush # plant 90–120cm high with three-cornered fruit

thupu smoke • *Thupuli nganinha muntjirla.* '[The fire]'s smothering us with smoke.' # See also **muki.**

thupu ngana (fire) smoke, be smoky # Yw

thupulu widower

thupurru heart # See also **ngarangara.**

thurla knife, stone knife, tula # SY. See **nalyba, thatji.**

thurna copi, white clay

thurratji Mitchell grass?

Thurratji Toolache Waterhole

thurrka gully, gutter # SY and Yw *ngarli*

thurrka singe the hair off

thurrka wear • *Ngala karrukarrulitji ngarru wirni yamunungulra, paladi wirnina thurrkarnanga ngarru pulyaldra.* 'On the other hand, the old men only wore a small string.' # See also **kadli, thulka.**

Thurrkapada placename, on Cooper's Creek # 'a crossing going into town'

Thurrkapirnta placename, a creek joining the Cooper at Thurrkapada or Ngunapirnta (?)

thurrpa ashes # See also **mudu.**

thurrpathurrpa ashy • *Thayiyindirnanga yartunarnangalatjini, walya padlapadla walya thurrpathurrpa, mardramitjingudatji.* 'They eat until they are full, [meat] from the stones, not dirty or ashy.'

thurrpa roll up, spin • *Ngapala kundikilili thana thurrparitji.* 'Then they roll it [the string] into a ball.' • *Ngala yamunu ngala thana wirnikamuratji thurrpininguda, yarnduldrangu, yarndu thana pirlitji, minhaya, karlukarlungadi.* 'They spin human hair into string, just as they make the string for fishing nets.' # See also **nhurrpa, kunyama, nhapi, pampuka.**

thurrpana spin (used for spinning something round and for spinning fibre into string) • *Ngapala yina wathi thinbanari mandawarra, ya wirni thurrpanari yinha mulhudungadilatji nhunu thawathalkiningadi warrkanga wathilatji yina karrtjikarrtjimari.* 'Well, he would cut and shape a stick from a plum bush and tie a string to it and whirl it around, so that someone would come and leave some food for him.' • *Wirnikamalka purupurriningudalatji thana parndringa* (word not clear) *wirningadi nga thurrpanga* ... 'They tease it up and make it into string by pounding it and then spinning it ...'

Thurrpayi Tooroopie Waterhole

thurrpu whirlwind # Also **makumarda.**

thuru belly, stomach • *thuru mawa* 'empty belly' # See also **thundru.**

thutjutju dog • *Kapada ngaldra thutjutjuli thawarla, tjukurru parndringa.* 'Come on, we're going with the dogs to kill a kangaroo.' • *Minhangadi thutjutju nhuliyi ngurra parndrirla yinhayi?* 'Why is this fellow always hitting his dog?' # *Pandi* was the preferred word for 'dog'. *Thutjutju* is perhaps more correctly 'pup'. See **tjutjutju, thirrtha**.

thuwa store • *Kuditharranhana nganyi thuwangaditji thawiningadi.* 'I forgot to go to the store.' # from Eng

thuwakipa storekeeper

tjada boomerang # Yw, H, Nh. See **yada**.

tjadla saddle # from Eng

tjalka be open (eyes) # Yw • *Kali nhunuyi mitji tjalkarlala.* 'His eyes are open.' # See **pindri, pirika, dingayindri, piltja**.

tjalparri pointed; sharp # Also **tjarrkarla**.

   tjalparrika sharpen • *Thiltja thana tjukurru pardrarla, ngapala thanadu pirditjirraritji nga palha mukuli tjalparrikininguda wirlpakanga nyinditji.* 'They hold the kangaroo sinew and strip it and poke the holes in the skin with a bird bone that has been sharpened.'

   tjalpatjalparri sharp • *mimi tjalpa-tjalparri windra* 'sharp point on the spear'

tjambaka, kathi tjambaka sheep • *Thayipadipadini ngani tjukurru; kathi tjampakala ngani thayirla.* 'We used to eat kangaroos, but now we eat sheep.' • *Kathi thambaka ngathu kilkarla; ngathu wakanarla thannganitjadu kathi tjipiyitji, minhayangadi yina, yamunu thana mulpiningadi, tjidali.* 'I know all about sheep; I work with those sheep, for whatsaname, for them to cut their wool, the shearers.' # = *tjipi.* BK,Yw *thambaka*, TG, H *tjambaka*. Loan word, but ultimate source unknown.

tjampa soft # H See **danthu, miltjamiltja**.

tjampitji pannikin # Yw. From Eng, probably 'jam pot'. See also **paynputu**.

tjapura pitchery bag • *Ngarru ngathu pirli tjapura yina wawalapurratji, thana drakininguda.* 'I only saw the pitchery bags they wove, a long time ago.' # Also described as 'half-moon bags they used to crochet'.

tjarnma shine • *Wawarla ngathu minha kara tjarnmarlayi.* 'I can see something shining.' # See also **para, dintji**.

tjarrkarla also heard *tjarrkari* (SY), *tjarrkula* (Yw) sharp # The endings of the two SY forms suggest that it may be a verb. See also **tjalparri**.

tjata shirt

tjawurra trousers

tjawutjawu carelessly, 'anyhow' # Yw

tjiba drink # Yw. The usual word in Yw seems to be *thapa*. See also **yiba**.

tjida shearer # from Eng • (see **tjipi**)

tjimada sister-in-law # Yw. See **yimadi**.

tjimpa black # Yw, H

tjinbiri scar

tjindra grandfather, father's father, (presumably also) grandchild, man's son's child, brother's son's child

tjindra chin # Yw. = **nganka**. Since *tjindra* also is a kinship term, it seems that touching the chin may be a sign-language way of saying this kinship term. (In Alyawarr the sign for father's father involves touching under the chin. Very little is known of hand-signs in Yandruwandha.)

tjin.gini beefwood (*Grevillea striata*) # Also **pirnta**.

tjingka laugh # Yw, H. • *Watja tjingka, nhungganinyi.* 'Don't laugh at him.' See **yingka**.

tjipi, kathi tjipi sheep # from Eng • *tjipi nhiwa* 'ewe' • *Kathi thambaka ngathu kilkarla; ngathu wakanarla thannga-nitjadu kathi tjipiyitji, minhayangadi yina, yamunu thana mulpiningadi, tjidali.* 'I know all about sheep; I work with those sheep, for whatsaname, for them to cut their wool, the shearers.' # See **tjampaka**.

tjirarri, tjiradi gum (from tree) # SY *ngulyi*

tjiri spring # ?, compare **ngapatjili**
• *Ngapa nhuniyi tjiri pararla.* 'There's a spring here.'

tjirra strip, peel off (for example, bark) # After you cut a gum tree down you bruise it all over and strip the bark off. See **pirditjirra**.

tjirrayindri get skinny

tjirri willow (type of Acacia) # grey willow in hilly country (?) # See also **parlayila**.

tjiwara woman # Yw, H. See **yiwa**.

tjukurru kangaroo • *Tjukurru ngathu windrali warrkanana.* 'I speared a kangaroo with a spear.' • *Kathi tjukurrutji, ngarru wathi windralildra warrkanarnanga.* 'As for kangaroos, one way is to just kill them with a spear.' • *Kathi tjukurru-nyadi thana walypalali, minhaya nganarla mayi, pirtipirtikarla darla yamunupani.* 'If they tanned the kangaroo skin with the fur removed, like the white men do, it would go red.'

tjulbi drip (water), leak (water)

Tjulkumindji place name (near Cutrabelbo Waterhole)

tjumbudu wild plum # vine, 30cm high, small fruit, in sandhills

tjumbutjurrkuru wild plum # similar to *tjumbudu*, but grows on hills

tjumpunya waxbill, zebra finch # or possibly swallow, see **pulyurru nyununyunu**.

tjumpurra waxbill, zebra finch

tjundurru crippled # SY

tjuru brain(?) # See **kuka thangka, puwa**.

tjurumindji sensible

tjuruntjuru marrow (of bone)

tjutama shoot # from Pidgin 'shootem', from Eng; see **dranyi**.

tjutjutju pup # SY. Compare **thutjutju**.

W

wadamarta (steel) axe # SY, Yw

wada, wadanhina wait for, await
• *Wadarla ngali yinha, ...* 'We're waiting for him, ...'
• *Thudayukarranga wadarnanga thakumani ngalyila.* 'He camped overnight while he waited for some stockmen.' • *Wadana ngathu thawawarriningadi kara nhukuyi thana, ay paningu.* 'I waited for them to come, but nobody yet.' # Often used with *mirni*, as in: *Mirni wada thawarlayi thana.* 'Wait till they go.' or: *Mirni wada, ngandjarri murdiningadi.* 'Wait till the rain stops.' # Yw and SY *kalka*

wadawada sit around waiting

wadayindri wait • *Mirni nganyi wadayindringa, puthakurnulatji nhunu thikiningadi, kara.* 'I'll wait for him to come back another time, maybe.'
• *Ngapala thana tharrapandhiri yada, ngala karna nhunu(?) wadayindrirla thadripalapala yadatji warrkanga.* 'Well, when they fly down towards the net, the men waiting there on both sides of the river throw their boomerangs.'

wadja or **wadji** (awake?) # H

wadjina wake up # H. See **yirrtji**.

wadjaka wake (someone) up # H

wadjina white woman # from Eng 'white gin'. Also **wadlumpada**.

wadla heap, pile # See also **kini**.

wadlaka heap up, pile up • *Padla ngathu yinha wadlakarla.* 'I'm piling up the sand into a heap.'

wadlangurru, walangurru type of plant # perhaps related to pigweed; a vine or prostrate plant, in flat sandy country, for example at the edge of a swamp.

It has black seeds, gathered when the plant is dying. • *Ngala pawa ngala kalildra dingarnanga, pawa kalpurru, pawa wadlangurru, pawa mitjimpa, pawa ngadli, pawa pidriyiltharri.* 'Then they used to grind seeds as well — coolibah seeds, wadlangurru seeds, puppa-grass seeds, pigweed seeds, frosty-arse seeds.'

wadlumpada white woman • *Nhandu nhandra wawarla wadlumpadali.* 'The white woman is looking at the horses.' # probably from Eng 'white lubra'. Also **wadjina**.

wadu hang

waduka (a) hang, be hanging # BK; (b) hang (something up) # SY • *Kathi yinhaku waduka; thirrthali thayiyi.* 'Hang the meat up, or the dog will eat it.'

waduwaduka hang upside down (like a bat)

waduwadukanmapandhi hang (your head)

waga move, shift • *wagari walarringadi* 'shifting into the shade' • *Wagaka yita!* 'Move over!' # This -ka is 'away', not causative.

wagaka, wagalka move over (yourself); move something, shift • *Ngalaaku, wagakanga kara ngathu yintjadu.* 'I don't know, maybe I can shift it.' • *Kali ngathu yinha wagalkana.* 'I shifted him.'

wagawindri move away (to live)

waka a word or ending that sometimes follows a word that tells where or which one; its meaning is not clear # Compare also **kanta, walha, widi** • *Karirri(yi?) pandhiwaka karlukarlu mandriyindrirla.* 'He's down at the creek fishing.' • *Minha kathi kara nhutjaduwaka.* 'There's some sort of animal over there.' • *Thawana thanawaka karawarrakadi.* 'They went north.' • *Ngapala ngapa marndrinilatji thanngani yulpu thawiningadi, padla*

yundrawaka ngapapaniyi. '[They use] their waterbags when they go on a journey in remote waterless country.'

waka, marna waka tooth • *Pandi nhutjadu marna waka madlantji.* 'That dog's got bad teeth.' # Also **marnardraku, dida**.

waka muku grinders, molars

waka work (noun)

wakaka make work • *Pidipidili nhulu wakakarla yintjadu.* 'He's working it [his horse] hard.'

wakana work (verb) • *Ngarnda-parlungi nganyi wakananhukada, nhinggikala.* 'I worked on Arrabury before.'

wakapurra hard worker

wakarramuku south # SY, Yw. See **mulhapundra**.

wakarri back of neck, nape # SY. See **purnda**.

wakiri see **kawalka**.

waku lame

wakuwaku catfish

wala grinding stone # the large one. SY. See also **mardra nhiwa**.

walangurru see **wadlangurru**.

walarri shade, shadow, reflection • *Walarriyi ngali nhuliyi pirripirrili nhinarla.* 'Me and this white fellow sitting in the shade here.' • *Walarri nganyi wawayindrirla ngapayi.* 'I can see myself in the water.' • *Walarri nganggaliyi nhunu yabali ngananhana.* 'His own shadow frightened him.' # See also **nguya**.

walawalarri shady, having plenty of shade

walha a word or ending that sometimes follows a word that tells where or which one; its meaning is not clear # Compare also **kanta, waka, widi** • *thalkatji walha* 'up there' • *Thawana nganyi kathi mandrithikanga nhungga-niyiwalha.* 'I went and got some meat from him.'

walhini boy ('16–17 years')

waliyuka or **waluyuka** type of water bird 'little blue crane' (white-faced heron?) # SY

walki, walkithalka climb • *Wathi payirriyi nganyi walkinhana kathi pildrangadi.* 'I climbed a big tree for a possum.' # See also **kari, kathi**.

walkithalkapada climb over

walpa humpy • *Minha nganarla yini nhinggudu muduwa, walpakurnuyitji? Dunka yada mayi!* 'What are you doing there, kid, in someone else's house? Come on out!' • *Walpangadi yada paka purtutji yinggani ngandjarripuru.* 'You'd better bring your swag inside in case it rains.' # See also **walparda, mambu, punga**.

walpakuku the inside of the humpy • *Yambarriyi ngali nhuludu yandha-yandhanhana, ngarlawu(?) kurnulitji nhulu ngalinha ngararlayi, walpakukunguda.* 'He and I talked outside, and someone else was listening to us from inside the humpy.'

walpamarna the front of the humpy • *Minhangadi nhunuyi walpamarnayi thanggurla?* 'What is he standing in front of the humpy for?'

walpanggarra north wind # Sometimes used for 'north'

walparda humpy # Yw. Also **walpa**. See also **mambu, punga**.

walpi when? • *Ey walpi yini thawa-warranhaneyey?* 'Hey, when did you get here?' • *Walpila yina ngathu wawangatji?* 'When will I see you again?' # Yw *wintja*

walpi kara I don't know when • *Thawawarrangatjinga walpi kara nhani.* 'I don't know when she's coming home.' • *Nganyi yandharla walypalayi nhungganiyi nhinggiyi, ngariningadi nganha yundru walpi kara.* 'I'm talking to this white fellow here, so you can listen to me, some time.'

walpirri over, over the hill • *kathi puluka walpirri miriyi thanggukarlatji.* 'tailing cattle over the sandhill.'

waltha bring, carry • *... ngala ngarndri-ngapirili thanha walthanarlayi karlu-karlutji, ngunyinga nhinggikala yarruyi.* '... while the birds feed on fish that their parents bring them and give them to them in the yard.' • *Pipa yintjadu walthathawana kundangalili; wayi kaka kara.* 'The wind blew the paper away; I don't know how far.' # Also **pakawarra, thuka**.

walthathika, walthathikawarra carry back, carry home • *Kathi ngali parndrinhana, nga kudlayukarranga yinha. Pandrala ngali walthathikana.* 'We killed [a kangaroo], and cooked him overnight, and then carried him home cooked.'

walthawindri take away • *Ngandra yaba ngunyinhana nganha yundru ngathutji purtupa walthawindrinhana winkarnanga yinggani kurnkipuru.* 'Oh! You frightened me and I took my swag away and ducked off for fear of you being a devil.'

walthayindri carry for yourself • *Ngapala parndringa palhatji, walthayindrithikangalatji.* 'Well, they kill the birds and carry them back home.'

waluyuka see **waliyuka**.

walya no, not; don't (let) • *Walya ngandra yurarla paldriningadi nhinggiyi.* 'We don't want (him) to die here.' • *Kayiditji walyala thana nhinarla.* 'They aren't living any more.' • *Ngararnanga pulhu yaraya(?) — walya ngathu pulhu nganandji.* 'I understood them but I didn't tell them.' • *Walya thana wawalapurra rabititji.* 'They never saw a rabbit [in the old days].' • *Yakarlala ngathu yina minhanganarla nhuniyi walya yandhiyandhini ngakaniyi.* "I'm asking you why he don't talk to me." • *Walya* *nhunu muka thudiningadi.* 'Don't let him sleep.' # Also **watja, watka** Yw; See also **pani**.

walya yurayindri be sad

walyangu not yet • *Mulhudu nganyi thayiyindrina, ngala walyangu nganyi yartu, ngurrangu nganyi mawali nganarla.* 'I had a feed but I'm not full yet; I'm still hungry.' # Also **kali paningu**; See also **paningu**.

walyawalyaka lose • *Kathi marngali ngathu wanthirla, walyawalyakanga yinha, kanthayi. Ay, nhutjadu kanparla.* 'I was after a goanna but I lost it in the grass. Hey, it's turned up!' # See also **nyulka, yikaka**.

walypala white man (from Eng 'white fellow') • *Ngapala yingkarnangala thili yabangunyiyindrininguda ngala pula walypalathili.* 'Well, they both laughed then, the two white men, at the way they had frightened one another.' • *Wilpadali nganyi thawalapurra, mandrithawari nganha walypalali.* 'Once I was travelling in a wagon — some white men picked me up.' • *Ngapala thana karrparnanga thirrithirri-nyadi yina walypalali kurrarlatji thana, thirrila karrpiningadi mirrka.* 'Then they weave it just like the cotton white people use for making their clothes.' # See **pirripirri**.

walypawalypala like a white man • *Walyala wawanga puthakurnu ngarru walypawalypala yina thana nhinarla kayiditji, ...* 'We won't see [that] again. They just live like white people now, ...'

wama woma, sandhill snake, carpet snake # Also **manga**; See also **mulhana**.

wamalurru grasshopper

wamba many, mob # SY. See **malkirri**.

wamba (1) hide, cover up • *Wambatharrarla nhulu padlatji.* '[The floodwater] is covering the land.' # See also **nhamba, purrilka,**

kudhikudhima, winkama (2) be unable to see (something) # *Wambarla ngathu = Pudlu ngathu wawarla.* 'I can't see.'

wambawamba be unable to see (something) # sometimes heard as *wambaamba* • *Wambaambarla ngathu.* 'I can't see it.'

wamiyami weak # SY. See **darnu**.

wandaparra ibis (black and white) # SY *wartamugali*

wandi leg # Nh

wandikila upper leg, thigh, hind leg • *Wandikila nganha yada ngunyi.* 'Give me the hind leg (of kangaroo).' # See also **thadamuku, kulayada, ngalpa**.

wandja see **wantja**.

wandukudra divide, split up, share # Compare **yalba, manggama-nggakurra**

wanga, wangangari, wangapandhi light (fire); heat something up • *Patjikurnutji makala ngala thana wangapandhirnanga ngapala ngapa kurrari mardrayi thana kudrakudrari makamakaniningudatji.* 'They light a good fire on the rock and after it has heated up they put water on it, to shatter the rock.' • *Kathi paladi parndriparndriyindrirnanga, ngala makatji wanginingudakathi yuka kara kuliningadi, ya karlukarlu kuliningadi.* 'They kill their own meat, and light a fire to cook their meat or maybe to cook fish.' • *Ngapa kuntha ngali wangarla.* 'We're making a drink of tea.' # See also **pulkapada, thalpapada, karadaka**.

wan.gu type of snake # SY

wani song, corroboree • *Ngapala nhulu wani drangayindrirnanga.* 'Well, he sang songs to himself.' • *Wani thambanini nhutjadu.* 'He's a good dancer.' [or 'He can dance.'] • *Yiwa walya wanitji wawiningadi, ngarru karrungadi yina.* 'The women aren't allowed to watch the corroboree, it's only for the men.' # See also **muda**.

wani paratharra corroboree ground

wankina feel for (something) # ?

wannganyi, warrnganyi on the left, left hand # See also **nguna warrku**.

wannganyikadi or **wannganyingadi** to the left

wantha past, passing

wanthamini run past

wanthathawa pass, go past • *Ngarru nhunu wanthathawanhana, walya kara nganha nhulu kilkanhanatji.* 'He walked straight past me, just like he didn't know me.' See also **ngardrawarrka, wawathawa**.

wanthawawa look past

wanthi, wanthiyindri look for • *Ngarndri nganyi wanthiyindrirla.* 'I'm looking for my mother.' (also *Ngarndri ngathu wanthiyindrirla.*) • *Muduwa nhunu wanthiyindrirla ngarndringadi.* 'The boy is looking for his mother' • *Ngapala pula yadatji yina wanthirnangala nga kurnutji nhunu thangguthalkawarranga wawa-yindripandhiringu.* 'They were looking for the boomerang. Then one of them stood up and looked down at himself.' # See Chapter 14 of *Innamincka Talk* for more information on the variety of ways in which this word can be used.

wantja, wantjangari, wantjapandhi (also heard as *wandja*) try, taste, test • *Kirri ngathu wantjangarirla, kandrakanga.* 'Will I try to lift it?' • *Kirri yinhayi wantja, patji kara.* 'Can you taste this and see if it's all right.' • *Kirriya nganha dramana, wantjiningadi, pandrala kara.* 'Will you cut [the meat] for me so I can see if it's cooked.' • *Ngapa kuntha yundru wandja yintjadu, makamaka yina ngakaniyitji.* 'You try that tea, it's too hot for me.' # SY *nhama*

wantjathawa touch in passing, graze

wantjiwantjina imitate • *Kawalka nhulu wantjiwantjinarla.* 'He's imitating a crow.'

wanyunka twist # SY, Yw. See **wapa**.

wapa twist • *Martardaku nganyi wapayindrina.* 'I twisted my ankle.' # See also **dulyi, wanyunka**

wapapandhi twist something round

wapawagawaga turn (something) around, twist it round and round

wapila type of grass (probably sandhill canegrass, *Zygochloa paradoxa*) # SY

wara who (subject of intransitive verb, object of verb or in a sentence without a verb), what (name) # Also **waranu, warnu** • (SY) *Wara yini darlatji?* 'What's your name?'

waralu = warlu, warali = warlu

warangi whose; who, whom (with inflectional suffix as in 'to whom', 'who from', 'from whom' etc.) • *Windra warangi nhuniyi, ngathu dan.gana?* 'Whose spear is this I found?' • *Muduwa nhutjadu yabali warangiyi?* 'Who's that kid frightened of?'

warangi kara someone's, I don't know whose • *Warangi kara nhutjadu pandi parlutji.* 'I don't know whose that white dog is.'

waranu who # = *wara, warnu* • *Waranu yini?* 'Who are you?'

wararri bottom of net • *Ngala ngapa kukuyitji ngari, wararriyitji, mardramitji karrininguda malkirri pardrangariningadilatji thanha, paltjakiningadi.* 'They tie a lot of stones [to go] deep down in the water, on the bottom of the net, to weigh it down and keep it tight.'

wardama calm, sheltered (from wind) • *Thawarla ngaldra kundangalipuru wardamayi nhinanga, yandhiyandhini-ngadilatji.* 'Let's go and sit [in the car] and talk out of the wind.'

wardayapa road # Yw (may be Wngu). See **palthu**, **kapitharra**.

wardi emphatic particle, usually heard as *-ardi*

wardla see **warla**.

wari see **wayi**.

wariwari sick # See also **mundja**, **patja**.
  wariwarina get sick • *Wakanarlala pirna, wariwarinarlatji nhutjadu.* 'He's working too hard and got sick.'

warla, wardla nest • *palha warla* 'bird's nest'

warlawaka, warlawaga mix # SY • *Puka yinhayi ngathu warlawakarla.* 'I'm mixing this dough.' # See **nguka**, **nhapi**.

warlga see **warlka**.

warli house, hut • *Ay ngandjarri kara warlkanga nganyi thawarla warli matjayi thudanga.* 'Oh, it looks like rain, I'll go and sleep in the old hut.' # Also **kundi**.
  warli marna door

warli help
  warlima, warliwarlima help; stop (for example, stop someone fighting) • *Thawa yada warlimanga nganha.* 'Come here and help me.' • *Ay warliwarlimana ngathu pulhudu(?) thirrirlayi.* 'I stopped them two from fighting.' • *Yiwa pula thawarla muduwa ngala thukarnanga warli-warlimayindringa.* 'Those two women are helping one another carry the child.'

warlka fall • *Warlkana nhutjadu wathinguda.* 'He fell out of the tree.' • *Ay ngandjarri kara warlkanga nganyi thawarla warli matjayi thudanga.* 'Oh, it looks like rain, I'll go and sleep in the old hut.' # SY and Yw also **warlga**, H **warlga**. See also **ngurli**, **ditjipurri**, **kudra**, **pundji**.
  warlkapandhi, warlkangari fall down (from a height) • *Ngapala palha pula dranyindji, nga yadatji*

nhunu thikawarranga ngapayi warlkapandhinga. 'They hit a bird, and the boomerang came back down and fell into the water.'
  warlkathalka fall (of rain)
  warlkatharra fall over

warlpa hit with something flexible (as a whip or flexible stick) # = *kuntji*

warlpara, warlpada learned, knowing, used to • *Ay kilkarla ngathu, matja warlpara nganininguda.* 'Oh, I know, I learnt a long time ago.' • *Ay warlpara nganyi malthiyitji thangguthanggunga.* 'Oh, I'm used to walking around in the cold.'
  warlparaka teach • *Nhuludu nganha warlparakanhana yada thinbiningadi.* 'That bloke taught me how to make a boomerang.' • *Wani nhutjadu drangayindrirla, nganhala warlparaka wanitji yintjadu.* 'You teach me that song you're singing.' # Also **kurrakurrana**, **ngana**.
  warlpada ngana learn • *Warlpada ngana muduwayi yini nhinarlayi.* 'Learn while you're young.'

warlu, waralu, warali who (subject of transitive verb) • *Warlu yina mitji yimpakanhana?* 'Who gave you a black eye?'
  warlu kara, waralu kara, warali kara someone, I don't know who (subject of transitive verb)

warlu, warluwarlu bark (of a dog) • *Warluwarlupani nhutjadu.* 'He never barks.' # See also **kaldrukaldru**, **wawurrka**, **marrtji**.
  warlu parndri bark # Lit. 'bark hit'

warnta short; for a short time; in a short time, shortly • *Karraringu thanha mulpininguda warnta, payipayirru yina, mara witju-nyadi.* 'They tie them on after cutting them into short lengths, about the size of a finger.' • *Ay ngarru nganyi warnta thuda-pandhinatji.* 'I was only asleep for a while.' • *Mundja muthu nhunu patjarla, paldringa kara nhutjadu warntala.* 'He's very sick; he'll be dead shortly.' (Can also be said with kayidi instead of warnta) # See also **ngurlu**. See also **maka warnta**.

warntatharra for a short time • *Thawawarranhana nhunu, nhinanga ngakaniyi, yandhiyandhinga ngali, warntatharrayi nhinala, thikangala yina nhunuyi.* 'He came to sit with me and have a talk; he's just staying for a while and then going back.'

warnu, waranu who (subject of intransitive verb, object of transitive verb or in a sentence without a verb) • *Waranu yini?* 'Who are you?' • *Kali thana wirninarnanga warnu nganyi.* 'They told them who I was.' • *Warnu ngala yundru ngunyinhana yinha?* 'Who did you give it to?'

warnu kara, waranu kara someone, I don't know who • *Warnu kara nhunuyi thawarla ngatjada ngalungganingadi.* 'Someone's coming to our camp.'

warnumayindri lean (on something)

warra see **dikilyarra**.

warra side # See **thili, thinka**.

warrakurnu on one side, on the other side • *Ngala nhunu thudapandhinga nhinggiyi maka warrakurnula.* 'Then he lay down on his side of the fire.' • *Ya palhatji thana yurari parndringa, pirli thana paladildrangu drakininguda, nga wathiyi pada karranga warrakurnutji, thadripalapala yina.* 'If they want to catch birds they make a net of a different mesh and tie it on to a tree on each bank of the river.'

warrayi, (Yw) warranyi never mind, leave it • *'Pirritjampanarla nhunu.' 'Warrayi nhunu yukarrapandhimalkayarndu.'* 'He's tired.' 'Oh, never mind, he can lie down.' • *Warrayi nhulu thayimalkayarndu.* 'It's all right,

he can eat it.' • *Warrayi, walya yurarla ngandjarritji.* 'I hope it doesn't rain.'

warrayi wawa (or **warrayi waw**) never mind

warrka throw, throw away; leave somewhere • *Ngapala thana tharrapandhiri yada, ngala karna nhunu wadayindrirla thadripalapala yadatji warrkanga.* 'Well, when they fly down towards the net, the men waiting there on both sides of the river throw their boomerangs.' • *Wilyaru thana pardraringu pakangalatji kanthayi warrkathikanga.* 'They took him into the bush and left him.' • *Yarru nhantjadu yundru wawarla, nhinggudungu nganha yadamanalitji warrkanhukada.* 'That yard you see there, that's where a horse threw me once.' • *Warrkawarrananhanatji ngathu yinha, ngala nhulutji maka wangangariningadi nganarlayi.* 'When I left him he was just about to light the fire.'

warrkana, warrkanapada spear • *Kathi tjukurrutji, ngarru wathi windralildra warrkanarnanga.* 'As for kangaroos, one way is to just kill them with a spear.' • *Pangkithirri nhulu yinha warrkananhana.* 'He speared it in the ribs.'

warrkapada throw to the other side

warrkapandhi, warrkanapandhi throw down • *Ngapala nhunu ngarru yankula mandriri, nga warrkapandhinga ngapala pulkanga ngala nhulu ...* 'So he just got some [dry] leaves and threw them down [on the hot coals] and started to blow them ...' • *Ngapala mardra thana warrkapandhi-warrkapandhingala makayi.* 'Then they throw all the stones into the fire.'

warrkawarra bring and throw down (for example, an armful of wood)

warrkatharra let go # Also given for 'leave'

warrkawarrkana throw from one to the other; dislike

warrkawarrkanayindri throw from one to the other; dislike one another

warrkawindri leave (someone or something), go away from • *Nga Kinipapayi nganha warrkawindringa ngapa yulpudu yina ngakarlayi.* 'They left me at Cooper's Creek because the river was in flood.'

warrkupada the other side # SY • *warrkupada widayi* 'on the other bank'

warru grey

warruwitji emu • *Ngapala thana kathi warruwitjingaditji thawari, kathi warruwitji yukatji parndringa.* 'They also go out for emus, to kill emus.' • *Ngapala pandhi wirlpinhinarnanga, ngala kathi thana ngarangaraminirlayila warruwitjilitji.* 'Then he whistles down there, and the emus hear him.' # Also **maltharrimindji, kiwada.** Emus are probably not classed as *palha* 'bird'.

warta larger end of anything long, butt (for example, of tree, yamstick, spear) • *windra warta* 'blunt end of a spear' • *Muduwa ngathu thanha wawarla nhinanhinarnanga wathi wartayi.* 'I'm sitting under the tree watching the kids.' # See also **nganku.**

wartamuku backside, hips # See also **pulumuku.**

wartamugali ibis # SY. See **wandaparra.**

wartaka go over • *miriwita wartakanga* 'to go over the sandhill'

wartari kangaroo rat (perhaps the desert rat kangaroo, *Caloprymnus campestris*) # SY, Yw?

Wartathulanini Wattathoolendinnie Waterhole

warumpudu swollen # Yw

warumpudu ngana swell up # Yw • *Warumpudu nganarla nhunuyi puka.* 'The damper's swelling up.'

waruwaru dark • *Thawayukarrana nganyi waruwaruyi.* 'I was walking in the dark.' # See also **milyaru, mabumabu, marri.**

wathara wind • *Wathara nhutjadu darrkarla.* 'The wind's blowing.' # See also **kundangali, thayirri.**

wathi make, erect, build, construct • *Palha purla pirnanarlayitji, ngapala yarru wathinaritji, marru kadawayi ...* 'When the young birds are getting big, they build a yard for them on the bank of the lake ...' # See also **daka, ngana, nhapi.**

wathi stick, log, tree, wood, firewood; machine • *Warlkana nhutjadu wathinguda.* 'He fell out of the tree.' • *Ngapala yina wathi thinbanari mandawarra, ya wirni thurrpanari yinha mulhudungadilatji nhunu thawathalkiningadi warrkanga wathilatji yina karrtjikarrtjimari.* 'Well, he would cut and shape a stick from a plum bush and tie a string to it and whirl it around, so that someone would come and leave some food for him.' • *... ya nhunggani yabali ngapala wathi drantha kurrari, blanket-li yinha purrilkatharranga, nga wathi thanggunari pantja thangguni-nyadi nhunu karna.* '... and, in his fear, put a forked log on the other side, and covered it over with a blanket, and stood a stick up so that it would look like a man's knee sticking up.' • *Minhangadi yundru wathi nhuludutji yada thinbarla; ngarru kudrayindrini yina nhutjadutji wathi.* 'What do you make a boomerang out of that wood for? It only breaks, that wood.' • *Wathi nhuniyi karrtjiwagawagarla.* 'This machine (tape recorder) is going round and round.'

wathi kala fork # Yw

wathi kaparri root

wathi karli limb of tree

wathi muku log; post # See also **thinka, maka warnta, pirta**.

wathi mutuka motorcar

wathi parndriparndrini hammer

wathi patjipatjikini mechanic

wathi thilpi twig # See also **witju**.

wathi thinka log (possibly also **wathi yinka**)

wathithirri # used in referring to sticks or logs put on or around grave, but meaning not clear • ... *nga yankala mandringa, yankala kurratharranga, ngapala wathithirrila warrkari, wathilardi kurranga thalkanga, ya thanggunatharrathalkaringu wathitji,* ... '... then [they] get branches, and put the branches all around, then they throw down logs(?), they put logs on top, and stand logs up all around, ...'

wathi warta butt of tree

wathi windra spear • *Karrukarruyi yintjadu ngathu mamathikana wathi windra.* 'I took the spear off that old fellow over there.'

wathi witju little stick • *Kurra-pandhiri purtutji yinhanga makali yina karrtjikarrtjimawarranga wathi witjuli.* 'He put the swag down by the fire and started to turn [the ashes] over with a twig.'

wathiwutju walking stick # not clear that *wutju* and *witju* are not the same

wathi pukapuka scrub # Also **pukapuka**.

wathiwathi scrubby

Wathiwathi Scrubby Camp Waterhole

wathi yinka see **wathi thinka**.

watja not # Yw. See **walya, watka**.

watjina hang up (for example, clothes) # SY, Yw

watka not # H; see **watja**.

wawa see, look • *Wawa parrariyi.* 'Look underneath.' • *Nga yarnduldrangu ngathutji wawana yina dunkarlayitji nga yabalildrangu winkanga yadamaningadila thannganiyi thudayukarranga.* 'And I saw you going out and I was frightened too and I ducked off down to the horses and spent the night with them.' • *Walarri nganyi wawayindrirla ngapayi.* 'I can see myself in the water.'

wawana, wawawawana watch, look after • *Purtutji yinggani wawawawanaw, winkamayila nhuludu.* 'Watch your things, or he'll take them.' • *Muduwa thanayi patjingu nhinarla wawawawanarlayitji thanha.* 'The kids are good while you're watching them.'

wawangalpirri look over (something you can't see through, for example, a fence)

wawatharra look, take notice • *Ngala pulyatji marndakurrapandhirlayi, nga walya yinha wawatharranga, karrtji-pandhiyila thana paninarla.* 'When the little ones stop halfway they don't take any notice of them, for fear the whole lot will turn back.'

wawathawa, wawathawawarra pass, leave behind • *Ngathu wawathawana yinha, palthuyi.* 'I passed him on the road.' # Compare **kurrawindri, ngardrawarrka, wanthathawa**.

wawathikathika, wawawagawaga look around

wawawawananhina expect, watch out for

wawu tea tree # SY. See **kayarri, thayarri**.

wawurrka bark (dog) • *Pandi ngathu purrtjinana, ngurra nhutjadu yabali wawurrkarla.* 'I frightened the dog; he's still barking at me.' # See also **warlu, kaldrukaldru, marrtji**.

wayaka myall # perhaps *Acacia calcicola*, but also given for acacia bush. See **kaltja**.

wayi how # in combined forms: *wayi kaka* 'how far?', *wayi patji* 'how good?', *wayi pirna* 'how big?'
• '*Yigatji wayi patji?*' '*Ay kaldringu thana. Walpi kara pirtipirtinangatji.*' '"What are the wild oranges like?" "Oh, they're bitter yet. Don't know when they're going to get ripe."'
Sometimes *wari*. See also **yarndu, yilaru**.

   wayi kara I don't know how ...
   • *Pipa yintjadu walthathawana kundangalili; wayi kaka kara.* 'The wind blew the paper away; I don't know how far.'

wayiludu mosquito • *Wayiludunguda nganha katjakatjarla.* 'I'm stinging from mosquito [bites].' # Also **kunthi**.

wayini how many, how much • *Ngathu yina mardra ngunyiwindringa; wayini yini yurarlatji?* 'I'll give you money before I go; how much do you want?'
• *Yakayindrini kalkayi, 'Mayi, karlukarlutji wayinila ngandra?'.* 'In the afternoon they ask one another, "How many fish did we get?".'

   wayini kara I don't know how many
   • *wayini kara dritji* 'I don't know how long (how many days)'

wayirri lignum # SY. See **pundrinya**.

wibu whip # from Eng. Also **wipayithi**.

wida bank (of river, creek) # SY, Yw; examples are SY • *nhinggiyi widayi* 'on this bank' • *warrkupada widayi* 'on the other bank' • *Widapulayi, kalpurru thanggurla.* 'There are coolibahs on both sides.' # The *-pula* in *widapulayi* may be a mistake; it is the Wngu dual suffix. See also **kadawa, thadri**.

widi a word or ending that sometimes follows a word that tells where or which one; its meaning is not clear # Compare also **kanta, waka, walha**

• *ngariwidi, ngaritji widi, pandhitji widi*, all translated 'down there'
• *Ngariwidi mayi Kilyalpa.* '[He's] down there at Kilyalpa. • *thalkatji widi* 'up there'

widi call to come # Yw. See also **kandri, mirrtjakurra, ngarndapandji, kaldripantji, karrka**.

wika clean # H *wirrkindri* 'to wash' may not be related.

   wikana, wikawikana clean (something), wipe (something)
   • *Wikawikananga, pinakanga, ya dringangalatjardi, nga thayi-yindringala yartunanga, ngapali ngunkukininguda.* 'They clean it, rock it, and grind it and then, after mixing it with water and making it into a ball, they eat their fill.' # See also **drangka, wirrk(a)**.

   wikapada wipe, wipe off • *Mulha yintjadu wikapada.* 'Wipe his face.'

wiki week # from Eng • *Wiki kurnu nganyi dritji parrkulu nhinathawan.ga.* 'I stayed there two days last week.'

wilarnku curlew

wilawarra sit on haunches

Wilbarrku Wilpancoo Waterhole

wiliwili shoulder # or perhaps collarbone (SY). See also **pinyi, thapini, kilkirri, pilpiri**.

wilka wild (animal) • *pandi wilka* 'dingo'

wilpada wagon # from Eng 'wheelbarrow' • *Wilpadali nganyi thawalapurra, mandrithawari nganha walypalali.* 'Once I was travelling in a wagon — some white men picked me up.' • *Walyala ngani purrkapadayi wilpadalitji, ngarrungu pula thawandji, thantjiyipangadi, nganyi nhinapadapadarlayi nhinggikala Kinipapayi.* 'We mightn't have got across with the wagon so they went on without me, to the town, and I stayed there at the river.'

wilpuru rope # SY. See **wirni, drupa**.

wilyaru exile, person who is exiled # According to S. Gason, Journal of the Anthropological Institute (1894) and A.P. Elkin, Oceania (1932) *wilyaru* means 'fully initiated man'

wilyaru pardra exile someone • *Wilyarula yina pardrari, thirri-thirrinarlayi nhunu ya nhipangurru nhulu parndrirlayi.* 'They would exile [a man] for stirring up trouble or beating his wife.' • *Wilyaru thana pardraringu pakangalatji kanthayi warrkathikanga.* 'They took him into the bush and left him.'

windawinda walking stick

windra owl, perhaps barn owl # SY. See **yurlawarra**.

windra, wathi windra spear • *Kathi tjukurrutji, ngarru wathi windralildra warrkanarnanga.* 'As for kangaroos, one way is to just kill them with a spear.' • *Wawarnanga ngapangadi ngari thawarlayi karna kulpina-yindrirlayila ngapatji yibarlayi nga wathi windrali warrkananga.* 'Well, when they see them going to the water the men surround them, and then spear them while they're drinking.'

windri paint, rub • *Maltji withi nganyi windrirla* (or *windriyindrirla*). 'I'm rubbing my sore leg.' • *Windringa ngathu yinhayi pirtipirti.* 'I'm going to paint it red.' # See also **marndra**.

windri, windripada, windritharra go in, enter, set (sun) • *Ngapala nhunu windripadari purtungurru.* 'Then he went in with his swag.' • *Ngarrungu nhunu kulkupathalkari purtu mandringa dunkawindringa nhunu windriwarrinitji yada warli.* 'So he just jumped up and grabbed his swag and went out the door he had come in by.' • *Nga pirliyi thana windriringu.* 'They [the ducks] go into the net.'

• *Palha purla pirnanarlayitji, ngapala yarru wathinaritji, marru kadawayi, ngapala thawarnanga puka windri-tharranga ngapa marruyitji palha purla thanhayi mapathikanga.* 'When the young birds are getting big, they build a yard for them on the bank of the lake and then go down into the water and herd the baby birds back [into the yard].' • *Windripadaka yita!* Or *windripadamalka!* 'Go right in!' # See also **wirri**.

windrima, windriwindrima, windrimawarra put in • *... ngapala thana windrimawarraringu wathininguda yarrutji thanngani.* '... and put them in the yard that they have built for them.' • *Ngala panipani(kari?) muku palgupalgu dukininguda, ngapala dultharri darlamurru windrimari, paltji-kiningaditji yina, pirtipirtikari darlatji yinha.* 'After they take out all the bone and muscle they put bloodwood bark in to make it supple and it makes the skin red.' • *Tjukurru darlatji windri-windrimawindrimalka.* 'You can fill up the kangaroo skin (water-bag).' # See also **kurrapada, winma**.

windrimapada bring inside

windripandhi go down in (hole); set (sun); get buried (slang?) • *Ngapala kudru pakuri ngari, nga yankula kurrawagandji nga windripandhinga palha mukuli.* 'They dig a hole and put boughs around it and [a man] goes down into the hole with a bird bone.' • *Dritji windripandhirlayi ngani kuthiwarranhana.* 'We got there at sundown.'

winka be lost, disappear, run away, duck off • *Ngapala nhunu winkarnanga yadamaningadila ngari.* 'Then he ducked back down to the horses.' • *Ngandra yaba ngunyinhana nganha yundru ngathutji purtupa walthawindrinhana winkarnanga* *yinggani kurnkipuru.* 'Oh! You frightened me and I took my swag away and ducked off for fear of you being a devil.' • *Yadatji ngathu mapanhana ngala nhunu winkarlayila.* 'I picked up the boomerang and he ran away.' # SY translated this word as 'hide away' and did not accept it for 'run away' # See also **nyulkayindri, miniwindri, putharrkawindri, kinyiwinka.**

winkama steal, run away with; hide • *Ay winkamana nhanha nhulu.* 'He ran away with her [my wife].' • *Ngathu yinha kapirla, yakayakanga yinha mardra ngakani winkamanhana, ngunyithikanga kara nganha nhulu, pani kara.* 'I'm going to follow him and ask him whether he took my money and whether he'll give it back to me or not.' • *Walpa nganggalili wawayila yina winkamarlayi kara yundru.* 'The owner of the house might see you and think you are stealing something.' • *Winkamana ngathu nhunggani wathitji, ngurra parndriyilatji nganinha.* 'I planted his stick so he won't belt us any more.' # SY and Yw *winkima.* See also **kudhikudhima, purrilka, wamba, minilka, mama.**

winkaminiwindri duck off

winkapada go inside, come inside • *Muduwa yada winkapadani ngandjarripuru.* 'Kids, come inside out of the rain.'

winkapandhi dive, go down # See also **kartiwirri.**

winkapani, winkawindri run away, go and hide • *Winkawindrinhana nhunu yilakadi kara.* 'He ran away and we don't know where he's gone.'

winkathawa disappear (into the distance), go out of sight

winma put in # SY, Yw. = *windrima, kurrapada* • *Kathi yinhaku winma, yakuthayi.* 'Put the meat in the bag.'

wintja when # Yw. • *'Wintjama yundru wathiya yinhaku punga?'* *'Kayidima.'* 'When are you going to put up that humpy?' 'Not long.' # The form with no suffixation is found only in RYn. See **walpi.**

wipa or **wipinga** sweep # from Eng; see **drangka** • *Yambarriyi kurranga, padla paltjapaltja yina wipinginingudatji yinha, patjikaringu padla, padla thaka mitji ngukangukayindriyi.* 'They put them on the hard flat ground, after sweeping it to make it clean so that the seeds don't get mixed with clay.'

wipa creek # Yw. See **karirri, kadri, kinipapa.**

wipayithi see **wibu.**

wirdi outside (for example, the outside one of a group) # See **thalka, yambarri.**

wirdiwirdika stir • *Ngapali wirdiwirdikari pukatji nhapinga.* '[They] stir the flour with water and roll it up.'

wirina tell • *Yandhiyandhinga ngali, nhunu nhinarlayitji. Minha kara, minha nganha wirinanga,* or *yakanga.* 'We're going to have a talk, while he's here. I don't know what about, whether he's going to tell me something, or ask me something.' # See also **ngana, pintaka.**

wiriwinma swap, exchange • *Wiriwinmarnanga karna thana pitjidi kumaningurrutji.* 'The people with the bags of pitchery exchanged [them].' • *Puladu kadringurru, wiriwinmanhana puladu ngathadi man.garri, nhipakiningadi.* 'Those two are brothers-in-law; they gave each other their young sisters to marry.' # See also **ngunyiyindri.**

wiriwinmayindri exchange (with someone)

wirlpa cave; hole (for example, in a dish) • *Wirlpangudali nhuliyi nganha wawarla.* 'He's peeping at me through a hole.' • *Nga yadala thana thinbari, yadatji thinbininguda nga wirlpa kurranga, mulha kurnuyi.* 'Then they make a boomerang and put a hole in one end of it.' • *Thana mukurdukalapurra thanha, ngarru ngaga yina nhunu pirnatji wirlpa.* 'They took the bones out through a hole only as big as the throat.' # See also **mingka, daba, thuka.**

wirlpaka pierce, drill (a hole), make an opening • *Thiltja thana tjukurru pardrarla, ngapala thanadu pirditjirraritji nga palha mukuli tjalparrikininguda wirlpakanga nyinditji.* 'They hold the kangaroo sinew and strip it and poke the holes in the skin with a bird bone that has been sharpened.'

wirlpa fast • *Karna wirlpa kanpamuthu nhutjadu minirla yabayi.* 'That man ran off really fast in his fear.' # See also **puthapika, puthapirna.**

wirlpi whistle # SY *wirlpa*; See also **payipaka.**

wirlpinhina be whistling • *Ngapala pandhi wirlpinhinarnanga, ngala kathi thana ngarangaraminirlayila warruwitjilitji.* 'Then he whistles down there, and the emus hear him.'

wirni string, rope • *Ngapala yina wathi thinbanari mandawarra, ya wirni thurrpanari yinha mulhudungadilatji nhunu thawathalkiningadi warrkanga wathilatji yina karrtjikarrtjimari.* 'Well, he would cut and shape a stick from a plum bush and tie a string to it and whirl it around, so that someone would come and leave some food for him.' • *Ngapala pirntathangkali nyanmari, marapardrini, wirnili ngukanguka pirntathangkali, karrangalatji yinha.* 'I'll bind the handle on with string and seal it with beefwood gum (mixed with the string).' • *Ngala karrukarrulitji ngarru wirni yamununguldra, paladi wirnina*

thurrkarnanga ngarru pulyaldra. 'On the other hand, the old men only wore a small string.' # See also **wilpuru, drupa, yinka, yulpudu.**

wirnika, wirnikamalka make string • *Wirnikamalka purupurriningudalatji thana parndringa* (unclear word) *wirningadi nga thurrpanga ...* 'They tease it up and make it into string by pounding it and then spinning it ...'

wirnikamura human hair string • *Ngala yamunu ngala thana wirnikamuratji thurrpininguda, yarnduldrangu, yarndu thana pirlitji, minhaya, karlukarlungadi.* 'They spin human hair into string, just as they make the string for fishing nets.' • *Drakarnanga yarnduldrangu wirnikamuratji yiwangaditji pirnaldra, karriningadi panikaldra nhambalkayindrindji.* 'On the one hand they make a big one [hair-string apron] for women to tie on, to cover themselves completely.'

wirni yinka a length of string or rope • *Yiwali nhandra wirni yinka mandrinhana karranga yinha panditji.* 'That woman got a piece of rope and tied the dog up.' # Said on one occasion to mean a ball (not a length) of string.

wirni tell a story # See **karrtjikarrtjima.**

wirnina tell about • *Kali thana wirninarnanga warnu nganyi.* 'They told them who I was.' • *Ay, ngathu yina walya wirninanhana thantjiyipangadi nganyi thawanhana yaba ngunyinga nganha thana.* 'Hey, I didn't tell you about how they frightened me in town.' • *Ngapiri nganha wirnina yinggani.* 'Tell me about your father.'

wirniwirni discuss, talk about • *Minha yula wirniwirnirla?* 'What are you two talking about?'

wirniwangka seagull

wirri duck down # See also **kartiwirri**.

wirri go in, enter, set (sun) # SY, Yw; see **windri**.

wirri type of weapon, like a club with a big sharp head # Yw 'When you hit anybody he turn the other way and he stick straight through you.' (Bob Naylon)

wirrk(a) wash, wipe # H. See **wika**; **drangka**, **wikana**, also **yika**, **panma**.

wita hill # See under **mardra**, **miri**.

witamuku backbone

withi sore, injury • *Maltji withi nganyi windrirla.* 'I'm rubbing my sore leg.' • *Ngapala nhunu purtu mandri-mandrirnanga milyaruyi, nga thawawindringa ngatjada kurnungadila, withi ngabayi-ngada, ya kuthiwarrarila mayi.* 'Well, he packed his swag in the dark and walked on to the other camp, while the injury was still fresh, and he got there.' # SY *dapa*

   withiwithina chafe • *Darla nganyi withiwithinarla.* 'My skin is chafed.'

witjipa put out to dry # SY. See **ditjipa**.

witju finger; twig • *Mitji nganyi draka-yindrinhana witju pulyali.* 'I poked my eye with my little finger.' # See **wathi** and **mara**, also **wutju**. It is not clear if *witju* and *wutju* are different.

witjukura east, east wind # Also heard *witjikura*; see also **dritjirdunka**.

wuldru narrow # Yw *yuldru*

wutju something long, perhaps used only to form compound words • *marawutju* or *marawitju* 'finger' • *wathiwutju* 'walking stick' # not clear if this is different from *witju*. Reuther has *wutju* 'long' (Yw).

Y

ya and • *Ngapala yina wathi thinbanari mandawarra, ya wirni thurrpanari yinha mulhudungadilatji nhunu*

thawathalkiningadi warrkanga wathilatji yina karrtjikarrtjimari. 'Well, he would cut and shape a stick from a plum bush and tie a string to it and whirl it around, so that someone would come and leave some food for him.' • *Pawangadi, pawa thungini ngunyirnanga ya ngarduparndrini ngunyirnanga.* 'They gave grinding stones, for seeds, and nardoo pounders.' • *Minhayangadilatji karlukarlu yukiningadi kara, ya kinipapayi kara kurriningadi, karlukarlu kara yamali.* 'That's what they're for, for catching fish while swimming in the water, and for putting across the river [to catch] fish in the cross net.' • *Ngala ngarru kathi tjukurruli thana nhinapadipadini, ya thalkaparlu, ya kathi pildra.* 'They only had kangaroo then, and kangaroo rat, and possum.' # See also **nga**.

yaba fear • *Karna wirrpa kanpamuthu nhutjadu minirla yabayi.* 'That man ran off really fast in his fear.' • *... ya nhunggani yabali ngapala wathi drantha kurrari, blanket-li yinha purrilkatharranga, nga wathi thanggunari pantja thangguni-nyadi nhunu karna.* '... and, in his fear, put a forked log on the other side, and covered it over with a blanket, and stood a stick up so that it would look like a man's knee sticking up.' • *Ngala nhunu karnatji yayinala yinda yabali.* 'Then the first man screamed out in fear.' # *Yaba* generally occurs with the ending *-li*. The cause of the fear may be marked with locative *-yi* or aversive *-puru* if it is a person or thing, or with purposive *-ini-ngadi* or potential *-yi* if it is an event; see examples of these in the **yabali** subentry below.

yabaka frighten, make timid • *Pandi yintjadu yundru yabakanhana, ngurra yinha parndriningadi nganarnanga yaba ngunyinga yinha.* 'You made that dog timid because you're always wanting to give him a hiding and frightening him.'

yaba mana frighten # SY

yabana get frightened

yaba ngana get frightened # SY

yaba ngunyi, yaba ngunyingunyi frighten • *Ngandra yaba ngunyinhana nganha yundru ngathutji purtupa walthawindrinhana winkarnanga yinggani kurnkipuru.* 'Oh! You frightened me and I took my swag away and ducked off for fear of you being a devil.' • *Ngapala yingkarnangala thili yabangunyi-yindrininguda ngala pula walypalathili.* 'Well, they both laughed then, the two white men, at the way they had frightened one another.'

yabakanpa, yabapika frightened person • *Ngala nhunu karnakurnutji thawawarrarlayi kilkarnanga yina karnatji yabapika.* 'Then this other man arrived and knew that this fellow was frightened.'

yabali frightened • *Yabali yini kathikathipuru?* 'Are you frightened of snakes?' • *Ngarru nhunu yabali minhayi kara.* 'I don't know what he's frightened of.' • *Yabali nhutjadu paldriningaditji.* 'He's afraid of dying.' • *Ngapala nhunu walypala-kurnutji yabalila nhungganardi karna-palhatji nhunuyi ngalardi, kali kuthiwarranatji.* 'Well this other white man was frightened [because he thought that] the devil had come.' • *Walthayindrithikangala kathi thana manggarlayila yabalilatji.* 'They carry the meat back to camp while the rest of the emus go for their lives.' # See also **purrtji**.

yabana get frightened, be afraid

yabapani unafraid, not frightened • *Yabapani muthu nhutjadu.* 'He's frightened of nothing.'

yabayabali a bit frightened

yabayabana become a bit frightened

yada boomerang • *Nga yadala thana thinbari, yadatji thinbininguda nga wirlpa kurranga, mulha kurnuyi.* 'Then they make a boomerang and put a hole in one end of it.' • *Ngapala thana tharrapandhiri yada, ngala karna nhunu(?) wadayindrirla thadripalapala yadatji warrkanga.* 'Well, when they fly down towards the net, the men waiting there on both sides of the river throw their boomerangs.' (Note that this sentence has both *yada* 'this way' and *yada* 'boomerang'.) • *Ngarrungu thanggu-thalkawarrandji dranyingalatji yadali.* 'The man just stands up and kills [one] with a boomerang.'

yada to here, hither, this way; towards the one(s) you are talking about • *Thawa yada warlimanga nganha.* 'Come here and help me.' • *Ngapa nganha yada ngunyi.* 'Give me some water.' • *Ngarrungu nhunu kulkupathalkari purtu mandringa dunkawindringa nhunu windriwarrinitji yada warli.* 'So he just jumped up and grabbed his swag and went out the door he had come in by.' • *Ngapala pula thingapadanga yada.* 'They pull it [the net] in.' # Opposite to *yita*.

yada paka bring • *Ngala thanatji walyala yartukari, ayi ngarndri-ngapirili yada pakarnanga karlukarlutji ngunyinga thanha.* 'They don't have to feed them; the parents bring fish and give it to them.'

yadamaka notched stick for messages

yadamani horse • *Ngala nhunu milimani thawawarrarlayila yadamanili Thayaparraringuda.* 'Meanwhile the mailman arrived on horseback from Durham Downs.' # See also **nhandu**, **pirndiwalku**.

yadhi (1) foetus, unborn baby # 'that's the baby in the bag, in the belly'; (2) born; (3) umbilical cord and afterbirth • *yadhi thundriyi, muduwatji kanpakari* 'the afterbirth is in the stomach (= womb) when the baby is born'

yadhi kurra give birth # See also **ngama mana, ngathanika, dan.ga.**

yadi like # Yw; see **nyadi**.

yaka, yakayaka ask • *Ngarrungu nhunu Diradili nganha yakapadanga nga walypala yawarrili, 'Yilangginguda yiney?'* 'Then he just asked me in Dieri, and then in whitefellow language, "Where are you from?"' • *Ngathu yinha kapirla, yakayakanga yinha mardra ngakani winkama-nhana, ngunyithikanga kara nganha nhulu, pani kara.* 'I'm going to follow him and ask him whether he took my money and whether he'll give it back to me or not.' • *Yakayindrini kalkayi, 'Mayi, karlukarlutji wayinila ngandra?'.* 'In the afternoon they would ask one another, "How many fish did we get?"' • *Thawarla nganyi, yaka-thikanga yinhayi yilanggi kara ngaldra thudiningadi.* 'I'm going over to ask him where we can camp.' # Yw also **yakana**.

yakutha bag # SY, Yw. See also **pirli, mirrka, paltja, thandji**.

yala same, alike (?) • *Puladutji nguthu-ngurru-nyadi mulha yala.* 'Those two are alike; you'd think they were brothers.' # See **marndu, nguya yala, yarnduldrangu**.

yalba split, divide (as a creek might divide two hills) • *Yalbangari yintjadu!* 'Split [the log]!' # See also **wandukudra, kudrikudrina**.

yalbana divide • *Yalbanarla ngathu nhanha.* 'I'm dividing [it] up for her.'

yalbanayindri divide, share amongst yourselves # See also **manggamanggakurra**.

yalbayindri split up, leave one another

yaliyali bicycle lizard # See also **karlantji**.

yalkada hopbush

yalkura Dreaming, Dreaming story # SY • *Yalkura nhulu nganha wirninana.* 'He told me the (Dreaming) story.' # = *mudamuda* (MN)

yalkura gall on limb of gum tree (?)

yama cross net • *Ngathu wawatharrana karlukarlungadi yukiningadi pirli yama yina karrparlayi.* 'I saw them make a bag net for catching fish while swimming in the water, and a cross net.' • *Minhayangadilatji karlukarlu yukiningadi kara, ya kinipapayi kara kurriningadi, karlukarlu kara yamali.* 'That's what they're for, for catching fish while swimming in the water, and for putting across the river [to catch] fish in the cross net.'

yambarri flat, flat place; outside; plain • *Yambarringadi thawa nhinanga.* 'Go and sit outside.' • *Kinikangatji ngala yiwalila yambarriyi kurranga.* 'The women heap them up on the flat ground.' • *Walya makayitji nhinawagawaga, kudlayindriyila yini. Makapani thambathambanakani mayi yambarriyi.* 'Don't stay near the fire, you might get burnt. Play away from the fire, out on the flat.' # See **thalka, wirdi, kunirri**.

yambarrikurra make flat

yambayambarri open place, open ground, flat # See also **paratharra**.

yampa strange; # SY and Yw also 'dingo, wild dog' • *karna yampa* 'stranger'

pandi yampa dingo, wild dog # Yw

thirrtha yampa dingo, wild dog # SY

yamunu wool, fur, hair (of body) • *Kathi tjukurru-nyadi thana walypalali, minhaya nganarla mayi, pirtipirtikarla darla yamunupani.* 'If they tanned the kangaroo skin with the fur removed, like the white men do, it would go red.' • *Ngala yamunumindjildra nhinggiyitji nyinyimulpiningudatji.* 'But our people [tan the hide] with the fur on, after turning the skin inside out.' • *Yilayarndu kara, minha yamunuli kara thana* (unclear word), *kathi pildrali kara thana nganapadipadini,* or *kathi tjukurruli.* 'I don't know how [they wove them] or what sort of hair they spun the thread from; maybe they used to use possum, or maybe kangaroo.' # Yw *nyurdu*

yandha say, talk; make its natural sound (for example, a bird to call) • *Minhala yini yurarla ngariningadi nganyi yandharlayi?* 'What do you want to hear me say?' • *Ngapala pula karlukarlungadi yada thawari nga yandhanga nhinanga karlukarlu parndrirnanga pula thadri parawadaldra, ...* 'Two of them came down to do some fishing. They sat and talked and caught fish on the other bank, ...' # See also **ngampa**, **ngana**.

yandhayandha talk, speak • *Yandruwandhatji nganyi yandhayandharla.* 'I talk Yandruwandha.' • *Yawarri pulganili ya(?) walya yawarri ngakanili, ngarru walypalayingu yawarri yandhayandharitji nganyi nganarnangatji pulhu.* 'I hadn't spoken to them in their language or in mine, only in the whitefellows'.' • *Minha yula yandhayandharla?* 'What are you talking about?'

yandjiyandji be shaky • *Wathi madlantji nhutjadu, yandjiyandjila yina nhutjadu.* 'The post's no good, it's too shaky.' # See **ngarra**, **yirrika**.

yandjiyandjilka shake

yandjiyandjina shake (something) # SY

yandri growl at, rouse on • *Muduwa ngathu yandrirla.* 'I'm rousing on the kids.'

yandriyindri swear at one another, abuse one another • *Ngarru puladu ngan.guli yandriyindrinhana.* 'They just roused on each other.'

Yandruwandha language name # often heard as *Yandruwantha* from MN

yanka, **yanku** bough, bush, bunch of leaves • *Ngapala nhunu ngarru yankula mandriri, nga warrkapandhinga ngapala pulkanga ngala nhulu ...* 'So he just got some [dry] leaves and threw them down [on the hot coals] and started to blow them ...' • *Ngapala kudru pakuri ngari, nga yankala kurrawagandji nga windri-pandhinga palha mukuli.* 'They dig a hole and put boughs around it and [a man] goes down into the hole with a bird bone.'

yapu, **yapuyapu** smooth, slippery # See also **yiliyili**, **yupurru**.

yarawarra naked • *Ngala thanayi kilkarla, ngarru yarawarrangu thawa-thawapadipadini ...* 'People now think they used to walk about naked ...' # Yw *parlu*

yarndu how, that way, for that reason • *Pin.gi pin.gi thana ngunyiyindripadipadini yarndu.* 'That's how they used to trade things.' • *Walya nhulu kilkanhana minha nganarnanga kara nhunu; walya yina nganha nhulu dranyiningadi. Yarndu nganha nhulu dranyinhanatji.* 'He didn't know what he was doing. He didn't intend to hit me. That's how he came to hit me.' • *Thayiyindringa palhatji yarndu thana parndri-padipadini karnalitji, palhatji ngala drakininguda ngala paladi.* 'That's how the Aborigines used to catch birds to eat, with a special type [of net] they had woven.' • *Ngan.gu kuthikuthidi nhinda ngunyingunyirnanga yinha. Yarndu nhunu walyatji yurarla yandhiningaditji.* 'His squeaky voice makes him shy. That's why he doesn't like talking.' # See also **wayi**, **yilaru**.

yarndudu how, like that, that way
• *Walya yarndudutji yandha.* 'Don't talk about that!'

yarndudungu like that, that way
• *Ngurra nhutjadu yandharla yarndudungu.* 'He always talks that way.'

yarndukala how, like that, that way
• *Pawathungini ngala pitjidi kumaningaditji ngunyiyindrirranga yarndukalangu thana nhinapadipadinitji.* 'They traded grinding stones for bags of pitchery; that's how they used to live.' • *Yarndukala ngali yinha thula-thulakanhana ay karna nganggalitji nhutjadu.* 'How could we reckon he was a stranger, when he's one of our own people.' • *Walypalatji walyaldra thanayi yarndukalatji nhinalapurra.* 'The whitefellows (on the other hand) never lived like that.'

yarnduldrangu, yarnduyildrangu the same, in the same way • *Yarnduyi-ldrangu yita thawarla.* '[He's] going the same way [as us].' • *Nhuludu nganathikathikarla madlantji nhukuyi nganyi ngala nhunutji yarnduldrangu.* 'He tells everyone I'm no good, but he's just the same.' • *Thimbiltji pakurnanga kulanga yarnduldrangu makamuduli.* 'They dig thimbiltjis and cook them the same way, in hot ashes.' # See also **yala**, **nguya yala**.

yarndunguda in that way, from that, that's how • *Pandi karranhana yintjadu kathipani, yarndungudala thuru mawa thirrithirrinarlatji.* 'The dog was tied up without any meat, that's how he got starved, and that's what made him savage.'

yarnduyi how, like this, this way
• *Ay, walya yarndudutji ngaldra yita thawa, ngala yarnduyi ngaldra yita.* 'Don't go that way, let's go this way.'

yarnduyildrangu the same way
• *yarnduyildrangu yita thawarla* 'going the same way [as me]'

yarra wide

yarrana spread (for example, open arms, spread legs) # Intransitive, but with object, perhaps only body part, as in *kupu yarranarnanga* 'opening the arms'

yarrkamarta devil # Yw. See **karnapalha**, **kurnki**.

yarru yard • *Palha purla pirnanarlayitji, ngapala yarru wathinaritji, marru kadawayi, ngapala thawarnanga puka windritharranga ngapa marruyitji palha purla thanhayi mapathikanga.* 'When the young birds are getting big, they build a yard for them on the bank of the lake and then go down into the water and herd the baby birds back [into the yard].'

yartu full • *Mulhudu nganyi thayi-yindrina, ngala walyangu nganyi yartu, ngurrangu nganyi mawali nganarla.* 'I had a feed but I'm not full yet; I'm still hungry.'# See also **marnamirri**, **pirna**.

yartuka feed (someone, something)
• *Ngala thanatji walyala yartukari, ay ngarndri-ngapirili yada pakarnanga karlukarlutji ngunyinga thanha.* 'They [the people] don't have to feed them [the young pelicans]; the parents bring fish and give it to them.'

yartuna become full (stomach), get full • *Ngapala nhinari yartunarnanga palhangudatji, ya palha paninarlayitji.* 'They eat their fill of them until the birds are all gone.' • *Thayiyindrirrnanga yartunarnangalatjini, walya padla-padla walya thurrpathurrpa, mardra-mitjingudatji.* 'They eat until they are full, [meat] from the stones, not dirty or ashy.'

yawa, yawapandhi spread • *manthi yawapandhi* 'spread bedding out'

yawathikathika, yawawagawaga
spread all around

yawayawa unroll • *Purtu yundru yawayawala thikandji yada yandha-yandhangalatji ngakaniyi.* 'Unroll your swag and then come back and talk to me.'

Yawarrawarrka language name, northern dialect of the Yandruwandha group

yawarri speech, language, word
• *Yawarri yintjadu yundru ngararla, pirripirri yintjadu?* 'Do you understand that language, that white bloke?'
• *Ngarrungu nhunu Diradili nganha yakapadanga nga walypala yawarrili, 'Yilangginguda yiney?'* 'Then he just asked me in Dieri, and then in whitefellow language, "Where are you from?"' # See also **ngan.gu, parlpa, yindri**.

yayi exclamation expressing fear

yayina call out 'Yayi!' (in fear)
• *Ngala nhunu karnatji yayinanga yina yabali.* 'Then the first man screamed out in fear.'

yiba drink • *Ngapa nhutjadu yibiningadi.* 'That water's for drinking.' • *Karrukarru, nhunuyi pada, ngapakaldringuda, yibanhana nhuluyi, thudarla nhunu, kurrayi nganarnanga, kurrayi nganarla.* 'This old fellow is inside, he's been drinking rum and now he's lying down, dead drunk.' • *Wawarnanga ngapangadi ngari thawarlayi karna kulpinayindrirlayila ngapatji yiba-rlayi nga wathi windrali warrkananga.* 'Well, when they see them going to the water the men surround them, and then spear them while they're drinking.'
• *Kilkalikarla thawanga ngapa-ngaditji, ngarru pulyala pakari tjukurru darla yibiningadi palthuyukala yitalayi thawarnanga.* 'They know it is there and they need carry only a small kangaroo skin

[waterbag] for drinking from while they are going along.' # See also **thapa**.

yibayiba suck # See **pardaparda**.

yibayindri suck (for example, a cut)

yidikurra groan # SY (exact meaning not clear)

(yidla) # see **yila**

yidlakadi where to? • *Yidlakadi yini yurarla thawanga?* 'Where do you want to go?'

yidlakadi kara I don't know where to, to somewhere

yidlanggi, yidlanggiyi where?
• *Nguthu ngakani yidlanggiyi?* (or *yidlanggi?*) 'Where's my brother?'

yidlanggi kara, yidlanggiyi kara somewhere, I don't know where
• *Ngalaaku yidlanggi kara nhunu nhinanga nhunggukalangu.* 'He's round about there sitting down somewhere.'

yidlangginguda where from? • *Karna yula yidlangginguda?* 'Where are you two from?'

yidlayarndu how?, what (saying)?; that way • *Yidlayarndu yinha yundru yakana?* 'What did you ask him?'

yidlayi where? • *Mayi, wawathikana yundru pani? Yidlayi nhunukukalangu thana?* 'Well, did you see anybody? Whereabouts are they?'

yidrayidra flower

yiga wild orange • *'Yigatji wayi patji?' 'Ay kaldringu thana. Walpi kara pirtipirtinangatji.'* '"What are the wild oranges like?" "Oh, they're bitter yet. Don't know when they're going to get ripe."' # Note that *yika* means 'fig' in Adnyamathanha.

yiga squeeze # SY. See **nyulka**.

yika wash • *Ngapa nhutjadu yibiningadi, walya mara yikayindriningadi.* 'That water's for drinking, not to wash your hands.' # See also **yirra, multhipa**.

(yika)

yikaka, yikayika lose; spill # SY
• *Ngathu yinhaku mardra yikakani.*
'I lost that money.' # See also
**walyawalyaka, nyulka, parrkuka,
pudla.**

yikayika the wrong way # SY
• *Nganyi thawanhana yikayika.*
'I went the wrong way.' # Also
manhamanha.

yila # possibly a non-specific inter-
rogative root. Heard as a separate
word only in *yila wayini* 'how many?'
— normally *wayini* — and as 'where
to?' (SY), each only once. Also **yidla.**

yilaadi see **yilayadi.**

yilaadinguda where from? # SY

yilakadi where to? • *Yilakadi yula
thawarla?* 'Where are you two going?'
• *Minha ngarrkanga kara ngandra?
Yilakadi ngandra pakanga?* 'What are
we going to do with her? Where will
we take her?'

yilakadi kara I don't know where to,
to somewhere • *Yilakadi kara nhunu
thawawindrinhanatji.* 'I don't know
where he's gone to?'

yilanggi, yilanggiyi where?

yilanggi kara, yilanggiyi kara
where; somewhere, I don't know
where • *Yilanggi kara thana pipatji.*
'I don't know where those letters are.'
• *Yilanggitji kara thana pitjidi
mandripadipadini, ngalaaku.* 'I don't
know where they used to get the
pitchery.' • *Thawarla nganyi,
yakathikanga yinhayi yilanggi kara
ngaldra thudiningadi.* 'I'm going over
to ask him where we can camp.'

yilanguda, yilangginguda where
from? • *Marrikudinhanala yini
yilanguda?* 'Where did you come from
to get here so early?' • *Ngapala pula
nganayindrirnanga 'Yilangginguda
nhutjadu?'* 'Well they asked one
another "Where's he from?"'

yilanguda kara, yilangginguda kara
I don't know where from, from
somewhere • *Kayidila thanadu thawa-
warranhana, yilangginguda kara.*
'They [rabbits] have only come lately
— I don't know where from.'

yilaru how?, what (say)? # Yw
• *Yilaru yini ngampiya?* 'What have
you got to say [about that]?' # See
wayi, yarndu.

yilayadi where? # SY • *Yilayadi-
ngadi ngaldra thawarla?* 'Where are
we going?' # Also heard as **yilaadi.**

yilayarndu how?; thus, that way;
what (saying)? • *Minha ngarrka-
nhana? Yilayarndu yundru
kudranhana wathi parndriparndrinitji
— ngandala?* 'What happened? How
did you break the axe — the handle?'
• *Yilayarndu yini yandharla? Walya
ngathuna ngaranatji. Thakuthakurru
yandha.* 'What did you say? I couldn't
understand you. Talk slowly.' # SY
also **yilarindu.**

yilayarndu kara somehow, I don't
know how • *Ngapala pakathikarnanga
darla pirnngandji yinha, yilayarndutji
kara.* 'Well, they carry them back to
camp and skin them — I don't know
how.' • *Yada nhuludu — yilayarndu
kara — warrkarlatji madlamadlantji.*
'He throws the boomerang a funny
way — no good.'

yilga see **yilka.**

yiliyili slippery # See also **yapu,
yupurru.**

yilka, yilga slip • *Mardrayi nganyi thina
yilgana warlkanga.* 'I slipped on a
stone and fell over.'

yiltharri frost # See **pudu;** froth; beer

yilthayiltharri frosty

yilyirri hurrying, in a hurry • *Walya
yilyirri nganatji mayi, nguni pirnangu
ngaldra.* 'Don't hurry, we've got all
day yet.' # Also **pakali, nhurrpa,
pawada.**

yilyirrika hurry (someone) up # Also **pakalika**.

yilyirri ngana get busy, be busy, be in a hurry • *Yilyirri nganana nhunu, walya ngarini nganha.* 'He was in too much of a hurry to listen to me.'

yimadi brother-in-law, husband's brother, sister-in-law, husband's sister # See also **kardri**.

yimpa black, brown • *Pandi yimpa nhutjadu warangi, thanggu-thikathikana.* 'Who does that black dog belong to, that's wandering around.' # = Yw *tjimpa*

yimpaka blacken • *Warlu yina mitji yimpakanhana?* 'Who gave you a black eye?'

yimpana (1) get black, go black • *Nganya thanadu yimpanapadalarla.* 'The clouds are getting black.'; (2) be bruised • *Kupu nganyi yimpanarla.* 'My arm is bruised.'

yina emphatic particle • *Walya yinha yirrtjinatjay, muka yina nhutjadu thudarla.* 'Don't wake him up, let him sleep.' • *Pulupulu ngathu yintjadu kandrakana mardri yina nhutjadu.* 'I couldn't lift that, it's too heavy.' • *Wanitji ngathu wawangala, karrula yina nganyi.* 'I can watch the corroboree now because I'm a man.'

yina you (object of verb) • *Walypala yintjadu ngana kathi yina ngunyiningadi.* 'Tell the whitefellow to give you some meat.'

yinba send • *Kilkanhanatji walya thana, kadli yina ngathu yawarri yinbininguda.* 'I had sent word, but they didn't know.'

yinbapada send across

yinbatharra send away • *Ngala thana ngarndri-ngapirilitji mulhudu mapaapininguda yinba-tharrapandhingalatji nhunggani.* 'His parents sent down food that they had collected for him.' • *Ngathu man.garri yinbana mandrithikiningadi*

purtu ngakani. 'I sent a girl to get my things.'

yinbathika send back home

yinbawindri send away

Yinbarrka Embarka Waterhole

yindri noise, thunder; language • *Yandruwandha yindri yurarla ngariningadi.* '[You] want to hear the Yandruwandha language.' # See also **yawarri, ngan.gu, parlpa, mirrtja**.

ngandjarri yindri thunder # See also **pildripildri**.

yinggani your, yours, belonging to you; you (as in 'with you', 'to you' etc.) • *Purtutji yinggani wawa-wawanaw, winkamayila nhuludu.* 'Watch your things, or he'll take them.' • *Yingganiyi nganyi thawarla.* 'I'm going to go with you.'

yingka laugh # perhaps a noun as well as an intransitive verb. Gerund is *yingkani*, not *yingkini* • *Ngapala yingkarnangala thili yabangunyi-yindrininguda ngala pula walypa-lathili.* 'Well, they both laughed then, the two white men, at the way they had frightened one another.' • *Wathinguda nganyi warlkanhana nga ngambutji ngakani yingkanga nhunu.* 'I fell out of a tree and my mate just laughed at me.' # Yw *tjingka*

yingka ngunyi, yingka ngunyi-ngunyi make (someone) laugh

yingkali amused(?)

yingki cry; neigh (horse) • *Muduwa nhutjadu yingkirla.* 'The baby's crying.' • *Yiwa nhatjadu yingkirla ngathaningadi.* 'That woman's crying for her baby.'

yingkiyingkina make (someone) cry • *Muduwa ngathu yingkiyingkinana, mirni yada mandrithakangay.* 'I made the baby cry, will you come and get it.'

yinha him, it, the (object of verb) • *Yarndukala ngali yinha thulathula-kanhana ay karna nganggalitji* *nhutjadu.* 'How could we reckon he was a stranger, when he's one of our own people.' • *Pangkithirri nhulu yinha warrkananhana.* 'He speared it in the ribs.' • *Wirni payirrikari yinha nga kunyayi kurranga.* 'They make the string long and put it on the spindle.'

yinhayi him (here), it (here), this (object of verb) • *Pudlupudlu ngathu nhandu yinhayi thilpathilparla, pirri-tjampanarla nhuniyi.* 'I can't get this horse going because he's tired.'

yini you (subject of intransitive verb or in a sentence without a verb) • *Yilakadi yini thawarla?* 'Where are you going?' • *Muduwa yini wanthiyindrirla; nhuniyi nhinarla ngalinggayi.* 'You're looking for the boy; he's sitting down here with me and him.'

Yinimingka Innamincka Waterhole (where the original Innamincka Station homestead was)

yinka string # Also used to form compounds *wirniyinka, pinyiyinka, wathiyinka*(?). See **wirni, yulpudu**.

yinma stick (something) in

yinma peel (something) # SY

yintjadu him (there), it (there), that (object of verb) • *Kilkarla ngathu yintjadu, ngarndri-ngapiri ngala nguthu-ngama.* 'I know him, and his parents and relations.'

yipi auntie, mother's sister

yirra wash • *Yirranhana nhanha thidharri.* '[She] washed the baby.' • *Yirrayindrina nganyi.* 'I washed myself.' # See also **yika, multhipa**.

yirrbandji something not allowed, forbidden # perhaps from a verb *yirrba* • *Nganggalildra thana wani thambanapadipadini, walya yiwali wawiningadi, yirrbandji yina.* 'They [the men] dance their own corroboree and the women don't watch, it's forbidden.'

yirrika shiver • *Pundrali nganyi yirrikarla.* 'I'm shivering with the cold.' # See **ngarra**.

yirrtji wake up • (SY) *Yirrtjila!* 'Wake up!' # H *wadjina*

yirrtjina wake (someone) up • *Walya yinha yirrtjinatji.* 'Don't wake him.' • *Ngapala nhulu drangayindrirnanga yirrtjinakaldri yina karnakurnutji, pani ngala nhunu karnatji ngarru wathildra thudarlayi.* 'Well he was singing to himself, to keep the other man awake, but there was no other man, only the log lying there.'

yirrtjithalka get up • *... yirrtji-thalkanga thawiningadilatji* '... get up to go'

yita over there, there; that way, away • *Ay, walya yarndudutji ngaldra yita thawa, ngala yarnduyi ngaldra yita.* 'Don't go that way, let's go this way.' • *Ngapala karrapadari yita.* 'Then they tie it [the net] on over there.' • *Ngandjarri mira yita wawaka!* 'Oh. look over there, there's a rainbow!' • *Ngali yitaldra thawarla ngala nhunu yadaldra thawarlayi.* 'We're going that way and he's coming this [opposite] way.' # Opposite to *yada*. See also **nhinggikala, nhukudu, kala**.

yitaka shift (something) # SY • *Yitaka yinhaku maka.* 'Shift that firewood.'

yitapandhi down there, further down a slope or bank

yitapandhiwarra ? # perhaps 'right down, all the way down' • *Ngapala pula karlukarlungadi yada thawari nga yandhanga nhinanga karlukarlu parndrirnanga pula thadri pada-warraldra, ngala nganyitji thadri yitapandhiwarraldra nhinarlayi.* 'Two of them came down to do some fishing. They sat and talked and caught fish on the other bank, while I was camped on the bank that sloped down opposite them.'

yitathalka up there, further up a slope or bank

yitayada back and forth; one another • *Yitayada ngali parndriyindrina.* 'We hit one another.' • *yitayada wawayindrirnanga* 'facing one another'

yiwa (Aboriginal) woman • *Kinikangatji ngala yiwalila yambarriyi kurranga.* 'The women heap them up on the flat ground.' • *Karnatji yiwa minha ngala karrukarru minha thawarnanga yulputji ngapatji marndrarnanga ngarru thanayi tjukurru darlalila.* 'Men and women and old men travel and they just cart water in the kangaroo skin.' • *Drakarnanga yarndu-ldrangu wirnikamuratji yiwangaditji pirnaldra, karriningadi panikaldra nhambalkayindrindji.* 'On the one hand they make a big one [hair-string apron] for women to tie on, to cover themselves completely.' # SY also 'female (animal)', See **nhiwa, tjiwara.**

yiwari body # See also **parlaka, marndra.**

yuda you mob, you (more than two) • *Wara yuda thawawarrana?* 'Who are you lot [who came here]?'

yudangga your, yours, belonging to you (more than two) # Yw, = *yunngani*

yudani your, yours, belonging to you (more than two); you (more than two) (as in 'with you', 'to you' etc.) # Yw. Also **yunngani.**

yuka catch (fish) by swimming with net • *Kapada yukathikanga ngandra, karlukarlu.* 'Come on, let's go fishing.' • *Ngathu wawatharrana karlukarlungadi yukiningadi pirli yama yina karrparlayi.* 'I saw them make a bag net for catching fish while swimming in the water, and a cross net.'

yuka so; too, also • *Ngapala thana kathi warruwitjingaditji thawari, kathi warruwitji yukatji parndringa.* 'They also go out for emus, to kill emus.' # Also **nguka.**

yukarra spend the night • *Tjukurru parrkulu kara, parrkulu-parrkulu kara karrpininguda nga kangu yukarrangatji.* 'It might be two skins, or maybe four and then they are warm at night.'

yukarrapandhi lie down • *'Pirritjampanarla nhunu.' 'Warrayi nhunu yukarrapandhimalkayarndu.'* 'He's tired.' 'All right, he can lie down.' # Also **thudapandhi.**

yula you two • *Karna yula yidlanggi-nguda?* 'Where are you two from?' • *Nhinanhinanhana yula ngurra walypalalitji nhuludu.* 'You and that white man were sitting there for a long time.'

yulani your, yours, belonging to you two; you (two) (as in 'with you', 'to you' etc.) # Yw, also **yulgani.**

yuldru narrow # Yw, see **wuldru.**

yulgani your, yours, belonging to you two; you (two) (as in 'with you', 'to you' etc.) • *Nhuniyi yulgani?* 'Does this belong to you two?' • (SY) *Ngathu mulhudu yulgani nhinalkarla.* 'I've got some food for you two.'

yulhu you two (object of verb) • *Wawana ngathu yulhu.* 'I saw you two.'

yulka swallow # Yw. See **yurrku.**

yulkuparlu river gum # Also used to refer to Cooper's Creek, perhaps because in Yandruwandha country they grow only there. • *Ngali pirnanalapurra yulkuparluyi, papangi nganha pirnakalapurra.* 'We grew up on the Cooper's Creek. My granddad reared me.'

yulpu travelling • *Ngapala ngapa marndrinilatji thanngani yulpu thawiningadi, padla yundrawaka* *ngapapaniyi.* '[They use] their waterbags when they go on a journey in remote waterless country.' • *Karnatji yiwa minha ngala karrukarru minha thawarnanga yulputji ngapatji marndrarnanga ngarru thanayi tjukurru darlalila.* 'Men and women and old men travel and they just cart water in the kangaroo skin.' # On a later occasion this word was said to be *yulpudu.*

yulpudu string # SY. See **wirni, yinka.**

yulpurru running (water)

ngapa yulpurru flood • *Nga Kini-papayi nganha warrkawindringa ngapa yulpurru yina ngakarlayi.* 'They left me at Cooper's Creek because the river was in flood.'

yulya policeman # See also **kandjipulu, pilimpara, pilitjimani, thandjipulu.**

yumbu upper back # 'the back, from the neck down, shoulders and that, and neck' • *yumbu durrurdurrunarlayi* 'with his head down, stooping'

yundayunda tadpole

yundra a long way away, far, remote • *Ngapa yundra nhunu ngatjadayi.* 'The water's a long way from the camp.' • *A'ay yundranguda nganyi, ngaandi, mayi yundrangudanga.* 'Oh, I'm from a long way away, yes, a long way.' • *Ngapala ngapa marndrinilatji thanngani yulpu thawiningadi, padla yundrawaka ngapapaniyi.* '[They use] their waterbags when they go on a journey in remote waterless country.'

yundrana get away (from somewhere), go away # SY • *Yundrana, walya nhuluyi yina wawiningadi.* 'Get away [from there] before he sees you.' # See also under **thawa.**

yundrayundra too far; a very long way

yundru you (subject of transitive verb) • *Minhangadi nganha yundru parndrina?* 'Why did you hit me?'

• *Ngandra yaba ngunyinhana nganha yundru ngathutji purtupa walthawindrinhana winkarnanga yinggani kurnkipuru.* 'Oh! You frightened me and I took my swag away and ducked off for fear of you being a devil.'

yunggudu blood • *Man.gili nhunu mundja, patjarla, thawanhana nhunu, kirringadi, kintha yunggudu ngakarnanga.* 'Benny's sick, his nose is bleeding and he's gone to the doctor.'

yunggudu kaparri vein

yunggudumindji menstruating

yungguyunggudu bloody

yunhu you mob, you (more than two) (object of verb) • *Walya ngathu yunhu kilkarla.* 'I don't know you lot.' • *Pulyala kara nhukuyi nhunu wathitji, yandhayandharlayitji nganyi nganarnangatji yunhu.* 'There must be only a little bit of tape left now, for me to talk to you fellows.'

yunka disgusted, with disgust • *Yunka nhunu thangguminiwindrina.* 'He stood up and walked away disgusted.' # SY also 'sulky'.

yunkali disgusted

yunkana be sulky # SY. See **thirrithirrina.**

yunka ngunyingunyi disgust, make disgusted

yunngani your, yours, belonging to you (more than two); you (more than two) (as in 'with you', 'to you' etc.) • *Yawarritji ngathu yinbininguda yunnganingadi walya yuda thawa-warranhukadatji. Wadanhana ngathu yunhu.* 'After me sending word to you you never turned up. I waited for you.' # Yw also **yudani.**

yupa give cheek, annoy, tease • *Madlantji nhutjadu; karna nhuludu yuparla.* 'He's no good, he's cheeky.'

yupurru, yupuyupurru smooth, slippery # See also **yapu, yiliyili**.

yura want, like # See Chapter 14 of *Innamincka Talk* for more information on the variety of ways in which this word can be used. • *Wayini yini yurarlatji?* 'How much do you want?' • *Walya ngandra yurarla paldriningadi nhinggiyi.* 'We don't want (him) to die here.' • *Walya ngathu yinhayi padla yurarla.* 'I don't like this place.' • *Minhala yini yurarla ngariningadi nganyi yandharlayi?* 'What do you want to hear me say?' • *Ya palhatji thana yurari parndringa, pirli thana paladildrangu drakini-nguda, nga wathiyi pada karranga warrakurnutji, thadripalapala yina.* 'If they want to catch birds they make a net of a different mesh and tie it on to a tree on each bank of the river.' • *Nhinggiwa thana thudamalka, yurarnangatjardi.* 'They can camp over there, if they want to.' • (SY) *Walya nganyi nhungganiyi karnayi yurarla.* 'I don't like that man.' # SY used *yura* only in negative sentences with *walya*, and *ngandja* in positive sentences.

yurayindri feel good about yourself (?, see **manu**)

yuri, yuriyi for a long time, a good while • *Ay yuriyi puladu yandhayandharla.* 'Those two are

talking for a long time.' # Possibly a loan from Eng 'hour'.

yuritja horn # SY, Yw • *Kathi thanaku yuritja payirri.* 'Those bullocks have got long horns.' # BK *yuruwitja*

yuritjamindji bullock, thing with horns # SY. See **puluka**.

yurlawarra mopoke, owl # At initiations the boys had to sit up all night without sleeping. To keep them awake they would hit them on the chest and say: • *Kapow! Yurlawarrali yina murna parndrina.* 'Bang! The night owl hit you in the chest.' # See also **windra**.

yurlu straight; true • *palthu yurlu* 'straight road' • *Ngarru nhulu wawanhana yurlu, walya kara nganha nhulu kilkanhana.* 'He just looked straight ahead, as if he didn't know me.' • (SY) *Yurlu ngampa mayi!* 'Tell the truth!'# See also **ngurraru, muthu**.

yurrku swallow

yurrkuyurrku dillybag # See also **pirli, mirrka, paltja, thandji, yakutha**.

yuru wallaroo, euro # SY. Also **thudu**.

yuruwitja horn # SY and Yw *yuritja*

yutha (meaning not clear, maybe 'hunting ability' or 'success in hunting')

yuthapani unsuccessful hunter

yuthapirna, yuthapurra good hunter

yutju throat # SY. See also **ngaga, ngayimala**.

3 English-Yandruwandha finderlist

Entries in this section are kept brief. You should go to the Yandruwandha to English section for more information. Where a word in the Yandruwandha to English section has a simple form and a more complex form, such as *drama, dramardrama* or *kantu, kathi kantu*, usually only the simple form is given in the English to Yandruwandha section. Alternative pronunciations are not given but alternative forms are, if one is not simply derived from the other. So, for example, *kulpinayindri* and *kulpinawaga* are both given. The Innamincka Yandruwandha form is given; a form from another dialect is given (but not identified as such) only if an Innamincka form is not known or if it is quite different. Some items are given in groups, such as 'birds, types of' or 'plants, types of', although many of the members of these groups also have their own entries, such as 'crow' or 'coolibah', and some appear instead in smaller groups, such as 'ducks, types of' or 'Acacias'.

Entries in this section are generally in alphabetical order, but where an entry consists of more than one word they are in alphabetical order of the important word or words. So, for example, to find 'give birth', look for where 'birth' would be; for 'the bush' look for 'bush'. In cases like these the word determining the place of the entry is underlined, so 'give birth'. Often such entries will be in two places.

Placenames are not included in this list. There is a separate list of them following it. Kinship terms are included in the list, but there is also a (very tentative) kinship chart at the end. This involves some assumptions based on the situation in other languages, and is probably not completely correct.

A

abdomen madru
able kirrikirri
(Aboriginal) person karna
(Aboriginal) woman yiwa
(initiated Aboriginal) man karru
about there nhukukala, nhunukukala,
  nhunggukala
be about to ngana
absence pani
abuse one another yandriyindri
acacia bush kaltja
acacias, types of kaltja, kalyu, kamburru,
  mandhirra, manharri, mardipirri,
  mardumanha, marlka, mawurra,
  parlayila, pararrka, tjirri, wayaka
across kunawarrku
active kirrikirri
adze thinbithinbini
be afraid yabana
afterbirth yadhi
afternoon kalka
again puthakurnu
aggression thirri
Alectryon oleifolius thayamarni,
  ngamikularri
alike marndu, yala(?)
alive thipi
all pani, purduku, pulpu
all over purru
all sorts mulhakurnu-mulhakurnu
all the time ngurra
something not allowed yirrbandji
alone kurnu
already kali
also yuka
altogether ngurrangurra
always ngurra, purra
amused(?) yingkali

and nga, ya
and then ngapala
animal kathi
animals (introduced) nhandu, pandi,
  pirndiwalku, puluka, rabiti, thirrtha,
  thutjutju, tjampaka, yadamani,
  yuritjamindji
animals (native) karndilgatha, kantu,
  kapitha, mayikurru, nganyipuntha,
  nguluwarnda, ngurrani, nharramuku,
  palyada, pildra, pindjipindjinhada,
  pundha, thalkaparlu, thudu,
  thukathayini, tjukurru, wartari, yuru
animatedly mampali
ankle martardaku, mukunkirri
annoy yupa
another kurnu
another country padla yundra
another one minha kurnu nguka
ant, types of marnkunu, matjurra,
  mithipudanda, pardi mirrka,
  pardimardri
Antechinomys laniger puntha,
  nganyipuntha, pundha
anthill kamba
anus pidri
any ngalyi
anybody karnakurnu-karnakurnu
anyhow tjawutjawu
anything minha kurnu nguka (with
  negative)
anywhere purru
apart (of feet) piriyarra
appear kanpana
appearance nguya, nhinda
argue kadiyindri, kaldriyindri
arm kupu, nguna
armpit kapurru
around there nhukukala, nhunggukala
arrive kuthiwarra, thawawarra
ascend kandrana

ashamed nhindali

ashes mudu, thurrpa

hot <u>ashes</u> maka kanya, maka mudu, maka
thurrpa

ashy thurrpathurrpa

ask ngana yaka

asleep muka

Atalaya hemiglauca ngurraputha,
kurrantjala

auntie yipi

await wada

get away yundrana

axe mardra thayithayi

(steel) <u>axe</u> wadamarta

B

baby muduwa, thidharri

back durru, kala, thuku, thumu

back (return) thika

at the <u>back</u> ngardra

back and forth yitayada

back of neck purnda, wakarri

bottom or <u>back</u> of net munthu

backbone witamuku

backside pidri, wartamuku

backwards durruli

bad madlantji, manha

go <u>bad</u> thunggana

bag mirrka, nindri, paltja, thandji,
yakutha, yurrkuyurrku

bag (in general) pirli

bag net pirli, pirli nindri, pirli yama

ball kundikili

ball (e.g. of clay) ngambu

ball (e.g. of tobacco or pitchery mixed
with ash, or dough) ngunku

ball (of flour and water)
damburdambu(ra?)

ball (of string) kunapampu

make into a <u>ball</u> kunapampuka,
ngunkuka, ngunkunhapi

bandage karrakarra

bang parndriparndri

bang (noise) karta

make a cracking or <u>banging</u> noise
kartaka

bank kadawa, wida, thadri

bare parlu

bark (dog) warlu parndri, kaldrukaldruna

bark (of a dog) warlu, kaldrukaldru,
wawurrka, marrtji

bark (of tree) darlamurru

bat pindjipindjinhada

be ngana, nhina

be (of something that typically stands,
such as a tree) thanggu

bean tree mudlu

beard ngan.ga

bearded dragon kani, kurla

beat time dranga

become ngana

bed manthi

bedded rock palparri

beefwood tjin.gini, pirnta

beefwood gum kandri palku,
pirntathangka

beer yiltharri

before matja, mirni, ngardra, ngurra,
purra

behind durruyi, ngalpirri, ngardra,
ngardratjika

from <u>behind</u> durrukadi

not <u>believe</u> someone padhaka

belly thuru

belonging to her nhanggani,
nhangganiyi, nhanggatjadu

belonging to him nhunggani,
nhungganiyi, nhunggatjadu

belonging to them pulgani, pulganiyi,
pulgatjadu, thanngani, thannganiyi,
thanngatjadu

belonging to us ngalungga, ngalingga,
ngaldrani, ngalini, nganungga,
nganingga, ngandrarni, nganini

belonging to you yinggani, yulgani, yulani, yunngani, yudangga, yudani

not belonging thula

belongings purtu

belt pilta

belt (someone) kartamatha

bend kurndikurndika

bend (arm?) dupurdupuka

bent kurndikurndi

get better manyuna, patjina

between thanu

between the legs piri

bicycle lizard karlantji, yaliyali

big pirna

become big pirnana

make big pirnapirnana

bigger, biggest, biggish, not very big pirnapirna

bindieye kurla, manharri

bird palha

birds (see also under **ducks**, **cockatoos** and **parrots**, and **water birds**) kandatjiri, karrawa, karriwara, karrupakarli, kawalka, kirrki, kukunka, kulikuliyada, kurrupakula, kuwukuku, malparu, maltharramindji, martimarti, milkiwaru, mulapada, pathada-pathada, palyakini thapithapini, pawayi, pirrki(?), pulyurru nyununyunu, purdathayini, purralku, putjaputja, thindrithindri, thirri, thiwildraka, tjumpunya, tjumpurra, wandaparra, warruwitji, wartamugali, wilarngu, windra, yurlawarra

give birth kurra, yadhi kurra, ngama mana, ngathanika, dan.ga

bite matha

bitter kaldri

black tjimpa

black bream thawirritji

black cockatoo murrumpadi

black duck dikarri, kunapika

black goanna kalamurru, makapari

black shag ngukumindji

black-headed python mulhayimpa

blacken yimpaka

blade (of spear) parlpa

blanket mirrka

blind putju

blind snake nyungumarlinya, mithinti

be blind, go blind putjuna

blister kima

block ngarndama, nyandama

blood yunggudu

bloodwood dultharri

bloody yungguyunggudu

blossoms thiwi

blow pulka

blow (nose) pulkayindri

blow (wind) darrka, ngaka

blowfly mundjurrunga

blue kunapantjiri

blue-tongue lizard kalta

blunt nyarna, parntu

become blunt parntuna

body parlaka, yiwari, marndra

body hair nyurdu

Bogan flea manharri

boggy palya

(water) boil parrtjini

bone muku

pull bones out mukurduka

bony bream pitjanka, parru

boomerang yada

tool for making (or grooving?) boomerang thatjithatji

boots thinaputa

born yadhi

be born kanpaka

boss mayatha

on both sides palapala

on both sides of the river thadripalapala

bottle kubala

bottom pandhi, ngari, pidri

bottom of the water ngapakuku
bottom or back of net munthu
bottom of net wararri
bough yanka
boulder palparri
bow vine punggu, kalu
boy kan.gu, walhini
little boy karruwali
brains kuka thangka, puwa, tjuru(?)
branch nguna
break kudrikudrina
break off kudra, dratji
break something kudra
black bream thawirritji
bony bream pitjanka, parru
breast ngama
breathe ngindra, pulhanga
breathe hard, be out of breath
  ngarawantina
breed kurrayindri
bridle puradlu
bring pakawarra, waltha
bring back pakathika
bring back (water) marndrathika
bring inside windrimapada
bring up pirnaka
brisket kuldru
broken kudrininguda
broken piece(s) of stone pilthirri
get broken kudrayindri
brolga purralku
brother, elder brother nguthu
younger brother ngathadi
brother's child ngathalki
brother's daughter's child papa
brother's son's child tjindra
brother-in-law kardri, yimadi
brown yimpa
be bruised yimpana
buckbush kurla kilthi
buckjumper pakitjampa

budgerigar pinyanku, thilbirrutja,
  thilinkurru
buggy pagi
build wathi
build up (a fire) thangkaka
bulldog ant pardimardri
bullet mardra, mardramitji,
  mardrathandra
bullfrog drukampada
bullock puluka, yuritjamindji
bullroarer thuburu
the sound of the bullroarer ngarlakurra
make the sound of the bullroarer
  ngarlangarlakurrana, ngarlakurraka
bully parndrinipurra
bulrushes karlku
bump thita
bunch of leaves yanka
bundle purtu
get buried windripandhi
burn thangkana, darra, mangga, ngarrtji,
  pidli
burn (not as being consumed by a fire
  but as being injured by a fire or
  heat) kudla
burn along (as a bushfire) manggaduda,
  ngarrtjirduda
burn away to ashes muduna
burn up thangka
burp kagayindri
burr kurla
burr (types of) kurla kilthi, kurla
  kurrumpa, kurla puntjiwarra, kurla
  purralku, manharri
bury nhamba, thudri
bush yanka
the bush kantha
bushfire maka kantha
bustard purdathayini
be busy, get busy yilyirri ngana
but ngala

butcher kathi dramidramini, kathi pirnngini, kathi parndrini
butt nganku
butt (e.g. of tree, yamstick, spear) warta
butt of a yamstick mudranganku
butterfly kalipilhipilhi
button padna
buy payama
by and by mirni
by oneself nganggali

C

cake puka kiki
call kandri, mirrtjakurra, ngarndapandji
call (someone something) drika, ngandja
call out kaldripantji, karrka
call out (as a galah) marrtji
call out (in fear) yayina
call to come widi
calm wardama
camp ngatjada, nguda
camp (for the night) thuda, muka thuda, thudayukarra
make camp kurrakurra
camping out marrka
can you? kirri
can't pudlu
canegrass wapila
capable kirrikirri
carefully patjipatji
carelessly tjawutjawu
carney kani, kurla
carpet snake wama, manga, mulhana
carry thuka, waltha
carry (water) marndra
carry away pakawindri
carry back walthathika
carry for yourself walthayindri
carry home pakathika, walthathika
carry under arm mungka

in case nguka
catch pardra
catch (a ball) dakunpa
catch (animals, birds or fish) parndri
catch (fish) parndriyindri
catch (fish) by swimming with net yuka
go and catch (fish) and come back parndrithika
caterpillar panga
catfish kirrapara, wakuwaku
small catfish kapi
cause ngana
cause pain draka
cave mingka, wirlpa
cave in hill mardrangumu
centipede thilthirri
a certain one paladi
chafe withiwithina
charcoal mukuru
chase kadi, thilpa
cheek ngulku, karditjidi, kidakida
give cheek yupa
cheeky thirripirna, thirripurra
chest murna
chew thayithayi
chew (tobacco) thayi
chicken hawk thirri
child muduwa
child (of a man) ngathalki
child (of a woman) ngathani
brother's child ngathalki
brother's daughter's child papa
brother's son's child tjindra
sister's child ngathani
woman's daughter's child kanyini
woman's daughter's daughter's child ngarlu
(woman's or sister's) daughter's daughter's child kayakaya
chin ngan.ga mudra, nganka, tjindra
chip palki

chips from making of grinding stone
  thayipilthirri
chisel thinbithinbini
chisel (something) thinba
choke puma, ngagapardra
chop (wood) parndri
church kundi muda
circumcise pantjika, pantjina
circumcised pantji
clapping of hands mara pabu
claws ngunpurru
clay padla thaka
claypan paratharra
clean wika
clean (i.e. finish) (a spear) thinba
clean (something) kurikapada,
  kuriyirrika, kuritharra
clean (something) wikana
clean (the guts out of a carcase) kun.ga
clench (fist) nganamayindri,
  ngarndamayindri
clever kirri
climb walki, kari, kathi
climb over walkithalkapada
clitoris thatji
close kaka
close to (in appearance) marndu
go close kakana
clothes mirrka
cloud nganya, ngandjarri, pariwirlpa,
  kudawarrala
cloudy ngandjangandjarri
cluster kini
hot coal maka kanya, maka mukuru
coarse (not fine) dragurdragu
coat kuta
cockatiel martimarti
cockatoos and parrots kakarrili,
  kilangkila, martimarti, murrumpadi,
  ngukumindji, nhadipintha, pinyanku,
  thilbirrutja, thilinkurru, palha parlu
cockerina kakarrili

cold malthi, pundra, kilpa
make you cold pundra ngunyingunyi
cold (sickness) kundrukundru
bad cold muda
collarbone pinyipinyi
come kuthiwarra, thawawarra
come (of a car) miniwarra
come and sit down for a while
  nhinanhinathawa
come apart kudrakudrayindri
come back thika, thikathika, thikawarra
come for a while thawaminiwarra
come inside winkapada
come on! kapada
come out dunka
company milparri
complete, completely panina, panika
do completely panina
construct wathi
cook (something) kudla, parndraka, darra
cook (something is cooking) kudlayindri
cook (in a ground oven?) kudlapandhi
cook (one who cooks) makawarlawagini,
  kukiyi
cook overnight kudlayukarra
cooked parndra
cool (someone, something) down
  malthika
coolamon pitji, nharra
coolamon, types of pitjingamburu,
  pitjiwiritji, nharramuku, kambu
coolibah kalpurru, pathada
copi thurna
copulate thani
corella palha parlu
cormorant maluda, ngukumindji
corroboree wani, muda
corroboree ground wani paratharra,
  muda
corrupt kinyi ngunyingunyi
cotton thirri
cough kundrukundru, kurrungkurruka

a <u>cough</u> kurrungkurru

make (someone) <u>cough</u> kurrungkurru ngunyi

count kandama

country padla

cousin (cross-cousin) kami

(cross-)<u>cousin's</u> daughter parli

(cross-)<u>cousin's</u> son ngapiri

cover nhamba, purrilka, wamba

crab mararrala, mundrupa

crack marnkana

crack (sound) karta

cracked (e.g. cracked mud) marnka, thaltha

become <u>cracked</u> marnkana

make a <u>cracking</u> or banging noise kartaka

cramp purrga

be <u>cramped</u> ngarnmayindri

cranky kurrari

be <u>cranky</u> kurrari ngana

crawl marrka

crayfish marnngani

creek karirri, kadri, wipa

crested pigeon mulapada

crippled tjundurru

crooked kurndikurndi, kurdikurdirri

cross kunawarrkuka, purrkapada

cross net yama

(river) <u>crossing</u> ngapangarrka

crossways kunawarrku

crotch drantha, thitha

crouch purri

crow kawalka

crown of head kukapidri

crush parndri

crutch *see* crotch

cry yingki

make (someone) <u>cry</u> yingkiyingkina

cure patjika

curl up kunapampuna

curled up dupurdupu

curlew wilarnku

curly (hair) munumunu

cushion for carrying coolamon on head kukapira

cut, cut up drama

cut and shape (wood) thinba

cut in halves mindimulpa

cut into little pieces ngurlupulya mulpamulpa

cut off, cut through mulpa

cut short ngurluka

D

damper puka

dance dranga, thambana

dance 'shake-a-leg' ngalpa

dance at night thambanayukarra

dark mabumabu, marri, milyaru, waruwaru

get <u>dark</u> mabumabuna, marringana

man's <u>daughter</u> ngathalki

woman's <u>daughter</u> ngathani

woman's <u>daughter's</u> husband patjiri

woman's <u>daughter-in-law</u> kalhidi

dawn padla marra

day dritji, kurli, nguni

day before yesterday ngananhinanhukada

daylight nguni, padlakanpa

become <u>daylight</u> kalkamarra, padla marra

daytime nguni

dazzle mitji parumandri

dead nhadi, thinka

dead finish pararrka

deaf thalpapuru

deafen thalpapuruka

death adder ngandrawandra

deep kuku, mikiri

deep (voice) pirna

deep water ngapakurna

defecate kunathika
dense mardri
devil karnapalha, kurnki, yarrkamarta
dew pudu
die nhadina, paldri
die down panina
die out, all die paldritharra
different paladildrangu, paladipaladi
dig paku
dig all around pakutharra
dig down pakungari, pakupandhi
dillybag (pirli) yurrkuyurrku
dim kalga
dingo pandiyapa, pandiwilka, pandi yampa, thirrtha yampa
dip up (water) marndra, kaluwa
directly kayidi
dirt padla
dirty manha, padlapadla
disappear winka
disbelieve padhaka
discuss wirniwirni
disgust (someone) yunka ngunyingunyi
disgusted yunka
make disgusted yunka ngunyingunyi
make dishonest kinyi ngunyingunyi
dishonestly kinyili
dishonesty kinyi
dislike warrkawarrkana
distribute ngunyithikathika
dive kartiwirri, winkapandhi
divide yalba, wandukudra
do ngana, ngarrka
do every day or for some time nhinathanggu
do well or successfully dakunpa, patjili
do what (to someone or something)? minha ngarrka
doctor kirri
dog pandi, thirrtha, thutjutju
wild dog pandiyapa, pandiwilka, pandi yampa, thirrtha yampa

dogwood thayamarni, ngamikularri
door marna
dotterel digirdigilyarra, thanpathanpa
dough puka
down ngari, pandhi
down there ngari widi, pandhi widi, yitapandhi
further down a slope or bank yitapandhi
go down winkapandhi
down (feather) thirripurdu
drag thingarduda
dream pukudu, dangguda
dream about dangguda pardra
Dreaming, Dreaming story yalkura
dress puruka
drill (a hole) wirlpaka
drink mura
drink (something) yiba, thapa
drip (water) tjulbi
drive kadi
drive (a vehicle) parndri
drive along (in a car) mininhina
driver mutuka pakini
drop purrina
drown (someone) nyunma
drown, get drowned nyunmayindri
drunk kurrari
be drunk kurrari ngana
dry muya, purudu
dry (become dry) purudungana
dry (something) kayinta, muyaka, puruduka
put in the sun to dry ditjipa
duck down wirri
duck off winka
duck, types of dikarri, kunapika, mingkanguda, mitjiparlu, tharralku, thawulu
dust kunuputha, puthurru, thayirri
duststorm, dusty puthurru

E

eaglehawk karrawa, karriwara

ear thalpa

early, early morning marrikudukudu,
  marriyungka(?)

do <u>early</u> marrikudhi

east dritjirdunka, witjukura

east wind witjukura

eat thayi

echidna karndilgatha

edge kadawa, ngudulu

edible grub pardri

egg pampu

egret mulpa

eh!, eh? mayi

elbow ngunamarnda, thintipidi

elder pirna

elder brother nguthu

elder sister kaku

eligible to marry nhipa mulha

emphatic particle yina

empty karla

empty (belly) mawa

empty out pudla

empty-handed marakarla, mara pani

emu warruwitji, maltharrimindji, kiwada

emu feathers maltharri

end mudra, ngulu, mulha, panina

end of a burrow or cave puru

enter windri, wirri

erect wathi

Eremophila gilesii pundri, dandhirri

euro thudu, yuru

even kala

get <u>even</u> kalaka

every day ngunikurnu ngunikurnu

everybody karnakurnu-karnakurnu,
  panina

everywhere padlakurnu-padlakurnu,
  purru

exchange ngunyiyindri, wiriwinma

exile wilyaru

exile someone wilyaru pardra

expect wawawawanhina

expert mara patji

explain ngana

eye mitji

eyebrow, eyelash mitjipilpa

F

face mulha

faeces kuna

fall warlka, ngurli, ditjipurri, kudra

fall (leaf or fruit from a tree) pundji

fall (of rain) warlkathalka

fall down (from a height) warlkapandhi,
  warlkangari

fall over warlkatharra

fallen leaves around a tree kurrthi
  thalpa

fan dadawa

far yundra

fart pithiri

fast puthapika, puthapirna, wirlpa

fasting mawamawa

fat (melted) kilthi

fat (person or animal) marnipirna,
  marnipika

get <u>fat</u> marnipirnana, marnipikana

fat (the substance) marni

father, father's brother ngapiri

father's elder brother ngapiri pirna

father's father tjindra

father's mother kami

father's sister parli

father's sister's child kami

father's sister's daughter nhipa

father's younger brother ngapiri pulya

father-in-law tharu, ngama

fatten marnipikana, marnipirnana,
  marnipirnaka

fatty marnimarni

fear yaba
feather thirripurdu
feed (someone) yartuka
feed (yourself), have a feed thayiyindri
feel (with the hand) pardrapardra
feel for (something) wankina
female animal nhiwa, yiwa
a few ngalyi
fight thirri
two-handed fighting stick ngandithirri
find dan.ga, mankamanka
fine, finely ground pupara
finger maramitji, witju
fingernail mara ngunpurru, marapirri, marapuku
finish murda, panika, panina
fire maka
build up (a fire) thangkaka
go out (fire) panmayindri
(fire) smoke thupu ngana
firelight maka paru
firestick maka thirra
firewood maka, wathi
first kambarri, ngakamarra
first shot kanpapardra
first time kanpangu, kayidi pardra
fish karlukarlu, kuya
fish (types, including crustaceans) kapi, kintha, kuya pardi, mararrala, marnngani, mundrupa, ngampurru, parru, pinthika, pitjanka, thawirritji, wakuwaku
fist maramuku
five mara
fix dakuka, patjika
flat palbarri, pali, pirrapirra, yambayambarri
flat place paratharra
make flat yambarrikurra
flat, flat place yambarri
flatten palika
flee putharrkawindri

flesh palku
float mindithanma, ngupa, tharraka
float off into the air milimiliwaduka, thinawaduka
flock ngami
flock pigeon malparu
flood ngapa yulpurru
flour pawa, ngardu
flower yidrayidra
flu kundrukundru
fly (insect) mundju
fly (in the air) tharra
fly across tharrapada
fly away tharrawindri
fly down tharrapandhi
fly in circles tharrawagawaga
fly up tharrathalka
foetus yadhi
fog mayiputha
fold (including legs) dupurdupuna
follow kapi
follow (someone) inside kapitharrapada
food mulhudu, puka
foot thina
for no reason ngarru
for that reason yarndu
forbidden yirrbandji
forehead ngarnda, ngurlu
foreskin pintha
forget kuditharra
fork wathi kala, wathi drantha
forked stick wathi drantha
four parrkuparrkulu, pulpapulpa
fresh ngaba
to get a fright purrtji
frighten purrtjina, thilpa, yabaka, yaba ngunyi, yaba mana
frightened purrtji, yabali
frightened person yabakanpa, yabapika
a bit frightened yabayabali
become a bit frightened yabayabana

get <u>frightened</u> yaba ngana, yabana

not <u>frightened</u> yabapani

frogs drukampada, durrkuwantha, kurrtjarrku, kutjarrku, kuyarrku, thinathina

from the back durrukadi

front mampa, marna

at the front kambarri

the <u>front</u> of the humpy walpamarna

in <u>front</u> marnayi

frost pudu, yiltharri

frosty yilthayiltharri

froth yiltharri

fruit on mistletoe palyakini

full marnamirri, yartu, pirna

become <u>full</u> marnaminina, yartuna

fur yamunu

G

galah nhadipintha, kilangkila

gall on limb of gum tree (?) yalkura

gallop putha

(make) <u>gallop</u> pangkiparndri

gather mapa

gear purtu

wood adder (type of <u>gecko</u>) ngapardalku

gentle slope murnurru

get mandri, pardraka

get (water) marndra

get (spear, shoot etc.) muthuka

get for yourself mandrithayi

get up early in the morning marrikudhi

get up to go thangguwindri

go and <u>get</u> mandrithika, minimandrithika

go and <u>get</u> (water) marndrathika

ghost karnapalha

gibber mardramitji

gidgea mawurra, mardumanha

gill net pirli mitji

girl purndapurnda

little <u>girl</u> man.garri

give ngunyi, mana

give a fright purrtjina

give around ngunyithikathika

give back ngunyithika

give to someone who is going away ngunyiwindri

be <u>glad</u> kandratjanggu

glasses mitjithulkini

go thawa

go across thawapada

go again thawakaldri

go at an angle thawardakapada

go away thawaka, thawawindri, yundrana

go away from warrkawindri

go back thika, minithika, thikathika, thikawarra

go down in (hole) windripandhi

go in windri, wirri

go out dunka

go out (fire) panmayindri

go out of sight winkathawa

go round and round karrtjiwagawaga

go to visit thangguthika

go up kandrana

make go thilpathilpa

goanna, types of kalamurru, karingkarra, kirriwali, makapari, man.gali

God muda yalkura

golden perch ngampurru

good patji, patjikurnu, manyu, ngumu

feel <u>good</u> about yourself yurayindri

good hunter yuthapirna, yuthapurra

good rider thukayindrini

a <u>good</u> job, a good thing manyu kurnu

a <u>good</u> while yuri

for <u>good</u> ngurrangurra

make <u>good</u> dakuka, patjika

grab pardrapada

grandchild kami, kanyini, papa, tjindra

grandfather papa, tjindra

grandmother kami, kanyini

grass kantha, kurrkari

grasshopper pindri, wamalurru

grassy country kanthakantha

graze (nearly hit) wantjathawa

grease thata

greasy thatathata, thatamindji

great grandchild, great grandmother
 ngarlu

greedy mundha

be greedy kalumarra

green kunapantjiri, kundakunda, kurrkari,
 pulayarra

green (unripe) purda

greenhead ant matjurra

grey warru

grey hair kuka pipi

grill pulka

grind thunga, kururrupa, dringa

grinders (teeth) waka muku

grinding stone thayi, wala, mardrakupu,
 pawathungini, mardra nhiwa

grip ngarnma

groan yidikurra

ground padla

ground seeds pawa

group kini, ngami

grow pirnana, punka

growl kaldrukaldru

growl at yandri

grown up pirna

edible grub pardri

edible grub, types of kananggu *or*
 kanunggu, kapukapu, pardri
 ngurraputhanguda, pirapardri

grumble kunakunana

grunt drulkurdrulkuna

guide paka

gully ngarli, thurrka

gum tjirarri, ngulyi

river gum (tree) yulkuparlu

gun makita

gut kun.ga

gutter thurrka

H

hailstone mardrapuru

hair (of head) karli, pada

body hair nyurdu, yamunu

half way marnda, marndakurnu, thanu

half-caste parlaka pirtipirti

hammer wathi parndriparndrini

hand mara

handle marapardrini

handle (as of axe) ngandala

hang wadu, waduka

hang on to one another
 ngarnmangarnmayindri

hang up (e.g. clothes) watjina

be hanging waduka

happy mangkiri

be happy kadhi

hard mampali, ngurru, paltja, pidipidi

hard worker wakapurra

be hard to follow (of someone's speech)
 ngarnmangarnmayindri

get hard, harden paltjaka, ngurru ngana

hat kabuta

have nhinalka, pardra

have (a baby) dan.ga, kurra, yadhi kurra,
 ngama mana, ngathanika

having rights over nganggali

chicken hawk thirri

kite hawk kandatjiri

types of hawk kirrhi, milkiwaru

hazy puthurru

he nhunu, nhuniyi, nhunudu, nhutjadu,
 nhunuwa, nhulu, nhuniyi, nhuludu

head kuka

crown of head kukapidri

forehead or upper part of head ngurlu

headband ngurluyapidi

heap kini, wadla

heap of dirt(?) padlawarna

heap up kinika, wadlaka

hear ngara, panga

heart thupurru, ngarangara

heart (perhaps only in the figurative sense) manu

heat makamaka

heat something up wanga

heavy mardri

heel thinawarta

help warli

her nhanha, nhanhayi, nhanhadu, nhantjadu, nhanggani, nhangganiyi, nhanggatjadu

here nhinggiyi, nhukuyi

here and there marndakurnu-marndakurnu

from here nhinggiyinguda

to here nhinggiyingadi, yada

heron malparu

hers nhanggani, nhangganiyi, nhanggatjadu

hiccough kagayindri

hidden kudhikudhi

hide (something) kudhikudhima, purrilka, wamba, winkama

hide (yourself) kudhi, purri

go and hide kudhithika

high kandra

hill wita

him yinha, yinhayi, yintjadu, nhunggani, nhunggatjadu

hind leg wandikila

hips pulumuku, wartamuku

his nhunggani, nhungganiyi, nhunggatjadu

hit parndri, thirri

hit (e.g. with bullet) dakunpa

hit (throwing) dranyi

hit back parndrithika

hit on the back of the head or neck purndaparndri

hit with something flexible warlpa, kuntji

hit yourself parndriyindri

hither yada

hobble kungka

hobble (a horse) papurlaka

hobbles papurla

hold pardra

hold high, hold up pardrathalka

hold tight ngarnma

hole daba, mingka, thuka, wirlpa; kudru

hollow in tree kukunu

honey pitjipampu

hook mila, milarrika, nguku

hop along (as a kangaroo) kulkumathawa, kulkupanhina

hop away (as a kangaroo) kulkupawindri

hopbush yalkada

horn yuritja, yuruwitja

hornet pirdrithiwirdi

horse nhandu, pirndiwalku, yadamani

hot makamaka, makamakali

hot ashes maka kanya, maka mudu, maka thurrpa

hot coal maka kanya, maka mukuru

get hot makamakana

house kundi, warli

how wayi, yarndu, yilaru

I don't know how yilayarndu kara, wayi kara

how about mirni, kara, kirri

how many, how much wayini

I don't know how many wayini kara

hug mungka

hug one another, hug (something) to yourself mungkayindri

human hair string wirnikamura

humpy walpa, walparda, mambu, punga

hunger mawa

hungry mawali

hungry person mawakanpa**

make you <u>hungry</u> mawa ngunyi
hunt ngandrangandra
hunter kathi parndrini
good <u>hunter</u> yuthapirna, yuthapurra
poor <u>hunter</u> murrupurlu
hunt away nharra
hurry tharratharra
hurry (someone) up yilyirrika, pakalika
hurry away tharratharrawindri
in a <u>hurry</u> pakali, yilyirri
be in a <u>hurry</u> yilyirri ngana
hurrying yilyirri
hurt katjakatja, mundjaka
husband nhipa
husband's brother kardri, yimadi
husband's father tharu
husband's mother patjiri, kalhidi
husband's sister yimadi
hut kundi, warli

I

I nganyi, ngathu
I don't know kara, ngalaaku
ibis wandaparra, wartamugali
if kirri
imitate wantjiwantjina
immediately pakali
indeed ngala
initiate pirnaka, karruka
initiated man karru
initiation ceremonies muda
injure mundjaka
injury withi
inoffensive murla
insects, types of (*see also* ant) kadra,
    kalipilhipilhi, kamba, kandirrtha,
    kanunggu, kinirdaka, kunthi,
    marangkarra, mirdiwiri, mulhakuna,
    mundju, mundjurrunga, nhardithi,
    padri, padri ngurraputhanguda, panga,
    parndilka, pidriputha, pindri, pintjidi,

pirapardri, pirdrithiwirdi, thilthirri,
    wamalurru, wayiludu
inside ngari, pada
the <u>inside</u> of the humpy walpakuku
go <u>inside</u> winkapada
intend to ngana
small <u>intestine</u> kunakadli
iron ngayana
something made of <u>iron</u> wathi ngayana
island thundi
it nhunu, nhuniyi, nhutjadu, nhunudu,
    nhulu, nhuluyi, nhuludu, yinha,
    yinhayi, yintjadu, nhunggani,
    nhunggatjadu
itchy purnunu
be <u>itchy</u> purnunuka
its nhunggani, nhungganiyi,
    nhunggatjadu

J

be <u>jammed</u> ngarnmayindri
jealous, jealousy thidri
make (someone) <u>jealous</u> thidri
    ngunyingunyi
jib ngarnmangarnmayindri
join someone kuthipada
join together marnduka
join up marnduna
juice, juicy kilthi
jump didjipirri, kulkupa
jump across kulkumawalpirri
jump out (as from a hole)
    kulkupathalkawarra
jump up kulkupathalka
just ngala, ngarru

K

kangaroo tjukurru
kick parndri
kidney pundrapundra

kill nhadika, parndri, parndripandhi, thinkaka

go and kill and come back parndrithika

kiss marna thapa, marna yiba, ngandja

kite hawk kandatjiri

knee pantja

kneel pantjakurra

get down on hands and knees purri

knife nalyba, thurla, thatji

knitted string cap kukawarnu

knob thita

knobby thitathita

knock or shake seeds off pudlapudla

knot (on tree) thita

knotty thitathita

know kilka

knowing warlpara

knowledgeable about something kilkakilka

kultarr puntha, nganyipuntha, pundha

L

lake marru, mitka

lake country, area with a lot of lakes marrumarru

lame waku

language parlpa, yawarri, yindri

language names Diradi, Matja, Ngananhina, Nhirrpi, Parlpakurnu, Parlpamardramardra, Pilardapa, Yandruwandha, Yawarrawarrka

lap ngalpa

larger end of anything long warta

last night nganayukarranhukada

lately kayidi

later ngardra

later on mirnimirningu

laugh tjingka, yingka

make laugh yingka ngunyi

lead paka

lead (a horse) thinga

in the lead ngakamarra

leaf thalpa

bunch of leaves yanka

leak pulayindri

leak (water) tjulbi

lean warnumayindri

lean (meat) palgupalgu

lean (something on something) thangguna

learn warlpada ngana

learned warlpara

leave (someone or something) purrka, warrkawindri

leave behind kurrawindri, ngardrawarrka, wawathawa

leave early in the morning kuthipada

leave it warrayi

leave one another yalbayindri

leave somewhere warrka

left hand nguna warrku, wannganyi

on the left wannganyi

to the left wannganyikadi *or* wannganyingadi

leg maltji

hind leg wandikila

lengthen payirrika

let go warrkatharra

let go (of something held) marapundji

letter pipa

level palbarri

liar manmini kanpa, mungini

lichen (?) munba

lick thapa

lie (down) parra

lie (of water) para

lie at night thudayukarra

lie awake thudathudanhina

lie down thudapandhi, yukarrapandhi

lie inside thudapada

lie on back thundruka, thundruthuka

lie on front murnapaka

lift kandraka, makumandri

light (weight) kanda, ngawada, ngalba
light nguni, paru
light (fire) wanga, pulkapada, thalpapada, karadaka
light up (fire) thangkathalka
get light kalkamarra
lightly (of eating) kalga
lightning kurni, parrikara
lignum pundrinya, wayirri
like (someone) ngandja, yura
like (similar) nyadi
like that yarndudu, yarndudungu, yarndukala
like this yarnduyi
limb of tree drantha, karli
lip mimi
little bit nganya, pulya
a little ngalyi
live nhina, thipinhina
lively kirrikirri
liver kalu, ngarangara
lizards (*see also* **goannas**) kalta, kaltjantada, kani, kurla, mardanpa, murlathi, ngapardalku, thadjingumini, thandakalini, yaliyali
local nhinggiyinguda
location nhinggi
log thinka, wathi, maka warnta, muku
long payirri, marrpu
make long payirrika
not very long payipayirri
long ago matja, manyanguda, pandja
a long way away yundra
for a long time ngurra, yuri
look wawa, wawatharra
look after wawana
look around wawathikathika, wawawagawaga
look for nhingka, wanthi
look out! kapow
look over wawangalpirri
look past wanthawawa

loose kalga
get loose dukayindri
loosen kalgaka
lose nyulka, walyawalyaka, yikaka, yikayika
lose (unborn) baby marayilka, thundruyilka
be lost nyulkayindri, winka
get lost kudhitharra, nyulkana, nyulkayindri
a lot malkirri, ngurra, pirna
loudly pidipidi
louse kadra
lower leg maltjimuku
lower part of body of kangaroo kapa
lower part of shin (?) maku
lucky (e.g. as a fisherman) kunparri
lump kima, malyu
lungs punnga
be lying thudanhina

M

machine wathi
mad kurrari
be mad kurrari ngana
madman kurrakurrari
maggot mirdiwiri, parndilka
magpie thiwildraka
mailman milimani
Major Mitchell cockatoo kakarrili
make (someone) sick mundja ngunyingunyi
make daka, ngana, nhapi, wathi
make (a fire) thangkaka
make (boomerang) thinba
make its natural sound (e.g. a bird calling) ngampa, yandha
make out kurrakurra
make sure of dakuma
male (animal) karrukarru
man karna

man (initiated, Aboriginal) karru
make a man of someone (initiate) karruka
man! (as a term of address) kan.ga
man's child ngathalki
man's daughter's child papa
man's son's child tjindra
many malkirri, wamba
mark malka
marpoo bush mandhirra
married nhipamindji
married couple nhipangurru
marrow (of bone) tjuruntjuru
marry mandripada, nhipaka
Marsilea drummondii ngardu
match maka matji
mate ngambu
matter (in boils and sores) ngampa
maybe kara
me nganha, ngakani
meat kathi, palgupalgu
social division ('meat') kamiri, mardu
meat ant marnkunu, pardi mirrka
mechanic wathi patjipatjikini
meet (one another) murnamandriyindri
melon pudhukani
mend patjika
mend (e.g. a torn dress) karrpa
menstruating yunggudumindji
make a mesh (net) milarrika
middle of the day nguni pirna, ngunipika
in the middle thanu
might kara
milk ngama
milk bush thupari
Milky Way Kadripariwirlpa
mine kamanti, ngakani
mirage nhilanhila
miscarry marayilka, thundruyilka
miss nyalka, pipi
make a mistake nyalka

mix nguka, nhapi, warlawaka
mob ngami, wamba, malkirri
molars waka muku
money mardra, mardra mani
month nyangi, pira
moon nyangi, pira
moonlight nyangi
mopoke yurlawarra
more marla, nguka
mosquito kunthi, wayiludu
moth pardri
mother ngarndri
mother's brother ngama
mother's brother's child kami
mother's father ngadra, papa
mother's mother kanyini
mother's mother's mother kayakaya, ngarlu
mother's sister ngarndri yipi, yipi
mother-in-law parli, patjiri
motorcar mutuka
get mouldy thunggana
mountain mardrawita
mountain devil thadjingumini
mountain duck mingkanguda, ngapa mingkanguda
mouse nganyipuntha, pundha
mouth marna
put into the mouth marnangadika
move waga
move away (to live) wagawindri
move fast putha
move over (yourself); move something wagaka, wagalka
mud pulyurru
mudlark kulikuliyada, martimarti, pathada-pathada(?)
red mulga marlka
mungeroo karlaka
murderer karna parndrini
muscle palgupalgu
mussel thuka, kudi

muster mandripandhi, mapa
my kamanti, ngakani
myall wayaka

N

nails ngunpurru
naked parlu, yarawarra
name drika, maya, tharla
nape purnda, wakarri
nardoo ngardu
stone for grinding nardoo
  ngarduparndrini
narrow pulya, wuldru
nasal mucus kintha ngamburru
navel mindra, pirda
near kaka
nearly kali walya, ngampu
neck ngaga
needlewood kuluwa
neigh yingki
nephew ngalari, ngathani
nest warla
net nindri, pirli mitji
net (in general) pirli
make a mesh (net) milarrika
never mind warrayi, warrayi wawa
new didamarra, kayidi
next kidla, puthakurnu
next day marri, marripathi
niece ngalari, ngathani
night mabumabu, milyaru
in the night marri
no pani, walya
no good madlantji, manha
noise mirrtja, yindri
noisy, make a noise mirrtja
noisy, make a noise mirrtja, mirrtja
  ngana, mirrtjakurra
none pani
north karawarra

north wind walpanggarra
nose kintha, mulha
not pani, walya, watja, watka
not at all muthu (with negative)
notched stick for messages yadamaka
nothing pani
for nothing ngarru
notify thilpawarra
now kali, kayidi, ngala
now and then kayidi-kayidi,
  marndakurnu-marndakurnu
nut in bloodwood tree thandra

O

occasion putha
red ochre kambada, milthi
yellow ochre parru
often ngurra
oh! ngandra
old matja, pandjanguda
old and feeble manhawakuru
get old and feeble manhawakura
old man karrukarru
get old (of a male) karrukarruna
old woman kurrupu
get old (of a female) kurrupu ngana
olden-days man karrukarru
olden-days woman kurrupu
on your own kurnu
once putha kurnu
one kurnu, paladi
one another yitayada
on one side warrakurnu
wild onion karlaka
only ngarru
open pindri, pirika
open (door) dabaka
open (eyes) dingayindri
be open (eyes) tjalka
open (mouth), be open (mouth) thangu

open (your eyes, mouth) piltja
open ground, open place yambayambarri
be <u>open</u> pirika
open your legs pirimayindri
make an <u>opening</u> wirlpaka
in the <u>open</u> kanpa
or kara
or not pani kara
wild <u>orange</u> yiga
orphan ngamurru
other nguka
on the <u>other</u> side (not visible) ngalpirri
on the <u>other</u> side warrakurnu
the <u>other</u> side pada, warrkupada
others ngalyi, ngariyuka
our, ours ngalungga , ngaldrarni,
     ngalingga, ngalini, nganungga,
     ngandrarni, nganingga, nganini
outside thalka, wirdi, yambarri
over walpirri
over there nhinggikala, nhukudu, yita
go <u>over</u> wartaka
owl windra, yurlawarra
own (something) nganggalika
own, owner nganggali

P

pain katjakatja
cause <u>pain</u> draka
paint milthi
paint (something) marndra, windri
palm of hand marathangka
pannikin paynputu, tjampitji
paper pipa
parents ngarndri-ngapiri
parrot, *see* cockatoos and parrots
part kala
particular paladi
pass ngardrawarrka, wanthathawa,
     wawathawa

passing, past wantha
go past wanthathawa
in the <u>past</u> matjanguda
paunch kunangarndri
pay puruka
peck drakardraka
peel (something) pirnnga, yinma
peel off (e.g. bark) tjirra
peep around ngulukayindriwaga
peep out nguluka
peewee kulikuliyada, martimarti,
     pathada-pathada(?)
pelican dakamirri, ngagangaga
penis kurni
pennyroyal kuntha
perentie kirriwali
(Aboriginal) <u>person</u> karna
person with a big appetite mawapika
photo (of a person) mulha malka
pick up mandri, mapa
pick up here and there mandrithawa
     mandrithawa
pick up on the way mandrithawa,
     mandrimini
picture malka
piebald malkamalka
little <u>pieces</u> ngurlupulya
pierce wirlpaka
pigeon kuwukuku
crested <u>pigeon</u> mulapada
flock <u>pigeon</u> malparu
pigeon-toed makudaka
pigweed ngadli
pile kini, wadla
pile up wadlaka
pillow purndawalkini
pinch milka
pintpot paynputu
pipe paypa
pitchery pitjidi
pitchery bag pirli tjapura, tjapura
pitchery bundle kumani

place padla

in the vicinity of a <u>place</u> that has been named or is known nhinggikala

plain kunirri, yambarri

plain turkey purdathayini

plainly visible kanpa

plant kudhikudhi

plants (*see also under* **acacias** and **burrs**) dandhirri, dultharri, kalpurru, karlku, kartakarta, kardra, karlaka, karnan.gu, kayarri, kuluwa, kuntha, kurla, kurrantjala, kurrumpala, mandawarra, mitjiyimpa, mudlu, mulhayimpa, munba, ngadli, ngamikularri, ngardu, nginyaru, ngurraputha, nharrtha, palyakini, patjiwarra, pidriyiltharri, pirnta, pitjidi, pudhukani, purdru, pundri, pundrinya, punggu, thayamarni, thayarri, thimbiltji, thupari, thurratji, tjin.gini, tjumburu, tjumbutjurrkuru, wadlangurru, wapila, wawu, wayirri, yalkada, yiga, yulkuparlu

play thambana

play around thambanawaga

play with thambaka

plug nyanma

plum bush mandawarra

wild <u>plum</u> tjumburu

point mimi, mudra

point (at something) thumba

point of beard ngan.ga mudra

pointed tjalparri

poisonous creature pardi

poke draka, pipa

poke out tongue thapa

policeman kandjipulu, pilimpara, pilitjimani, thandjipulu, yulya

poor fellow ngidlayi, ngurrani

porcupine karndilgatha

possessions pin.gi

possum pildra

post pirta, wathi muku

potato putiyita

pouch thandji

pound parndri

pour kima, pirrpa, pudla

pregnant thundrumindji

prentie kirriwali

present kanpa

pretend manma

on a <u>previous</u> occasion matja

prick draka

proper muthu

properly patji

do <u>properly</u> dakuma

be <u>proud</u> kadhi

pull duka, thinga

pull bones out mukurduka

pull in thingapada

pull out duka

pull to pieces dukatharra

pull up mandrithalka

pup tjutjutju

puppa-grass mitjiyimpa

pus ngampa

push thadra

push along thadrarduda

put kurra

put around kurrawaga

put down kurra

put in kurrapada, windrima, winma

put in the sun to dry ditjipa

put into the mouth marnangadika

put on (clothes) kadlinayindri

put on top of nhangkapandhi

put out (fire) panma

put to sleep mukaka

put together marnduka

put under kurrapada

put up kurra

black-headed <u>python</u> mulhayimpa

Q

quarrion martimarti
quick paka
quickly nhurrpa, pakali, pawada
quiet murla, ngapu, pilpangurru
become quiet, be quiet ngapuna
quietly pilpangurrulu, kalga

R

rabbit rabiti
race putha
rag mirrkapiki
rain ngandjarri
rainbow kurrikira, mira
raise pirnaka
rat mayikurru
raw kimba, purda
get ready ngana
real muthu
really muthu
for no reason ngarru
for that reason yarndu
recognise kilka
reconcile manu patjika
red pirtipirti
red mulga marlka
red ochre kambada *or* kambadi, milthi
get red marra
make red pirtipirtika
reeds (on river bank) karnan.gu
reflection nguya, walarri
related to one another in such a way
    that you can't marry one another
    pirni nguru
relations ngarndri-kaku, nguthu-ngama
relaxed kalga
remote yundra
repair dakuka
the rest ngariyuka

return nhinathika
in return kidla
revenge party pinya
ribs diparri, pangki
ride (a horse) thukayindri
good rider thukayindrini
right patjikurnu
on the right pinhaniwa
to the right pinhanikadi
having rights over nganggali
ripe parndra, parrkini, pirtipirti
ripen, get ripe pirtipirtina
ripple ngamanyalpi, marndikila
river karirri, kinipapa, karitjurru, kadri
river gum yulkuparlu
river wattle kamburru
(river) crossing ngapangarrka
road palthu, wardayapa
roast darra
rock mardra
bedded rock, big flat rock palparri
rock (as in a coolamon) pinaka
rock wallaby kantu
rockhole mardrakipani
roll over karrtji
roll up kunyama, nhapi, thurrpa
roll up into a ball (e.g. string) pampuka
roly-poly kurla kilthi
root of tree kaparri
rope wirni, wilpuru, drupa
rot thunggana
rotten kutawirri, thungga
rough kurtukurtu, thitathita
rough (voice) kaldrukaldru
round dupurdupu
round up kulpina
rounded pampaampu
rouse on yandri
have a row kadiyindri
rub windri
rub (hard) kururrupa

rubbish kanthiri
ruin madlantjika
rum ngapa kaldri
run mini
run (of liquid) ngaka
run and spear miniwarrkana
run around miniminithika
run away miniwindri, putharrkawindri, winka, winkapani
run away (stealthily) kinyiwinka
run away with minilka, winkama
run back minithika
run down ngakangari, ngakapandhi
run past wanthamini
running (water) yulpurru

S

be sad walya yurayindri
saddle tjadla
saliva ngaltja
salt thaltu
saltbush, types of mulhayimpa, kartakarta
same yala, nguya yala, yarnduldrangu
the same place nhinggingu
in the same way yarnduldrangu
sand padla, padla muthu, thipari
sand goanna karingkarra
sandfly pidriputha
sandhill miri, miriwita
sandhill snake wama
satisfied patjikurnu
be savage thirrithirrina
say ngana, yandha
scar tjinbiri
scatter mangga
scatter (them, e.g. people) pirnpi
scoop up (water) kaluwa
scorpion kinirdaka
scrape dringa

scrape all over dringatharra, dringawaga
scratch mirra
scream kirdra
scrub pukapuka, wathi pukapuka
scrubby wathiwathi
sea thaltuwata
seagull wirniwangka
seal nyanma
search ngandrangandra
second finger mara payirri
see wawa
see properly kurrakurra
seed mitji
seeds (probably only edible seeds) pawa
send yinba
send across yinbapada
send away yinbatharra, yinbawindri
send back home yinbathika
send for kandri
sensible tjurumindji
separate paladipaladi, punthipunthipa
set (sun) windri, wirri
sever mulpa
sew karrpa, milpi
shade, shadow walarri
shady, having plenty of shade walawalarri
shag (= cormorant) maluda
black shag ngukumindji
shake ngarra, yandjiyandjilka, yandjiyandjina
knock or shake seeds off pudlapudla
shaking legs/knees (in corroboree, after a death) kuma
be shaky yandjiyandji
shallow kanda, putha
shame nhinda
shame (someone) nhinda ngunyingunyi
shape nhinda
share kala, wandukudra, yalba, manggamanggakurra
sharp tjalparri, tjarrkarla

sharpen tjalparrika

shatter druka, kudrakudrayindri, pilthipilthirrika

she nhani, nhaniyi, nhatjadu, nhanidu, nhaniwa, nhandra, nhandrayi, nhandradu

shear mulpa

shearer tjida

sheep tjipi, tjampaka

shell of egg darla

sheltered (from wind) wardama

shield nharrathitha

shield shrimp pinthika

shift waga, wagaka, wagalka

shift (something) yitaka

shine dintji, para, tjarnma

shirt tjata

shiver ngarra, yirrika

shoot dranyi, tjutama

short ngurlu, warnta

in a short time warnta

for a short time warnta, warntatharra

shorten ngurluka

shortish payipayirri

shortly warnta

shoulder kilkirri, pilpiri, pinyi, thapini, wiliwili

shovel nharra

show thumba

show (by pointing) thumbalka, thumbatharra

show around thumbalkathikathika, thumbalkawagawaga

show up kanpana

shrimp kintha

shield shrimp pinthika

shut (eyes) ngarndamayindri, ngupina(?)

shut (mouth) dapa, munma, ngapuka

be shut (eyes) putjuna

be shut (mouth) ngapuna

shy nhindali

make shy nhinda ngunyingunyi

shyness nhinda

sick mundja, wariwari

become sick, get sick, be sick patja, mundjana, wariwarina

make (someone) sick mundjaka

side diparri, pangki, thili, thinka, warra

at the side thiliyi

on one side warrakurnu

on this side nhinggiyipada

on both sides palapala

on both sides of the river thadripalapala

sideways thinkali

in sight kanpa

in a similar way marndunangu

sinew thiltja

sing dranga, parndri

sing out kaldripantji, ngarndapandji

sing to yourself drangayindri

singe the hair off thurrka

sister, elder sister kaku

younger sister ngathadi

sister's child ngathani

sister-in-law yimadi

sit nhina

sit (in tree, of a bird) thanggu

sit around nhinawagawaga

sit around waiting wadawada

sit down nhinapandhi

sit on haunches wilawarra

sit on heels (with knees on the ground), sit (as emu) manpakurra

sit on something nhinana

sit with legs straight out ngurrukutha

size nguya, nhinda

skin darla, nyindi

skin (something) pirnnga, nyinyimilpa

get skinny tjirrayindri

sky pariwirlpa

sleep muka, thuda

sleepiness muka

sleepy mukali

make (someone) <u>sleepy</u> muka
  ngunyingunyi
sleepyhead mukapurra
slip yilka
slip along dikilyarra warra
slippery yapu, yiliyili, yupurru
slipping dikilyarra
not <u>sloping</u> much palbarri
slow marnka
slow (someone or something) down
  marnkaka
slowly marnka, thakurru
small pulya, purla
small intestine kunakadli
smell, have a smell parni
smell (especially, perhaps,
  characteristic smell, as of a person)
  kamiri
smell (something) panthama, parnima
smoke thupu, muki *or* muku
smoke (tobacco) puba
smoky cloud pirli
be <u>smoky</u> thupu ngana
smooth palbarri, palurru, yapu, yupurru
smoothe palurruka
smother muntji
snake kathikathi, pardi
snake, types of kadrantji, manga,
  mithinti, mulhana, mulhayimpa,
  ngandrawandra, nyungumarlinya,
  pardingunthu, wama, wan.gu
sneak off kudhiwindri
sneak up para
sneaky kudhikudhi
sneeze thuntjirri
snot kintha ngamburru
so yuka
soak ngapatjili
soap thupa
social division ('meat') kamiri, mardu
soft danthu, miltjamiltja, tjampa
soldiers pinya

sole thinathundru
some ngalyi
somehow yilayarndu kara
someone warlu kara, warnu kara
someone's warangi kara
something kurnu nguka, minha, minha
  kara
something else minha kurnu nguka
something not allowed yirrbandji
somewhere yidlanggi kara, yilanggi kara
be <u>somewhere</u> for a while
  thangguthikathika
from <u>somewhere</u> yilanguda kara
to <u>somewhere</u> yidlakadi kara, yilakadi
  kara
man's <u>son</u> ngathalki
woman's <u>son</u> ngathani
son-in-law ngalari, patjiri
song wani
soon kayidi
sore dapa, withi
sorrow ngidla
sorry purlkali
sorry (for someone) ngidlali
be <u>sorry</u> ngidlali ngana
make (someone) <u>sorry</u> ngidla
  ngunyingunyi
sort nguya
soul ngapitja
make its natural <u>sound</u> (e.g. a bird to
  call) ngampa, yandha
the <u>sound</u> of the bullroarer ngarlakurra
make the <u>sound</u> of the bullroarer
  ngarlangarlakurrana, ngarlakurraka
soup kilthi
sour kaldri
source of water ngapa
south mulhapundra, wakarramuku
in the <u>space</u> between the legs
  pirithanuthanu
speak ngampa, yandhayandha
spear windra

spear (something) warrkana, draka
run and <u>spear</u> miniwarrkana
speech ngan.gu, yawarri
have a <u>spell</u> pipi
spend nights on the road while travelling thudathawa
spend the night yukarra
spider marangkarra
spike thilpi
spiky stick wathi thilpi
spill parrkuka, pudla, yikaka, yikayika
spin (something) thurrpa, nhurrpa
spindle kunya
spinifex kurrumpala
spirit of a person ngapitja
spit, spit at drintha
spit, spittle ngaltja
splinter druka
split kudrikudrina, yalba
split something into splinters pilthipilthirrika
split the end (of a stick, to make a handle) kakayalba
split up wandukudra, yalbayindri
spoil madlantjika
spoil (?) pika
spongy palya
spotted dragurdragu, malkamindji
spread yawa
spread (e.g. open arms, spread legs) yarrana
spread all around yawathikathika, yawawagawaga
spring tjiri
spur thinapara
square-ended nyarna
squash dralyama
squashed dralyardralya
squat manpakurra
squeak kirdra
squeaky kuthikuthidi
squeal kirdra, ngalamarra

squeeze nyulka, yiga
stab draka
stack firewood makawarrka
stand thanggu
stand (someone, something) up thangguka
stand (something) up thangguna
stand around thangguwagawaga
stand on head kukali thanggu
stand right up thangguthalkawarra
stand up thangguthalka
stand up and walk away thangguminiwindri
be unable to walk freely or stand ngarnmangarnmayindri
star dritji, dritji dandra
stare nguduthalpa
start papana
start to burn thangka
stay nhina
stay a while nhinanhina
steal mama, winkama
stealth kinyi
stealthily kinyili
stealthy kudhikudhi
(steel) axe wadamarta
(steel) knife nharrpa
steep slope ngarnarri
step cut in tree trunk thathi
step on nhangka
stick wathi
stick (something) in yinma
stick with a big knob on (used to stop a boomerang) pirnta
little <u>stick</u> wathi witju
sticky pinngapinnga
stiff paltja
be <u>stiff</u> **(e.g. leg)** ngarnmayindri
still ngada, ngurrangu
sting katjakatja, thalpa
stink parni
stinking thungga

stir wirdiwirdika

stock up with kinikinika

stockman thakumani

stomach thundru, thuru

become full (stomach) yartuna

stone mardra

stone for grinding nardoo ngarduparndrini

stone knife thatji, thurla

stoop durrurdurruna, durruthanggu, purringari

stop murda, parndriyindri

stop (and turn around?) darrpi

stop (e.g. stop someone fighting) warlima

stop for a minute on the way past thanggumini, thangguthawa

stop halfway marndakurra

stop someone doing something (by telling) dadirdadima

store thuwa

store up kinikinika

storekeeper thuwakipa

storm kura, ngandjarri kura

story mudamuda

straight ngurraru, yurlu

straight away kanpangu

strange minhamindji, thula

strange yampa

strange country padla thula

stranger thula

strengthen paltjaka

stretch (arm, leg) out nguthangutha

strike (a match) thalpa

string wirni, yinka, yulpudu

make string wirnika

strip tjirra, pirditjirra, pirditjinga

stripe malka

striped malkamindji

strong ngurru, paltja

get strong, be strong; be strong enough (to cope with a situation) ngurrungurruna

be stuck for words ngarnmangarnmayindri

be stuck together ngarnmayindri

stupid kurrari

suck thapa, pardaparda, yibayiba

suck (e.g. a cut) yibayindri

sugar ngapa palyakini, thipi *or* thipiwa

sugarbag pitjipampu

be sulky thirrithirrina, yunkana

summer makamaka

sun dritji

sunrise ditjirdunka

sunset dritjiwindripandhi

supper thapa

supple paltja, danthu

make supple paltjaka

support (as for a humpy) pirta

suppose kilka

surround kulpina, kulpinayindri, kulpinawaga

susceptible to kanpa

swag purtu

swagman purtupakini, purtuwalthini

swallow yurrku

swallow (bird) pulyurru nyununyunu, tjumpunya(?)

swan kudri

swap ngunyiyindri, wiriwinma

swear at kaldrithayi

swear at one another yandriyindri

sweat kanyi

sweep drangka, wipa *or* wipinga

swell kimana

swell up warumpudu ngana

swim ngupa, thanma

swim across thanmapada

swing (something, such as a rope) around karrtjimawagawaga

swollen warumpudu
swoop kartiwirri

T

tadpole yundayunda
tail kurni, nhura
tail (stock) thangguka
take mandri, paka
take away walthawindri
take by force mama
take it easy mirni
take notice wawatharra
take off (your clothes) dukayindri
take out duka, mandritharrapada
take the part of someone (in a fight or argument) kanbi
talk yandha, ngampa, yandhayandha
talk about wirniwirni
tall payirri
tame murla
taste nhama, wantja
tea kuntha
tea tree kayarri, thayarri, wawu
teach kurrakurrana, ngana, warlparaka
tear purra, daba
tear up purrapurrana, purrapurraka
tears mitji kilthi, mitjiyindri
tease (fibre) purupurra
tease (someone) purnunuka, yupa
teat (e.g. of kangaroo) ngama
tell ngana, pintaka, wirina
tell (a lie) manma, munga
tell (a story) wirni, karrtjikarrtjima
tell about wirnina
tell everyone nganathikathika
tell someone back nganathika
tell someone not to do something dadirdadima
test wantja
testicles dambu

that nhanhadu, nhantjadu, nhanidu, nhatjadu, nhutjadu, nhandradu, nhuludu, nhunuwa, yintjadu
that way yarndu, yita
in that way yarndunguda
from that yarndunguda
that's how yarndunguda
the nhandra, nhanha, nhani, nhulu, nhunu, yinha
the (more than two) thana, thanha
the (two) pulhu, pula
their, theirs pulgani, pulganiyi, pulgatjadu, thanngani, thannganiyi, thanngatjadu
them (more than two) thanha, thanhayi, thanhadu, thanngatjadu, thanngani
them (two) pulhu, pulgani, pulhiyi, pulganiyi, pulhudu, pulgatjadu
then ngala, ngapala
there kala, nhinggiwa, nhinggudu, nhukuwa, yita
there in the distance ? nhukurra
around there nhukukala, nhunggukala
from there nhinggiwanguda, nhinggudunguda
to there nhinggiwangadi, nhinggudungadi
these (more than two) thanayi, thanhayi
these two pulayi, pulhiyi
they (more than two) thana, thanayi, thanadu
they (two) pula, pulayi, puladu
thick pirna
thief kinyikanpa, kinyipurra
thigh thadamuku, wandikila, kulayada, ngalpa
thin mukukarta, ngawada
be thin, get thin kirrayindri
things purtu
think kilka, kukathanggu
think about kilka, kilkanhina
thirst mura
thirsty murali

thirsty person murakanpa
make thirsty mura ngunyingunyi
this nhaniyi, nhandrayi, nhanhayi,
  nhuniyi, nhuluyi, yinhayi
this morning ngarathalkana
this way yada, yarnduyi
on this side nhinggiyipada
thorn thilpi
thorny devil thadjingumini
those (more than two) thanadu,
  thanhadu
those two puladu, pulhudu
three parrkukurnu
throat ngaga, ngayimala, yutju
throw warrka
throw (in wrestling) padlangarika
throw away warrka
throw down warrkapandhi
throw from one to the other
  warrkawarrkana, warrkawarrkanayindri
throw to the other side warrkapada
thunder yindri, ngandjarri yindri,
  pildripildri
thunder cloud ngandjarri mitji
thus yilayarndu
tickle kilyikilyika, kilyikilyipa, thithidika
tickly feeling purnunu
tie, tie up karra
tie here and there karramini
tie on karrapada
tight paltja
tighten paltjaka
time putha
with time to spare mirnimirningu
in time mirnimirningu
make timid yabaka
tip up parrkuka
get tired pirritjampana
tobacco paka
toenails thina ngunpurru, thinapirri
toes thinamitji
together marndu

get together mandripandhi, marnduna
tomahawk mardrathaki
tomorrow ngaranhina nhukadani,
  marripathi, marnathunga
tongue parlpa, thanhani, tharli
too nguka, yuka
too far yundrayundra
tool for making (or grooving?)
  boomerang thatjithatji
tooth marnardraku, waka
front tooth dida
top kamarra, kandra, kudu
top (of hill) kukapidri
torch maka paru
torn daba
be torn purrayindri
get torn dabana
tortoise nharra
totem kamiri, mardu
touch nhama
touch in passing wantjathawa
touchy (of horse) purrtjipurrtji
towards the one(s) you are talking
  about yada
town thantjiyipa
track kapi, kapitharra, palthu
track of foot thina
travel thawa
travelling yulpu
tree wathi
trip someone makumandri
tripe kunangarndri
trousers tjawurra
true muthu, yurlu
trunk (of tree) kurrpa
try wantja
tucker mulhudu, puka
tula (stone knife) thurla
turkey purdathayini
turkey bush dandhirri, pundri
turn (something) around
  wapawagawaga

turn around karrtjiwaga

turn back darrpithika

turn back (down) darrpingari, darrpipandhi

turn back, turn around karrtjingari, karrtjipandhi

turn inside out nyinyimilpa

turn off (the way or track) dirrkapandhi

turn over purri

turn something over purrilka, karrtjikarrtjima

in turn kala, kadla, kidlali

turtle nharra

twig wathi thilpi, witju

twist wanyunka, wapa

twist (e.g. ankle) dulyi

twist something round wapapandhi, wapawagawaga

two parrku, parrkulu, pulpa, thili

two days later marriparrkulu

two of them pula

two-handed fighting stick ngandithirri

type of fish kuya pardi

U

umbilical cord yadhi

be unable pudlupudluka

be unable to see (something) wamba

be unable to walk freely or stand ngarnmangarnmayindri

unafraid yabapani

unawares kudukudu

unborn baby yadhi

uncircumcised pinthapurru

uncle ngama

under, underneath pada, parrari

understand ngara

unrelated nhipa mulha

unripe purda

unripe fruit puka purda

unroll yawayawa

unroll swag purturdukarduka

unsuccessful hunter yuthapani

untie yourself dukayindri

up thalka

up there thalkatji walha, thalkatji widi, yitathalka

further up a slope or bank yitathalka

get up yirrtjithalka

upper back yumbu

upper leg wandikila

upper part of body (e.g. of kangaroo) kuldru

be upside down kukali thanggu, purri

upstream kandrakandra

urinate puda, pudathika

urinate on puduma

urine puda

us ngalunha, ngalungga, ngalinha, ngaldrarni, ngalingga, ngalini, nganunha, nganungga, nganinha, nganingga, ngandrarni, nganini

use ngana

used to warlpara

useless madlantji

useless (small?) growth pukapuka

V

vagina ngunuwirlpa

vein yunggudu kaparri

very kanpa(?), kanpamuthu, muthu

vigorously mampali, pidipidi

go and visit nhinatharrathika

voice ngan.gu, ngaru

vomit ngukuwarra

vulva dirrpa, ngunutjarrpa

W

waddy ngandithirri

wagon wilpada

wait wada, kalka

sit around <u>waiting</u> wadawada

wait on! mirni, thakurru

wake (someone) up wadjaka, yirrtjina

wake up wadjina, yirrtji

walk thawa

walk about thangguthanggu

walk around thawathawa

walking stick kunya, pirtapirta, wathiwutju, windawinda

rock <u>wallaby</u> kantu

wallaroo thudu, yuru

want yura

war pinya

warm kangu

warriors pinya

wash yika, yirra, multhipa

wash (hands) panma

wasp kandirrtha

watch wawana

watch out for wawawawanhina

water ngapa

water birds (other than ducks) dakamirri, digidigilyarra, dirrmi, karrukarru, kilki, kudri, maltjimarrini, maluda, mulpa, thanpathanpa, thundruputha, waliyuka *or* waluyuka, wirniwangka

water rat thukathayini

water snake pardinguntu

(water) boil parrtjini

waterbag ngapa mandrini

waterhen dirrmi, kilki, maltjimarrini

waterhole ngapakurna

wattles *see* Acacias

wave kupitji, kupu warrka

wave to someone going away kupu warrkapada

waves marndikila, ngamanyalpi

waxbill tjumpunya, tjumpurra

we ngaldra, ngali, ngandra, ngani

weak darnu, wamiyami

weapon, type of wirri

wear kadli, thulka, thurrka

weave draka, karrpa

week wiki

weigh down mardringari

well patji, manyu, muthu

well! mayi, malka, ngandra

well (for water) thuka

well built nguyamindji

west dritjiwindrini

wet ngaba

wet something ngabaka

get <u>wet</u> ngabana

whack kartamatha

what? minha

what!, what?, what now? mayi

what (name)? wara

what (saying)? yidlayarndu, yilaru

what for? minhama, minhangadi

what happen to? minhangana

what is it? minhayarndu

do <u>what</u>? minhangana

I don't know <u>what</u> minha kara

when? walpi, wintja

I don't know <u>when</u> walpi kara

where? yidlanggi, yilanggi, yilayadi, yidlayi

I don't know <u>where</u> yidlanggi kara, yilanggi kara

where from? yidlangginguda, yilaadinguda, yilanguda

I don't know <u>where</u> from yilanguda kara

where to? yidlakadi, yilakadi

I don't know <u>where</u> to yidlakadi kara, yilakadi kara

which? minha

a <u>while</u> ago ngakamarra, mirni

in a <u>while</u> mirni

whip wibu, wipayithi

whirl (something) around karrtjikarrtjima

whirlwind makumarda, thurrpu

whisky ngapa kaldri
whistle payipaka, wirlpi
be **whistling** wirlpinhina
white parlu
white (only in compounds) putha
white clay thurna
white man pirripirri, walypala
white woman wadjina, wadlumpada
white-eyed duck mitjiparlu
whitewood ngurraputha, kurrantjala
who? wara, wamu, warlu, warangi
I don't know who warnu kara, warlu kara
whose? warangi
I don't know whose warangi kara
why? minhangadi
wide pirna, yarra
widow mangawarru
widower thupulu
wife nhipa
wife's brother kardri
wild (animal) wilka
wild dog pandiyapa, pandiwilka, pandi yampa, thirrtha yampa
be **wild** thirrithirrina
will I? kirri
willow parlayila, tjirri
willy wagtail thindrithindri
win mandrithayi
wind kundangali, thayirri, wathara
windbreak kankunu
winding kutikutirri
wing kutja, nguna
wing feathers kutja
winter pundra, malthi, kilpa
wipe drangka, wikana, wirrk(a)
wipe off wikapada
witchetty grub kananggu *or* kanunggu
with her nhangganiyi, nhanggatjaduyi
with him, with it nhungganiyi, nhunggatjaduyi

with them pulganiyi, pulgatjaduyi, thannganiyi, thanngatjaduyi
without looking, without seeing kudukudu
woma (snake) manga
(Aboriginal) woman yiwa, tjiwara
woman! (as a term of address) purdupa
woman's son's child kami
women's genitals ngunu
wood wathi
wood adder (type of gecko) ngapardalku
wood duck kunapika
wool yamunu
word ngan.gu, yawarri
work (n.) waka
work (v.) wakana
work out kurrakurra
make work wakaka
worrying purlkali
wrestle pumayindri
wrinkly nyununyunu
write draka
the wrong way manhamanha, yikayika
wrongly manhamanha

Y

yabby marnngani
yam kardra
yamstick mudra
yard yarru
yawn didamangga, kagayindri
year malthi
yell karrka
yellow parru
yellow goanna marngali
yellow ochre parru
yellowbelly ngampurru
yes kawu, ngaandi
yesterday kalkayi, ngananhinanhukada
not yet kali paningu, walyangu

you yini, yundru, yina, yinggani, yula, yulhu, yulgani, yulani, yuda, yudani, yunhu, yunngani

young purla

young man pangga

younger pulya

younger brother or sister ngathadi

your own paladi

your, yours yinggani, yulgani, yulani, yunngani, yudangga, yudani

for <u>yourself</u> nganggali

yower karlaka

Z

zebra finch tjumpunya, tjumpurra

4 *Appendix*

4.1 Naming of new concepts

Concepts introduced by the white men may be expressed by one of three methods, or by a combination of two of these:

  (a) extension of the meaning of an existing word,

  (b) coining of an expression from existing words,

  (c) borrowing of the English word (not necessarily directly).

Examples of (a) include *kuntha*, the name of a herbaceous plant growing at the water's edge in waterholes, and called by the whites 'pennyroyal' or 'tea bush' (because a drink was brewed with it), and extended to mean 'tea'; *purtu* 'goods', 'belongings', extended to mean 'swag'; *yurrkuyurrku* 'dilly bag', extended to 'port' (i.e. 'suitcase'); *mardrathandra* 'stone' (*mardra* is 'stone' in general; *thandra* 'nut in bloodwood tree') and *mardramitji* 'stone' (*mitji* 'eye', 'seed', may be used as a compound element for small rounded objects) both extended to include 'bullet'; and *wathi* 'tree' to any machinery, tools or other metal or wooden objects. (It is likely that *wathi* also had, traditionally, a meaning 'thing (in general)', as the corresponding word has in Arremte and Western Desert languages, among others.) Other probable cases, in which the original meaning of the word is not known, are *wardama* 'motor car' and *yulya* 'policeman' (which is found also in Diyari). A verb whose meaning has been extended is *draka* 'to pierce', also now 'to write'.

Examples of (b) include a number involving the gerund formative *-ini*, which nominalises the verb. For example, *ngapa patjikini* 'sugar' (*ngapa* 'water', *patji* 'good', *-ka* 'causative', literally something like 'water-improver'), *purtuwalthini* 'swagman' (*purtu* cf. (a), *waltha* 'to carry', lit. 'swag-carrier'), *padla warrkini* 'shovel' (*padla* 'ground', *warrka* 'to throw', 'ground-thrower'), *wathi patjipatjikini* 'mechanic' (*wathi* cf. (a), *patji* 'good', *-ka* 'causative', 'machine-fixer'). Examples not of this type include the verbs *mininhina* 'to drive along (e.g. in a car)' (*mini* 'to run', *nhina* 'to sit') and *thukayindri* 'to ride (a horse)' (*thuka* 'to carry', *-yindri* 'reflexive/reciprocal/intransitiver/applicative', something like 'carry yourself') and the nouns *puka patji* 'cake' (*puka* 'tucker', *patji* 'good') and *ngapa kaldri* 'alcoholic drink' (*ngapa* 'water', *kaldri* 'bitter').

Examples of type (c) can be further classified, imprecisely, according to how fully they are assimilated into Yandruwandha — changed so that they fit the Yandruwandha sound system. Words which are unassimilated or only slightly assimilated, include [stɔːkiˑpa]

166

'storekeeper' (also [tɔːkiˈpa], a little more assimilated, and compare *thuwa* 'store'; *bagi* 'buggy' (also *pagi*, which is fully assimilated) and [puˌlǽŋkət] 'blanket'. These are probably on-the-spot borrowings by the informant, as may be some of the next group.

Words which are partly assimilated — in that, for example, a fricative has become an affricate but not yet a stop, or a consonant cluster has been broken up but the main stress has not been transferred to the new initial syllable so formed, or a final vowel has been added but a consonant cluster not normally permissible in Yandruwandha remains — include [tʃúgɐ] 'sugar' (also *tjuga*, which is fully assimilated), [buˌɹádlu] (or [búˌɹádlu]) 'bridle', *mitji padna* ([pádṇa]) 'button' (for *mitji* see in examples of (a)), *tjadala* 'saddle' (also *tjadla*, which although closer to the English form also conforms more closely to Yandruwandha phonotactics), *paypa* 'pipe', [páynʔputu] 'pannikin' (pintpot), *dhibila* 'devil', [ḍáˈpɐ] 'supper', *rabiti* 'rabbit'. Perhaps *walypala* 'white man' should be included here, as *lyp* does not occur in native words.

Most of the borrowed words attested are fully assimilated. In some cases they are compounded with an appropriate classifier, as *puka paka* 'tobacco' (*puka* 'vegetable food'), *wathi mutuka* 'motorcar' (*wathi* 'wooden — and now also metal — object'), *wathi ngayana* 'a piece of iron', *maka matji* 'matches' (*maka* 'fire'), *kathi puluka* 'bullock'. The origin and meaning or function of the addition *yithi* in *wipayithi* 'whip' (also *wibu*) are not known. There are very few verbs: two have verb stem formatives added — *wakana* 'to work' (*-na* 'inchoative', often meaning 'become') and *kandama* 'to count' (*-ma* 'causative') — while one seems to be derived from the English present particle/gerund — *wiping*V 'to sweep' (the final vowel, written V here, is unknown because only the nominalised form has been heard).

The origin of *tjambaka* (the well-known word jumbuck) 'sheep' is not known (see Dixon, Ramson and Thomas (1990) *Australian Aboriginal words in English: their origin and meaning*, p.67). Words which have come into Yandruwandha from other Aboriginal languages via English include *kundi* 'house', *wadlumbada* 'white woman' ("white lubra") and *kabuta* 'hat' (Dixon, Ramson and Thomas pp.199, 170 and 198 — re 'cobra').

Fully assimilated borrowed words not already mentioned are listed below:

tjawurra	'trousers'
pilta	'belt'
tjata	'shirt'
kuta	'coat'
puruka	'dress' (from 'frock')
drupa	'rope'
wilpada	'wagon' (from 'wheelbarrow')
makita	'rifle' (from 'musket')
mayatha	'boss' (from 'master')
thakumani	'stockman'
milimani	'mailman'
pakitjamba	'buckjumper'
papurla	'hobble'
thaltawata	'sea' (from 'saltwater')
thantjipa, thantjiyipa	'town' (from 'township')
thuwa	'store'

tjida	'shearer'
thupa	'soap'
thirri ~ thirritha ~ thirrithirri	'cotton' (from 'thread')
pipa	'paper', 'letter'
tjipa	'sheep'

Many of the adaptions exemplified by these borrowings are obvious, such as replacement of English initial /b/ by *p*, /tʃ/ (usually written *ch* or *tch*) by *tj*, final /ə/ (often written *er*, as in *better*) by *a*. Others are not so obvious but the majority are predictable; these include, for single consonants, /ʃ/ (= *sh*) by *tj*, /s/ by *th*, initial /t/ by *th* (since initial /t/, /rt/, /d/ and /dh/ are not permitted in Yandruwandha the only other possibility is /rd/), /z/ by *rr* and initial /r/ by *rdr*; for consonant clusters /st/ replaced by *th* (medially as well as initially), /sk/ by *k*, /sw/ by *w*, /nsh/ by *ntj* and /fr/ by *pVr* (V represents any vowel); for vowels /au/ by *a* (or in one case *awu*), /ə/ by *a*, /ɒ/ (the sound of *o* in *got*) by *a* (except that it is *u* in *puruka*), /ɛ/ (the sound of *e* in *get*) by *i*, /iː/ (like the *ee* in *sheep*) by *i*, /ou/ by *u*. The final vowel added when the English word ends in a consonant is usually *a*, although there are three examples of *i* and one of *u* (*wipu*). Final /z/ has been deleted in two words. *ng* has been preposed before initial /a/ (in *ngayana*). Other less easily explained correspondences are between initial /tr/ and *tj*, initial /θr/ and *thirr*, /aː/ and *aya*, (*aa* also heard), /ɒ/ and *u*, /i/ and *iyi* [iˑ]

4.2 Place names

With references to 1:250,000 maps: Inna = Innamincka, Cord = Cordillo, Strz = Strelecki, DurD = Durham Downs, Barrolka. IY means said by BK to be Yandruwandha, Yw Yawarrawarrka and SY said to be Pilardapa but probably actually Strzelecki Yandruwandha.

Dalan.garanyi	Dullingari Waterhole (?)	Strz 357528	
Dalintji	Daralingie Well (?)	Strz 338479	
Dampunu	Dampoona Waterhole	Cord 324655	
Didawalkali	Derawalkillie Waterhole	Inna 351620	Yw
Didawandrini	Derawantana Waterhole	Inna 354576	
Kadripariwilpa	Cutrabelbo Waterhole	Inna 322581	
Kadrimitji	Kudriemitchie Waterhole	Inna 314605	IY
Kadripayirri	Cuttapirie Station	Inna 295595	
Kakurrthunggayi	Gidgealpa Oilfield	down from Gidgealpa, in the sandhills	
Kalumurayi	place name	somewhere near Moomba oilfield towards the Strzelecki	
Kalyamarru	Callamurra Waterhole	Inna 385563	
Karitjurru	Coongie Lake	Inna 310625	Yw
Kathipidi	Cuttaberrie Lake	Inna 321615	Yw
Kilyalpa	Gidgealpa Waterhole	Inna 309548	
Kinipapa	Coopers Creek		

Kukuyi	Cooquie Waterhole	Inna 336567	
Kunathi	Coonatie Waterhole	Inna 327593	
Kuyapidri	Queerbidie Waterhole	Inna 370557	
Madlali	Mudlalee Waterhole	Strz 344493	
Mardamarda	Murtamurta Well	Strz 323454	SY
Mardrantji	Mudrangie Waterhole	Inna 318575	
Mardrapirna	Planet Downs or Tibbooburra		
Makulpi	Marqualpie Waterhole	Cord 382660	
Malkanpa	Mulkonbar Waterhole (Innamincka)	Inna 374561	
Maramilya	Merrimelia	Inna 318559	
Marnanhi	Merninie Creek	Inna 392586	
Marrpu	Marpoo Waterhole	Inna 353557	
Marrukatjani	Lake Maroocutchanie	Inna 315631	Yw
Mingkayi	Minkie Waterhole	Inna 360555	
Mitkakaldrathili	Mitkacaldratillie Lakes	Inna 337629	Yw
Mitkapatjithili	near Cordillo Downs		Yw
Mudrangankuthili	Scrubby Camp Waterhole	next to Wathiwathi	
Munba	Lake Moonba	Strz 343480 (or 330486 'Big Lake Moonba')	
Ngagapugina	Ooga-Boogina Waterhole	Inna 288566	
Ngandaparlu	Arrabury	Barrolka 403677	
Ngapamiri	Nappamerry	DurD 411576	
Ngapatjiri	Lake Apachurie	Inna 304626	
Ngapawirni	Nappaoonie Waterhole	Inna 397566	
Ngunapirnta	Oonabrinta Creek	Inna 375567	
Nhanthanini	Yantandana Waterhole	Inna 327611	
Palkarrakarani	the name of the sandhill from which the spirits of the dead float off into the air		SY
Pardlaparli	Burlieburlie Waterhole	Inna 370550	
Patjiwarra	Patchawara Creek	Inna 365608	Yw
Pukapurdayi	Bookabourdie Waterhole	Inna 344582	
Pulupulu	Booloo Booloo Waterhole	DurD 409575	
Thadani	?		
Thala	Della Waterhole	Inna 363534	
Thayipin.gini	Typingine Waterhole	Inna 328603	
Thayipingginyi	w.h. on Patchawara Creek (?)	Inna 365608	Yw
Thilka	Tilcha Waterhole	Inna 358557	
Thirriwarra	Tirrawarra Waterhole	Inna 308595	Matja
Thundilawarani	Lake Toontoonawaranie	Inna 310637	Yw
Thuntjimintji	?		
Thurratji	Toolache Waterhole	Strz 337485	

Thurrpayi	Tooroopie Waterhole	Inna 367543	
Tjulkumindji	near Cutrabelbo		Yw
Wartathulanini	Wattathoolendinnie Waterhole	Inna 336540	IY
Wathiwathi	Scrubby Camp Waterhole	Inna 333569	
Wilbarrku	Wilpancoo Waterhole	Inna 326601	
Yinbarrka	Embarka Waterhole	Inna 313566	
Yinimingka	Innamincka Waterhole	Inna 371557?	

4.3 Kinship

The kinship system, the way people talk about family, is very different in Aboriginal languages in general from the way things are organised for speakers of English. As a result, the translation of a kinship term (a name for a type of relation) can be misleading. For example, *ngarndri* is translated as 'mother', but in English when we use the word 'mother' it generally refers to one particular person; for me, my mother is the one who gave birth to me, and nobody else. In the Aboriginal system, at least in many parts of Australia if not everywhere, everyone in the whole of society can be called by a kinship term. The word that we translate as 'mother' refers also to 'mother's sisters' (in our English system) and to 'mother's mother's sisters' daughters' and to various other people. Similarly, *ngapiri* means 'father' but also 'father's brother' and various others. The same sort of thing (with differences in the details) applies to all other kinship terms.

In Yandruwandha, the variety of ways of talking about kinship were probably very complex, as they are or were in other languages of inland Australia, but the last speakers did not have a full grasp of them. This is a common situation when a language is going out of use and being replaced by another; speakers forget terminology when there is no-one in their community to whom it would apply. This is worse when the replacement language is English because of the radically different kinship system — the rules by which people decide how they are related to others, what to call them and how to behave with them are very different.

Some details could be filled in from knowledge of closely related languages. For example, a term used for a grandparent can be assumed to have been used also for the grandparent's brothers and sisters, and to have been used also by the grandparent for the corresponding grandchild. Thus, for example, I call my mother's mother *kanyini*, and she also calls me by the same name. I would probably also call her brothers and sisters *kanyini*, and they would all call me by the same term. However, no attempt is made in the dictionary entries here to describe the full range of likely meanings of any kinship term, and usually only the most basic meaning is given.

Some other differences between Yandruwandha and English are:

Yandruwandha has a word for 'elder brother', a word for 'elder sister', and a word for 'younger brother or sister' (they are not distinguished, unless you add a word like 'male' or 'female') while English has just the words 'brother' and 'sister' (although, of course, you can add words like 'elder', 'younger', 'big', 'little');

Since my father's brother is also a father to me, the word that would normally be translated as 'uncle' (*ngama*) applies only to my mother's brothers (and certain others more distantly related), and similarly my aunties are my father's sisters but not my mother's sisters;

Instead of having a word equivalent to 'son' and a word equivalent to 'daughter', Yandruwandha has a word *ngathani* that a woman uses for her own children (sons or daughters) and her sisters' children, and a man would use this word also for his sisters' children, and a word *ngathalki* that a man uses for his own children or that people of both sexes use for their brothers' children;

Yandruwandha has four separate words for grandparents — *kanyini* 'mother's mother', *papa* 'mother's father', *kami* 'father's mother' and *tjindra* 'father's father', while English has the same words, grandfather and grandmother, that are used for grandparents on both the maternal and the paternal side;

A *kami* in your own generation is equivalent to a cousin, but is used only for father's sister's children and mother's brother's children (and certain others more distant); father's brother's children and mother's sister's children are regarded as brothers and sisters.

Some other differences can be discovered by studying the kinship chart, which, however, is incomplete and in some parts unreliable. In this chart, the conventional symbols for male, a circle with an arrow on the upper right, and female, a circle with a cross underneath, are used. A + sign means 'marries' and a line going down from this, or sometimes down and across and down again, leads to the children of that couple. EGO means 'me'.

Yandruwandha kinship chart

♀ represents females; ♂ males; EGO means me; + means marries

5 *Stories and texts*

The following two sections comprise (§5.1) an account of some features of the life of the Yandruwandha before contact with Europeans, told by Benny Kerwin, and (§5.2) a collection of stories and fragments of stories, mostly from Benny Kerwin but with three short ones by Tim Guttie.

The texts are broken up into numbered sentences; the Yandruwandha text of each comes first, and under each line of this there is an interlinear translation — a line giving a detailed literal translation, word by word. This is mainly for the use of those people who are particularly interested in the grammar and would have a copy of the grammar volume, *Innamincka Talk*. Other readers can skip these lines. Some Yandruwandha words have hyphens to help people who are using the interlinear translation. At the end of each sentence (in §5.1), or at the end of each story (in §5.2) a free (plain English) translation is given. The text is broken up into sections according to the topic.

A question mark in an interlinear translation denotes that the meaning or function of a suffix (or, less commonly, a stem) is unknown, or that a word cannot be heard clearly and I am guessing. (?) after a translation means that I am particularly unsure of it.

Many sentences are introduced by *ngapala*, glossed 'well' or 'then', or *ngala* 'then' and these words are often more or less meaningless (like, for example, English 'well') and need not appear in a free translation.

Marking of words for number in Yandruwandha (equivalent to putting *s* on the end of a word in English, as in *boys*) is optional and not common; thus the use of plural number in the free translation is governed usually by the sense of the sentence and not by the use of a plural form in the original text.

5.1 An ethnographic text [A][1]

The following description of some features of the life of the Aboriginal people of the Innamincka area before its disruption by white settlers is a corrected and adapted version of the paper 'The land of stone chips' (Kerwin & Breen 1981). Most of it was given in a single long Yandruwandha text in 1972, repeated with modifications a few days later. It was translated by Breen, with substantial help from Kerwin. Unfortunately, Ben Kerwin died before all details of the translation could be checked. The texts were edited and

---

[1] Cross-references to sentences in this section are prefaced by 'A' in the companion volume, Innamincka Talk.

combined by Breen to give the following account.[2] The first text, in substantially unedited form, has been published (together with biographical notes on Ben Kerwin) in Hercus and Sutton (1986).

The title of the Oceania paper is based on the name that the Innamincka people called themselves: *Thayipilthirringuda*. This comprises the word *thayi* 'grinding stone', usually used in conjunction with the generic term *mardra* 'stone', as *mardra thayi*, *pilthirri* 'stone chips' and *-nguda* 'from'. This name arises from the presence at Innamincka of deposits of sandstone from which grinding stones were quarried, and refers to the waste material — stone chips — from the quarrying. The name can, therefore, be freely translated as 'people from the land of stone chips'.

The text is broken up into sentences according to the topic. A more or less free translation follows each sentence. This is sometimes by Kerwin, sometimes by Breen; Kerwin's translations are usually freer. The translation of a sentence is often followed by an explanatory note or notes. These are cross-referenced to the number of the sentence, and often include additional information given by the narrator. Many of these notes have been deleted as unnecessary now, given the grammar and dictionary.

Usage of tense in the Yandruwandha text does not seem to be entirely consistent; however, this impression may be due to my lack of knowledge of the range of uses of the various tense and other inflections.

No attempt has been made to compare this text with other published material on the culture of this or similar areas. Craig (1970)[3] gives many references to such material.

A. Nets made from bow vine

1   *Karrukarrundjali nganha.*
     old.man-PL-ERG   1sg:ACC
     The old men [told] me [how they did it].

     Karrukarrundjali nganari nganha was intended; *nganari* means 'told'.

2   *Ngathu wawatharrana karlukarlu-ngadi yukini-ngadi   pirli   yama*
     1sg:ERG see-fly-IP   fish-DAT   catch-GER-DAT bag.net cross.net

     yina   karrpa-rlayi.
     EMPH weave-SIM
     I watched them make a bag net for catching fish while swimming in the water, and a cross net.

     -tharra, in the second word, denotes completeness of the action: 'I saw it all'. (See also note to 63.) *Yuka* means 'catch fish by swimming with the net and sweeping the fish up into it'. A cross net is a net that is stretched across the river.

---

2   The text as published here contains three long unbroken extracts from the first version (transcript D): lines 1–37, 99–121, 141–160. Most of the remainder is from that version, but not in the original order. Lines taken from the second version (transcript E) are: 54–57, 63, 77, 78, 82, 85, 86, 89, 92, 95, 161–168. Material from other sources is lines 122–133 and 177–189. An aim of the editing was to produce a logically ordered account of some aspects of Yandruwandha culture.

3   *North-West-Central Queensland: an annotated bibliography*, Canberra, Australian Institute of Aboriginal Studies.

3   *Minhaya-ngadilatji*   *karlukarlu* *yukini-ngadi*   *kara, ya*   *kinipapayi*
     what-DAT-EMPH-EMPH   fish   catch-GER-DAT maybe and river-LOC

     kara   *kurrini-ngadi, karlukarlu kara*   *yamali.*
     maybe   put-GER-DAT   fish   maybe cross.net-INST
     That's what they're for, for catching fish while swimming in the water, and for
     putting across the river [to catch] fish in the cross net.

4   *Pungguli*   *ngala.*
     bow.vine-INST then
     [They make it] out of the bow vine.

5   *Punggu mulpini-ngudatji*   *ngapala kurrari ngapayi,*   *wiki*   *parrkulu*
     bow.vine cut-GER-ABL-EMPH then   put-UNSP water-LOC week two

     kara,   *thunggani-ngadi.*
     maybe   rotten-CAUS-GER-DAT
     They cut the bow vine and put it in water for maybe two weeks, so that it will rot.

     The last word should be *thungganiningadi.*

6   *Kali*   *thana*   *thukaringu*   *ngapa-ngudatji ya* *pirditjirranga*
     already 3pl:NOM take.out-UNSP-THEN   water-ABL-EMPH and strip-FUT

     thanha.
     3pl:ACC
     Then they take it out of the water and strip it.

     It is not clear whether *pirditjirra* means 'strip the leaves off' or 'peel'.

7   *Ngapala kururrupa-rnanga nga nhurrpanga ngalpayi*   *kunya* *payirrili.*
     then   rub-CONT   then spin-FUT   thigh-LOC spindle long-INST
     Then they rub it with stones and spin it on their thighs, using a long spindle.

     Kururrupa normally means 'grind' but here refers to rubbing with stones to separate
     the fibres.

8   *Ngapala kundikilili thana*   *thurrparitji.*
     then   ball-INST   3pl:NOM roll-UNSP-EMPH
     Then they roll it into a ball

9   *Wirni payirrikari*   *yinha*   *nga kunyayi*   *kurranga.*
     string long-CAUS-UNSP 3sg:ACC then spindle-LOC put-FUT
     They make the string long and put it on the spindle.

10 *Ngapala thana*   *karrpa-rnanga thirrithirri-nyadi* *yina* *walypalali*
     then   3pl:NOM weave-CONT   cotton-like   EMPH white.man-ERG

     kurra-rlatji   *thana,*   *thirrila*   *karrpini-ngadi mirrka.*
     put-PRES-EMPH 3pl:NOM cotton-EMPH weave-GER-DAT clothes
     Then they weave it just like the cotton white people use for making their clothes.

11 *Ngapala wirnitji* *yamatji*   *thana* *drakaringu*   *wathili*
     well   string-EMPH cross.net-EMPH 3pl:NOM weave-UNSP-THEN stick-INST

kunyali.
spindle-INST
They weave it into a cross net with a stick and a spindle.

The stick is held parallel to the spindle.

12   *Paltjapaltjakari   thana   karlukarlu-ngadi kurranga kinipapayitji.*
strong-make-UNSP 3pl:NOM fish-DAT   put-FUT river-LOC-EMPH
They make it strong and put it across the river to catch fish.

13   *Ngapala yamalitji   mandriri malkirri.*
well   cross.net-INST-EMPH get-UNSP many
They got a lot of them in the cross net.

14   *Minhaya ngala?*
what   then
What next?

15   *Kurra-rnanga kandratji   mirndithanmini-ngaditji   thana   (or thanha)*
put-CONT   top-EMPH   float-GER-DAT-EMPH   3pl:NOM (or 3pl:ACC)

yamatji,   karnanku yina.
cross.net-EMPH   reed   EMPH
They put reeds on top of the cross net so that it will float.

The procedure described in this and following sentences of course preceded the use
of the net (12, 13).

16   *Karraringu   thanha   mulpini-nguda warnta, payipayirru yina,   mara*
tie-UNSP-then 3pl:ACC cut-GER-ABL   short   long-long   EMPH hand

witju-nyadi.
finger-like
They tie them on after cutting them into short lengths, about the size of a finger.

The word *payirri* 'long' is reduplicated here and the resulting word means 'not very
long'.

17   *Ngapala karramini-rnanga.*
well   tie-run-CONT
They tie them here and there.

Mini 'run' is used here as a modifier of the verb to denote 'do in a number of
places', i.e. 'here and there'.

18   *Ngananga kurranga kinipapayitji,   ngapala thana   mirndithanmari.*
do-FUT   put-FUT   river-LOC-EMPH then   3pl:NOM float-UNSP
Then they put them in the river and they float.

Mirndithanma 'float' is a compound verb which incorporates *thanma* 'swim';
mirndi, however, is not known elsewhere.

19   *Ngala ngapa kukuyitji   ngari, wararriyitji,   mardramitji*
then   water deep-LOC-EMPH down bottom-LOC-EMPH stone-pebble

karrini-nguda   malkirri,   pardrangarini-ngadilatji   *thanha,*
tie-GER-ABL   many   hold-down-GER-DAT-EMPH-EMPH   3pl:ACC

paltjakini-ngadi.
strong-CAUS-GER-DAT
They tie a lot of stones [to go] deep down in the water, on the bottom of the net,
to weigh it down and keep it tight.

20   *Ngapala kurra(rla?), marripathi   thana   marrikurukurutji*
     then   put(-PRES?) next.day   3pl:NOM   early-EMPH

     minipandhiringu   *mandrithalkangalatji   karlukarlu,   pitjanka   yina.*
     run-down-UNSP-THEN   get-up-FUT-EMPH-EMPH fish   bony.bream EMPH
     Then they put it in [at night] and next morning, very early, they run down and pull
     up the fish — bony bream.

21   *Pitjanka.*
     bony.bream

22   *Ngarru pitjanka   pardrarlatji.*
     only   bony.bream hold-PRES-EMPH
     They only catch bony bream.

23   *Mukupika   yina   thana   pitjankatji.*
     bone-much   EMPH   3pl:NOM   bony.bream
     Those bony bream are the very bony ones.

24   *Ngala pirlili   ngampurru-ngaditji   paladildrangu thana*
     then   net-INST   yellowbelly-DAT-EMPH type-BUT-YET 3pl:NOM

     drakini-nguda,   kurrarla yarnduldrangu kinipapayi kurrapadari   yita.
     weave-GER-ABL   put-PRES way-BUT-YET   river-LOC   put-in-UNSP there
     They use a net that they have woven with a different mesh, and that they put into
     the water in a different way, for yellowbelly.

25   *Nga yarnduldrangu thana   ngampurru paladildra pardranga,*
     then way-BUT-YET 3pl:NOM yellowbelly type-BUT hold-FUT

     ngampurru minhaya, drakini-nguda   ya   pitjanka-ngadi   drakini-nguda,
     yellowbelly what   weave-GER-ABL and bony.bream-DAT weave-GER-ABL

     ya   yama yukini-ngadi   drakini-nguda.
     and net   catch-GER-DAT weave-GER-ABL
     They have a net woven in one way for yellowbelly, and another kind for bony
     bream, and another kind for catching fish while swimming.

     The words *yama* and (perhaps) *pirli*, here translated 'net', may be used incorrectly
     here. Earlier *pirli* meant 'bag net' and *yama* 'cross net' but the meanings are
     reversed in these sentences. In fact, *pirli* probably means 'net (generic)'; see 28, 31,
     34, 40, 42.

26   *Pulya, ngapala,   karna parrkulu pula   thanmaritji   yukangatji.*
     small then   man   two   3du.NOM swim-UNSP-EMPH catch-FUT-EMPH
     It [the last] is a small one and two men swim with it to catch [the fish].

27   *Ngala yamali   thana   ngunipika   kurraringu,   kalkayi,*
    then   cross.net-INST   3pl:NOM   daylight-much   put-UNSP-THEN   afternoon-LOC

    marripathi minipandhingayayi   mandrithalkanga karlukarlulatji,   ngampurru
    next.day   run-down-FUT-DISTORT   get-up-FUT   fish-EMPH-EMPH   yellowbelly

    kara,   ya   kathi   nharra-mindji   kara,   ya   palha   kara,   ya   kathi
    maybe   or   animal   coolamon-PROP   maybe   or   bird   maybe   or   animal

    thanayi —   minhaya yina,   kathi —   mayatji   nganyi
    3pl:NOM-HERE   what   EMPH   animal   name-EMPH   1sg:NOM

    kuditharrarlala,   kathi   thukathayini,   thana   drika-lapurrayi thanha.
    forget-PRES-EMPH   animal   mussel-eat-GER   3pl:NOM   call-REMP-?   3pl:ACC
    Well, with the cross net, they put it down in the daytime, in the afternoon, and next
    morning they run down and pull up the fish — maybe yellowbelly, or maybe a
    turtle, or maybe a bird, or maybe one of those animals — what is it — I forget the
    name — mussel eater they used to call them.

    Here *kathi* 'meat, edible animal' is used in a generic-specific construction, as was
    mardra 'stone' in 19, but in that case the two were pronounced as a single word.
    The bird the narrator had in mind was a shag (cormorant). The 'mussel eaters' are
    water rats. This is probably a nickname, not the real name.

28   *Thanatji —   minhaya, paldriyi —   pirliyitji.*
    3pl:NOM-EMPH   what   die-POT   net-LOC-EMPH
    They might have died in the net.

    The verb wanted was probably 'drown', not 'die'.

29   *Patjikurnu   thayingatji   thana.*
    good   eat-FUT-EMPH   3pl:NOM
    They are good eating.

    Thayiningaditji 'eat-GER-DAT-EMPH' may have been meant.

30   *Kulari   thana(ma?)   makamuduli.*
    cook   3pl:NOM(-?)   hot-ash-INST
    They cook them in hot ashes.

    29 and 30 seem to refer to the water rats.

31   *Ngapala thikaringu   ditjipawindriringu   thana   pirlitji*
    then   return-UNSP-THEN   put.in.the.sun-away-UNSP-THEN   3pl:NOM   net-EMPH

    thanha   ngapa kadawayi.
    3pl:ACC   water edge-LOC
    Then they go back and spread the net out on the bank to dry in the sun.

32   *Yuka-yindri(ni?) kalkayi,   'May, karlukarlutji wayinila   ngandra?'*
    ask-RR(-GER?)   afternoon-LOC   well   fish-EMPH   how.many-EMPH   1pl.in:NOM
    In the afternoon they ask one another, 'How many fish did we get?'.

33   *Ay malkirringu thanayi!*
    oh   many-YET   3pl:NOM-HERE
    'Oh, plenty!'

34   *Ay marripathi ngandra   pirlitji   kurranga   ngapayitji.*
     oh next.day   1pl.in:NOM   net-EMPH   put-FUT   water-LOC-EMPH
     'Well we needn't put the net in the water again until tomorrow'.

35   *'Kawu.'*
     Yes

     In English, of course, the answer would be 'No'.

36   *Ngapala thana   thayi-yindrinhinaringu   ngurra karlukarlutji, nhaningu*
     then   3pl:NOM   eat-RR-sit-UNSP-THEN   always fish-EMPH   ?

     kanta walarriyi.
     DEM   shade-LOC
     Then they sit in the shade all the time, eating fish. (?)

     If *walarri* is a feminine noun (which very few words are, other than those referring
     to female humans or animals), *nhaningu* could possibly be *nhaniyingu*
     '3sg:fem:NOM-HERE-THEN'.

37   *Thayi-yindringa thana   ani nhinanhinanga.*
     eat-RR-FUT   3pl:NOM   ?   sit-sit-FUT
     They just sit and eat.

     (36–37) Here *-yindri* focuses on the action 'having a feed' rather than just 'eating'.
     The word written *'ani'* is probably English 'only'.

B. Nets made from bulrushes

38   *Karlkuli   ngala yamatji mikimana, ngana-lapurra thana   yamali*
     bulrushes-INST then   net-EMPH make-IP   do-REMP   3pl:NOM   net-INST

     ngala karlkuli,   karlku.
     then   bulrushes-INST bulrushes
     Well they made nets of bulrushes; they used to use nets made of bulrushes.

     Mikima 'to make' is a loan-word from English.

39   *Minhaya warrka-rnanga pirditjirranga thanha,   kathi   thukali.*
     what   throw-CONT   strip-FUT   3pl:ACC   animal   mussel-INST
     They cut them down and strip them with a mussel [shell].

40   *Wirnika-malka puru — purupurriningudalatji   thana   parndriparndringa*
     string-CAUS-OPT ?   tease-GER-ABL-EMPH-EMPH 3pl:NOM   hit-hit-FUT

     wirni-ngadi nga thurrpanga, yarnduldrangu drakini-ngadilatji
     string-DAT   then spin-FUT   way-BUT-YET   weave-GER-DAT-EMPH-EMPH

     pirli yamatji   kurrini-ngadi kinipapayitji.
     net   net-EMPH   put-GER-DAT river-LOC-EMPH
     They tease it up and make it into string by pounding it and then spinning it, in the
     same way as for making the nets they put across the river.

     The second word, *puru*, may be simply an anticipation or false start of the following
     word.

C. Catching ducks

41   *Ya   palhatji   thana   yurari   parndringa, pirli   thana*
    and   bird-EMPH   3pl:NOM want-UNSP   kill-FUT   net   3pl:NOM

    paladildrangu   drakini-nguda,   nga   wathiyi   pada   karranga
    type-BUT-YET   weave-GER-ABL   then   tree-LOC   in   tie-FUT

    warrakurnutji,   thadri-palapala   yina.
    side-other-EMPH   bank-both.sides EMPH
    If they want to catch birds they make a net of a different mesh and tie it onto a
    tree on each bank of the river.

    Birds, i.e. ducks.

42   *Nga — yarnduldrangu nhinda, pirli ngunthuya mayi,   minha-ngadildra,*
    then   how-BUT-YET size   net   back-?   well   what-DAT-BUT

    wathi nhutjadu   kakaldra,   ngala wathi pirna   puladu
    tree 3sg:NOM:THERE   near-BUT   then tree big   3du:NOM-THERE

    kalpurru thanggurla, yarndu nhinda ngulutji.
    coolibah stand-PRES how   size   end-EMPH
    They make the net of such a size that it stretches right across from a coolibah on
    this side to a big one standing [on the other side].

    The exact translation of this sentence is not clear; in particular the reference to
    ngunthu (translated as 'the back [of the net]').

43   *Ngapala   kurrapadari yita.*
    then   tie-in-UNSP over.there
    Then they tie it on over there.

44   *Nga yadala   thana   thinbari,   yadatji*
    then boomerang-EMPH 3pl:NOM make-UNSP   boomerang-EMPH

    thinbini-nguda   nga wirlpa kurranga,   mulha kurnuyi.
    make-GER-ABL   then hole   put-FUT   nose one-LOC
    Then they make a boomerang and put a hole in one end of it.

    They put a hole in one end so that it would whistle when thrown. The hole is in the
    end which is not held.

45   *Ngapala palhatji   thana   thilparingu,   karna malkirri thawini-nguda*
    then   bird-EMPH   3pl:NOM   chase-UNSP-THEN man   many   go-GER-ABL

    nga thilpanga thanha   palhatji.
    then chase-FUT 3pl:ACC   bird-EMPH
    Then a lot of men go and chase the birds down.

46   *Ngapala thana   tharrapandhiri   yada, ngala karna nhunu(?)*
    well   3pl:NOM   fly-down-UNSP   hither then   man   3sg:NOM(?)

    wada-yindrirla thadripalapala   yadatji   warrkanga.
    wait-RR-PRES   bank-both sides   boomerang-EMPH throw-FUT
    Well, when they fly down towards the net, the men waiting there on both sides
    of the river throw their boomerangs.

The pronoun *nhunu* here (if it is that) seems to be referring to the group as a single entity.

47   *Ngapala palhatji   thana   kariwirriringu.*
     then   bird-EMPH 3pl:NOM   dive-UNSP-THEN
     Then the birds dive down.

48   *Minhaya-puru yina?*
     what-AVER   EMPH
     What for?

49   *Palha thirri-puru.*
     bird   chicken.hawk-AVER
     Because [they think] it is a chicken hawk.

The birds think the whistle of the boomerang is the whistle of a chicken hawk.

50   *Nga pirliyi thana   windriringu.*
     then net-LOC 3pl:NOM enter-UNSP-THEN
     They go into the net.

51   *Ngala karna parrkulutji pula   warrkapandhi-rlayila   pirlitji.*
     then   man   two-EMPH   3du:NOM throw-down-SIM-EMPH   net-EMPH
     Then the two men throw the net down.

52   *Ngapala pula   thingapadanga yada.*
     then   3du:NOM pull-in-FUT   hither
     They pull it in.

53   *Palha yina mandriringu   malkirrilatji.*
     bird   EMPH get-UNSP-THEN many-EMPH-EMPH
     They get a lot of birds.

54   *Karna thana   thikarila(?),   minhangananga kayidila,   thana*
     man   3pl:NOM return-EMPH   what-do-FUT   now-EMPH 3pl:NOM

     thilpini-ngudatji.
     chase-GER-ABL-EMPH
     The men who were chasing them come back, and what do they do then?

55   *Ngapala parndringa palhatji,   waltha-yindrithikangalatji.*
     well   kill-FUT   bird-EMPH carry-RR-return-FUT-EMPH-EMPH
     Well, they kill the birds and carry them back home.

-yindri here denotes action for one's own benefit.

56   *Ya   manggamanggakurraringu.*
     and   divide-divide-put-UNSP-THEN
     They share them out.

57   *Thanayildra   pakangala   ngalyitji,   thanayildra* (word not clear),
     3pl:NOM-HERE-BUT carry-FUT-EMPH some-EMPH 3pl:NOM-HERE-BUT

     thanayildra   yarndu.
     3pl:NOM-HERE-BUT thus
     Each group takes a few.

The exact translation is not clear; perhaps 'these ones take a few, and these a few, and these likewise'. The suffix *-ldra* corresponds to English 'as for' — 'as for these, they take a few' or 'on the one hand ... on the other hand' (except that here there are three hands; cf. note to 151–152).

58   *Thayi-yindringa palhatji   yarndu thana   parndri-padipadini*
      eat-RR-FUT   bird-EMPH thus   3pl:NOM kill-HAB-GER

      karnalitji,   palhatji   ngala drakini-nguda   ngala paladi.
      man-ERG-EMPH bird-EMPH then   weave-GER-ABL then   type
      That's how the Aborigines used to catch birds to eat, with a special type [of net] they had woven.

D. Harvesting pelicans

59   *Yarndu ngathu   wagarla,   palha ngala thana   dakamirritji,*
      thus   1sg:ERG shift-PRES bird   then   3pl:NOM pelican-EMPH

      marrumarruyitji.
      lake-lake-LOC-EMPH
      I'm shifting now [to a new topic]; those pelicans in the lake country.

      The exact meaning is not clear.

60   *Palha purla pirnana-rlayitji,   ngapala yarru wathinaritji,*
      bird   baby   big-INCH-SIM-EMPH then   yard   build-APP-UNSP-EMPH

      marru kadawayi, ngapala thawa-rnanga puka   windritharranga ngapa
      lake   edge-LOC then   go-CONT   ?   enter-fly-FUT   water

      marruyitji   palha purla thanhayi   mapathikanga.
      lake-LOC-EMPH bird   baby   3pl:ACC-HERE muster-return-FUT
      When the young ones are getting big, they build a yard for them on the bank of the lake and then go down into the water and herd the baby birds back [into the yard].

      -na, in *wathina*, denotes that the action is for the benefit of another or others. This seems to be a strange use, since the yards are hardly for the benefit of the birds. *-tharra*, see note to 2.

61   *Mapari   panipanika   thanha   purlatji.*
      muster-UNSP none-none-CAUS 3pl:ACC baby-EMPH
      They muster all the young ones.

62   *Pirritjampana-rlayi nhunu   karrtjipandhinga pulyatji   nhunu   nga*
      tired-INCH-SIM   3sg:NOM turn-down-FUT   small-EMPH 3sg:NOM then

      thikanhinanga thundi-ngadi, ngala thana   kadi-rlayi palha ngalyitji,
      return-sit-FUT island-DAT   then   3pl:NOM chase-SIM bird   other-EMPH

      pirnapirnatji, ngapala thana   windrima-warraringu
      big-big-EMPH then   3pl:NOM enter-CAUS-arrive-UNSP-THEN

      wathini-nguda yarrutji   thanngani.
      build-GER-ABL yard-EMPH 3pl:GEN

If a little one gets tired it turns around and heads back to the island, while they hunt the rest of them, the biggest ones, on and put them in the yard that they have built for them.

63 *Ngala pulyatji   marndakurrapandhi-rlayi, nga walya yinha*
    then   small-EMPH stop.halfway-down-SIM   then not   3sg:ACC

    wawatharranga, karrtjipandhiyila   thana   paninarla.
    see-fly-FUT   turn-down-POT-EMPH 3pl:NOM all-INCH-PRES
    When the little ones stop halfway they don't take any notice of them, for fear
    the whole lot will turn back.

    Wawatharra here means 'notice' and the implication is that they see it but do not
    take any notice. Compare 2, in which it was necessary to take notice.

64 *Ngapala wiki   parrkulu wiki   parrkukurnu kara   nhina-padapada-rnanga*
    then   week two   week two-one   maybe sit-HAB-CONT

    thayi-rnanga palhatji   thanha,   ngala ngarndri-ngapirili   thanha
    eat-CONT   bird-EMPH 3pl:ACC   then   mother-father-ERG   3pl:ACC

    walthana-rlayi karlukarlutji, ngunyinga nhinggikala   yarruyi.
    carry-APP-SIM fish-EMPH   give-FUT location-about yard-LOC
    Then for two or maybe three weeks they camp there, living on birds, while the birds
    feed on fish that their parents bring them and give them in the yard.

65 *Ngala thanatji   walyala yartukari,   ay ngarndri-ngapirili yada*
    then   3pl:NOM-EMPH not-EMPH full-CAUS-UNSP oh mother-father-ERG hither

    paka-rnanga karlukarlutji ngunyinga thanha.
    carry-CONT fish-EMPH   give-FUT 3pl:ACC
    They don't have to feed them; the parents bring fish and give it to them.

66 *Ngapala thana   thayi-yindri-rnangari marnipikana-rnanga.*
    well   3pl:NOM eat-RR-CONT-?   fat-much-INCH-CONT
    While they are eating [some, the rest] are getting fat.

    It seems to be more likely that *thana* here refers to the young birds, not the people,
    and the meaning of this sentence is: 'They feed and get fat'.

67 *Pirnapirna thanhayey,   tharrini-ngaditji   ngana-rlayi,*
    big-big   3pl:ACC-HERE:DISTORT fly-GER-DAT-EMPH do-SIM

    purndaparndringa kudlanga yina   thayi-yindri-rnangatji.
    nape-hit-FUT   cook-FUT EMPH eat-RR-CONT-EMPH
    The biggest ones, that are nearly ready to fly, they kill and cook and eat.

68 *Yarndu thana   nhina-padipadini.*
    thus   3pl:NOM sit-HAB-GER
    That's how they used to live.

69 *Panika-kaldri   thawakaldringa mapathika   puthakurnula.*
    none-CAUS-again go-again-FUT   muster-return time-other-EMPH
    When they finish them off they go down again and muster some more.

The verb *mapathika* should have some inflectional suffix. Maybe the *-nga* on the second verb was meant to go there; *-kaldri* is not known to combine with *-nga* elsewhere.

70   *Ngurra yina   kurra-yindrirla   mayi,   purla,   palhatji   thana.*
always EMPH   put-RR-PRES   well   baby   bird-EMPH   3pl:NOM
Those birds are breeding all the time.

71   *Ngapala nhinari yartuna-rnanga palha-ngudatji,   ya   palha*
well   sit-UNSP   full-INCH-CONT   bird-ABL-EMPH   and   bird

panina-rlayitji.
nothing-INCH-SIM-EMPH
They eat their fill of them until they are all gone.

They used to eat the eggs as well.

E. Killing emu

72   *Ngapala thana   kathi   warruwitji-ngaditji thawari,   kathi   warruwitji*
well   3pl:NOM   animal   emu-DAT-EMPH   go-UNSP   animal   emu

yukatji   parndringa.
too-EMPH   kill-FUT
They also go out for emus, to kill emus.

The generic term *kathi*, glossed 'animal', here refers to the emus.

73   *Ngapala kudru pakuri   ngari,   nga yankala   kurrawagandji   nga*
well   hole   dig-UNSP   down   then   bough-EMPH   put-around-FUT   then

windripandhinga   palha   mukuli.
enter-down-FUT   bird   bone-INST
They dig a hole and put boughs around it and [a man] goes down into the hole with a bird bone.

74   *Ngapala pandhi wirlpinhina-rnanga,   ngala kathi   thana*
then   down   whistle-sit-CONT   then   animal   3pl:NOM

ngarangaramini-rlayila   warruwitjilitji.
hear-hear-run-SIM-EMPH   emu-ERG-EMPH
Then he whistles down there, and the emus hear him.

He uses the bird bone as a whistle.

75   *Thawawarranga thangguwagawaganga,   ngala karna nhunu*
go-arrive-FUT   stand-around-around-FUT   then   man   3sg:NOM

purrinhina-rlayi ngari   mingkayi.
hide-sit-SIM   down   hole-LOC
They go and stand around the hole, while the man hides in it.

Emus are notorious for their curiosity.

76   *Ngarrungu thangguthalkawarrandji dranyingalatji   yadali.*
only-THEN   stand-up-arrive-SEQ   kill-FUT-EMPH-EMPH boomerang-INST
The man just stands up and kills [one] with a boomerang.

The combination of *thalka* 'up' with *warra* 'arrive' gives the meaning 'right up'.

77   *Kanpangu, purnda yina   dranyiri.*
right-then   nape   EMPH   hit-UNSP
He hits it right then, on the back of the neck.

78   *Waltha-yindri-thikangala kathi   thana   mangga-rlayila*
carry-RR-return-FUT-EMPH meat   3pl:NOM scatter-SIM-EMPH

yabalilatji.
fear-INST-EMPH-EMPH
They carry the meat back to camp while the rest of the emus go for their lives.

F.   Killing kangaroos

79   *Kathi   tjukurrutji,   ngarru wathi windralildra   warrkana-rnanga.*
animal   kangaroo-EMPH only   tree   spear-INST-BUT   spear-CONT
As for kangaroos, one way is to just kill them with a spear.

80   *Minhaya-nyadi yina?*
what-like   EMPH
How do they do it?

81   *Wawa-rnanga ngapa-ngadi ngari thawa-rlayi karna kulpina-yindri-rlayila*
see-now   water-DAT   down   go-SIM   man   surround-RR-SIM-EMPH

ngapatji   yiba-rlayi nga wathi windrali   warrkananga.
water-EMPH drink-SIM then tree   spear-INST spear-FUT
Well, when they see them going to the water the men surround them, and then spear them while they're drinking.

In 79 and 81 *wathi* 'tree' or 'stick' is used as a generic term preceding the specific term *windra* 'spear'. (See note to 27.) *Windra* is the noun 'spear' and *warrkana* the verb.

82   *Ngapayi   nhulu   warrkana-pandhiri yita,   kanpangu   kara, nyalkari*
water-LOC 3sg:ERG   spear-down-UNSP   there   right-THEN   maybe miss-UNSP

kara.
maybe
They spear them at the water, and they might get one straight off or they might miss.

83   *Ngapala mini-yukarra-rlayi thana   warrkana-pada-rlayi-ldrangu, kanpangu.*
well   run-at.night-SIM   3pl:NOM spear-in-SIM-BUT-YET   right-THEN
They chase them at night too and spear them then, straight off.

84   *Ngalyi thana   yadali   dranyi-rnanga.*
some   3pl:NOM boomerang-INST hit-CONT
Some people kill them with boomerangs.

85   *Yarndu thana   kathitji   parndri-padipadini.*
      thus   3pl:NOM animal-EMPH kill-HAB-GER
      That's how they used to kill them.

G. Making waterbags

86   *Ngapala pakathika-rnanga   darla pirnngandji yinha,   yilayarndutji   kara.*
      well   carry-return-CONT skin   skin-SEQ   3sg:ACC   how-EMPH   maybe
      Well, they carry them back to camp and skin them — I don't know how.

87   *Yilayarndu kara   nyinimilpanga.*
      how   maybe   turn.inside.out-FUT
      I don't know how they turn [the skins] inside out.

88   *Walya ngathu   wawa-lapurra rabiti-nyadi yina   thana   walypalali*
      not   1sg:ERG   see-REMP   rabbit-like   EMPH   3pl:NOM white.man-ERG

      nyinimilparla,   darla pirnnga-rnanga.
      turn.inside.out-PRES   skin   skin-CONT
      I never saw it, but they might have done it like white men turn rabbit skins inside
      out as they skin them.

89   *Thana   mukurduka-lapurra   thanha,   ngarru ngaga yina   nhunu*
      3pl:NOM bone-pull-REMP   3pl:ACC   only   throat EMPH   3sg:NOM

      pirnatji   wirlpa.
      big-EMPH   hole
      They took the bones out through a hole only as big as the throat.

      86 and 89 are taken from one version and 87 and 88 from the other.

90   *Yarndu ngala thana   kathi   tjukurrutji*   (word not audible), *ngapala*
      thus   then 3pl:NOM animal   kangaroo-EMPH   well

      thana   ngapa marndrini.
      3pl:NOM water dip.up-GER
      This is how they make a kangaroo [skin] into a waterbag.

      Ngapa marndrini here 'thing for dipping up water', i.e. 'waterbag'. It could also
      mean 'one who dips up (or scoops out) water'.

91   *Dultharrili.*
      bloodwood-INST
      They used bloodwood.

92   *Ngala panipani*   (not clear) *muku palgupalgu dukini-nguda,*
      then none-none —   ?   bone muscle   pull-GER-ABL

      ngapala dultharri   darlamurruli windrimari,   darlamurru
      well   bloodwood   bark-INST   enter-CAUS-UNSP bark

      paltjakini-ngaditji   yina,   pirtipirtikari yinha,   darlatji
      strong-CAUS-GER-DAT-EMPH   EMPH   red-CAUS-UNSP   3sg:ACC   skin-EMPH

yinha.
3sg:ACC
After they take out all the bone and muscle they put bloodwood bark in to make
it supple and it makes the skin red.

92 is not taken from the same version as 93 and 94 and there seems to be a slight
contradiction. The suffix -*li* on *darlamurru* seems to be wrong; perhaps this is why
the word is repeated without it.

93 *Pirtipirti kathi   tjukurru-nyadi thana   walypalali,   minhaya nganarla*
    red   animal kangaroo-like 3pl:NOM white.man-ERG what   do-PRES

    mayi, pirtipirtikarla   darla yamunu-pani.
    well   red-CAUS-PRES   skin   hair-less
    If they tanned the skin with the fur removed, like the white men do, it would go red.

94 *Ngala yamunu-mindjildra nhinggiyitji   nyinyimulpini-ngudatji.*
    then   hair-PROP-BUT   location-HERE-EMPH turn.inside.out-GER-ABL-EMPH
    But our people do it with the fur on, after turning the skin inside out.

    Note that the verb 'turn inside out' is not exactly the same in form here
    (*nyinyimulpa*) as in 87 and 88 (*nyinimilpa*).

95 *Ngapala ngapatji   waltha-yindringangu maltjitji   kurnu karrini-nguda*
    well   water-EMPH carry-RR-FUT-THEN leg-EMPH one   tie-GER-ABL

    thiltjali.
    sinew-INST
    They carry water in it, after tying up one leg with sinew.

    This sentence is not from the same version as the several sentences preceding and
    following.

96 *Ngapala ngapa marndrinilatji   thanngani yulpu   thawiningadi,*
    well   water dip.up-GER-EMPH-EMPH 3pl:GEN travelling go-GER-DAT

    padla yundra-waka ngapa-paniyi.
    country far-DEM   water-PRIV-LOC
    [They use] their waterbags when they go on a journey in remote waterless country.

97 *Ngapala tjukurru darla karna parrkululi pula   wathili   pinyiyinkali*
    well   kangaroo skin   man   two-ERG   3du:NOM stick-INST shoulder-INST

    walthangatji.
    carry-FUT-EMPH
    Two men carry the kangaroo skin [waterbag] on a stick resting on their shoulders.

98 *Karnatji   yiwa   minha ngala karrukarru minha thawa-rnanga*
    man-EMPH woman what   then   old.man   what   go-CONT

    yulputji   ngapatji   marndra-rnanga ngarru thanayi
    travelling-EMPH water-EMPH dip.up-CONT   only   3pl:NOM-HERE

    tjukurru   darlayila.
    kangaroo skin-LOC-EMPH
    Men and women and old men travel and they just cart water in the kangaroo skin.

The purpose of *minha* here is not clear; perhaps it is used as a hiatus filler although there was no hesitancy.

H. Native wells

99 *Ngapala, pakuthawakaldriri mardra minhaya.*
well   dig-go-again-UNSP stone   what
While they're going along, they dig out [the holes in] the rocks again.

100 *Patjikurnutji   makala   ngala thana   wangapandhi-rnanga ngapala*
good-one-EMPH fire-EMPH then 3pl:NOM   light-down-CONT   then

ngapa kurrari mardrayi   thana   kudrakudrari   (thana ?)
water put-UNSP stone-LOC 3pl:NOM break-break-UNSP (3pl:NOM ?)

makamakanini-ngudatji.
hot-INCH-GER-ABL-EMPH
They light a good fire on the rock and after it has heated up they put water on it, to shatter the rock.

101 *Ngapa pundrali   warrkini-nguda, ngapala thana,   kurli   parrku,*
water cold-INST   throw-GER-ABL   then   3pl:NOM day   two

mandrathayi pilthirri   thana   warrkathalkangatji.
get-eat   chips   3pl:NOM throw-up-FUT-EMPH
After they pour cold water on, after a couple of days, they pick up the broken pieces of rock and throw them out of the hole.

The fire is kept burning for a couple of days because it takes this long for the rock to heat up properly. The rock is sandstone. He actually said *ngapa kaldri*, which means 'saltwater' but cold water, *ngapa pundra*, was intended. *Thayi* 'eat' in *mandrathayi* has the same function as *-yindri* with some verbs (see notes to 36, 37); it means 'do for one's own benefit'. It should have an inflectional suffix.

102 *Kudru thana   yarndu pakupurringarini.*
hole   3pl:NOM thus   dig-?-down-GER
That's how they make the wells deeper.

Purri is a verb 'hide' and also means 'upside down'; its function here is not known.

103 *Ngandjarri warlka-rnanga ngapala nhunu   ngapa   marnamininari.*
rain   fall-CONT   then   3sg:NOM water   brim.full-INCH-UNSP
When it rains the water fills it to the brim.

104 *Kathi   tjukurru-purutji,   ya   mardra pirrapirra kurrathalkaniya*
animal kangaroo-AVER-EMPH and stone   flat   put-up-?-?

kandratji.
top-EMPH
They get a flat stone and put it over the top to keep kangaroos out.

105 *Ngala ngapatji   nhunudu   para-rlayi ngurra.*
then   water-EMPH 3sg:NOM-THERE lie-SIM   always
Then the water stays there for a long time.

106   *Karnakurnu-karnakurnu   ngarru   palthu   kurnuyi   thawa-rnanga*
      person-one-person-one   only   road   one-LOC   go-CONT

      ngapangadilatji   pakuni-nguda   thana   matja.
      water-DAT-EMPH-EMPH   dig-GER-ABL   3pl:NOM   long.ago
      Anyone using this road can get water from the well they dug long ago.

      The construction *N-kurnu-N-kurnu* means 'all Ns'.

107   *Kilkalilkarla   thawanga   ngapa-ngaditji,   ngarru   pulyala   pakari*
      know-know-PRES   go-FUT   water-DAT-EMPH   only   small-EMPH   carry-UNSP

      tjukurru   darla   yibini-ngadi   palthuyukala   yitalayi
      kangaroo   skin   drink-GER-DAT   road-too(?)-EMPH   there-EMPH-EMPH

      thawa-rnanga.
      go-CONT
      They know it is there and they need carry only a small kangaroo skin [waterbag]
      for drinking from while they are going along.

108   *Yibathawanga   yita   ngapa   muralitji   nganari.*
      drink-go-FUT   there   water   thirst-INST-EMPH   do-UNSP
      They drink it when they get thirsty.

109   *Ya   thawawarranga   ya   thudathawa-thudathawanga   marri-parrkulu   kara*
      and   go-arrive-FUT   and   sleep-go-sleep-go-FUT   next.day-two   maybe

      marri-parrkulu   kara   thudathawari   kaku-pani,   ngarru   tjukurru
      next.day-two   maybe   sleep-go-UNSP   (water?)-PRIV   only   kangaroo

      darlali   walthini-nguda.
      skin-INST   carry-GER-ABL
      They might have only two or three nights on the road with no water, apart from
      what they carry in the waterbag.

      The first two words should perhaps be omitted. *Kakupani* was repeated as
      ngapapani 'water-without'. *Kaku* means water in a nearby language (Kungkari) but
      not in Yandruwandha.

I. Stone knives

110   *Minhayali   ngala   thana,   pirna   palparrinitji   mardra   pilthirrili*
      what-INST   then   3pl:NOM   big   boulder-?-EMPH   stone   chip-INST

      palkini-nguda.
      chip-GER-ABL
      Now what do they [skin animals] with; with a stone chip that has been broken
      off a big boulder.

111   *Ngapala   thana   kathi   nalybali-nyadi   dramirdramini-nguda*
      well   3pl:NOM   animal   steel.knife-INST-like   cut-cut-GER-ABL

kilkari.
think-UNSP
You would think it had been done with a steel knife.

112   *Yilayarndu   kara   thana   pirnngi-padipadinitji   mara   patjikurnuli*
how   maybe   3pl:NOM   skin-HAB-GER-EMPH   hand   good-one-INST

yina   karrukarrutji   nhina-padipadini   ngapangaditji.
EMPH   old.man-EMPH   sit-HAB-GER   water-DAT-EMPH
I don't know how they did it, but the old men used to be good hands at skinning
[kangaroos] for water [bags].

J. Getting pitchery

Pitchery is a narcotic prepared from the leaves of the plant *Duboisia hopwoodi*. It was
mixed with the ashes of certain leaves or barks (differing according to area) and chewed. It
is often spelt 'pituri'; however the spelling 'pitchery' is preferable as it is less susceptible to
gross mispronunciation.

113   *Ngapala thana* (word not clear) *padlakurnu-ngadi-yuka ya*
well   3pl:NOM   country-other-DAT-too   and

nhinatharrathikarlangu,   Yandruwandha   thana   thawa-padipadini
sit-fly-return-PRES-THEN   Yandruwandha   3pl:NOM   go-HAB-GER

ngapa nhuludu   tjukurruli.
water   3sg:ERG-THERE   kangaroo-INST
The Yandruwandha people used to travel and visit other countries, with a
kangaroo [skin to carry their] water.

The exact translation of this sentence is not clear. *Tharra* 'fly' here seems to denote
that the stay is brief, just a visit.

114   *Nhingguwa-ngadi   pitjidi   kumani   mandrithikanga.*
location-THERE-DAT   pitchery   pitchery.bundle   get-return-FUT
They used to go over there to get bundles of prepared pitchery.

115   *Yilanggitji   kara   thana   pitjidi   mandri-padipadini, ngalaaku.*
where-EMPH   maybe   3pl:NOM   pitchery   get-HAB-GER   I.don't.know
I don't know where they used to get the pitchery.

116   *Ngarru ngathu   pirli tjapura   yina   wawa-lapurratji,   thana*
only   1sg:ERG   net   pitchery.bag   EMPH   see-REMP-EMPH   3pl:NOM

drakini-nguda.
weave-GER-ABL
I only saw the pitchery bags they wove, a long time ago.

Pirli 'net' here seems to be used as a generic term specified by *tjapura* 'pitchery
bag'.

117   *Yilayarndutji kara,   minha yamunuli kara   thana*   (word not clear), *kathi*
how-EMPH   maybe   what hair-INST maybe 3pl:NOM   animal

pildrali   kara   thana   ngana-padipadini, or kathi   tjukurruli.
possum-INST maybe 3pl:NOM do-HAB-GER   or animal kangaroo-INST
I don't know how they wove them or what sort of hair they spun the thread from;
maybe they used to use possum, or maybe kangaroo.

118   *Rabiti-pani yina   thana   nhina-padipadini matjardi.*
      rabbit-PRIV EMPH 3pl:NOM sit-HAB-GER   long.ago-EMPH
      They didn't have any rabbits in the old days.

Yandruwandha lacks both a verb 'to be' and a verb 'to have', and *nhina* 'to sit' can
function as either. Here and in 121 it denotes a type of possession (which is negated
by *pani* in this sentence: 'they used to sit without rabbits'). Its use as a verb 'to be'
is illustrated in 112.

119   *Walya thana   wawa-lapurra rabititji.*
      not   3pl:NOM see-REMP   rabbit-EMPH
      They never saw a rabbit.

120   *Kayidila thanadu   thawawarra-nhana, yilanggi-nguda kara.*
      now-EMPH 3pl:NOM-THERE go-arrive-NP   where-ABL   maybe
      They have only come lately — I don't know where from.

121   *Ngala ngarru kathi   tjukurruli   thana   nhina-padipadini, ya*
      then   only   animal kangaroo-INST 3pl:NOM sit-HAB-GER   and

      thalkaparlu,   ya   kathi   pildra.
      kangaroo.rat and   animal possum
      They only had kangaroo then, and kangaroo rat, and possum.

K. Trade

This section is a separate text, recorded in 1974.

122   *Nhina-padipadinitji thana.*
      sit-HAB-GER-EMPH   3pl:NOM
      [This is how] they used to live.

123   *Pitjidi-ngaditji,   pitjidi   kumani.*
      pitchery-DAT-EMPH pitchery bag
      For pitchery, bags of prepared pitchery

This sentence is incomplete; a brief explanation in English of what pitchery bags
were was then given: 'I'll tell you about that. That bundle in them half moon bags
they used to crochet'.

124   *Pawa-ngadi, pawa thungini   ngunyi-rnanga, ya   ngarduparndrini*
      seed-DAT   seed   grind-GER give-CONT   and nardoo-hit-GER

      ngunyi-rnanga.
      give-CONT
      They give seed grinders [grinding stones] and nardoo pounders.

125   *Wiriwinma-rnanga karna   thana   pitjidi   kumani-ngurrutji.*
      exchange-CONT   person 3pl:NOM pitchery bag-PROP-EMPH
      The people with the bags of pitchery traded [them].

126   *Ya ngarduparndrini ya   pawathungini, ya   mardrathaki.*
      and nardoo-hit-GER and seed-grind-GER and stone-axe
      Nardoo pounders and seed grinders, and axes too.

127   *Mardrathaki-ngadi thana   ngunyi-rnanga parndriparndri-yindrini-ngadilatji*
      stone-axe-DAT   3pl:NOM give-CONT   hit-hit-RR-GER-DAT-EMPH-EMPH

      thana   yada   waka thinbathinba-yindri-rnanga.
      3pl:NOM boomerang   ?   chisel-chisel-RR-CONT
      They give axes and they use them to make boomerangs for hunting.

      The meaning of this sentence is doubtful; in particular it is not clear if *thana* refers
      to the same or different 'they' on its two occurrences. *Waka* also is a problem.

128   *Yarndu thana   wiriwinma-yindri-padipadini karrukarrundjatji.*
      thus   3pl:NOM exchange-RR-HAB-GER   old.man-PL-EMPH
      That's how the old people used to trade.

      Karrukarru 'old man' here refers to 'man of the olden days' rather than 'aged man'.
      The same usage has been noted on other occasions, for example 141. A false start,
      ngunyipadipadini ya, is omitted from this sentence.

129   *Kayiditji walyala   thana   nhinarla.*
      now-EMPH not-EMPH 3pl:NOM sit-PRES
      They aren't living any more.

130   *Paldritharra-nhana yina thana   panina, karnatji.*
      die-fly-NP   EMPH 3pl:NOM all-INCH person-EMPH
      They've all died out, the Aborigines.

131   *Walyala(?) karangu(?)   wawanga puthakurnu,   ngarru*
      not-EMPH(?) maybe-YET(?) see-FUT   occasion-other only

      walypawalypala.
      white.man-white.man
      We won't see [that] again. They just live like white people now, no Aborigines.

132   *Pin.gi-pin.gi thana   ngunyiyindripadipadini yarndu.*
      things-things 3pl:NOM give-RR-HAB-GER   how
      That's how they used to trade things.

133   *Pawathungini ngala pitjiri   kumani-ngaditji ngunyi-yindri-rnanga*
      seed-grind-GER then pitchery bag-DAT-EMPH give-RR-CONT

      yarndukalangu   thana   nhina-padipadinitji.
      thus-about-THEN 3pl:NOM sit-HAB-GER-EMPH
      They traded grinding stones for bags of pitchery, that's how they used to live.

      A one-word false start, *ngardungadi,* is omitted here. Shields were another item
      obtained by trading grinding stones.

L. Grilling meat

134 *Kathi paladi parndriparndri-yindri-rnanga, ngala makatji wangini-nguda*
  meat own kill-kill-RR-CONT   then fire-EMPH light-GER-ABL

  kathi yuka kara kulini-ngadi, ya karlukarlu kulini-ngadi.
  meat too maybe cook-GER-DAT and fish   cook-GER-DAT
  They kill their own meat, and light a fire to cook their meat maybe, or to cook fish.

135 *Ngapala maka pirna thangkakari, nga mardramitji mandringa malkirrili,*
  well fire big make-UNSP then stone-pebble get-FUT many-ERG

  karnakurnu-karnakurnuli.
  person-other-person-other-ERG
  Well, they make a big fire, and everybody collects stones.

136 *Ngapala mardra thana warrkapandhi-warrkapandhingala makayi.*
  then stone 3pl:NOM throw-down-throw-down-FUT-EMPH fire-LOC
  Then they throw all the stones into the fire.

137 *Makatji nhunu muduna-malkaya.*
  fire-EMPH 3sg:NOM ash-INCH-OPT-?
  The fire is allowed to burn away to ashes.

138 *Nga ngarru makathurrpala thana dringa-rnanga and drangkanga*
  then only hot-ash-EMPH 3pl:NOM scrape-CONT and sweep-FUT

  nganangatji.
  do-FUT-EMPH
  When there are only hot ashes left they scrape and sweep them away.

  The use of *ngana* 'do' here is unusual; see §11.3.1 in the grammar volume.

139 *Kathi thanayi pulkapulkaringu maka-mukuruli-nyadi, ngala*
  meat 3pl:NOM-HERE grill-grill-UNSP-THEN hot-coal-INST-like then

  mardramitjili ngala.
  stone-pebble-INST then
  They grill their meat on the stones and you would think it had been grilled on the coals.

140 *Thayi-yindri-rnanga yartuna-rnangalatjini, walya padlapadla walya*
  eat-RR-CONT   full-INCH-CONT-EMPH-EMPH-? not dirt-dirt not

  thurrpathurrpa, mardramitji-ngudatji.
  ash-ash   stone-pebble-ABL-EMPH
  They eat until they are full, [meat] from the stones, not dirty or ashy.

M. Beds

141 *Ngapala, kurrupu karrukarru* (word not clear, possibly *thana*) *pundrayi*
  well old.woman old.man   3pl:NOM cold-LOC

  kara, makamakayi kara, ngapala ngarru kankunu kurraringa
  maybe hot-LOC maybe then only windbreak put-UNSP-?

makawarrkanga   kunawarrkutji   thuda-yukarrangatji.
firewood-throw-FUT   crossways-EMPH   sleep-at.night-FUT-EMPH
Well, the old women and old men, in winter or summer, only put up a windbreak,
throw some firewood down and sleep all night crossways.

The reference is to 'women and men in the olden days'; see note to 128.
Crossways: i.e. at right angles to the windbreak, with heads towards it.

142   *Ngarru mirrka ngala thana   kathi   tjukurru darlali.*
      only   blanket then   3pl:NOM animal   kangaroo skin-INST
      They have only a kangaroo skin for a blanket.

This sentence should have a verb; perhaps *thudayukarranga* is understood (see
preceding sentence).

143   *Mirrkatji   milpi-rnanga, marndumarndukana pulhu   tjukurru*
      blanket-EMPH   sew-CONT   join-CAUS-IP   3du:ACC   kangaroo

      thiltjali.
      sinew-INST
      They sew two [skins] together with kangaroo sinew [to make] the blanket.

144   *Thiltja thana   tjukurru   pardrarla, ngapala   thanadu*
      sinew   3pl:NOM   kangaroo   hold-PRES then   3pl:NOM-THERE

      pirditjirraritji   nga   palha mukuli   tjalparrikini-nguda
      strip-UNSP-EMPH   then   bird bone-INST sharp-CAUS-GER-ABL

      wirlpakanga   nyinditji.
      hole-CAUS-FUT   skin-EMPH
      They hold the kangaroo sinew and strip it and poke the holes in the skin with
      a bird bone that has been sharpened.

145   *Ngapala windrimari   karrpangalatji.*
      Then   enter-CAUS-UNSP   sew-FUT-EMPH-EMPH
      Then they put it in and sew it.

146   *Tjukurru parrkulu kara,   parrkulu parrkulu kara   karrpini-nguda*
      kangaroo two   maybe two   two   maybe   sew-GER-ABL

      nga kangu yukarrangatji.
      then warm spend.night-FUT-EMPH
      It might be two skins, or maybe four, and then they are warm at night.

147   *Padlayi   yina kurnutji   kurrari   ngala kandraldra nhambalka-yindriri*
      ground-LOC EMPH one-EMPH   put-UNSP then top-BUT   cover-RR-UNSP

      kurnulitji.
      one-INST-EMPH
      They put one on the ground and cover themselves over with another.

148   *Kangu   thuda-yukarrangani.*
      warm   lie-at.night-FUT-?
      They sleep warm at night.

N. Clothes

149   *Ngala thanayi   kilkarla,   ngarru   yarawarrangu   thawathawa-padipadini,*
       then   3pl:NOM-HERE   think-PRES   only   naked-THEN   walk-walk-HAB-GER

       mirrka   thana   (word not clear)   karrpa-padipadini   paladi.
       clothes   3pl:NOM   sew-HAB-GER   own
       People now think they used to walk about naked, but they used to sew their own
       clothes.

150   *Ngala yamunu   ngala   thana   wirnikamuratji   thurrpini-nguda,*
       then   hair   then   3pl:NOM   human.hair.string-EMPH   spin-GER-ABL

       yarnduldrangu,   yarndu   thana   pirlitji,   minhaya,   karlukarlu-ngadi.
       thus-BUT-YET   thus   3pl:NOM   net-EMPH   what   fish-DAT
       They spin human hair into string, just as they make the string for fishing nets.

       The human hair string was used for a belt.

151   *Draka-rnanga   yarnduldrangu   wirnikamuratji   yiwa-ngaditji*
       weave-CONT   thus-BUT-YET   human.hair.string-EMPH   woman-DAT-EMPH

       pirnaldra,   karrini-ngadi panikaldra   nhambalka-yindrindji.
       big-BUT   tie-GER-DAT   none-CAUS-BUT   cover-RR-SEQ
       On the one hand they make a big one for women to tie on, to cover themselves
       completely.

       Wirnikamura here seems to be a mistake; the apron worn by the women was made
       of possum fur, and was hung on the human hair string-belt, as was the smaller
       covering worn by the men. The women's garment covered the front of the body
       below the waist, not the whole body as this sentence implies.

152   *Ngala karrukarrulitji   ngarru wirni yamununguldra, paladi wirnina*
       then   old.man-ERG-EMPH   only   string   hair-YET-BUT   own   string-?

       thurrka-rnanga ngarru pulyaldra.
       wear-CONT   only   small-BUT
       On the other hand, the old men only wore a hairstring, but theirs was only small.

       (151–152) The suffix *-ldra* is used in these two sentences as an equivalent to the
       English 'on the one hand ... on the other hand'. In 152 *-nguldra* seems to have the
       same meaning as the more common *-ldrangu* (see, for example, 24, 41, 83). Both
       are compound suffixes made up of *-ldra* and *-ngu*. *-nguldra* may be a mistake.

O. Yams

153   *Kurrupu   thana   pakupadipadini   kardra.*
       old.woman   3pl:NOM   dig-HAB-GER   yam
       The women used to dig yams.

       Re 'old woman', see note to 128. *Kardra* is not identified and may be a generic
       term.

154   *Putiyita-nyadi   thayingatji.*
      potato-like   eat-FUT-EMPH
      They eat them like potatoes.

155   *Makamuduli   kulari,   mulhudu   patjikurnutji.*
      hot-ash-INST   cook-UNSP   tucker   good-one-EMPH
      They cook them in hot ashes, and they are good tucker.

      In the English of Aborigines in many parts of Australia 'tucker' means 'vegetable
      food' and does not include meat or fish or other food from animal sources.

156   *Thimbiltji   paku-rnanga kulanga   yarnduldrangu makamuduli.*
      yam.species dig-CONT   cook-FUT   thus-BUT-YET   hot-ash-INST
      They dig *thimbiltji*s and cook them the same way, in hot ashes.

157   *Ya   karlakala   paku-rnanga malkirri   thana   kulanga*
      and   yower-EMPH   dig-CONT   many   3pl:NOM   cook-FUT

      makakanyayildrangu.
      hot-ash-LOC-BUT-YET
      They dig yowers and cook them in hot ashes too.

158   *Yarndu thana   yartuna-padipadini.*
      thus   3pl:NOM   full-INCH-HAB-GER
      That's how they used to fill themselves up.

P. Seeds

159   *Ngala pawa ngala kalildra   dinga-rnanga, pawa kalpurru, pawa*
      then   seed then   already-BUT grind-CONT   seed   coolibah seed

      wadlangurru, pawa mitjiyimpa, pawa ngadli,   pawa   pidri-yiltharri ya —
      wadlangurru seed eye-black   seed pigweed seed   anus-frost   and
      Then they used to grind seeds as well — coolibah seeds, *wadlangurru* seeds,
      puppa-grass seeds, pigweed seeds, frosty-arse seeds and —

160   *Ngalyitji   nganyi   kuditharralarla   pawa thana   dinga-padipadini.*
      other-EMPH 1sg:NOM forget-NOW-PRES seed 3pl:NOM grind-HAB-GER
      I forget the other seeds they used to grind.

161   *Yarndu thana   pawala   dinganga, ya pawa parndriparndringa.*
      thus   3pl:NOM seed-EMPH grind-FUT or   seed   hit-hit-FUT
      They grind the seeds, or crush them.

      The purpose of *yarndu* in this sentence is not known.

162   *Ngala yiwalitji   kardraldra paku-rlayi, ngala ngarru karruli*
      then   woman-ERG-EMPH yam-BUT   dig-SIM   then   only   man-ERG

      thana   pawatji   kudra-rlayi.
      3pl:NOM   seed-EMPH break-SIM
      Only the men crush the seeds, while the women dig yams.

This sentence lacks a main verb (both verbs being marked as complements) and the exact translation is not clear.

163   *Kinikangatji*   *ngala yiwalila*   *yambarriyi*   *kurranga.*
       heap.up-FUT-EMPH   then   woman-ERG-EMPH   flat.ground-LOC   put-FUT
       The women heap them [the seeds] up on the flat ground.

164   *Yambarriyi*   *kurranga, padla paltjapaltja yina wipingini-ngudaatjinha,*
       flat.ground-LOC   put-FUT   ground   hard   EMPH   sweep-GER-ABL-EMPH-?

       patjikaringu   *padla, padla thaka mitji ngukanguka-yindriyi.*
       good-CAUS-UNSP-THEN ground ground clay   seed   mix-RR-POT
       They put them on the hard flat ground, after sweeping it to make it clean so that the seeds don't get mixed with clay.

While *mitji* and *pawa* seem to be interchangeable in this text, it was said on another occasion that *mitji* (basically 'eye', also, in *mardra mitji*, 'pebble') means 'seed' and *pawa* 'ground seeds, flour'.

165   *Ngapala thana*   *kurrupulila*   *mandrithikathalkangardi kantha*
       well   3pl:NOM   old.woman-ERG-EMPH   get-return-up-FUT-EMPH   grass

       pudlapudla-rnanga thanha,   *ya*   *warrkakaldri(?)*   *karlitji,*   *wathi*
       spill-spill-CONT   3pl:ACC   and   throw.down-again(?)   limb-EMPH   tree

       karlitji.
       limb-EMPH
       Well, the women get grass and separate the seeds, and throw down limbs of trees.

The meaning of *pudla* in this sentence is obscure; it is assumed that it refers to shaking or otherwise dislodging the seeds from the grass. The tree branches are broken off, taken to the collecting place, shaken to remove the seeds and then thrown aside.

166   *Ngala ngarru pawala*   *thana*   *mapaapanga*   *pinakaringu*
       then   only   seed-EMPH 3pl:NOM   gather-gather-FUT   rock-UNSP-THEN

       pitjiyilayi.
       coolamon-LOC-EMPH
       They just gather up the seeds and rock them in the coolamon.

The material from the heaps is 'rocked' in a coolamon so that the seeds go to one end and the rubbish (which is lighter) goes to the other end.

167   *Wikawikananga, pinakanga,*   *ya*   *dringangalatjardi,*   *or*
       clean-FUT   rock-FUT   and   grind-FUT-EMPH-EMPH-EMPH or

       thungangalatji,   *nga thayiyindringala yartunanga,*   *ngapali*
       grind-FUT-EMPH-EMPH   then eat-RR-FUT-EMPH full-INCH-FUT   water-INST

       ngunkukini-nguda.
       ball-CAUS-GER-ABL
       They clean it, rock it, and grind it and then, after mixing it with water and making it into a ball, they eat their fill.

The two verbs meaning 'grind' are given (linked by the English 'or') as alternatives, with the same meaning.

168   *Makamuduyi   ngalyitji   kudlari,   ngunku pirnatji,   ngala ngarru*
hot.ashes-LOC   some-EMPH   cook-UNSP   ball   big-EMPH   then   only

ngunku pulya thanha   thayi-rnanga kartitji.
ball   small   3pl:ACC   eat-CONT   ?-EMPH
They bake some of them in hot ashes, the big balls, only the little ones are eaten raw.

The word *karti* is not known; the translation 'raw' seems reasonable but the normal word for 'raw' is *kimba*. The word 'cook' is heard sometimes, as here, *kudla*, sometimes, as in 176, *kula*. These are alternative pronunciations.

169   *Ngardu ngala,   parndringa ngandra,   nga pinakanga   nhulu*
nardoo then   hit-FUT   1pl.in:NOM   then rock-FUT   3sg:INST

pitjili.
coolamon-INST
Then there is nardoo; we crush it and then rock it in the coolamon.

Note the change to first person.

170   *Ngapala ngapa kurrari   nga thayinga ngapali.*
then   water put-UNSP then   eat-FUT   water-INST
Then we pour water on it and eat it with the water.

171   *Kathi   thukali   ngala thayi-rnangatji   marna-ngadikinitji*
animal   mussel-INST then   eat-CONT-EMPH   mouth-DAT-CAUS-GER-EMPH

mandri-rnanga.
get-CONT
We eat it by spooning it into our mouths with a mussel [shell].

172   *Kathi   thukali,   walya kalpurru thalpali   or   walya darlamurruli,*
animal   mussel-INST not   coolibah leaf-INST   or   not   bark-with

ngarru kathi   thukali   mandri-rnanga.
only   animal mussel-INST   get-CONT
We don't spoon it up with a coolibah leaf or with bark, only with a mussel [shell].

Q. Grubs

173   *Muduwa pulyali   ngathu   wawatharrana kurrupu   karrukarrutji*
child   little-ERG 1sg:ERG   see-all-IP   old.woman   old.man-EMPH

nhina-rlayi ya   thayi-yindri-rlayi.
sit-SIM   and   eat-RR-SIM
When I was a little boy I saw how the old people lived and how they fed themselves.

See note to 63, 128.

174   *Pardi yuka thana mulhakuna thayi-padipadini ditjipini-nguda ngapala*
      grub   too   3pl   nose-faeces eat-HAB-GER   dry-GER-ABL then

     ngunkunhapiri.
     ball-roll.up-UNSP
     They used to eat a brown-nosed grub which they dried in the sun and rolled into
     a ball.

     After drying them, they pounded them with a stone, added water and then made
     them into a ball. The grub is green with a brown nose and a sharp tail.

175   *Ngapala marnatji   nhinari mayi pulapulayarra thayini-ngudatji*
      then   mouth-EMPH   sit-UNSP well   green   eat-GER-ABL-EMPH

     pardi   mulhakunatji.
     grub   nose-faeces-EMPH
     Their mouths were green after eating the brown nosed grub.

176   *Ngarru kathi   kanangku   ngala duka-rnanga kulanga*
      only   animal witchetty.grub   then   pull-CONT   cook-FUT

     makamuduyitji,   mardrathakili parndrini-nguda.
     hot-ashes-LOC-EMPH stone-axe-INST chop-GER-ABL
     And they pulled out witchetty grubs from trees, after chopping them out with
     a stone axe, and cooked them in hot ashes.

     Parditji dukari thana milali 'They pull the grubs out with a hook (*mila*)'.

R. Putting the handle on an axe

    This is a separate text, recorded in 1972. It is in the first person, and was an answer to
an elicitation of 'I put the handle on the axe with gum'.

177   *Mardrathakiyi ngathu   marapardrini kurranga, wathi ngukalatji*
      stone-axe-LOC 1sg:ERG hand-hold-GER put-FUT   tree   too-EMPH-EMPH

     nganyitji   parndrini-ngadi.
     1sg:NOM-EMPH chop-GER-DAT
     I'll put the handle on the axe so I can chop some wood.

     A partial English translation was interpolated here. The use of *nganyi* instead of
     ngathu 'I (as subject of a transitive verb)' may be incorrect. Normally the subject of
     the verb in a subordinate clause like this is omitted.

178   *Marapardrinitji   kurrini-nguda, wathi yina kakayalbari   pulya,*
      hand-hold-GER-EMPH put-GER-ABL   stick EMPH split.the.end-UNSP small

     mardra ngapala kurrapadaringu nhungganiyi mardrathakiyi.
     stone   then   put-in-UNSP-THEN 3sg:GER-LOC stone-axe-LOC
     After putting the handle down, I split the end of the stick a little and put the axe
     head in it.

A one-word false start is omitted here. The meaning of *kurrapadari* was explained in English at this point. The function of the first phrase (the first two words) is not clear.

179   *Ngapala   pirntathangkali   nyanmari, marapardrini   wirnili*
     well   bloodwood.gum-INST   seal-UNSP   hand-hold-GER string-INST

    ngukanguka pirntathangkali   karrangalatji   yinha.
    too-too   bloodwood.gum-INST   tie-FUT-EMPH-EMPH 3sg:ACC
    I bind the handle with string and mix it with bloodwood gum to seal it.

The exact translation is not clear.

S. Treatment of an antisocial person

This text was recorded in 1971 and again in 1972; this is the later version. The first sentence could not be translated (by either storyteller or linguist) and has been omitted.

180   *Wilyarula   yina   pardrari,   thirrithirrina-rlayi nhunu   ya   nhipa-ngurru*
     exile-EMPH EMPH hold-UNSP fight-fight-APP-SIM 3sg:NOM and   wife-PROP

    nhulu   parndri-rlayi.
    3sg:ERG   hit-SIM
    They exile [a man] for stirring up trouble or beating his wife.

181   *Wilyaru   thana   pardraringu,   pakangalatji   kanthayi*
     exile   3pl:NOM   hold-UNSP-THEN carry-FUT-EMPH-EMPH grass-LOC

    warrkathikanga.
    throw-return-FUT
    They exile him — take him into the bush and leave him.

The transitive verb 'leave' in this and a number of other Australian languages is based on the verb root 'throw'. This does not, however, imply any violence.

182   *Ngapala yina   wathi   thinbanari   mandawarra, ya   wirni*
     well   EMPH   stick   chisel-APP-UNSP   plum.bush   and   string

    thurrpanari   yinha.
    spin-APP-UNSP 3sg:ACC
    Well, they cut a stick from a plum bush to shape for him and make some string for it.

The bullroarer, or stick referred to here, is called *thuburu*, and its sound is described as, approximately, voowoovoowoovoovoowoovoo.

183   *Mulhudu-ngadilatji   nhunu   thawathalkini-ngadi warrkanga,*
     food-DAT-EMPH-EMPH 3sg:NOM   go-up-GER-DAT   throw-FUT

    wathilatji   yina   karrtjikarrtjimari.
    stick-EMPH-EMPH EMPH whirl-whirl-CAUS-UNSP
    He whirls it around so that someone will come and leave food for him.

184   *Ngapala nhunu   kirdrari,   ya   mulhudutji yina   thana*
     well   3sg:NOM whistle-UNSP and   food-EMPH   EMPH 3pl:NOM

nguthu-ngamalitji   *pakana-pandhi-malka.*
elder.brother-mother's.brother-ERG-EMPH   carry-APP-down-OPT
Well, it whistles, and his relatives can carry food down for him.

Nguthu-ngama is a group term which seems to comprise more than just elder
brothers and mother's brothers, but it is not clear just what it does mean. *Kirdra* is
not the most correct verb; *ngarlakurra* (or *ngarlangarlakurra*) should have been
used as this refers specifically to the sound of the bullroarer.

185   *Ngarru ngamalitji.*
      only   mother's.brother-ERG-EMPH
      Only his mother's brothers [can carry it down].

186   *Ngala thana   ngarndri-ngapirilitji   mulhudu mapaapini-nguda*
      then   3pl:NOM   mother-father-ERG-EMPH   food   gather-gather-GER-ABL

      yinbatharrapandhingalatji   nhunggani.
      send-all-down-FUT-EMPH-EMPH   3sg:GEN
      His parents send down food that they have collected for him.

      Nhunggani 'his' here means 'for him'.

187   *Waltha-yindrithikaringuna   mulhudutji.*
      carry-RR-return-UNSP-THEN-?   tucker-EMPH
      He carries the food back for himself.

188   *Thayi-yindringa nhinathanggu-rnangalatji.*
      eat-RR-FUT   sit-stand-CONT-EMPH-EMPH
      He lives on it while he's staying there.

      Nhina here means 'stay' and *thanggu* denotes 'for some time' (here the period is up
      to two or three months). See §12.19 in the grammar.

189   *Yilayarndu kara   yina ngatjada-ngadi thika-lapurratji,   walya yina*
      how   maybe EMPH camp-DAT   return-REMP-EMPH not   EMPH

      ngathu   ngaran.ga.
      1sg:ERG   hear-FARP
      I don't know how he came back home; I never heard.

T. Burial

They used to dig a hole and put him in it, and they cover him over with a big heap of
dirt, then they lay sticks on top, four or five or six, then they lay a couple on the side so it
won't slip off, then they stand up all the other little sticks all around it, stick it up; and
they'll build a mound up; on top of the gum leaf here, they put sand, gumleaves, then these
logs they put on top, and these fellows on the side sticking up. Do it neat, you know.

Because of Ben Kerwin's untimely death it was never possible to fully analyse the
Yandruwandha text of this description, which in any case contains less detail than his
English version, given here. The phrase 'on top of the gum leaf' is, of course, a slip of the
tongue; it should be 'on top of the mound'.

5.2 Yandruwandha stories [S][4]

The texts below include three short ones by Tim Guttie and seven of various lengths by Ben Kerwin. English translations are interpolated at times in texts as recorded; these are omitted but their location is marked /—. An 'interlinear' literal translation follows each line of Yandruwandha, but the free translation is given at the end of each story.

Text 1: Tim Guttie, 1968. (T11)

1. *Putha thana   minithalkarla, marripathi, dritji   parrkulu,*
    races 3pl:NOM run-up-PRES   tomorrow   day   two

    nhandu thanayi   putha-pika. /—
    horse 3pl:NOM-HERE speed-CHAR

2. *Mardra-ngadi,   mandrithayinga pirna. /—*
    stone-DAT   get-eat-FUT   big

3. *Walya nganyitji   thawanga putha-ngaditji. /—*
    not   1sg:NOM-EMPH   go-FUT   races-DAT-EMPH

4. *Ay kurrupu   kara   nhaniyi.*
    eh old.woman maybe 3sg:NOM-HERE

5. *Ey! Thawanga yini?*
    hey go-FUT   2sg:NOM

1. There's races on tomorrow, for two days, these racehorses. 2. They're going to win a lot of money. 3. I'm not going to the races. 4. Maybe this old woman is. 5. Hey, are you going?

Text 2: Tim Guttie, 1968. (T14)

Karrukarru nhuniyi   pada, ngapakaldri-nguda, yiba-nhana nhuliyi,
old.man   3sg:NOM-HERE in   water-bitter-ABL   drink-NP   3sg:ERG-HERE

thudaarla   nhunu,   kurrayi ngana-rnanga kurrayi nganarla.
lie-NOW-PRES 3sg:NOM mad   do-CONT   mad   do-PRES
This old fellow is inside, he's been drinking rum and now he's lying down, dead drunk.

(TG's translation: "Old Joe Smith, he's been on the rum, now he's choked down now, and he's asleep.")

---

[4]   Cross-references to sentences in this section are prefaced by 'S' in the companion volume, *Innamincka Talk*.

Text 3: Tim Guttie, 1968. (T14)

Man.gili   nhunu   mundja, patjarla;   thawa-nhana nhunu
Ben.Kerwin 3sg:NOM sick   be.sick-PRES go-NP   3sg:NOM

kirri-ngadi, kintha yunggudu ngaka-rnanga. /—
clever-DAT nose   blood   run-CONT
Benny's sick, his nose is bleeding and he's gone to the doctor.

Text 4: Ben Kerwin, 1971. (W3–4)

1. *Pipa yilanggi kara   thana,   yilanggi kara   thana   pipatji.*
   paper where maybe 3pl:NOM where   maybe 3pl:NOM paper-EMPH

2. *Nhanggani   man.garri-ngaditji.*
   3sg:fem:GEN girl-DAT-EMPH

3. *Ngarru mulha malka ngathu thanhayi   pardrarla nhanggani.*
   only   face mark 1sg:ERG 3pl:ACC-HERE hold-PRES 3sg:fem:GEN

4. *Pipatji,   pipa drakini-nguda nhandra,   yilanggi kara   nhunu.*
   paper-EMPH paper pierce-GER-ABL 3sg:fem:ERG where   maybe 3sg:NOM

5. *Mirni ngaldra   wawarla man.garri nhani   thikawarrini-ngadi.*
   wait   1du:in:NOM see-PRES girl   3sg:fem:NOM return-arrive-GER-DAT

6. *Yakarlalatji   ngathu.*
   ask-PRES-EMPH-EMPH 1sg:ERG

7. *Nhandrayi   pardrarla nhinggiyi.*
   3sg:fem:ERG-HERE hold-PRES location-HERE

8. *Minhayatji nhanggani   mayatji   ya — malka pipatji*
   what-EMPH 3sg:fem:GEN name-EMPH ?   mark paper-EMPH

   drakini-ngadi. /—
   pierce-GER-DAT

9. *Ngathu yina   nganarla, man.garri nhani   thikawarra-rlayi ngapala*
   1sg:ERG 2sg:ACC tell-PRES girl   3sg:fem:NOM return-arrive-SIM well

   yinana   minhaya ngunyiri, man.garri nhani. /—
   2sg:ACC-? what   give-UNSP girl   3sg:fem:NOM

10. *Kuditharrarla yina nganyi, kuditharrarla nganyi. /—*
    forget-PRES   EMPH 1sg:NOM forget-PRES   1sg:NOM

11. *Kuditharrarla nhukada ngathu.*
    forget-PRES   before 1sg:ERG

12. *Minhala   ngathu yina   nganangatji, minhala   ngathu yina*
    what-EMPH 1sg:ERG 2sg:ACC tell-FUT-EMPH what-EMPH 1sg:ERG 2sg:ACC

ngananga.
tell-FUT

13. *Minhala   yini   yurarla   ngarini-ngadi nganyi   yandha-rlayi.*
    what-EMPH 2sg:NOM want-PRES hear-GER-DAT 1sg:NOM talk-SIM

1. I don't know where those letters are. 2. They belong to that girl. 3. I've only got these photos of hers. 4. I don't know where the letter is that she wrote. 5. We'll watch for her to come home. 6. I'll ask her. 7. She's got it here. 8. She'll write down her address.(?) 9. I'm telling you, when that girl comes home she'll give it to you. 10. I've forgotten it. 11. I forgot it before. 12. What else will I tell you? 13. What do you want to hear me say?

Text 5: Ben Kerwin, 1971. (W6)

1. *Ngali   nhinarla nhinggiyi   yandhayandhanga nhutjaduyi.*
    1du:ex:NOM sit-PRES location-HERE talk-talk-FUT   3sg:NOM:THERE-LOC

2. *Wathi   nhuniyi   karrtjiwagawagarla.*
    machine 3sg:NOM-HERE turn-around-around-PRES

3. *Ngala nganyi   yandharla walypalayi   nhungganiyi, Yandruwandha yina.*
    then 1sg:NOM talk-PRES white.man-LOC 3sg:GEN-LOC Yandruwandha EMPH

4. *Yandharla nganyi,   ngararla   ngala yundru.*
    talk-PRES 1sg:NOM listen-PRES then 2sg:ERG

5. *Minha-ngadi yina.*
    what-DAT   EMPH

6. *Yandruwandha nhulu   ngarini-ngadi   yurarla.*
    Yandruwandha 3sg:ERG listen-GER-DAT want-PRES

7. *Nganyi   yandharla yingganiyi,   nhungganiyi, karrukarru nh — walypala*
    1sg:NOM talk-PRES 2sg:GEN-LOC 3sg:GEN-LOC old.man   white.man

    nhuniyi.
    3sg:NOM-HERE

8. *Well, nganyi   yandharla ngan.gu   yina, karna   yawarri, Yandruwandha.*
        1sg:NOM talk-PRES language EMPH person language Yandruwandha

9. *Ngathuna   nganarla.*
    1sg:ERG-2sg:ACC tell-PRES

10. *Minhaya-ngadi yina?*
    what-DAT   EMPH

11. *Yandruwandha yundru   yurarla   ngarini-ngadi, nganinha,   karna,*
    Yandruwandha 2sg:ERG want-PRES hear-GER-DAT   1pl:ex-ACC person

    Yandruwandha, Thayipilthirringuda.
    Yandruwandha   Thayipilthirringuda

12. *Ngathuna   nganarla.*
    1sg:ERG-2sg:ACC tell-PRES

13. *Nganyi   yandharla walypalayi   nhungganiyi nhinggiyi,   ngarini-ngadi*
    1sg:NOM   talk-PRES white.man-LOC 3sg:GEN-LOC location-HERE listen-GER-DAT

    nganha   yundru,   walpi kara.
    1sg:ACC   2sg:ERG   when   maybe

1. We're sitting here talking to that thing. 2. This machine (tape recorder) is going round and round. 3. I'm talking to this white fellow, Yandruwandha. 4. I'm talking and you're listening. 5. What for? 6. He wants to listen to Yandruwandha. 7. I'm talking to you — to him, to this old man — white man. 8. Well I'm talking the language, Aboriginal language, Yandruwandha. 9. I'm telling you. 10. What for? 11. You want to hear Yandruwandha, us lot, Aborigines, Yandruwandha, Thayipilthirringuda. 12. I'm telling you. 13. I'm talking to this white fellow here, so you can listen to me, some time.

Text 6: Ben Kerwin, 1971, repeated 1972.
The later version is given here. (E1)

1. *Panggapangga-thili   pula.*
   young.man-DU   3du:NOM

2. *Karruwali nhina-lapurratji,   pinthapurru.*
   boy   sit-REMP-EMPH   foreskin-PROP

3. *Ngapala pula   yada   thinbari,   nga palha-ngadi thawanga.*
   well   3du:NOM boomerang chisel-UNSP then bird-DAT   go-FUT

4. *Ngapala palha pula   dranyindji,   nga   yadatji   nhunu*
   well   bird 3du:NOM hit(throwing)-SEQ then boomerang-EMPH 3sg:NOM

   thikawarranga   ngapayi   warlkapandhinga.
   return-arrive-FUT water-LOC fall-down-FUT

5. *Ngapala pula   yadatji   yina wanthi-rnangala,   nga kurnutji*
   well   3du:NOM boomerang-EMPH EMPH look.for-CONT-EMPH then one-EMPH

   nhunu   thangguthalkawarranga wawa-yindripandhiringu.
   3sg:NOM stand-up-arrive-FUT   look-RR-down-UNSP-THEN

6. *Ngandra panytjila   ngala nganyardi!*
   oh   circumcised-EMPH then 1sg:NOM-EMPH

7. *Nhinathikapandhingaldra ngapayi.*
   sit-return-down-FUT-BUT   water-LOC

8. *Ngapala pardrapardra-rnanga-thili, nganandji nhulu   ngathadi-maladinyi,*
   well   hold-hold-CONT-DU   tell-SEQ 3sg:ERG younger.sibling-2KIN-?

   'Thangguthalka, wawa-yindringalatji!'
   stand-up   look-RR-FUT-EMPH-EMPH

9. *Nga thangguthalkanga   nhunu,   wawa-yindriringu.*
    then stand-up-FUT   3sg:NOM look-RR-UNSP-THEN

10. *Ngandra pantjila   ngala nganyardi!*
    oh   circumcised-EMPH then 1sg:NOM-EMPH

11. *Ngaandi.*
    yes

12. *Mirni ngaldra   ngapirila   ngalungga   karrukanga.*
    wait 1du:in:NOM father-EMPH 1du:in:GEN man-CAUS-FUT

13. *Thika(?) karrukanga   mirni kara.*
    return man-CAUS-FUT wait maybe

14. *Karrukarrutji yinheyey   pakawindriringu.*
    old.man-EMPH 3sg:ACC-DISTORT carry-enter-UNSP-THEN

15. *Karrukarrulatji   yinha,   ngapala yinha   karrukarnanga.*
    old.man-EMPH-EMPH 3sg:ACC well   3sg:ACC man-CAUS-CONT

16. *Mirni t —* ngapala pula   pakarila   thanha,   ngapiri-maladitji —*
    wait   well   3du:NOM carry-UNSP-EMPH 3pl:ACC father-2kin-EMPH

    wanilatji   yina — mudalatji   yina dranga-rnanga —
    corroboree-EMPH-EMPH EMPH corroboree-EMPH-EMPH EMPH dance-CONT

    pantjina-yindririlatji.
    circumcise-CAUS-RR-UNSP-EMPH-EMPH

17. *Ngapala — paka — thawawagawaga-rnangadi karruka-thikathikana —*
    well   go-around-around-CONT-? man-CAUS-everywhere-?

    padlakurnu-padlakurnu.
    country-one-country-one

18. *Karrulatji   thana   nhinatharrathikarla.*
    man-EMPH-EMPH 3pl:NOM sit-fly-return-PRES

19. *Pintha-purru   panila,   ngarru Malkanpa karru nhina-padipadi —*
    foreskin-PROP none-EMPH only Innamincka man sit-HAB-(GER)

    pulya-padipadinitji.
    ?-HAB-GER-EMPH

20. *Pirnala thana   karrukarrula nhinarlatji,   ngala panggarala*
    big-EMPH 3pl:NOM old.man-EMPH sit-PRES-EMPH then young.man-?-EMPH

    thana   nhina-padipadinitji, pintha-purru, muduwa.
    3pl:NOM sit-HAB-GER-EMPH   foreskin-PROP child

1. There were two young men. 2. They were still boys, with foreskins. 3. Well, they made a boomerang and went out hunting birds.

4. They hit a bird, and the boomerang came back down and fell into the water. 5. They were looking for the boomerang. Then one of them stood up and looked down at himself. 6. "Oh! I've been circumcised!"

7. He sat down again in the water. 8. Well, the two of them were feeling about (for the boomerang) and he told his brother, "Stand up and look at yourself." 9. So he stood up and looked at himself. "Oh! I'm circumcised now! Yes!" 12 & 13. "Come on, we'll go back and make a man out of our father."

14 & 15. Then they took the old man away (into the bush) and made a man of him. 16. Well then they took all their fathers, and they had a corroboree and circumcised one another. 17. They went everywhere and circumcised all the men in every place. 18. They went and visited the men [in all the other places]. 19. Only at Innamincka did none of the men have foreskins. 20. The old men [at other places] used to be like young fellows (?), with foreskins, like children.

Addendum. The following song, associated with circumcision, was sung when the story was told in 1971. It is given in phonetic transcription with probable phonemic transcription and an attempt at translation. The language is not all modern Yandruwandha and BK did not understand it all.

[miːn̪aː jalɛj   in̪teːwɛɹɛj   n̪t̪aːt̪ʲiːliː]
minhayali   *?*   *thatjili*
what-INST   knife-INST

[jæpaːwa   jæreːriːnmaːwaː   jat̪aːla]
yapawa   *yarririnmawa*   *yathala*
fear(?)-   stick.stone.in-

[kaːliya   juːkaːwaː   japeːnʲeːjeː   jaːliːnaː   waːjukeːɹenʲdʲi]
kaliya   *yukawa*   *yapanyiya*   *yalinawa*   *yukarrandji*
                        fear-*   *   lie-SEQ(?)

The song was repeated as follows:

[miːn̪aː jalɛj   n̪t̪ɜːwejən̪t̪adʲeːleː]
minhayali   *thatjili*
what-INST   knife-INST

[japaːwaː   jarɛiɹi.nmajwɜː]
yapawa   *yarririnma*
fear(?)   stick.stone.in

[jæt̪aːlaːwa   jaleːn]
yathala   *yalina*
*

[kaːlʲei   joːkaːwaː]
kaliya   *yukawa*

[jæbaːndʲeːweː   jarjɛnda]
yapanyiwi
fear- *

[ŋuːluːjɑːbeːɾeːweːɪ jɑlɛ.n]
          yalina

* "*Yalina* means finish in the song, but not in the proper language." *Yapanyi* is
"something to do with frightened".

Text 7: Ben Kerwin, 1973. (B25)

1. *Karna   nhunu   thawa-lapurra, mukathudathawanga.*
   person   3sg:NOM   go-REMP   sleep-lie-go-FUT

2. *Ngapala nhunu   pukudu pardrari   thuda-rlayi nhun — thudanga nhunu*
   well   3sg:NOM dream   hold-UNSP lie-SIM   lie-FUT   3sg:NOM

   pantja thanggu-rnanga, nga nganndithirri nhulu   mandringa nga
   knee   stand-CONT   then nulla-nulla   3sg:ERG get-FUT   then

   pirnta nhulu   mandringa purndawalkiniyi,   ngarrungu
   waddy   3sg:ERG get-FUT   nape-climb-GER-LOC only-THEN

   kartamatha-yindriri pantja, pantja parndri-yindriringu
   belt-RR-UNSP   knee   knee   hit-RR-UNSP-THEN

3. *Ngapala nhunu   nguthangutha-rnangala, katjakatja-rlayilatji*
   well   3sg:NOM stretch.out-CONT-EMPH   ache-SIM-EMPH-EMPH

   parndri-yindrini-nguda nganggali, karna   palhanyadi wawawawari.
   hit-RR-GER-ABL   own   person   bird-like   see-see-UNSP

4. *Ngapala nhunu   purtu mandrimandri-rnanga milyaruyi, nga*
   well   3sg:NOM(?) swag get-get-CONT   dark-LOC then

   thawawindringa ngatjada kurnu-ngadila,   withi ngabayi ngada, ya
   go-enter-FUT   camp   other-DAT-EMPH   sore   wet-LOC while and

   kuthiwarrarila   mayi.
   come-arrive-UNSP-EMPH   eh!

5. *Minha yini   marrikudhiwarrarlayey?*
   what   2sg:NOM   come.early-arrive-PRES-DISTORT

6. *Ay parndri-yindri-nhana nganyi,   pirntali,   pantja-puru.*
   eh hit-RR-NP   1sg:NOM   waddy-INST   knee-AVER

7. *Karna palha-nyadi wawa-rnanga nhinawarra-rlayi ngakaniyi,   pukuduli*
   person bird-like   see-CONT   sit-arrive-SIM   1sg:GEN-LOC   dream-INST

   pukuduli   ngathinha —   parndri-yindri-nhanatji nganyi.
   dream-INST 2sg:ERG-3sg:ACC hit-RR-NP-EMPH   1sg:NOM

1. This man, a long time ago, was travelling, and camped along the way. 2. Well, he had a
dream, while he was lying there with his knee up, and he got his waddy from under his
pillow, and just belted himself on the knee. 3. Well, he stretched out his leg because of the
pain, because he had hit himself, thinking it was a devil he had seen. 4. Well, he packed his

swag in the dark and walked on to the other camp, while the injury was still fresh, and he got there. 5. [He was asked,] "What are you coming in here so early for?" 6. "Oh, I hit myself with the waddy, because of my knee. 7. I thought I saw a devil sitting with me, in my dream, and I hit myself."

Text 8: Ben Kerwin, 1973. (B26)

Interpolations in the translation are from the English version of the story.

1. *Ngakathunggayi nhinggiwa,   yarnduldrangu karna   thawa-lapurra kurnu.*
   Nockatunga-LOC location-THERE   how-BUT-YET person go-REMP   one

2. *Thuda-yukarranga, wada-rnanga karn — thakumani ngalyila.*
   lie-at.night-FUT   wait-CONT   stockman few-EMPH

3. *Nga kankunu pirna nhulu   kurranga.*
   then windbreak big   3sg:ERG put-FUT

4. *Yabakanpa ngala nhunu   karnatji.*
   fear-visible then   3sg:NOM person-EMPH

5. *Nga, manthi nhuya warrakurnu maka warrakurnu ya — ya nhunggani*
   then bed   3sg.? side-other   fire side-other   and   and 3sg:GEN

   yabali(?), ngapala wathi drantha kurrari,   purlangkitli yinha
   fear-INST well   stick   fork   put-UNSP blanket-INST 3sg:ACC

   purrilka-tharranga,   nga wathi thanggunari,   pantja thangguni-nyadi
   cover-CAUS-fly-FUT then stick stand-CAUS-UNSP knee   stand-GER-like

   nhunu   karna.
   3sg:NOM person

6. *Ngala nhunu   thudapandhinga nhinggiyi,   mak — warrakurnula.*
   then   3sg:NOM lie-down-FUT   location-HERE   side-other-EMPH

7. *Ngapala nhulu   wani dranga-yindri-rnanga.*
   well   3sg:ERG song sing-RR-CONT

8. *Ngala nhunu   karnakurnutji   thawawarra-rlayi, kilka-rnanga yina*
   then   3sg:NOM person-other-EMPH go-arrive-SIM   know-CONT   EMPH

   karnatji   yabapika.
   person-EMPH fear-CHAR

9. *Ngapala nhulu — dranga-yindri-rnanga nhunu   ya — yirrtjinakaldri*
   well   3sg:ERG sing-RR-CONT   3sg:NOM and   wake-INCH-again

   yina karnakurnutji,   pani ngala nhunu   karnatji   ngarru
   EMPH person-other-EMPH none then   3sg:NOM person-EMPH only

   wathildra thuda-rlayi.
   stick-BUT   lie-SIM

10. *Ngarru kurnula(?) nganandji kurnu nhunu   we — karna   muthu kurnu*
     only   one-EMPH do-SEQ   one   3sg:NOM   person very   one

     nhunu   kankunu   durru-nguda   kulkuma-walpirringa (or kulkumangalpirringa)
     3sg.NOM windbreak back-ABL   jump-across-FUT

11. *Ngala nhunu   karnatji   yayinala[5] yina   yabali.*
     then 3sg:NOM person-EMPH scream-? EMPH fear-INST

12.[6] *Murra nganha-yandru   mardri-yala tjidi.*
     well   1sg:ACC-ERG?   grab-PRES(?) now

13. *Yooi matja nganha-yandru   mardri-yala tjidi kurnki-yandru!*
     oh   already 1sg:ACC-ERG(?) grab-PRES(?) now   devil-ERG

1. It was at Nockatunga,[7] and again[8] there was a man travelling on his own. 2. He camped overnight while he waited for some stockmen. 3. He put up a big windbreak. 4. He was a very frightened fellow. 5. Then [he made] his bed on one side of the fire and, in his fear, put a forked log on the other side, and covered it over with a blanket, and stood a stick up so that it would look like a man's knee sticking up.

6. Then he lay down on his side [of the fire]. 7. Well, he sang songs to himself [and talked to himself, to make out that there was someone with him]. 8. Then this other man arrived and knew that this fellow was frightened. 9. Well he was singing to himself, to keep the other man awake, but there was no other man, only the log lying there. 10. Then the other real person [sneaked up as close as he could] behind the windbreak, and jumped over [and grabbed him].[9] 11. Then the first man screamed out(?) in fear. 12. "He's got me now, 13. Oh, the devil's got me now."

Text 9: Ben Kerwin, 1974. (R3–4)

1. *Thawa-lapurra milimani nhunu   Tibupara-nguda, nga thudathawanga*
    go-REMP   mailman 3sg:NOM Tibooburra-ABL then lie-go-FUT

    marndayitji,   Thanangarrpira.
    half way-LOC-EMPH Tenappera

2. *Thudathawari padla maya Thanangarrpira.*
    lie-go-UNSP place name Tenappera

3. *Thawandji nhunu   Thayaparrari-ngadi, ngala nhunu*
    go-SEQ   3sg:NOM Durham.Downs-DAT then 3sg:NOM

    Ngapamiri-ngudaldrangu walypala kurnutji   thawa-rlayi.
    Nappamerry-ABL-BUT-YET white man other-EMPH go-SIM

---

5   I suspect that *yayinanga* 'scream-FUT' was intended here.
6   Sentences 12 and 13 are in Parlpakurnu, the language of the Durham Downs area.
7   Nockatunga is *ngaka thungga* (or *ngakathungga*), lit. 'stinking water'.
8   This 'again' is a reference to text 9, which also involved a man travelling alone.
9   This extract translation of this sentence is doubtful.

4. *Nga thuda-yukarranga nhunu,   ey   thudathikanga   nhunu*
   then lie-at.night-FUT 3sg:NOM eh lie-return-FUT 3sg:NOM

   Thayaparraritji.
   Durham.Downs-EMPH

5. *Mayi, ngapala nhunu   thikangaldranguya,   ngala nhunu*
   eh! well   3sg:NOM return-FUT-BUT-YET-? then 3sg:NOM

   walypalatji   thawa-rlayi yita —   thinalildra.
   white.man-EMPH go-SIM   that.way foot-INST-BUT

6. *Kurrakurrawarralanga   warli matjayitji.*
   put-put-arrive-NOW(?)-FUT hut   long.time-LOC-EMPH

7. *Nga, maka nhulu   thangkaka   ya   thudapandhiringu,   thapa*
   then fire 3sg:ERG light-CAUS-? and lie-down-UNSP-THEN supper

   thayini-nguda thudapandhiringuri.
   eat-GER-ABL   lie-down-UNSP-THEN-?

8. *Ngala nhunu   milimani —   thawawarra-rlayila yadamanili*
   then 3sg:NOM mailman   go-arrive-SIM-EMPH horse-INST

   Thayaparrari-nguda.
   Durham.Downs-ABL

9. *Ay ngandjarri kara   warlkanga, nganyi   thawarla warli matjayi*
   eh rain   maybe fall-FUT   1sg:NOM go-PRES hut   long.time-LOC

   thudanga.
   lie-FUT

10. *Ngapala mabaabili nhunu   kuthiwarra-rnanga, nga kurrakurrawarranga,*
    well   dark-INST 3sg:NOM come-arrive-CONT then put-put-arrive-FUT

    purturdukardukarnanga   pap — yadamani papurlaka-tharrari   yita.
    swag-pull.out-pull.out-CONT   horse   hobble-CAUS-fly-UNSP that.way

11. *Ngapala nhunu   windripadari   purtu-ngurru.*
    well   3sg:NOM enter-in-UNSP swag-COM

12. *Kurrapandhiri   purtutji   yinha   nga makali yina*
    put-down-UNSP swag-EMPH 3sg:ACC then fire-INST EMPH

    karrtjikarrtjima-warranga,   wathi witjuli.
    turn-turn-CAUS-arrive-FUT   stick finger-INST

13. *Ngarrungula   nhulu — 'Ngandra maka ngala nhunuyardi*
    only-YET-EMPH 3sg:ERG oh   fire then 3sg:NOM-HERE-EMPH

    thangkanarla   ngurrangu. Walya panma-yindrina ngathu   yinha
    burn-INCH-PRES always-YET not   put.out-RR-IP   1sg:ERG 3sg:ACC

    thangkaka-nhina-nhukadatji.
    burn-CAUS-sit-RECP-EMPH

14. *Ngapala nhunu ngarru yankula   mandriri, nga warrkapandhinga*
    well   3sg:NOM only leaves-EMPH get-UNSP then throw-down-FUT

    ngapala pulkanga ngala nhulu, marnali   pulka-rnanga nhulu,   ngala
    well   blow-FUT then 3sg:ERG mouth-INST blow-CONT 3sg:ERG then

    nhulu — karrukarrukurnulitji ngararila.
    3sg:ERG   old.man-other-ERG-EMPH hear-UNSP-EMPH

15. *Thibila ngala nhunu — parrari — maka kaka.*
    devil   then 3sg:NOM under   fire near

16. *Ngapala nhunu walypalakurnutji,   yabalila   nhungganardi*
    well   3sg:NOM white.man-other-EMPH fear-INST-EMPH 3sg:GEN-EMPH

    karnapalhatji   nhunuyi   ngalardi,   kali   kuthiwarranatji.
    person-bird-EMPH 3sg:NOM-HERE then-EMPH already come-arrive-IP-EMPH

17. *Ngapala nhunu(?) thangguthalkawarrananga patjipatjingu   nga purtu*
    well   3sg:NOM stand-up-arrive-?-FUT   good-good-YET then swag

    nhulu   kunyamanga, nga kupuyi yinha   kurrapadaringu,
    3sg:ERG roll-FUT   then arm-LOC 3sg:ACC put-in-UNSP-THEN

    munka-yindriri yina   purtutji.
    hug-RR-UNSP   EMPH swag-EMPH

18. *Ngala nhulu   walypalakurnutji   ngarari,   ngapala nhunu*
    then 3sg:ERG white.man-other-EMPH hear-UNSP well   3sg:NOM

    dunkawindri-rnangala   yita.
    go.out-enter-CONT-EMPH that.way

19. *Ngala nhulu   milimanilitji   ngararila   yinha.*
    then 3sg:ERG mailman-ERG-EMPH hear-UNSP-EMPH 3sg:ACC

20. *Ngaldra! karnapalhatji   nhuniyi   ngalardi.*
    oh   person-bird-EMPH 3sg:NOM-HERE then-EMPH

21. *Ngala nhulu, walypala dunka-rlayila   yita,   walpamarna*
    then 3sg:ERG white.man go.out-SIM-EMPH that.way house-mouth

    kurnuyi, warli marna kurnuyi ngala nhunu —
    one-LOC hut   mouth one-LOC then 3sg:NOM

    ngararlandra kurnkitji   nhunuyi   ngalardi.
    hear-PRES-BUT devil-EMPH 3sg:NOM-HERE then-EMPH

22. *Ngarrungu nhunu — purtuldra mandri — kulkupa-thalka purtu mandringa,*
    only-YET 3sg:NOM swag-BUT get   jump-up   swag get-FUT

    dunkawindringa, nhunu windriwarrinitji   yada warli.
    go.out-enter-FUT 3sg:NOM enter-arrive-GER-EMPH hither hut

23. *Ngapala   nhunu   winka-rnanga*[10] *yadamani-ngadila,   ngari.*
    well   3sg:NOM disappear-CONT horse-DAT-EMPH   down

24. *Yadamani   thannganiyi   thuda-yukarraringula,   ngala   nhunu   walypala*
    horse   3pl:GEN-LOC lie-at.night-UNSP-THEN-EMPH then 3sg:NOM white.man

    kurnutji,   purtu walthinitji,   minhaya.
    one-EMPH swag carry-GER-EMPH what

25. *Thinaputa-panildra nhunu   miniwindriri,   yabali,   nga thuda-yukarranga,*
    foot-boot-PRIV-BUT 3sg:NOM run-enter-UNSP fear-INST then lie-at.night-FUT

    ngandjarritji warlkaringu,   ngabangabakaringu   pulhu.
    rain-EMPH   fall-UNSP-THEN   wet-CAUS-UNSP-THEN 3du:ACC

26. *Ngapala   nhunu —   purtuwalthini   karla — ngapala   nhunu*
    well   3sg:NOM   swag-carry-GER   well   3sg:NOM

    thikaminiwarrana   purtu kunyamanga thikaminiwarranga   warliyitji
    return-run-arrive-IP(?) swag roll-FUT   return-run-arrive-FUT hut-LOC-EMPH

    makala   yina   thangkaka-thalkanga.
    fire-EMPH EMPH burn-CAUS-up-FUT

27. *Ngala nhunu   yadamani mapa-yindri-rlayi milimanityéyi*
    then 3sg:NOM horse   muster-RR-SIM   mailman-EMPH-DISTORT

    thikaringu   yada, ya   warlitji kuthiwarranga   ya   purtulatji
    return-UNSP-THEN hither and   hut-EMPH come-arrive-FUT and   swag-EMPH-EMPH

    ngapala karrakarraniya yadamani nhulu   karra-thikathika-rnanga
    well   tie-tie-?-?   horse   3sg:ERG   tie-everywhere-CONT

    thanha, windripadanga.
    3pl:ACC enter-in-FUT

28. *'Ey! Walpi yini   thawawarra-nhaneyey?*
    hey   when   2sg:NOM   go-arrive-NP-DISTORT

29. *'Marrikudi-nhanala   yini   yilanggi-nguda?'*
    come.early-NP-EMPH 2sg:NOM where-ABL

30. *'Ay nhinggiwa   nganyi   thuda-nhana yambarriyi.'*
    eh   location-THERE 1sg:NOM lie-NP   far-LOC

31. *'Nga walpala   yinitji   kuthiwarra-nhana?*
    then house-EMPH(?) 2sg:NOM-EMPH come-arrive-NP

32. *'Ay ngananhina-nhanaldreyi yini.'*
    eh   do-sit-NP-BUT-?   2sg:NOM

33. *Ngampu!*
    ?

---

10 Or *winkananga* 'disappear-TVR-FUT', with *-na* used in the same way as in (11) in Chapter 13 in
    Innamincka Talk. Also in sentence 36.

34. *'Yina   ngala ngathu   wawanhana — makatji   pulka-rlayi.'*
    2sg:ACC then   1sg:ERG   see-NP   fire-EMPH   blow-SIM

35. *'Ngaandi, ngathutji   maka pulka-nhana.'*
    yes   1sg:ERG-EMPH   fire blow-NP

36. *'Ngandra, yaba   ngunyi-nhana   nganha   yundru   ngathutji   purtupa*
    oh   fear   give-NP   1sg:ACC 2sg:ERG 1sg:ERG-EMPH swag-?

    walthawindri-nhana(?)   winka-rnanga   yinggani kurnki-puru.'
    carry-enter-NP(?)   disappear-CONT   2sg:GEN devil-AVER

37. *'Nga yarnduldrangu   ngathutji   mandrinhana wawana   yina*
    then how-BUT-YET   1sg:ERG-EMPH   get-NP   see-IP   2sg:ACC

    dunkarlayitji,   nga yabalildrangu   winkanga   yadamani-ngadila
    go.out-SIM-EMPH   then fear-INST-BUT-YET disappear-FUT   horse-DAT-EMPH

    thannganiyi   thuda-yukarranga.'
    3pl:GEN-LOC   lie-at.night-FUT

38. *Ngapala yingka-rnanga-thili   yabangunyi-yindrini-nguda   ngala pula,*
    well   laugh-CONT-DU   fear-give-RR-GER-ABL   then 3du:NOM

    walypala-thili.
    white.man-DU

39. *Kurnki ngala pani.*
    devil   then nothing

1. A long time ago, a mailman was travelling from Tibooburra, and he spent the night halfway, at Tenappera. 2. He camped at this place called Tenappera. 3. Then he went straight on to Durham Downs, while another white man was going down from Nappamerry. 4. Then he stayed the night at Durham Downs and then went back, 5. Well he went back while this white man was going that way, on foot.

6. He [the other man] made camp at an old hut [which was believed to be haunted]. 7. Then he made a fire and had his supper and went to bed. 8. Meanwhile the mailman arrived on horseback from Durham Downs. 9. "Oh, it looks like rain, I'll go and sleep in the old hut."

10. Well it was dark when he arrived, and he unloaded his things and hobbled the horses. 11. Then he took his swag inside. 12. He put the swag down by the fire and started to turn [the ashes] over with a twig. 13. "Oh! Well this fire's still alive!" 14. So he just got some [dry] leaves and threw them down [on the hot coals] and started to blow them. He was blowing them and the other old man heard him. 15. "It's the devil, near the fire!"

16. Well this other white man was frightened [because he thought that] the devil had come.

17 & 18. Then he got up, very carefully, and rolled up his swag and put it under his arm — hugged it in his arms — and started to sneak out. 19. Then the mailman heard him. 20. "Oh! Here's the devil!" 21. [The hut had a door at each end] Then while the white man sneaked out one door he [the mailman] could hear [what he thought was] the devil there.(?)

22. So he just jumped up and grabbed his swag and went out the door he had come in by. 23. Then he ducked back down to the horses. 24. He spent the night with the horses, while

the other white man, the swagman — what? 25. He ran away without his boots, frightened, and camped [in the open], and the rain came down and wet them both.

26. Well, [next morning] the swagman rolled up his swag and went back up to the hut, and lit up the fire, 27. Meanwhile the mailman was rounding up his horses, and then he came back to the hut and ... (?) and tied up all the horses and went in, 28. "Hey, when did you get here?

29. Where did you come from to get here so early?" 30. "Oh, I camped down there."(?) 31. "Then you got to this place yesterday? 32. So it was you who did it."(?) 33. ? 34. "Then it was you I saw blowing the fire." 35. "Yes, I was blowing the fire," 36. "Oh! You frightened me and I took my swag away and ducked off for fear of you being a devil." 37. "And I saw you going out (?) and I was frightened too and I ducked off down to the horses and spent the night with them."

38. Well, they both laughed then, the two white men, at the way they had frightened one another.

39. There was no devil at all.

Note: re 33, *ngampu* means 'nearly' in Strzelecki Yandruwandha, but its meaning in this dialect is not known.

Text 10: Ben Kerwin, 1974. (R9)

1. *Wilpadali   nganyi   thawa-lapurra, mandrithawari nganha   walypalali.*
   wagon-INST 1sg:NOM go-REMP   get-go-UNSP   1sg:ACC white.man-ERG

2. *Nga, Kinipapayi   nganha   warrkawindringa, ngapa yulpurru yina*
   then Coopers.Creek-LOC 1sg:ACC throw-enter-FUT   water flood   EMPH

   ngaka-rlayi.
   run-SIM

3. *Walyala   ngani — purrkapadayi   wilpadalitji,   ngarrungu pula*
   not-EMPH 1pl:ex:NOM cross-across-POT wagon-INST-EMPH only-YET 3du:NOM

   thawandji, thanytjiyipa-ngadi, nganyi   nhina-padapada-rlayi nhinggikala,
   go-SEQ   town-DAT   1sg:NOM sit-HAB-SIM   location-about

   Kinipapayi.
   Coopers Creek-LOC

4. *Ngala karna   thana   nhina-rlayi — thundiyi.*
   then person 3pl:NOM sit-SIM   island-LOC

5. *Ngapala pula   karlukarlu-ngadi yada thawari, nga yandhanga*
   well   3du:NOM fish-DAT   hither go-UNSP then talk-FUT

   nhinanga karlukarlu parndri-rnanga pula   thadri padawarraldra,
   sit-FUT fish   kill-CONT   3du:NOM bank   other.side-BUT

> *ngala nganyitji   thadri yitapandhiwarraldra   nhina-rlayi.*
> then   1sg:NOM-EMPH bank   that.way-down-?-BUT   sit-SIM

6. *Ngapala pula   ngana-yindri-rnanga, 'Yilanggi-nguda nhutjadu?'*
   well   3du:NOM tell-RR-CONT   where-ABL   3sg:NOM:THERE

7. *'Ngalaaku.'*
   I.don't.know

8. *Yakapadaka   yinha   may!'*
   ask-across-AWAY 3sg:ACC eh!

9. *'A'ey, nhindalitji   nganyi, yundru   kay!'*
   uhuh shame-INST-EMPH 1sg:NOM 2sg:ACC maybe

10. *'A'ay, yundrungu   yakapada   may!'*
    uhuh 2sg:ERG-YET ask-across   eh!

11. *'A'ay yundru   kay!'*
    uhuh 2sg:ERG maybe

12. *Ngarrungu nhunu — Diradili   nganha   yakapadanga, nga walypala*
    only-YET   3sg:NOM   Diyari-INST 1sg:ACC ask-across-FUT   then white.man

    yawarrili,   'Yilanggi-nguda yiney?'
    language-INST where-ABL   2sg:NOM.DISTORT

13. *'A'ay yundra-nguda nganyi, ngaandi, mayi yundra-ngudanga.'*
    uhuh far-ABL   1sg:NOM yes   eh!   far-ABL-EMPH(?)

14. *'Thaltawata-nguda ngala nhunudu,   padla   yundra-ngudatji(?).*
    sea-ABL   then 3sg:NOM-THERE country far-ABL-EMPH(?)

15. *'Thaltawata-nguda nhutjadu,   karna   thula.'*
    sea-ABL   3sg:NOM:THERE person   stranger

16. *Ngapala Diradili   pula   yandha-rnangatji, ngala ngathutji*
    well   Diyari-INST 3du:NOM talk-CONT-EMPH   then 1sg:ERG-EMPH

    ngara-rlayi pulhu.
    hear-SIM   3du:ACC

17. *Thulathulaka-rlayi   nganha.*
    stranger-stranger-CAUS-SIM 1sg:ACC

18. *Ngara-rnanga pulhu   yaraya — walya ngathu   pulhu   nganandji.*
    hear-CONT   3du:ACC ?   not   1sg:ERG 3du:ACC tell-SEQ

19. *Nhina-padapadanga nganyi — nhinathanggu-rnanga(?).*
    sit-HAB-FUT   1sg:NOM   sit-stand-CONT(?)

20 *Dritji kurnuyitji,   karna malkirri thawawarrandji, ngalyila.*
    day   one-LOC-EMPH person many   go-arrive-SEQ   other-EMPH

21. *Nga thawapadanga thundiyi   thannganiya   thudaringu.*
    then go-across-FUT island-LOC 3pl:GEN-LOC-DISTORT(?) lie-UNSP-YET

22. *Kali — thana wirnina-rnanga warnu nganyi.*
     already 3pl:NOM tell-APP-CONT who:NOM 1sg:NOM

23. *'Malkanpa-nguda nhutjadu karna.*
     Innamincka-ABL 3sg:NOM:THERE person

24. *'Kilkarla ngathu yintjadu, ngarndri-ngapiri ngala*
     know-PRES 1sg:ERG 3sg:ACC:THERE father-mother then

     nguthu-ngama.'
     elder.brother-mother's brother

25. *'Ngaandi yabayitjardi!*
     yes fear-LOC-EMPH-EMPH

26. *'Yarndukala ngali yinha thulathulaka-nhana, ay karna*
     how-about 1du:in:NOM 3sg:ACC stranger-stranger-CAUS-NP eh person

     nganggalitji nhutjadu!
     owner-EMPH 3sg:NOM:THERE

27. *'Kinipapa nhinggiyi-ngudaldrangu.*
     Coopers.Creek location-HERE-ABL-BUT-YET

28. *'Malkanpa ngala nhunu, ngathani-ka-lapurratji yintjadu.*
     Innamincka then 3sg:NOM child.(of.woman)-CAUS-REMP-EMPH 3sg:ACC:THERE

29. *'Ngaldra yabayitjardi, nhindalila nganyi!'*
     oh fear-LOC-EMPH-EMPH shame-INST-EMPH 1sg:NOM

30. *Ay yingkangala thana.*
     oh laugh-FUT-EMPH 3pl:NOM

31. *Pula kilka-nhukada walya-nyadi ngathu ngara-rlayi.*
     3du:NOM know-RECP not-like 1sg:ERG hear-SIM

32. *Ngathu ngara-rlayi pulhu nga walya pulhu nganangatji.*
     1sg:ERG hear-SIM 3du:ACC then not 3du:ACC tell-FUT-EMPH

33. *Yawarri pulganili ya(?), walya yawarri ngakanili, ngarru*
     language 3du:GEN-INST and(?) not language 1sg:GEN-INST only

     walypalayingu yawarri yandhayandharitji nganyi ngana-rnangatji
     white.man-?-? language talk-talk-UNSP-EMPH 1sg:NOM tell-CONT-EMPH

     pulhu.
     3du:ACC

34. *Nhindalila pula ngana-lapurratji.*
     shame-INST-EMPH 3du:NOM tell-REMP-EMPH

35. *Ayi yingkanga kara nhukuyu thana, ngaldratjila.*
     oh laugh-FUT maybe location-?(?) 3pl:NOM after-EMPH-EMPH

36. *Nganangandji padawarraldra nhina-rlayi wilpadalitji.*
     tell-?-? other.side-BUT sit-comp wagon-INST-EMPH

1. Once I was travelling in a wagon — some white men picked me up. 2. They left me at Coopers Creek because the river was in flood. 3. We mightn't have got across with the wagon so they went on without me, to the town, and I stayed there at the river.

4. Meanwhile there were some blackfellows camping on an island.

5. Two of them came down to do some fishing. They sat and talked and caught fish on the other bank, while I was camped on the bank that sloped down opposite them. 6. Well they asked one another, "Where's he from?" 7. "I don't know." 8. "Well, ask him." 9. "Uh-uh, I'm shy, you do it." 10. "Uh-uh. You ask him." 11. "Uh-uh, you do it." 12. Then he just asked me in Dieri, and then in whitefellow language, "Where are you from?" 13. "Oh, I'm from a long way away, yes, a long way." 14. "He's from the sea then, from a far country. 15. He's a stranger, from the sea." 16. Well they were talking in Dieri, and I understood them. 17. They reckoned I was a stranger. 18. I understood them but I didn't tell them.

19. I stayed there for a while [Story-teller's translation: "stopping for a week or two"]. 20. One day another mob — another group — of blackfellows arrived. 21. They went across to the island and camped with them [i.e. the original ones]. 22. They told them who I was; 23. "That fellow's from Innaminacka. 24. I know him, and his parents and relations." 25. "Oh my God! [Story-teller's translation.] 26. How could we reckon he was a stranger, when he's one of our own people. 27. He's from this river. 28. He was born at Innamincka. 29. Oh my God, I'm ashamed!" 30. They all laughed then. 31. Those two had thought I didn't understand. 32. I understood them and I didn't tell them. 33. I hadn't spoken to them in their language or in mine, only in the whitefellows'. 34. They had been very shy. 35. Oh, they must have laughed later on. 36. [Meaning not clear.][11]

www.ingramcontent.com/pod-product-compliance
Lightning Source LLC
Chambersburg PA
CBHW061245270326
41928CB00041B/3424